A Kernel in the Pod

A Kernel in the Pod

*The Adventures of a
"Midlevel" Clinician in a
Top-level World*

J. MICHAEL JONES, PA-C

To order additional copies of this book, contact:
Xlibris Corporation
1-888-795-4274
www.Xlibris.com
Orders@Xlibris.com
14990

Contents

To Physician Assistants and Nurse Practitioners
who have dared to find their own place in the pod

Acknowledgments

My first real supervising physician, Dr. Joel Saper, gave me the encouragement to start writing and publishing as a new PA graduate in 1982. I owe him my gratitude. I am also grateful for a long line of physicians, all of whom were fine doctors, but beyond that they were fine people. I pay tribute to Dr. Charles Bantle, Dr. Jerry Napier, Dr. Dick Bohjanen, and to the greatest supervising physician any PA could hope to have, Dr. Jerry Swanson. They stand like beacons of hope in a career troubled with many not-so-fine physicians.

I also want to thank those who selflessly lent a hand during the colossal task of writing this manuscript. What started as a six-month project became a three-year mission. I want to especially thank Mary Ettari, Charles Reed, Michelle Heinan, Charlene Morris, Sharon Bahrych, Steven Tiger, and Judi Colver. These individuals reviewed my manuscript from the perspective of practicing Physician Assistants and provided many invaluable ideas for improvement.

Karl Monger gave the manuscript invaluable insights and guidance from the perspective of a professional writer and editor. Alfredo Portales is a talented artist whose cartoons capture visually the stories I have tried to weave with words. We have worked together on several projects and I consider him a friend and a great person.

I owe my heartfelt gratitude to those who read my manuscript and had the courage to give me their endorsement. Their names are listed on the back cover.

My sister Sandra gave hours of her precious time to proofreading the manuscript, creating the cover art, and most of all, encouraging me when I was ready to throw in the towel. She is a great artist, but more than that, a wonderful sister.

In my best attempt to avoid sounding like a winner on Oscar night, I really want to thank my family. My wife and my five kids have been crucial to the content of this book, reminding me of my struggles as a PA. A father could be no prouder than I was when my son Ramsey, at four years of age, wore a T-shirt that read, "My PA loves me." The older boys, Bryan, Dan, and Tyler, had to forego the computer many nights so dad could work on his "stupid book." Amy was often frustrated when her dad could not give her his complete attention because he was so distracted by revisions and more revisions.

Naturally, my greatest support has come from my wife, Denise. She is a tremendous person and, as you will soon see, stood by my side though some extremely trying times.

J. Michael Jones, PA-C

Introduction

What's it like to practice medicine in America–legally–without having the abbreviation "M.D." after your name? And I don't mean prescribing herbal supplements or massage therapy. I mean mainstream, conventional, state-licensed Western medicine–seeing patients, taking histories and performing physician exams, ordering laboratory tests, and making diagnoses. Of course, along with making a diagnosis comes prescribing appropriate treatments, including writing prescriptions for medications.

How is it someone can look like, act like, and, as one patient told me, "smell like" a physician, but not be one?

This is the life of a Physician Assistant (PA), a Nurse Practitioner (NP), or a Clinical Nurse Specialist, all of whom are lumped together under the unofficial heading of "midlevel" clinicians. It is not a name that we necessarily like. For one thing, it implies a hierarchical relationship of medical professions, rather than a team. Nurses are certainly not low-level professionals. But it is a name that is widely used and understood and one that we have to live with until something better comes along.

As so-called midlevel clinicians we must try to thrive in a world that is dominated by the much more prestigious profession of physicians, which is considered the top level in that same hierarchical model. Midlevel life is like being a square peg in a round hole, a fish out of water, a kernel of corn between two peas in a pod. But a kernel of corn is also a seed, something that starts small but has great promise–another characteristic of the midlevel clinician.

The seed of this book took root in the soil of incertitude during the summer of 1997. I had just experienced two back-to-back terrible PA job experiences that had just about finished me (as well as my family) off. I was ready to throw in the towel on my career and apply as a greeter at a discount department store, or the guy that drives the Tiny-Tots Train around an oval track at a city park.

Around this time, I accompanied my wife to her 20-year high school reunion. This gave me the idea of setting up my own 20-year undergraduate college reunion. For this I used the various people-search services on the Internet to look up the three Physician Assistants who had encouraged me to enter the young profession. To my surprise, all three occupied, apparently happily, the same positions they had back in 1977.

What the heck is wrong with me? I thought. I'm not proud in claiming that in my eighteen years of being a PA, I have been through nine positions. In one stretch I went through four positions in a row in which the practice soon started to fall apart after my arrival (not my fault—I promise). It was like a bizarre take on the movie *Ground Hog Day,* in which the character lives through the same scenario over and over.

The Internet also introduced me to many other PAs through an e-mail bulletin board called the "PA Forum." It was a wonderful opportunity to dialog with PAs and a few NPs from across the country on a daily basis. We swapped stories and shared laughs and I soon realized that my professional plight wasn't so unusual after all. Certainly there were those, like my three mentors, who found wonderful supervising physicians to work with from the beginning. However, there were many more, like myself, whose career paths had proved much more serpentine and uphill.

With the encouragement of some Internet buddies, I published some of my more colorful stories in national PA journals and was surprised by the positive response I received. Many PAs came out of woodwork to say how much they related to me. It was at this point that the president of the American Academy of Physician Assistants (AAPA) approached me about writing a book.

My first book effort was a collection of stories submitted by various authors. I had a difficult time gathering enough stories, so I decided to share the stories that grew out of my own life and convoluted career.

I have written many technical articles for professional journals and consider it pure joy when writing something that doesn't require footnotes and references, and making sure the tables are exactly right. In technical writing, a misplaced decimal point, for example in a drug dose (even by 3 mm), could do a lot of damage. It's enough to take all the fun out of writing. The hardest part of writing an autobiographical book is that one day you wake up and find the intimate details of your life exposed like a filleted codfish. It leaves you feeling vulnerable.

The stories in this book are true, but most of the names and places been changed to protect the privacy of the people behind them. In some cases, I use their real names as a tribute to them, because I say great things about the great people they are.

So return your seats and trays to their upright and locked position and fasten your seat belts. There is adventure and turbulence ahead, throughout this journey of enlightenment as a midlevel clinician in a top-level world.

Chapter One

But Mama, I Don't Want to Be No Doctor

I took a seat in an antique wicker and leather chair. I glanced back from my front row seat to see the stuffy auditorium quietly filling with men in gray and navy tailored suits and camel hair sports jackets. A few women, also conservatively attired, were scattered among the group.

I carefully studied the formal, museum-like auditorium. It was dimly lit by recessed lighting and on the walls hung portraits of prestigious, stone-faced men in dark suits. Among the portraits hung large color photos of dendrites and axons that seemed woefully out of place. Certainly these photos had some significance besides what I could garner from a casual glance.

A tall, distinguished gentleman with bifocals hanging from his neck approached the podium. As he cleared his throat, the room grew silent. His deep voice carried a distinctly Canadian accent. "Today, we want to welcome J. Michael Jones. He is a Physician Assistant and has recently joined our department as a headache consultant." He paused to slip on his bifocals and look down at the podium. "He will be addressing us today on the subject of Transformed Migraine."

When he pronounced "J. Michael Jones," I felt the flutter of intestinal butterflies. I exchanged places with the gentleman and surveyed the audience. *Who am I to be lecturing in the most prestigious department of neurology in America, if not the world?* Rarely would anyone but an MD stand at this sacred podium. *Should I pinch myself to see if I am really awake? Was I still a little boy tucked under my quilted blankets deep in the mountains of East Tennessee?* It seemed like just yesterday I was that little boy. At the same time, it felt like I had lived enough lifetimes to satisfy a dozen men. As that young boy, never in a dozen lifetimes would I have dreamed of choosing medicine as a career.

I will never forget my first encounter with real-life gore and the beginning of my disdain of all things medical. It was during a camping trip with my parents. Our family never did things the easy way. My dad, Explorer Scout leader that he was, preferred to rough it. Commercial campgrounds like KOA or Jellystone apparently were too luxurious. Dad would just pull our beige station wagon to the side of the road near a patch of woods or a lake. My parents, two sisters, brother, and I would load up our gear and march down through nature until we found a suitable spot to set up camp for a week or two.

Dad was also a great innovator, always coming up with new ideas for camping equipment. When clear polyethylene hit the market, he thought it was the greatest thing since sliced bread. Driven by a singular vision, he got out the sewing machine and scissors and spent several weeks making clear plastic tents for his scout troop. His family was awarded the dubious distinction of testing the prototypes, warmed by the implication that clear tents held for hungry bears.

A favorite camping spot was the shore of Cherokee Lake–a TVA reservoir created by the damming of the Holston River. The long narrow waters of the lake meander through the green Tennessee hills following the path of the old streambed. On both sides gnarled inlets sweep up the dark hollows forming great bass habitats, but not-so-great swimming holes. Upstream from the lake can be found several major cites as well as such sprawling industrial sites as the Tennessee Eastman Chemical Plant, the Holston Defense Plant, and the occasional paper mill. In those days, scant effort was made to clean up wastewater prior to dumping it back into the river. As a result, most lakes in Tennessee consisted of a brownish-green slimly sludge. You couldn't see two inches below the surface. Not until my mid-twenties, as I stood ankle-deep in the frigid waters of Lake Superior, did I discover that water in the wild was meant to be clear.

During our trips to Cherokee Lake, my dad was mostly involved in fishing. He must have thought it better to ingest the poison from the polluted water directly through your food than to absorb it through your skin by swimming.

Dad, a tall thin man with a receding dark head of hair, usually wore khaki trousers and no shirt around camp. When he did slip on a shirt, it would likely be a tank-top, in some circles referred to as a "wife-beater." He would stand for hours on the red clay bank, a cigarette dangling from his lip, casting his line out between the stumps in the hollow.

On one trip, when I was six years old and my sister nine, I begged my parents to let me go swimming. Understand: their biggest fear wasn't the polluted water, but the garbage in the lake. In our local Appalachian culture of the 1960s, it was common practice to throw your trash anywhere it couldn't be seen–often the woods, sink-holes, or lakes. It seemed many adults never grew out of the "out of sight, out of mind" phase. With such a mindset, it was no big deal to dump your trash in the out of doors.

I was relentless. "Please let us go swimming. I promise I will be careful. I promise to clean your fish if you catch any."

Finally Dad caved in. "Go ahead and swim–but please, be very careful. You have to take your sister so you can be on the buddy system."

My sister, Susan, was not in the mood for swimming so I faced yet another lobbying effort. Finally, she hesitantly donned her swimsuit. We hiked down through the woods to the muddy lakeshore. When you weren't swimming you could beach comb for old tires, plastic milk jugs, broken beer bottles, and Kotex boxes. It was a redneck's Waikiki. I took off my shoes and waded in. As soon as I was ankle-deep, my toes had already vanished in the mucky waters. When I was in up to my waist I shouted for my sister to join me.

Susan had waded in up to her knees and the cold water had finally coaxed a big smile out of her. With her next step, her smile suddenly transformed into a horrible scream. She turned and darted out of the water. Immediately I thought, *Sharks!* I caught up with her about the time she reached camp, screaming her lungs out. When dad picked her up I saw something red dripping from her foot. Dad took her to a tent and laid her on an air mattress.

Mom was a classic beauty–we're talking Elizabeth Taylor–with short dark hair and baroque-looking glasses inlaid with fake diamonds and mother of pearl. She held my face against her belly to cover my eyes. I looked up and saw the worried look in her eyes behind her ornate spectacles.

Dad came tearing out of the tent. "She is cut really bad. I have got to take her to the hospital." Mom let me go and went to help dad find his shirt and car keys. She came out of her tent holding one of dad's dress shirts. Dad meanwhile had found the keys hidden in the glove compartment of the old Plymouth.

Once out of mom's grip, I slowly approached the tent where Susan was. She lay spread out on the air mattress on the floor of her tent. She looked pitiful, like the bubble-boy from the infamous "Sienfield" episode. I quietly opened the door of the tent and peeked in. Susan was still in her muddy, wet, yellow two-piece swimsuit with little blue mermaids on it. Her chocolate brown eyes were red from crying–like cherry-covered chocolates, if you will. Her right foot had a huge cut on it. I knew nothing about anatomy at the time, but I could have sworn I saw intestines hanging out of her gapping foot wound. It was awful. About this time she raised her head from the pillow, her eyes swollen and her hair a mess. She had a terrible look on her face. "I hate you!" she shouted. "You did this to me! You are going to die when I get home!" Fortunately for me, the cut was on her foot, meaning I could easily outrun her for the foreseeable future–there's no telling how long it would take for her temper to calm down. After it was over, I vowed in my heart to avoid gore at all costs.

**The author and his sister ready themselves
for a swim in Cherokee Lake.**

Aside from the gore, I didn't care to study medicine because of the violation of personal space that appeared to go along with it. As a high school kid, there was nothing I dreaded more than our pre-sport physicals. Whenever I went to my family doctor, he just listened to my chest and, at most, looked in my ears. I considered even that much personally intrusive. But, the pre-sport physical took me to new heights of personal intrusion when the doctor performed a traumatic maneuver called a "hernia check." It gave me nightmares. In junior high, I would

come out of those exams feeling as violated as a fair-skinned juvenile in a Turkish men's prison.

I was a total stranger to Buddhism, but during these exams I would meditate intensely, trying to transcend the situation. I would hear a faint voice in the distance say, "Now, drop your drawers." I would painfully reach down and slide my briefs down about an inch. Then the voice would repeat more harshly, "I said, drop your drawers!" Closing my eyes, I would slide them down, exposing my purest privacy. Then came the probing rubber glove. I lost more respect for the man every time. I imagined him after the exam returning to his office, laying back in his chair, putting his feet on the desk, and lighting up a cheap cigarette. I could see him there, a big smile on his face, blowing smoke rings. Of course it was only a hurt child's perspective.

I could under no circumstances imagine myself in a profession in which I would have to touch other people's bodies, especially their most private parts. So armed with my reasons, I failed to seriously consider a career in medicine. Yet even if I had wanted to study medicine, in those days such a goal seemed beyond the reach of mere mortals like me.

In my mind, doctors had a mystique that was larger than life. It was common in Middle America for mothers to dream of their little boys growing up to be part of that mystique. Short of being a doctor, you might set your sights on something lessor—say, president of the United States. Besides being one of the richest people in town, the doctor was also considered the smartest and, overall, most respected citizen. And not just when it came to matters of medicine, but in everything. This belief may have had its roots in TV shows like "Ben Casey" and "Marcus Welby, MD," which, if I've heard correctly, the AMA helped script.

I remember my mom taking my brother to our pediatrician when he turned eighteen, just to get advice on how to keep him from having to go to Vietnam. She wasn't looking for a medical wavier, just his advice. Dr. Brown recommended the Coast Guard or Navy. As it turned out, it was sound advice. My brother was never drafted but was assigned to a small boat, guarding the coast of . . . the Mekong River!

The townsfolk also considered doctors a different species altogether. It seemed unreasonable to believe a doctor could mate with one of the local girls and actually have children, so vivid was the apparent genetic incompatibility. Doctors were considered a "higher life form" and usually took wives from such exotic places as Paris, New York, and Knoxville.

I don't recall when mom first asked me to consider being a doctor. I was probably two or so. I do remember that each time I changed majors in college, she would always suggest that I go to medical school.

I had always loved science, particularly anything having to do with rockets and space. My goal was to work for NASA. The movie *October Skies* was like a mirror held up to my adolescence. I was always making rockets, competing in and winning science fairs, and occasionally simply blowing things up.

My high school guidance counselor, on the other hand, believed that everyone should be . . . high school guidance counselors. She had very little advice for a future NASA rocket scientist. I finally decided to go into engineering, thinking it would be the best approach to becoming a rocket scientist. I enrolled in the nearby East Tennessee State University and made plans to start in the fall of 1973. I had my dream wagon hitched to a star. I couldn't be positive it was the right star, but I knew one thing for sure: the medicine star was in a completely different galaxy. At that point, I could never have imagined the set of circumstances that would soon change my fate completely.

Chapter Two

My Polka Dot Parachute

The drive up old Highway 11 E from the town of Fall Branch to Johnson City was breathtaking, especially in the autumn. The thirty-mile trip takes you from a high plateau down a long sweeping valley to Johnson City, which nestles at the foothills of Buffalo Mountain, a rounded mountain of 3,500 feet that has the appearance of its namesake. At the highest point is a cluster of tall radio and TV transmission towers—a thorny crown on the bison's head.

The highway follows an old pioneer trail, twisting like a snake, crossing rocky creeks and maneuvering old oak trees—some with trunks the diameter of a wagon wheel. To the east, in the direction of Johnson City, the Appalachian Mountains rise abruptly from the rolling hills and farmland in the Nolichucky River Valley. By September, the tops of the mountains have a light yellow dusting, a soft touch by the Autumn Fairy, and a foretaste of what is to come.

This stretch of highway contains many imaginary mileposts drawn from my childhood memories. I spent my youth in Fall Branch. Although Johnson City wasn't a common destination for shopping, it was a common destination for school functions. From the third grade on, we made quarterly school trips to the Johnson City Roller Rink. Later would come many trips aboard the school basketball team bus. Two high school friends died along this road in separate car accidents. I could never pass this way without thinking about Charlie and Amanda.

The 1973 trip was the most profound I would take along the old two-lane blacktop. My red Plymouth Duster was loaded to the brim with my life possessions, heading for college. At 18, I couldn't grasp how profound this drive really was, for I would never live at home with my folks again. The thirty miles covered that day would prove a distance vast beyond measurement.

After being agnostic for most of my young life, I turned and became a Christian just before graduating high school. I was quite the theistic-determinist for many years. I really believed, as did many of my contemporary Christian friends, that every event, down to a leaf falling from a tree, was so ordered by God for some grand purpose. The problem with this type of thinking is that it leads readily to becoming very superstitious. If the car won't start on the first try, does it mean the Eternal Creator of the Universe didn't want me to go to the store to buy milk . . . or was the engine simply flooded? If the former, and I did get it started, was I going to be killed in a car wreck for brooking His will? This kind of thinking had a great influence on my college years and eventually my choice to become a Physician Assistant.

That first night in Johnson City, I settled in an off-campus rental with three friends. The next morning I would be registering at East Tennessee State University. My heart was bent toward NASA and my intent was to be a mechanical engineer.

Registration in the pre-computer age entailed actually having to go to each teacher and pick up cards for open slots in their classes. I had just visited my academic advisor in the math department. Dr. Getting was an odd looking little fellow, about five foot six, who had no forehead. I don't mean he was anencephalic, but the top of his head went straight back from the crest of his bushy brown eyebrows. I couldn't imagine much space for a brain in his cranium. It must have been packed in there somehow, however, because he was the dean of the school of mathematics and a brilliant thinker.

Although I loved science, I never cared much for math. I hated memorizing formulas and hadn't taken advanced math in high school. As a freshman engineering student, I had my choice of pre-calculus or calculus. I didn't know the first thing about calculus. Unlike the "I don't know much about science books" song, I did know what a slide rule was for, but not much beyond that. The choice was simple for my adviser: "Mr. Jones, I strongly encourage you to start with pre-calculus."

As I was leaving the math building that afternoon, I happened to run into my high school math teacher on the stairs of the tiny, two-story, red-brick building. Mr. Evans was a tall, thin man in his late twenties. He had light blond hair he kept combed in such a way as to hide his pre-frontal balding. He was quite feminine in his gestures and voice and could have easily passed himself off as a woman with the simple addition of a wig. "Hi Michael, what are you doing here?"

"I was just on my way to sign up for pre-calculus."

Mr. Evans fiddled with his comb-over and smiled. "Oh, Mike, don't waste your time with pre-calculus. You did well in algebra. You will have no problem going straight into calculus."

"Really?" I said sheepishly.

"Absolutely!" came his confident reply.

Believing in theistic-determinism, I felt nothing happened by chance. God put Mr. Evans on the steps of the math building at that precise moment to direct me to calculus. My high school was 30 miles away, so it struck me as very odd to run into him like I had. So, my question was, Do I follow my own judgment and the judgment of the headless head of the math department and take pre-calculus, or do I follow the advice of the high school teacher—whom I now believed had been put there by the Creator of the Universe? I did follow the high school teacher's advice and signed up for calculus—a class that soon would dispel any aspiration of being a mechanical engineer with NASA.

As soon as the calculus class started, I was lost. I couldn't grasp the terminology and concepts, so I couldn't follow the logic from the beginning. It had been over three years since I had taken algebra. Also, and unfortunately, the same brilliant, tough, headless professor, none other than Dr. Getting—the one who had clearly instructed me *not* to take calculus—was my calculus instructor. To make matters worse, I sat beside an older scary-looking fellow who resembled Charles Manson—the recent version of Manson, with the long tangled hair and beard. He wore sandals, ragged bellbottom jeans, and a tie-dyed T-shirt. He always had a self-rolled cigarette–of tobacco, I assume–tucked behind his left ear.

The guy was very restless. He kept moaning and acting frustrated. At first I thought he was like me, on the verge of total confusion. I would look at him and smile. I felt a kind of kinship with him in what I thought was a mutual struggle to understand the difficult lectures. We would occasionally moan together. Suddenly one day he shouted out, "This class is a waste of my time!" Even I was not willing to go that far.

Looking quite astonished, Dr. Getting said, "I beg your pardon?"

The scary, freaky-looking guy went on. "When are you going to get to real calculus? You are moving too slow. We already know all of this stuff!"

My heart sank. I saw the image of me in my coat and tie, cheering as my first interplanetary space vehicle was being launched from Cape Kennedy fading. It was fading into a picture of a toothless me, wearing overalls, standing barefoot behind my trailer, trying to light a Fourth of July skyrocket with my corncob pipe. It wasn't pretty.

There would be one exam prior to the last course drop date. I decided to stick it out and see if the professor's exams were any easier than his lectures. They weren't. I remember the day he handed out the test scores. I opened mine and saw the score of 62. I had never scored so low on a test in my entire academic career.

The professor offered a brief glimmer of hope when he said, "I usually grade on a curve. With this class it was hard to know how to score. While most of you were in the 60s and 70s, a few were in the low 80s. The problem is that one of you scored 98. He only missed a minor point on one problem."

Guess who that was? Charles Manson. The paradox confounded me. How could someone so ugly and unkempt be so smart? OK, if I really believed in this theistic-determinism, how did I explain the outcome of that divine encounter with Mr. Evans on the math building steps? Was this some kind of cruel joke, a real Divine Comedy? Again, theistic-determinism has some problems, not the least of which is explaining the tragic deaths of innocent children and other such horrors. My only conclusion was that, for some mystical reason, the Creator of the Universe did not want Mike Jones to be a mechanical engineer.

Now I was confronted with a real quandary. I met with Dr. Getting. "Mr. Jones, I suggest that you go to the university book store and buy *What Color Is Your Parachute?* and read it." He pulled a scrap of paper from his desk and scribbled down the title and handed it to me. "This book can give you direction in looking for a career."

I never found a copy of the book in the university bookstore. Either the book didn't really exist, or a lot of other students were in the same boat as me. I am certain that the Physician Assistant profession wasn't mentioned, at least not in the 1973 edition.

I had a good friend named Gary who was in computer science. He had dark brown curly hair parted in the middle and wore brown horn-rimmed glasses, looking a little like the infamous Harry Potter. He always wore dress shirts with a stack of IBM cards in his front shirt pocket. Gary said to me, "I think you should consider going into computer science. That field is getting ready to take off." One day, while at his apartment, Gary showed me a new invention. A huge black box with two large holes. He dialed a number to the university computer from his big black rotary phone and slammed the handset down into the holes. In a few minutes, he could type on a giant keyboard, from his apartment, right into the university computer. I thought it was interesting. However, I didn't want to spend my career in a hot room filled with huge noisy vacuum tube contraptions. It wasn't like computers would ever become a household item. After starting a business software company, Gary retired at age 40 and now lives on the beach.

During the quarter break I decided to make a huge shift, and switched my major to psychology. Why not? I had always liked psychology, especially when it came to trying to figure out what the hell was wrong with me. I have heard that 90% of those who study psychology do so because they themselves are screwed up in the head. On the other hand, I identified with Bob Newhart, who played a Chicago psychologist on TV. Like him, I often felt like the last sane person left alive. This was the first time I imagined myself in a career in which I would be seeing patients.

I did well in psychology although I was disappointed in what I was learning–our program being profoundly influenced by B.F. Skinner. It seemed like the only thing I was learning was how to train animals. For class projects I would go down to the University School, a large two-story red-brick structure just down the hill from the center of campus. It looked like any other classroom building, except it had a playground outside. The kids there were constantly chasing college students off the swings and slides so they could use them.

The University School was like a fish bowl school for grades 1-12. Many of the professors' kids attended. Classes like my psychology unit could go there to conduct cognitive experiments on the naive little brats.

One assignment I had was to "shape" an 8-year-old's unruly behavior. I was to give him an M&M every time he went 10 minutes without saying a four-letter word. The objective was for him to go a full day without saying "dirty words." After 45 minutes the kid had only earned a couple of candies. He just looked at me and said, "I'll give you a buck for the whole damn bag." Well, I was a poor college student. I guess my behavior was open to being shaped as well.

During my sophomore year I became a real outdoors enthusiast. A friend named Don asked me to ride along as he took a couple of friends up to the Appalachian Trail. It was October. The leaves were golden yellow and orange and the sky was a brilliant blue. I rode shotgun, with the two backpackers crammed in the back of Don's International Scout. The drive on the dirt back roads, high in the mountains, would have a profound influence on me. Through the open windows wafted the organic smell of leaves in the cool, crisp autumn air. At one point, we drove through a large apple orchard. The smell of ripe apples compelled us to pull over and pick a few–after chasing away the yellow jackets. The backpackers loaded up the outer pockets of their packs with the fresh fruit.

In 1974, I became so much of an outdoor nut that it began to consume me. I was buying backpacks, sleeping bags, and climbing rope with every spare dime. I traded my car for a Jeep CJ-7. In such a state, I reasoned, a career in the out of doors is just what I needed.

Rather than working in some stuffy office trying to shape the behavior of armed psychopaths with M&Ms.

At the beginning of my junior year, I decided to major in wildlife management. I switched my classes to biology, geology, and General Outdoor Studies. I imagined myself high in the Rockies in a log cabin, living like Grizzly Adams. Reality soon opened my eyes to the fact that the job market was not promising. My new academic advisor told me, "Do you realize that for every 10,000 graduates in wildlife management there's only two job openings? One of those job openings could be counting squirrels in a city park in Detroit, the other working in a stuffy museum in Biloxi." He added, "If you are lucky enough to land a job in the field, the salary would start just below that of a burger monkey." Although I enjoyed that quarter of school, I was too practical to continue down that route. I decided to teach science instead.

In the second quarter of my junior year, I switched again, this time to Secondary Education. I could still major in Psychology and combine it with General Science studies. School started to become really fun. Things were going well and I seemed to have direction–that is, until I had a visit from my friend, Tom Hall.

Tom was a wonderful guy and looked every bit the typical hippie and Jesus Freak of the early 70s. He had long curly blond hair and drove a VW micro-bus. I had met him during my senior year of high school. He was doing his student teaching in my psychology class. He had a true calling for working with kids with problems. It was the attraction of his faith that started me down the path that eventually led me to becoming a Christian.

Tom was a secondary school psychology teacher who had been out of school for about four years. He came through for a visit while on his way from Jackson, Mississippi, where he was teaching, to visit his parents in Washington, DC. He had one strong piece of advice for me: "Mike, get the heck out of education." He had grown quite disillusioned with it. The job market was very tight at the time.

Now what was I going to do? I was ready to finish my junior year of college and faced with the fact that, believe it our not, some people had actually chosen a major by this point. I felt confused and directionless. Should I take Tom's advice to heart? He was always someone I deeply respected.

One spring morning I was sitting in my Jeep on Watauga Street, waiting to look at a house I was interested in renting for a group of friends. I was reading in my Bible and came across a verse in I Timothy 5:8 that says, in my paraphrase, "If you don't provide well for your family, you are worse than a pagan." I appreciated this verse on two levels. On the one hand was its face value. It was simply a good teaching; you might even call it common sense. Provide well for the needs of your family. But my theistic-deterministic superstitions urged me to take this on another level. I saw the verse as a sign from God to change my major from education to something else. "But to what, God?" I prayed.

The house tour didn't last long. The owner showed up—a nice man in his mid forties, just starting to gray. His hair was cut and combed to perfection—like those plastic heads of hair on GI Joe dolls. He was dressed in a shiny silk, three-piece light green suit with a wide (stylish back then) yellow tie. He told me that he was an attorney and bought this house next to his mom as an investment. As we walked up the sidewalk, Debi, one of my future housemates, met us. I saw an old lady next door peaking through her curtains, watching us like a hawk. Debi was married to another one of my future housemates, Edward. Debi had long blond hair and wore long "granny" style dresses, resembling in my mind Michelle Phillips of the Mamas and the Papas.

The owner had just started to give me the grand tour when the woman from next door shuffled up to the house with the help of her walker. The man addressed her. "Hi Mom, is everything OK?"

"I don't want college students living next to me with their loud music and wild parties. And I don't want boys and girls living together here. It ain't right," she croaked. Little did she imagine we were all evangelical Christians. I hope she eventually got her wish and found a nice, quiet, stable, middle-aged couple—say, Mick Jaeger and Tina Turner—to move in.

When I got back to my dorm, I purchased a city newspaper. Dismissing the *What Color is Your Parachute?* book, I decided to measure the employment want-ad columns of the paper. Whatever the longest ad was for, that's what I would become. I wanted to have a marketable trade and to be a good provider for my family.

The winner of the longest ad contest, hands down, was RNs. There was twenty-three inches of ads in all. The runner-up ad was "Earn $$$$$ in the Privacy of Your Home." I am glad that one didn't win. If it had, I would have been ordering $500 "Home Business Starter Kits" for years to come.

This constituted the first time I ever seriously considered a medical career. I looked out my dorm window and imaged myself wearing a white shirt and pants and one of those silly white, stunted-wing Flying Nun hats.

I immediately marched over to the Health Sciences Building and up to the nursing department. I approached the secretary. "I would like to see the dean of nursing." I was taken into a waiting area outside of a plush office. In a few minutes, a well-dressed middle-aged woman walked in. "I am Dr. Nelson, the dean of the College of Nursing. May I help you?"

"Yeah. I want to become a nurse."

"What do you know about nursing?"

"Absolutely nothing."

She was wise enough to not invite me into the program based on such impulsiveness. In her wisdom she suggested, "Mr. Jones, you should get a job for the summer in a hospital. Then, in the fall, if you are still interested in nursing, come back and see me."

"How can I get a job in a hospital? What can I do there?"

She smiled. "Oh, there are things you can do in a hospital that don't require a lot of medical training." Little did I know at the time what things she meant.

She picked up the phone and called one of her close friends, the director of nursing at the local hospital. When she got off the phone she came out and handed me a piece of paper. "Go to the hospital to see this person, Mrs. April Johnson."

I soon found myself in Nursing Assistant training. This passage, from the normal civilian world into the medical care realm, is a psychological phenomenon, something akin to culture shock. Suddenly you find yourself exposed to blood, urine, feces, guts, and gore. You also find yourself invading strangers' very personal space on a regular basis. These were exactly the things I had wanted to avoid at all cost— ever since almost cutting off my sister's foot.

I will never forget my first day on the floor at the hospital. I was to work with a seasoned 50-year-old male nursing assistant, whom they still called "orderly." We were assigned to cover the entire spectrum of the hospital from the ER to the extended care facility.

With our first page we were called to extended care to look after a patient "with a BM." I wasn't sure what "BM" meant but I would soon find out. All I had to do was hold the patient on his side. The seasoned guy did all the work, cleaning up the patient using wash clothes . . . and all without gloves. He was like Rambo in Turdsville. Here I was looking the other way, gagging with each breath, praying very hard that I would not barf on the dear little old man.

Next we were called to "dc a catheter." On the way, I cautiously asked the orderly, "What does 'dc a catheter' mean?"

"A catheter is a tube that goes into the kidneys to keep them drained."

My imagination went wild trying to figure that one out. Once we arrived in the patient's room, the orderly explained to the man what we were doing. Then he pulled back the blankets, revealing his naked body. Feeling embarrassed, I simply wanted to look out the window.

At least the man with the "BM" had been incoherent. This man was wide awake and sported a beige garden hose going up to the end of his penis. It may seem strange, but in our society, if you walk up to stranger and suddenly rip his clothes off, you could go to prison. However, as long as you are wearing white it seems to be OK. The brazen orderly took hold of the man's privates and snipped off the little branch to the garden hose and started to pull it out. I felt certain that we were looking at just the external part of the hose. Once it entered his penis, I assumed it would be the diameter of a coat hanger wire. As he pulled, a huge garden hose came sliding out of his urethra; I felt myself becoming lightheaded with empathetic pain.

Over the two weeks I was exposed to other interesting nursing assistant activities such as morgue care, dressing changes, enemas until clear, bed baths, patient lifting, and foley insertions. The foley insertion was like trying to cram a garden hose down the throat of a dead toad. Not much fun.

The ER duty had no BMs to deal with, but was obviously much gorier. While covering the ER, I was checking in a patient who was holding a dirty bath towel around his waist. "What is troubling you today?" I asked.

He said, in a rather calm voice, "I just got in a fight and . . . I was cut with a razor."

"Can I see your cut?" I said and pulled the dirty towel off him. His abdomen was sliced open and his intestines were hanging out. This time, unlike with my sister's foot, these were real guts. I handed him his towel and left the room before I became the next patient.

During this initiation into the medical realm, I felt myself undergoing a kind of metamorphosis. It was a stressful time characterized by little sleep and strange dreams—Freud would have gotten a lot of mileage out of those dreams. Several times, I felt like quitting and going into construction or something similarly removed from private body parts and excrement. But after two weeks, I experienced an amazing adaptation. I actually started liking it, especially the ER. I liked seeing the wounds and mangled limbs. It was exciting; I was becoming accustomed to the EMERGENCY high.

I started taking first aid classes through the university's summer program. The next thing I knew I was putting fire extinguishers and rescue equipment in my jeep, as well as rappelling ropes and rock climbing gear. I carried a pair of bandage scissors in my back pocket, occasionally stabbing myself in the butt when I sat down too hard. My logic went like this: if I came across a collapsed citizen I could rapidly cut off all their clothes. I'm not sure what I was supposed to do next, but whatever it was, at least there would be no clothes in the way. I could imagine myself arriving on the scene with a crowd of people surrounding a person on the sidewalk. I would rip open my coat, revealing my white smock and name tag. I would say, "Have no fear, the Nursing Assistant is here." This is the phase when you know just enough to be dangerous.

By the end of the summer, I was feeling more and more confident about medicine, and was on the verge of signing up for nursing. My one hesitation was the preponderance of females in the profession. Not that I didn't like being around women. But, in our entire hospital there was only one male nurse. He wore little white button-up sweaters with the sleeves pushed up past his elbows. I am not making assumptions about his sexual orientation, but he was certainly effeminate. The older conservative patients would often refer to him as the "queer nurse." I had nothing against the guy; he was a good nurse. However, I guess I didn't feel secure enough in my own masculinity to be hounded by nursing stereotypes of the 1970s.

When a friend who was just graduating from nursing showed me her class picture, I counted 150 women and 2 men. At that point I had very serious doubts about nursing, but at least I had narrowed it down to medicine. This same friend had a fiancé named Terry. Terry and I were becoming good buddies. He was an out-of-doors kind of guy. He even looked a lot like John Denver, my folk hero. I knew that Terry worked for a large VA hospital and that he was a "PA," but I assumed this was some sort of administrative function. One night he was over at my place and his pager went off. In those days, only people with important jobs carried pagers–unlike today, when even the homeless carry pagers . . . not to mention cell phones.

Terry borrowed my phone and called the hospital. "Yes, why don't you get a CBC and lytes, start an IV of D-5 W with a large bore needle and I will be over to see him." Then he hung up and turned to me. "I've got to run over to the hospital. I have a patient who is pale and clammy. He has a history of a GI bleed and I want to make sure he's OK."

I was a little surprised that someone in the business office would be micro-managing a seriously ill patient via telephone. Of course, those were the days prior to HMOs and aggressive third-party payers.

The next time I saw Terry I asked him to explain what he did for a living. A humble guy, he had never talked about his work. He was kind enough to fill me in on what it meant to be a PA. Dr. Eugene Stead Jr.

had started the first Physician Assistant program at Duke University Medical School in the 1960s. Terry was a graduate from one of Duke's early classes. The concept of a medical career that included fun things like suturing, minor surgery, writing prescriptions, and ordering someone else to give enemas until clear intrigued me, especially when that profession had plenty of male role models.

Terry went on to point out that there were two other PAs in town. Both of them worked in the same hospital as me. I knew these guys and had assumed they were physicians. One worked with the orthopedist and the other with the neurosurgeon. I had seen them doing some amazing things in the hospital, such as putting in a trach in ICU and placing wires in broken bones in the ER. The nurses loved them and treated them with the utmost respect, and the professionalism went both ways.

Over the next couple of weeks, I spent time with each of these PAs, asking a lot of questions. In those days, it was like a top-secret program—like something you would see on the *X-Files*. Very little information was available to the public. No web sites, brochures or toll-free numbers. It would have taken me two additional years to become an RN. In about the same time period, I reasoned, I could be a PA. The choice was becoming clear.

It was time to sign up for fall classes. Fortunately, I had nearly completed my entire requirement for a major in psychology and a minor in general science. I withdrew from the secondary education program. This freed me from a lot of education requirements. I began to fill my elective spots with every medical course I could find. Anatomy, Advanced Human Anatomy, Advanced First Aid (now I would really be dangerous), Human Physiology, and Advanced Human Physiology. My senior year was a lot of fun. Finally I knew what color my parachute was: PA blue. I had started down the daring road to becoming a real Certified Physician Assistant. But the road was going to be much longer and serpentine than I could have ever imagined. There would be days when I saw the ground fast approaching and I was left wondering if the chute would ever really open.

Chapter Three

A Real Kentucky Kernel

It was the spring, and the apocalypse that was college graduation stood menacingly on the horizon. The occasion would force me to deal with three major issues: getting into PA school, finding spiritual training, and earning a living.

After writing to the few PA schools I knew of, I was discouraged to find out that each required two years of health care experience. By graduation, in August, I would only have one year of experience under my belt. I would have to defer PA school for another year.

The other big issue in my life at this time was spiritual training. I was involved with a Christian organization during my college years that I will refer to as ICO (for International Christian Organization). ICO at East Tennessee State had been a very positive experience. It consisted of 30-40 kids from all walks of life who honestly cared for others and who took their faith seriously. ICO placed great emphasis on training in ministry. After college I wanted to find a place where I could get this kind of training.

The third issue was money. I didn't have nearly enough saved to pay for PA school and I was determined not to take out loans. In my undergraduate days, the students I knew were constantly short of money. This included my roommate, also named Mike. We ate macaroni and cheese three times a day–bought for 15 cents a box on sale. We were always looking for "alternative" food sources. I tried eating the dandelions from the dorm yard. According to *Mother Earth News*, they make a great salad. I found them to be terribly bitter. In a quest for more protein, Mike and I came up with a plan.

Across the street from campus was the large Veteran's Mountain Home Facility. It stretched out over hundreds of acres in the middle of town. The front of the property, facing away from the university, had a cluster of 1940s and 50s era brick buildings, including a hospital, where my PA friend Terry worked. It also had a long-term care facility. Next to this was a huge military cemetery. The back half of the grounds consisted of many beautiful acres in a park-like setting of grassy hills and old oak and maple trees. In the center of this was a large pond that the staff kept stocked with carp and goldfish. Some of the veteran residents would fish in the pond to help pass the time. Outsiders were not allowed to fish there, as if any would want to. After all, carp isn't usually considered a trophy fish, or even edible, being bottom feeders.

Mike and I went over and sat with the older men, hoping they might give us a carp if they caught one. They never thought we were serious, although clearly we were. We would reason with them: "Chinese eat carp, so it can't be that bad."

Our plan was to clean the carp in the dorm bathroom and make carp-mac and cheese dinners. Finally we gave up on the carp but came across some cheap mackerel at a grocery store. So we cooked up a mess of mac-mac and cheese, which I guess could be shortened to mac^2 and cheese. You might say we invented it. It wasn't bad. At least it was better than the dog food Mike had tried once.

Mike was a coffee drinker but couldn't afford real ground coffee. Acting on another tip from *Mother Earth News* he roasted barley and made "coffee" from it, filtering it through bathroom tissue.

I could picture Martha Stewart, Mike, and me sitting on the crates we used for furniture, eating mac^2 and cheese for breakfast while drinking toilet paper barley coffee and discussing the finer things in life. Martha: "This is really living!"

The people in the ICO fellowship looked after one another. If someone's car broke down and there was no money to fix it, within a few days they would find money-filled envelopes slipped under their door. The other kids would go without food, sell their clothes, or do whatever needed doing to help one another. If someone had a problem, others would be there, offering help day or night. It was a magical time in my life. And it wasn't just turned inward to help those within the group. It was also about helping others who were down and out from all walks of life.

During my junior year, I lived off campus in a house (we finally found one that would rent to us) with Edward, Debi, and two other guys. We opened our large Victorian home to the homeless and frequently had strangers staying with us. We would feed them, clothe them, and give them a warm bed to sleep in. By the grace of God we never woke up to find ourselves dead, our throats cut, and our belongings gone. Of course, the homeless people probably had more belongings than we did at the time.

Our small group had loose connections with ICO. We attended conferences sponsored by the organization and used Bible study materials produced by them; however, we were never an official chapter. ICO was no far-out religious cult. It worked closely with such traditional hometown churches as Baptist, Methodist, and Presbyterian. ICO was considered the "Navy Seals" of evangelicalism: tough, committed, and well disciplined. Their emphasis was on training, training, and more training to become a real "Man of God."

The best popular example I can think of for this Man of God paradigm is the Jedi in *Star Wars*. Becoming a Jedi required many years of special training under a qualified staff trainer. In my desire to know God and to serve Him, I really wanted to be a Jedi. Therefore, I needed to get more spiritual training.

As I approached ICO and voiced my desires to go to the next level, they recommended a man in Louisville, Kentucky. He was an older man, in his fifties. Many of the ICO staff members were in their twenties and thirties. I met with the man and liked him. He seemed to me like an older version of Yoda.

The idea of going to Louisville was starting to mesh with my desire to go to PA school. The University of Kentucky in Lexington had a PA program. I could go to Louisville for a year for "Jedi" training; meanwhile

I could continue my brilliant nursing assistant career, meeting the PA school requirements, and obtain in-state status for tuition purposes.

The decision became clear. Again, from my theistic-deterministic perspective, all these things had come together for a purpose. So I loaded up my jeep and moved to Louuuey . . . . ville that is, but no swimming pools or movie stars. And the kinfolk didn't say, "Jedi, get away from here." My parents considered this whole spiritual training business strange. They were afraid I was joining a cult, but I convinced them I wasn't. It turned out, unfortunately, that they were more right than I was.

My time in Louisville was tough. It was my first experience living in a big city in which I didn't know anyone. I had a tiny one-room efficiency apartment. My only furniture was a desk and a sleeping bag. The Yoda guy lived on the other side of town, about an hour away in traffic. I only saw him once a week for Jedi training, which consisted mostly of Bible study and talking about ministry techniques. It was a very scheduled time and quite formal. It was a very lonely time in my life.

The main difference about working in a hospital in Kentucky was the anti-PA feelings of many of the nurses. When I told them I was going to PA school, they thought it was a poor choice. It was obvious they had been brainwashed. The Kentucky Nursing Association (KNA) was engaged in a bitter legislative fight against PAs at the time. I kept hearing the same thing from nurse after nurse: "PAs should be banned. Twelve weeks of training after high school and they think they can start giving orders." Nothing I said could change their minds. Nurses had been fighting their own battle for a century—a well-deserved battle to be considered professionals rather than handmaidens. The appearance of PAs on the scene seemed to threaten some. They tried to persuade me to go to medical school. Some even suggested that PA school would be a good stepping stone to nursing school. This was a real disappointment, especially after my positive experience with the nurses in Tennessee who shared a mutual respect with PAs.

I went to dinner with a nice couple from church. It was the first social invitation I had accepted since moving to Kentucky, and I thought, finally, someone was trying to be friendly. She was a registered nurse and he was an Army officer. From my experience in the hospital, I was a little hesitant to talk about my ambitions around them because of her background. Sitting at the table with them that evening left a lasting impression on me. Up until this point, they had been very polite. Then the husband asked me, "So, Mike, what are your plans? Are you going back to school?"

"I am applying to Physician Assistant school," I said.

I noticed his wife was very quiet and her face turned a shade of red that went well with her long, straight, strawberry-blond hair. She pushed away from the table and walked into the kitchenette to stick a lukewarm bowl of corn back in the microwave, watching me out of the corner of her eye all the while. Then her husband asked, "What's a Physician Assistant?"

Knowing that he must be familiar with the nursing profession, I asked him, "Do you know what a Nurse Practitioner is?"

"Certainly," he said with confidence.

"A Physician Assistant is a lot like a Nurse Practitioner."

Immediately his wife turned and screamed, "That's not true! They're nothing alike. An NP has a master's degree and a PA has 12 weeks training out of high school! PAs are much more like medical assistants who think they can order nurses around!" At that moment the microwave bell went "ding," marking the end of the first round of a prizefight of words.

I was shocked by her hostility but—out of politeness—decided to disengage from the sparing match with her. But her attitude had frustrated me. I had a lot of respect for nurses. I didn't understand why they couldn't reciprocate. Why didn't they want another professional in their state who could improve the accessibility of patients to medical care?

As consolation, I did get the blessing for PA school from the Kentucky Patron Saint . . . Colonel Sanders, at least in an indirect way. I was working at the hospital and received a page to the EEG lab to help a patient climb onto the exam table. When I arrived at the lab, there sat Colonel Sanders. I couldn't believe it. He looked just like his pictures in KFC, complete with cane, except he was wearing silk PJs and a housecoat rather than a white suit. I was still staring when the EEG tech said, "Would you please help Mr. Sanders onto the table." I had to forget that this was Colonel Sanders and think of him as a patient.

As I put my hands under his arms to help him stand up, he said, "What's your name, boy?"

"Mike Jones," I replied. He was unusually direct.

"So, what are you doing with your life? Are you going to go to college or just be an orderly until the day you die?"

"Well sir, I have already finished college."

"Well, then, why the hell are you working here as an orderly?"

"Uh, I am waiting to get into PA school. Do you know what a PA is?"

"No, I guess I don't, but you better get back in school and make something out of yourself–no matter how long you have to wait to get in. On the other hand, education never did me a damn bit of good." Then he laughed out loud.

Unfortunately the tech asked me to leave and I never had a chance to explain what a PA was. Harland Sanders died the following year. Every time I visit a KFC, I think of that encounter.

Speaking of chickens, I had put all my eggs in the UK basket in applying only to their PA program. Now I had been invited for an interview. The experience turned out to be an intimidating one. We were scheduled to visit in groups of twenty. As I sat in the lobby with the other well-dressed kids, we nervously eyeballed one another. Out of a few hundred applicants, sixty were invited for interviews. Out of the interviewees, twenty would be selected to enter the PA program.

Two PA alumni helped during the interview process. One PA, Rob, seemed to revel in his position of power. He struck me a little like Caesar at the Coliseum. In the end, the emperor would give the thumbs up or down. Your life was at his mercy.

The fun stuff came for me in the morning: a tour of the campus and a luncheon. Then came my one-on-one interview in the afternoon. When I got into the room with Rob, he was tough. "Why did you change majors so often? Why didn't you go to medical school? Do you really think you can hold up to studying 80 hours per week for two very long years? Why did you only have one course of Chemistry?" Then came the trick question: "How would you function in a subordinate role such as a Physician Assistant."

I tried my best to answer each of these questions, but he didn't seem to like my answer to the last one. Finally, at the end of the interview, he voiced his opinion of the "correct" answer to the last question: "PAs are *not* subordinate professionals!"

It was three longs months before I got word. I remember coming home from work one day and finding a card for a registered letter. It was Friday evening and I could not go by the post office until next week.

To my horror, the letter simply stated, "We are sorry to inform you that you were not chosen to enter the Clinical Associate Program for the fall of 1978." When a letter starts with "sorry," it is usually not a good sign. My heart sank. What was I going to do? My basket of eggs just got run over by a Mac truck.

A confusing few weeks followed. I had made friends with a psychiatrist who attended my church, and he strongly urged me to go to medical school. I was still tainted by that Kentucky atmosphere of putting low value on the PA profession. I started looking into medical school. After all, isn't medical school what happens to all PA school rejects?

One day that spring, I learned through the grapevine that Yoda was moving to Lexington. I decided to move there as well. Since I was considering medical school, I could start taking the pre-med requirements that I was missing at UK. Also, I could hang around the PA program and maybe increase my chances for the next year. The first pre-med course I took was Chemistry.

I found a job as an "aide" in the University of Kentucky Medical Center Post Operative Recovery Room. My name badge was eighteen inches long, just to hold my department name. It was certainly more interesting than being a nursing assistant in Louisville. When I wasn't busy, I had arranged with the surgeons to allow me to observe cases at close range.

The ICO chapter in Lexington was larger and more defined. Also, Yoda was moving to town with the intention of setting up a major training center for the organization. This was going to be like a Protestant monastery—or even like the Taliban, but without the turbans, beards, guns, and the only ones we would learn to hate was ourselves. Qualified people started moving in from around the southern states, by invitation from Yoda. The training was going to be intense and take somewhat of a cultic turn. The common thread in most cults is the abuse of authority. ICO seemed to have taken as its model the military rather than anything Jesus of Nazareth may have said.

Although I was part of this inner circle that was coming to town for special training, I never quite fit in with the others. ICO put a great emphasis on finding "sharp" people for training, real leaders for the future. I never fit that definition.

When you have a sub-culture made up of mere mortals who value being "godly," one of two things can happen: either you go insane from the overriding pressure of guilt, or you shift into a type of superficial façade that gives you the appearance of godliness. But first I must define what being godly meant in this context.

Godliness meant being almost perfect, having the correct attitude all the time, and never getting angry. It also meant loving everyone, no matter how they treat you, never telling a lie, while, on a sub-conscious level at least, being a prolific liar to maintain the godliness façade. Most importantly, it meant being sexually pure. Never even a thought about sex. Keep in mind, we were all 20-25-year-old hot-blooded men and women.

My mother is a very honest and transparent woman. With such genes, I couldn't live in this façade. I would be with a group of the ICO guys and ask them a question like, "Guys, sometimes I will be talking to one of the sisters (girls in ICO) and have terrible thoughts. For example, she might be telling me something very serious about something she was reading in the Bible. I would be listening very intently trying to focus on what she was saying, then boom, I would suddenly get an image in my head of the two of us in a hot tub, drinking cheap wine from a paper bag. How do you guys handle these kinds of thoughts?"

They would look at me in horror and say, "That is terrible. We would never have such thoughts about our dear sisters."

So, I didn't look very "sharp." I also hung out with some "undesirables." Some of these were even people involved with ICO or the churches we attended, but they weren't "core people."

One such friend was a girl named Val, who had grown up in a very conservative, evangelical family in Kentucky and attended a conservative Bible college in the Chicago area. Val had made some poor choices, like we all had. She had undergone an abortion when she was at Bible college because she felt too ashamed to let her parents and her friends know that she was pregnant. This was especially devastating for her because she personally opposed abortion. After finishing two years of Bible school, she decided to come home to Lexington to work for a while. Soon after arriving, she got pregnant during a one-night stand with a guy from another Christian group. This time she decided to tell her family and carry the baby to term, putting it up for adoption.

Her family was deeply shaken. Also, Val was having a difficult time being accepted by the ICO people. It is hard to cover up a pregnancy while maintaining a godliness façade. I felt a lot of compassion for her and became her best friend. We played racquetball every day throughout her pregnancy. Although we were just friends, Yoda frowned on the relationship.

Toward the end of her pregnancy, Val asked me to be her birthing partner. The father of the baby was suffering from an odd case of "amnesia." He didn't remember meeting Val before.

On the night when her labor began, I met her mom and dad for the first time at the hospital. The three of us sat with her for four hours during the delivery. Her dad wasn't a very friendly man. It was several weeks later when I asked Val what she had told her parents about getting pregnant.

She said, "Well, I could never have told them it was a one-night stand."

"What did you tell them?"

She hesitated, you might call it a pregnant pause. Then she blurred out, "I told them that YOU were the father!"

"Me!" I cried. "Why me?" Now I realized why her dad didn't speak to me that night. It is a wonder he hadn't choked the living daylights out of me!

My interest in medical school didn't last long. I had a good friend, Steve, whom I had met through ICO. He had just finished the U.K. PA program and encouraged me to continue on the PA path, which is what I did.

I applied again for the fall 1979 semester. Eventually I received the infamous registered letter, but this time it began, "We are pleased to inform you . . ." My future as a PA was sealed. I was boarding the PA train with only a vague notion of my final destination, but I clearly knew the next two years would be uphill the whole way.

Chapter Four

Journey to Planet PA

Twenty nervous strangers began to assemble in the sterile classroom at 8:00 a.m. We took our seats at one of the colorful plastic and chrome desks. Before that moment, none of us had met, but we would fast become friends. We sat for about ten minutes waiting on the instructor, during which time you could hear a pin drop. Within the next twelve short months we would have to find a way to cram enough medical facts into our heads so we could start seeing real patients in our clinical rotations. The task ahead was daunting.

In walked Rob, the interrogator from my interview the previous year. As far as I could tell, he didn't remember me. He gave us a pep talk like a Marine drill sergeant. "It is going to be tough and some of you aren't going to make it. Some of you will flunk out and others won't be able to handle the pressure."

After Rob's speech, Dr. Wilcox, the program director, arrived. Measuring in at about five foot five, Dr. Wilcox sported a salt and pepper beard–perfectly befitting his age, which I put at late sixties. A once-chronic smoker, he wheezed with every breath. He was dependent on inhalers, which he carried in his shirt pocket, and prone to coughing fits.

Finally, we were introduced to each other. The PA program had an interesting blend of people. A few were just out of college. A couple had a master's degree in art or other non-medical topic. One was a forty-five-year-old songwriter for Bobby Goldsboro. For the next two years this strange mixture would be my surrogate family.

Dr. Wilcox was one of the authors of our core textbooks. Most of us considered the books the Achilles heel of the program. They had been developed with the attitude of trying to teach complex concepts of human medical physiology to blooming idiots. They were filled with cartoons to illustrate the points. For example, take the introduction to rheumatology. The chapter was titled *Anatomy of an Inflamed Brick*. It had a cartoon of a brick in its natural state and in an inflamed state. It spoke of, "This cell wasn't happy" or "This cell wanted to do this bad thing," etc. Maybe these were precursors to the *Books for Dummies* series. The textbooks seemed to aptly reflect Dr. Wilcox's attitude toward PAs, which was that we were all too simple-minded to ever have made it in medical school. Once I got to know my classmates, none of them struck me as simple-minded; on the contrary, most seemed very bright and confident. They had chosen PA school for the same reasons I had—issues of timing, money, and other circumstances.

Each textbook came with a large stapled pack of papers with corrections. The corrections were as extensive as the book itself. Even the corrections had corrections. You had to sit down with the book and go through it with the corrections, marking each mistake with a pen. For example, the peds book might include, "If a child presents to the emergency department with a fever of 103, severe headache, stiff neck, diminishing mental status and a positive Kernig's sign (strong evidence of meningitis) the most likely diagnosis would be school avoidance behavior." That might be an exaggeration, but the point is, the mistakes were often considerable. We rubbed shoulders everyday with medical and dental students and medical residents, so we learned to carry our books in brown paper bags.

I also had a unique burden among the other students because I was in the ICO training program, which demanded six nights a week. I had decided earlier that I would only be able to give the PA program from 8:00 a.m. to 5:00 p.m., because the one night a week not claimed by ICO was *my* time. I would fill it with basketball or video games or whatever it took to keep my sanity. Many nights, my classmates were having late night anatomy cramming sessions that I never participated in because I had an obligation to the ICO group.

Gross Anatomy–this was certainly the most interesting course. This class posed another psychological metamorphosis. The human cadavers we had as PA students were hand-me-downs: the medical students got to cut them up; we got to take them apart, study them, and put them back together. Going into Anatomy class the first day was an eerie event. It was held in a large room, maybe 20 by 40 feet, with two rows of 3-by-8-foot stainless steel tables. Each table was draped with a large opaque sheet of plastic through which you could see the gray outline of body parts. The room was otherwise bare except for florescent lights hanging from the 10-foot ceiling. The smell of formaldehyde was stifling. The lab instructor spoke to us for a while in the back of the room, then led us to the tables. One by one we uncovered the bodies. Some tables contained upper extremities. Some had hips and some whole bodies.

The University of Kentucky PA class of 1981

The worst table was the head table. And I don't mean head table as in the table where the Captain sits. This table held 8-10 large jars with human heads in them. You pulled them out with a device like a meat hook. I felt like I was in Dr. Frankenstein's lab. To complete this macabre scenario was the fact the man in charge of the bodies was right out of a Frankenstein novel. He was about six-four and heavy, rough looking, and walked with a limp. He was dressed in a gray lab coat that was always buttoned to the hilt. On top of this, he wore a plastic apron and rarely spoke. We called him Igor behind his back because we never knew his real name. Igor worked in a back room where none of us were allowed to go. There he prepared the bodies. His was an abnormal occupation to say the least.

The eeriness of the class wore off with each passing lab. Since the lab was held right after noon, some of us started coming to class early to study and eat our lunch. By February 14th things were so light-hearted that someone came in early, took apart a cadaver, and replaced his real heart with a heart-shaped box of chocolates. Then they put his chest back together. We came in and peeled back his skin and subcutaneous fat layer. The thorax had been sawed so you could lift it out in one piece, exposing the heart and lungs. We were surprised (to say the least) when we took him apart and found the box of chocolates. Written on the cover was, "Will you be my Valentine?"

At this time, I lived in an apartment with several guys who had moved to town for ICO training. When I told them about anatomy lab, they couldn't believe me—especially the part about the head table. Gary, an elementary school teacher, was a bit impulsive. He was an ex-Green Beret sergeant and did nothing halfway. He was like the Arnold Schwarzenegger character in *Kindergarten Cop*, except he wasn't nearly that big. He wanted to see this head table for himself. I had to come up with a plan to sneak Gary into the lab without being caught.

We went to the medical school building at 6:30 p.m. after classes were over and it was dark. I put on a lab coat and gave Gary one as well. We slipped up to the third floor where the lab was located. I tiptoed down the hall and checked the anatomy door and was surprised to find it unlocked. I motioned for Gary to follow. He rapidly tiptoed down the hall, looking really goofy in the lab coat, which was at least two sizes too small for him. The sleeves reached only to his elbows. The way he wore it would jump out to any self-respecting habitual lab coat wearer. I opened the door to the large room. It was dark except for the streetlight shining through the windows. There was also a light coming from beneath the back room door. I took Gary to the back of the room, where the head table was, next to the door. I pulled back the sheet and Gary said, "Oh gross! Those really are human heads. You can see their little eyeballs hanging out. Hey, can you pull one out for me?"

I was reaching for the little meat hook when the back room door came flying open. There stood Igor in his long, stained lab coat, wearing elbow-length black rubber gloves and his plastic apron. The light coming through the open door gave him a surreal penumbra. Igor had caught me with my hand in the cookie jar . . . so to speak.

"What are you doing?" he yelled.

"Uh, uh" (I was waiting for my brain to come up with some reasonable sounding excuse. It didn't). "I am just looking."

"Are you an anatomy student?" he said.

"Yes I am, Gross Anatomy 403," I proudly said.

"Is he an anatomy student?" he said, pointing his long grimy finger at Gary.

There stood Gary in his lab coat wearing a silly grin and his hands in his pockets. I said convincingly, "No . . . uh . . . he is an elementary school teacher."

Igor raised his voice. "Get him out of here now!"

We split. It occurred to me that all those tables might be covered, not with the bodies of kind people who had donated them to science, but with bodies belonging to people like Gary and me who wandered into Igor's lab after hours.

One nice thing about the PA program was that it tried to integrate real patients with course study from the very beginning. We were assigned to small groups of three students with a senior medical resident. Our resident, Dr. Snow, was about five feet tall and weighed about eighty pounds soaking wet. She was pushing twenty-eight but could have passed as twelve. We made rounds with her in the morning. We were just starting to learn about the inflamed brick. This resident would talk to a patient about the tests that should be ordered, etc. The patient would then look at us, Curley, Larry, and Moe, and ask, "What do you think?" The patient, out of layman's naivete, was much more confident of what we had to say–perhaps because we were male. This certainly annoyed her. We would simply respond in a confident deep tone. "Yes, we concur with Dr. Snow." I am sure that our resident felt relieved to have our approval. Actually, I could not imagine her expression if a patient asked this question and one us of had said, "We think Dr. Snow is full of crap."

Later, after we had a couple of months worth of physical examination and history-taking classes under our belts, we began to go to the hospital and do histories and physicals (H&Ps) on poor, unsuspecting patients. However, as beginners, the task was quite laborious. I remember spending about three hours one afternoon with a single patient. He was exhausted by the time I had asked him about every intimate detail of his miserable life and had poked my finger into every bodily orifice. I don't remember what his specific diagnosis was; however, after such a grueling H&P, I am sure his condition must have deteriorated. I wouldn't be surprised if a good percentage of our patients were transferred to intensive care by the time we were through with them.

After we were through, the first-year resident would come in and do the real H&P. Then the senior resident would repeat at least part of it. When the patient had just a little more life left in him, the attending physician would come in and do his H&P, just to finish him off. The way in which this process played out clearly made us look bad.

When we would record up our H&P in the chart, we would write, "The patient is alert, orientated, and cooperative." Our physical exams would be almost normal. However, by the time the patient came to their fourth complete H&P on the day of admission, he or she would be disoriented, ataxic, tender all over from the poking and prodding, and actually bleeding from their orifices. If the patients were not hemoccult positive (a test for blood in their stool) when they came in, we would make sure they were by the time we were through. For all we knew our erroneous textbooks led us to believe we should be able to palpate their splenic flexures (about 18 inches inside the colon) on a good rectal exam; and we ALL wanted to do good rectal exams.

The history also made us look bad through a phenomenon called historical drift. When we interrogated patients they might tell us one story, but, by the time the attending physician reviewed their history, the story was quite different—a sort of good-cop, bad-cop maneuver.

In doing the medical history, the PA student is the good-cop. We were trying to be kind and would ask the patient gently, in a nonjudgmental tone, "Do you smoke?"

"No, I don't," he would reply.

And you write on the history, "Non-smoker."

Then the resident comes in and asks with more confidence, "Do you smoke?" The same answer is given. Then the resident asks, "Did you ever smoke?"

The patient pauses for a minute and says, "Yeah."

"When did you stop smoking?"

The patient waits a really long time and whispers in shame, eyes cast down at the hem of his mini-skirt, tie-in-the-back gown, "Well . . . about 2 minutes before you came into the room."

"OK, then you are a smoker. How much do you smoke?"

"I am cutting back. I only smoke a pack . . . uh . . . a pack a week!" he stammers, wiping the sweat from his forehead with tar-colored fingers.

Next you give the patient enemas until clear, draw his blood five times in two hours, and do a urethral catheterization, barium enema, and an upper GI. After this, you separate him from his loved ones for days, then feed him elementary school left-over lunches at $50 a plate and put him in a room with a roommate who constantly sucks his snot back into his throat and spits it into the garbage can. This roommate also happens to have the TV remote on his side of the room and insists on viewing the 24-hour Polka channel . . . for 24 hours a day. The same roommate screams for "Margaret" throughout the night at the top of his lungs and is on oxygen—so if your patient even thinks about sneaking a smoke, the two of them would be cremated on the spot. About this time, the attending physician walks in the room and starts his history. "How much do you smoke, you little sleazeball of a man?"

The patient starts sobbing and says, "I smoke four packs a day and have since I was seven." Your PA student history starts to look pretty silly by this time. The next morning, you go to grand rounds. The attending reviews the case in front of fifty physicians. "Well, the dumb Medical Assistant . . . er . . . I mean Physician Assistant student said the patient was a nonsmoker when actually he has 200 pack-years of smoking history. Because of the PA student's mistake, we ordered the wrong test and treatment, costing the patient $100,000 in un-reimbursable medical expenses and resulting in a delay that has turned his treatable illness into a terminal one."

About this time, a harsh overhead spotlight illuminates you, and the rest of the staff turn around and stare as you quietly download your three cups of café lait into your brand new Fruit of the Looms.

H & P

Pharmacology was one of the most difficult classes; however, the instructor managed to make it captivating. She wasn't an ivory tower pharmacologist, but she and her husband were both small-town pharmacists outside of Lexington. Between the lectures on the pharmacokinetics of various agents, she would relay funny stories from her long and colorful career.

She talked about the challenge of being the first female pharmacist in her town. She and her husband rotated shifts so they rarely worked together. She told one story about men who would come into the pharmacy and loiter for a while. They would wander up and down each aisle as if looking for something. Eventually they would approach her. "Can I speak to a male pharmacist?"

"Sorry, I am the only one here today, but I can help you. What do you need?"

Some men would simply leave at this point. A few of them would then ask, red-faced, "Uh . . . do you have rubbers?"

This was well before the arrival of AIDS and the mass marketing of condoms. Nowadays condoms hang on racks right next to the hard candy and car air freshener. In those days, they were kept out of sight, behind the pharmacy counter.

Our instructor would reply, "Sure." Then she would walk to the back of the store filled with townsfolk. Once she reached the back of the pharmacy she would shout out, "Did you want lubricated rubbers or dry ones?"

One of our instructors, a practicing psychiatrist, was a walking Rolodex of fascinating cases. Dr. Bell's favorite story was about a nice woman who was *not* crazy. The referring gynecologist thought she was delusional. During her annual pap smear, she brought up the fact that she was coughing up "hair balls."

Dr. Bell's first impression was that she was a pleasant, sensible lady. Rather than digging into her childhood, trying to dislodge some repressed memory about an abusive mother who forced her to eat cat food, he simply said, "Can you cough up some hair for me."

"Maybe."

She took some really deep coughs and started snorting, like she was trying to bring something up. Dr. Bell quickly handed her a Kleenex. She spit a wad of hairy phlegm on the white tissue. A chest X-ray of her chest revealed a tumor, which turned out to be a dermoid cyst connecting to her right main bronchus. A dermoid cyst is a tumor right out of a sci-fi thriller. Inside its hollow shell, it can grow skin, teeth and, yes, even hair. The point, well taken, was to respectively listen to what the patient was telling you.

Speaking of X-rays, a radiological PA taught a class on the interpretation of radiographs. This guy worked really hard to make the class interesting. He spent a lot of time in the radiograph archives, pulling examples of interesting cases, and he would end each class with an amazing story.

One film of a barium enema revealed a large rectal tumor. This PA narrated that the patient noticed a change in the pitch of the sound of his farts. That was his only symptom. He kept bugging his family doctor about it, who by this time was thinking he was just plain nuts, that is, until he did a digital rectal exam. His doctor felt something strange, like a stool except that is was hard and didn't move when he pressed on it. This eventually led to the barium enema and the discovery of the tumor. So in summary, he may be the only person who's musical farts saved his life.

The first year of PA school came and went quickly. By this time, we had been desensitized to body excrement, sickness, and death, so we were ready to become clinical PA students. As we waited for the assignments for our clinical rotations, there was one rotation we feared more than all the others: the emergency room (ER).

The ER site was at a large intercity hospital in Louisville. We had heard rumors that you were simply thrown into the chaos with little supervision and expected to care for seriously ill patients. Well, I lucked out. My partner Lilly and I pulled the ER as our first rotation. We were quick to find out that the rumors were . . . well . . . true. We were to start our year of being gypsy clinicians in the hellhole of medicine.

Chapter Five

The Gypsy Clinician

I pulled my chocolate jeep down the dark Lexington alley, very slowly. I saw a gray metal door open into the alleyway and Mr. James stepped out. I pulled just past him and jumped out, opened the swing-out spare tire on the back, and popped the hatch door.

Mr. James was a short man in his late forties with coal-black hair–slicked back LA-style. He always wore a dress shirt and tie with jeans, and I never saw him without his reading glasses dangling from his neck on a gold chain. He glanced over both shoulders. "OK Mike, let me see what you got."

I pulled the sheet back to reveal a nice telescope, gold class ring, Cannon SRL camera, plus a few other items. Mr. James kept looking over his shoulder, first left then right.

Again I reassured him, "These things are really not stolen. They're mine. I have to hock everything I own as I am going on clinical rotations for PA school."

He didn't appear convinced but reached into his pocket and pulled out a roll of twenty-dollar bills. "OK Mike, here's $180 for everything. Take it or leave it." I took it.

When I moved to Kentucky, I had only a few items of value. I had to sell all of them. I would be moving from town to town every six weeks, so I wanted to streamline my possessions to the bare minimum. I didn't own a single piece of luggage, just a backpack. I went to the local grocery store to look for good cardboard boxes. I found four heavy-duty waxed boxes, the kind that lettuce comes in. These would serve me well over the next fifteen months.

One box held my medical books; one my kitchen supplies, which consisted of a backpacking cook set, a plate, cup, and glass. The other two boxes contained my entire wardrobe.

With my boxes neatly stacked in the back of my Jeep, I headed off to Louisville. Driving into town on I-65 was a bit of deja vu; however, this time I knew that I would be too busy to be lonely. I was thinking, too, no matter how bad the ER experience might be it would only last six weeks. Although I was nervous, I was also excited to start practicing clinical medicine. I had waited three years for this moment. When I arrived in downtown Louisville, I was given a room in the medical school dorm, which was next door to the ancient hospital.

My first shift as a clinical PA student was a major milestone of PA career. It was the graveyard shift on a busy Saturday night. The yellow brick facility had been built in the thirties and was far from state-of-the-art. It was four stories high and took up a whole city block. Ground had already been broken for a new facility scheduled for completion in two years.

I arrived at the ER at 10:45. The huge waiting room was packed. A few of the patients were actually sober. I figured this was unusual for this time of night, on a Saturday in downtown Louisville. The butterflies in my stomach were as active as Jim Carey on a caffeine high. I checked in.

The little lady at the front desk saw me approach, but pretended to ignore me while she finished talking about her dog with a couple of other ladies sitting behind her. While she spoke, with her head still turned away from me, she reached out and slowly slid open the small window. She finally turned, making eye contact with me. "Yes, can I help you?"

"I am a PA student, and I am here for my ER rotation."

"OK, just go on back," she said, motioning with her head and quickly closing the window and resuming her canine conversation.

I went through the double doors to the back. The ER was one

huge area divided into male and female wards by a cinder block and tile wall you could walk around at either end. At one end, running perpendicular to the dividing wall, was a long desk. A wall surrounded the desk with windows from the waist up and provided the staff a little asylum from the chaos of the two wards, yet offered a good observation point for both.

Each ward contained 20 beds that lined the outside wall. Dark green curtains with white, fish-net tops separated each of the beds, but were rarely drawn. On the wall beside each bed was an assortment of oxygen flow meters, suction adapters, and greenish transparent tubing. Randomly placed around the wards were rolling chrome bedside trays and dirty linen hampers. The corner beds, which had more space, had an additional array of monitors and a large red, tool cabinet on wheels that served as the crash cart.

I held in my hand a letter from the Emergency Medicine director, Dr. Smith. It stated that I was to report to a Dr. Jackson, who was the chief resident. When I arrived at the desk, a nurse in traditional white dress and hat told me, "Take a seat and Dr. Jackson will be back in a moment."

Momentarily a tall, lanky, bushy-red-haired guy came around the corner holding a Mr. Pibb. He resembled Bill Walton, the ex-NBA center, but was about six inches shorter. A nurse addressed him as Dr. Jackson and showed him some lab results and they began discussing a patient. While he stood listening to the nurse and sipping his soda, I studied his attire carefully. He was dressed in a scrub shirt and jeans cut off just below the knees. On his feet were iodine-stained white socks and sandals. An assortment of pens and cigars populated his shirt pocket.

When the nurse finished her business with Dr. Jackson, she paused and said, "Oh, this is Mike Jones and he is joining us tonight as a medical student."

Dr. Jackson stepped over to me. "Welcome to the ER, Dr. Jones."

"Thanks, but I'm not a medical student, I'm a PA student from the University of Kentucky."

"Great! Welcome aboard. I hope you have your running shoes on."

I rather enjoyed my six weeks working with Dr. Jackson. He was in charge of the night shift since the attending physicians worked 8:00-

5:00 Monday through Friday. He was one of the most laid back physicians I ever worked with. He quickly eased my nervousness. No matter how chaotic the emergency room became, I never saw Dr. Jackson become unraveled. And this ER could be very chaotic.

The TV series "ER" gives the closest impression of what this experience was like. Car wreck causalities poured in through one door while a full-blown cardiac arrest was being played out in the other corner. In between was a roiling collage of people and action, experienced experts in various fields: fourth-year medical students, residents from all specialties, interns, and of course, one PA student still wet behind the ears. Dr. Jackson was like an orchestra conductor trying to create order in a most disorderly place. He sent providers in this direction or that. The only sign of stress was when he stuck one of his cigars in his mouth and started chewing on it.

I will never forget the night I sutured a living human being for the first time. I had just arrived for my shift carrying my backpack full of medical reference books when Dr. Jackson greeted me. As I walked into the staff desk area, he looked up and said, "Hey Mike, do you know how to suture?"

"Well, I think so. I have practiced on cows' tongues and pigs' feet but never on a real person."

"Well, tonight is your lucky night. Now put down your books and follow me."

I did as he said and followed Dr. Jackson over to the equipment area. I assumed he would show me step by step how to suture, with him doing most of the actual work. Then he turned to me and said, "What size gloves do you wear?"

"Uh . . . seven and a half."

He pulled a pair of seven and a half, sterile gloves from the box. "Now, grab a suture tray. You are going to do the suturing on a young woman who just fell through a glass door."

I was starting to feel nervous. As we walked toward the women's ward, I asked him, "Do you think she will mind if I sew her up?"

"Well," he said, "it is all in the introduction–the fact that she is drunk helps a bit, too."

When we arrived at the girl's bed, we found her sound asleep. Both of her forearms were wrapped in blood-soaked four-by-fours. Dr. Jackson grabbed her by the shoulders and shook her. "Miss Boyd, wake up."

The patient slowly opened her bloodshot eyes and raised up her head. Dr. Jackson said, "Miss Boyd, this is Michael Jones, he is a famous plastic surgeon that we flew in from Cincinnati to close up your cuts real pretty." A big smile came to her face. "Wow," she whispered with bourbon-scented breath.

Dr. Jackson looked at me and winked. "Like I said, it is all in the introduction."

I stood in disbelief.

I unwrapped the patient's forearms. Both of them looked like ground chuck. I put on my gloves and set up the suture tray and injected the area with lidocaine. My hand had a small tremor as I tried to approximate the ragged pieces of flesh. I put in my first suture and tied my knot. Dr. Jackson patted me on the back. "It looks great, keep up the good work." Then he walked away, leaving me to figure things out on my own. I started to sweat.

I looked up to see the commotion across the room. A woman, her hair in curlers and wearing a housecoat with fuzzy pink house slippers, was executing ballet moves in the center of the ward, obviously waiting for the psychiatry resident. A couple of beds away from me was a fourth-year medical student working on a car accident victim. The patient's head had gone through the windshield and the sharp glass had nearly scalped her. Her scalp was completely separated back to the ears. The poor medical student, like me, was trying to get things to line up.

It took me almost an hour to close up the nasty wounds. My patient slept most of the time, awakening now and then to ask questions about life in Cincinnati. I mumbled yes or no in response while trying to keep my focus.

During this first rotation I came face to face with a phenomena I will call CYI (cover your ignorance). This is a strong temptation for medical students of all types. It is when you are presenting your patient, for example someone with numbness, to the attending physician and he says something like, "You did do a protein electrophoresis to make sure we are not dealing with a polyneuropathy associated with monoclonal gammopathy of undetermined significance, didn't you?"

It isn't just the question, but the tone of voice, especially when the inflection rises when he says the words, "Didn't you?" You feel a strong temptation to nod and say, "Of course," while, at the same time, you are thinking, *What the hell is he talking about?*

The truth is, students in this situation don't know a lot, and what they do know is usually still pretty sketchy. That is the purpose of preceptorships. But, the blame shouldn't be placed solely on the student's shame and ignorance, but also on the teacher's attitude. If it pushes the teacher's pleasure button to make others look like fools, the CYI temptation is huge. Yet, if the teacher is like Dr. Jackson, the temptation is much less, and the patient much safer. Dr. Jackson would always say, "The only dumb question is the question that you had but didn't ask."

When PA students ask me for advice about starting their rotation, I advise them, "Never fall into the CYI trap. Be humble; be willing to look like a fool rather than pretending to know something that you don't and jeopardizing a patient's health."

One confidence-boosting ER experience was realizing how close I was to the fourth-year medical school students. We would seek each other out for advice and insight routinely. I was gaining a deeper appreciation for the rigors of PA school and the pre-PA school mandatory requirements. I also realized quickly that one of the greatest attributes of a medical clinician is judgment. Judgment can't be taught in school. In the years to come I would meet physicians and PAs alike who, although bright, lacked good clinical judgment.

Lilly and I survived the reckless six weeks in the ER and moved onto our next assignments. I was assigned to work with Dr. Short, a 65-year-old thoracic surgeon in a small town near Lexington. He stood about five-ten and was stocky. His white hair was cut in a very short flat-top and he had a husky loud voice. He was the "franchise player" for his small hospital. He single-handedly accounted for a huge portion of the struggling hospital's earnings.

Unfortunately, this gave Dr. Short—in his mind, at least—the license to display the demeanor of a two-year-old. It wasn't beyond him to have someone fired if the coffee in the doctor's lounge wasn't perfect. His darkest aspect was that he wrote the book on sexual harassment.

The first morning I scrubbed in with this surgeon I watched him gown up. The scrub nurse held the surgical gloves open for him so he could slide his hands in. He slipped them on and then went directly for her breasts, pulling on them and moaning until everyone laughed. I didn't think it was funny, especially when I realized he did it every time he put on gloves. I would think after years of this the humor would fade. Surely the nurses thought complaining would end up in him making life hell for them and possibly cost them their jobs.

One morning I asked one of the nurses, "How do you feel about having your breast grabbed by this guy every time you turn around." She then handed me a line that sounded like it must have been the hospital's official position on the issue. "That is just the way he is. We just have to learn to deal with it."

The major lesson from this rotation had nothing to do with surgical skill; it was that hospital administrators' ethics are sometimes driven by the bottom line. This Dr. Short could abuse anyone he liked and they just had to "deal with it." Yet, if a nurse did something that offended the man, she could get fired on the spot. The administration viewed nurses as a dime a dozen while knowing it would be very hard to recruit another thoracic surgeon to such a small hospital. I am glad to find that in the new millennium, this kind of behavior can get you sued really fast.

Although I had observed surgery many times while working in the recovery room, I had never scrubbed in before. The first case was a lung biopsy. I had just been talking to the patient before they put him under. Then I went through the process of scrubbing in and gowning up. Next thing I knew, I was at the table across from Dr. Egomaniac. He was kind to me, but it really bothered me the way he treated the nurses and other staff. He yelled at the OR tech right from the beginning. "I said, give me the damn Betadine! Are you deaf or just an idiot?" Then he sliced open the left side of the patient's chest, cut out a rib, and put in a spreader. Before I knew it, he'd grabbed my hand and thrust it inside the patient's chest. "Now, PA student, grasp the guy's beating heart." He never called me by name, no doubt because he didn't know it.

All of this was becoming too much for me. My adrenal glands kindly gave me a huge dose of adrenaline, but I was in no position to either fight or take flight. My heart rate shot up to about 180 beats per minute. The next thing I knew, I was growing short of breath. I knew what was happening and tried to fight it. It seemed hopeless, like I had just run a hundred-yard dash. I was hyperventilating inside my mask. The room was growing distant and my hands felt numb. I was begging my body not to do this to me. I just couldn't faint in the OR, not across from Dr. Short.

I could just picture what would happen if I fell face-forward onto the table. My head would go right between the rib spreaders, into the man's chest, and get stuck. The OR would have to call the fire department to bring the Jaws of Life to get my head out of this man's thoracic cavity. After the demise of the patient, the reporters from "Hard Copy" would be banging on my mother's door late at night. She would be standing there in her curlers and bathrobe, crying, "He was such a nice boy. I'm not sure what happened. He isn't a bad kid, just a klutz."

By God's grace I came back from the brink of syncope to reality. I heard Dr. Short calling me in the distance, "PA . . . hey, PA student!" By now the surgery was almost over. The surgeon had about 15 threaded curved needles resting on a towel. He quickly put the sutures through the intercostal muscles. He looked at me, giving me a nod, and said, "You can tie."

Fortunately there was a real surgical PA scrubbed in on the case. She had initially stepped back, allowing me to assist in her place. I tied four or five of the interrupted sutures and the PA elbowed me. "Move over Mike, let me tie." She rapidly finished tying the sutures then stapled the skin closed.

As I left the OR, the PA pulled down her mask and mouthed to me, "I want to talk to you."

"Sure," I said, wondering what this was about. I imagined that she was going to tell me, "Mike, you performed really well. I think you have a natural talent in the OR." I started to visualize myself in a mission hospital in Nepal doing the first human head transplant.

When we got into the locker room she pulled me aside. "Mike, where did you learn to tie knots like that?"

I thought for a moment. "Well . . . the Boy Scouts."

"The Boy Scouts!" she screamed. "You must be kidding me. You don't know how to tie surgical knots?"

"Uh . . . what are surgical knots?"

To make a long story short, she found me a knot tying practice kit. It consisted of two parallel rubber tubes stretched on a board with one end close together and one about an inch apart, like the edges of a surgical wound. She gave me a roll of suture thread and showed me two-hand ties and one-hand ties. I took the kit home and practiced like crazy for the next few days, rapid two-hand ties, right-handed ties, left-handed ties, and even behind-the-back ties. I was a little concerned about the patient with the five Boy Scout knots holding his ribs together over his heart. I imagined him sneezing and finding his heart in his shirt pocket.

Dr. Short's bedside manner wasn't much better than his professional conduct with the nurses. Most of our patients were in for lung biopsies to see if they had lung cancer. It was a very sobering time for the families. After mornings in the OR, we would make rounds in the afternoon. As we walked into each patient's room, I could see the fear in their eyes. Dr. Short would announce, "That was a beautiful surgery. I did a fantastic job in the OR." He would then laugh, half-jokingly. "You were lucky to have a skilled surgeon like me."

The patient or family would nervously ask, "Doctor . . . is it cancerous?"

Dr. Short would become slightly more sober and say, "Yep, it is cancer and I will refer you to the oncologist." He would turn and walk away, leaving them in tears. I would often stay behind to try and console them the best I could.

I remember more than once a patient or the family following us down the hall with more questions. Dr. Short didn't have much time for them. I remember one little man coming down to the nursing station where we were charting. He had just been given the bad news. He was pushing his IV pole in his left hand and had a pack of Marlboros in his right. He came up to Dr. Short. "I've decided to stop smoking." The frail man's eyes were holding back the tears and he crushed the red box in his fist and threw it in the trash can at Dr. Short's feet. It was like some kind of ritual, an appeasement of the cancer god that could somehow change his fate. Dr. Short, his scrub mask still dangling from his neck, looked at the trash can and then back at the patient. He then cracked an untimely joke: "Hey, don't throw those away, my friend. Cigarettes are what keep me in business." Then he laughed so loud you could hear down to the end of the long, aseptic hall. It broke my heart every time.

The nurses told me, "Dr. Short has been in practice so long his emotions have been hardened." Now that I have been in practice for twenty years and have seen some terrible things, I feel my heart is more compassionate than ever. I have a different theory. I think Dr. Short's real problem had to do with his mother dropping him on his head when he was a baby.

At this hospital was another surgeon, Dr. Thomas. He was from India and was a very nice man. He treated the nurses with respect and they loved him for it. He had a wonderful bedside manner, spending a great deal of time answering the patients' questions. Although he was not a franchise player, doing more minor procedures than thoracotomies, I hung out with Dr. Thomas for the last couple weeks of my rotation.

My next rotation was pediatrics. I have always loved kids and was really looking forward to it. The location was a pretty little town nestled on a steep hill beside the Ohio River. The place had been established as a trading post in the late 1700s. The brick streets lined with old Victorian homes imparted loads of character. The late autumn leaves were tinged golden yellow and flaming orange. The PA school had arranged for me to stay in an all-women's nursing dorm beside the hospital. The only problem with this arrangement was that there was only one community bathroom on each floor. So, obviously, I could only use the bathroom when it was completely vacant. I had an agreement with the nursing students: the last person out would leave the bathroom door propped open.

I didn't realize how long it takes fifteen college-aged women to use the bathroom in the morning. I had to set my alarm for about 4:30 a.m. to get into the "time share" bathroom; otherwise I wouldn't get in until 10:00.

This worked out fine until my little patients so generously began sharing every virus they had with me, taking my immune system by surprise. At the end of my first week in the pediatrician's office, I started with a runny nose followed by the worse case of tonsillitis I have ever had. About the same time I developed bronchitis, then a viral intestinal infection. I had never felt so bad. I couldn't breathe through my nose. My throat felt like I had swallowed molten lead. I was coughing my head off, puking my brains out, and pooping my colon inside out. It was charming. I missed three days of work. During this time I faced a real dilemma. My colon wanted to expel everything inside me, up to my baseball-sized tonsils. It took all my strength to keep everything inside. Still, I had to lay prone to succeed. After an hour, quivering with exhaustion, I would feel the urge to make a run for the bathroom. Once I was in standing position, it would be too late. Yet, I had no choice but to take the risk that the bathroom would be unoccupied. There is nothing less sexy than having anal leakage in front of a bunch of cute women. It would leave a lasting impression, but that wasn't quite what I wanted for them . . . or me. Somehow I survived the rotation with my health intact. I got to work with an excellent pediatrician and learned a lot. I really enjoyed working with the children.

Next came psychiatry. I was more than ready for this after weeks of blood, gore, and sickness. The idea of sitting in offices where the patients wore clothes and didn't bleed, barf, cough, or pee on you appealed to me in a big way.

My psych rotation was in a small town about two hundred miles from Lexington—a neat little burg right out of a novel . . . a Stephen King novel.

I arrived on a Sunday afternoon and wanted to get settled. I was assigned to live with a middle-aged divorcee named Anna. Since her children were grown, she rented out her three upstairs bedrooms to the University of Kentucky and a local technical school.

When I met Anna, she seemed like a very pleasant lady. She was short, about 5' 2", and quite heavy. I would soon learn she was completely obsessed with dieting. She ate Weight Watcher's meals three times a day, plus Weight Watcher's cakes, ice cream, and other snacks. She hated being heavy but had no idea how to take the weight off. I know it wasn't that simple, and that it had more to do with her body weight thermostat being genetically set at about 100 pounds above her ideal weight.

My weight is set about fifteen pounds too high, and I know how hard it is to even keep that off. I will starve myself and exercise like crazy and lose only three pounds. Then I eat one stinking four-ounce cookie and—boom—I jump up two pounds. Instinctively, it seems to violate one of Newton's laws.

Anna took me upstairs. Acting as my tour guide, she said, "This room on the right is your room." It was a very comfortable looking room and it was nice to be in a home decorated in something rather than Repo-Dumpster—the style of my apartment in Lexington.

We continue the tour. "Down here is the bathroom. I keep my towels in this hall closet. At the end of the hall is Beth's room. She is a student at the vocational school. She is studying to be a mortician's assistant."

I met Beth later that night. She was about the same size as Anna except a little taller. She was very quiet. Not just shy, but oddly quiet.

Bright and early the next morning I showed up at the office of Dr. Singh, the psychiatrist. I sat with him and observed. I have to say, I was a little disappointed in his office practice. He didn't do any psychotherapy that I observed. Patient after patient would come into his office. He simply renewed Valium prescriptions all morning. It seemed like the whole town was on Valium, which was still something of a novel drug.

He told me to meet him at the "day care program" after lunch. I thought he was talking about little kids. Once we got there, I found it was the closest thing the town had to an inpatient psych ward and was located on the grounds of the community hospital. These patients were mostly nonfunctional in general society. They slept at their own homes but then came and spent the day at the "day care" facility, complete with an LPN who dispensed medications.

I looked around the room at the dozen or so patients. Several were obviously schizophrenic, sitting in the corner, rocking and chain smoking while mumbling to themselves. Others had different levels of psychosis and a few were there just because they were seriously depressed. It reminded me of *One Flew Over the Cuckoo's Nest*. I found this a much more interesting place than the office with the line of people coming in for their vitamin "V" (Valium) refills. I got Dr. Singh's permission to spend some time here. This would be were I spent the bulk of my psych rotation.

The LPN at the Day Care was Sandy, a small woman in her late twenties with short sandy-blond hair. She introduced me to a 60-year-old, very neatly dressed red-haired woman named Betty, who was the spitting image of George Costanza's mother on "Seinfield." She was the activities director. The mornings were made up of crafts, art projects, board games, and dancing. I'm not sure why dancing was so popular with them, but there is nothing more entertaining than disco dancing with a room full of lunatics. I did get to know them well, though. I also got to observe how they related to one another. I would spend part of the morning reading their charts and familiarizing myself with their drugs and illnesses. I also helped to care for some of their more general medical problems.

One morning, Sandy asked me to take a look at Alice–a client who was about my age and had an affect as flat as a wooden puppet. I can't remember her psychiatric diagnosis. I took her into the little examining room and took a history. She had been feeling bad for about a week, displaying a productive cough and running a low-grade fever. I listened to her chest and thought I heard a few rales, which are wet sounds indicative of pneumonia. I sent her to the hospital for a chest X-ray. When she returned, I told her that I was going to go look at her films. "I want to talk to you in private first," she said.

"Sure, let's go back to the exam room."

Once there she started to speak. "I have something very personal I must tell you. I don't want to go into details because my psychiatrist knows all about it."

"OK," I said.

"Well, I used to do a lot of sewing."

"Yeah, go ahead"

"Well, when I sewed, I used my breast for pin cushions and many of the needles are still in them."

Now, when someone tells you something like that, the normal reaction is to tell him or her something on the same level to ease the potential embarrassment. Something like, "Oh that is nothing, dearie, I keep my extra set of car keys in my rectum." But in this case, I was speechless. I went over to radiology and, sure enough, her breast tissue was full of small metallic foreign bodies.

Around this time I asked Betty how long she had worked in the Day Care. She looked at me funny and said, "I don't work here, I am a client."

That was a shocker. She seemed every bit the nice middle-aged woman. She was dressed well and kept her appearance immaculate. She had also done a good job lining up artists and musicians for the programs. I couldn't figure out her diagnosis. She certainly didn't appear to be psychotic, overly depressed, or anxious. She was very friendly to me and we spent a lot of time talking. I believe her husband was an attorney.

One day she said, "Would you like to go to the Elk's Club this Thursday? It's surf and turf night. Dr. Abbott, the gynecologist, flies the lobsters back—fresh from Boston—in his own private plane. He belongs to the Elk's Club and does his lobster trip once a year. Surf and Turf night is a big deal around here."

I found that very kind of her. Here I was, the new kid in town. I said, "Sure. Will you and your husband pick me up or should I drive?"

"My husband?" she said. "I would never tell my husband we are going." At first, I was puzzled, but I felt a nagging urge to turn down her invitation.

That afternoon I was in the town public library. I pulled down a book and there was Betty in the next aisle peering through at me. I spoke to her. Later, I went to the YMCA to play basketball. When I came out, there was a note under the windshield wiper: "Hi Mike. I was here at the Y and saw your jeep. Do you come here often? Maybe we could exercise together. Betty."

The next night I went to play basketball and there was Betty decked out in spandex waiting for me. I tried to be nice, but I ran on the inside track for three miles to lose her. She stood on the side trying to talk to me as I lapped. It was frustrating. Then I got in a pick-up basketball game, ignored her, and finally she left. After the Y, I went to the grocery store to get food to cook for dinner and there she was again.

After a few days of this, I began to worry. I asked Sandy, "What is Betty's diagnosis?"

"I'm not sure. I do know that Betty used to see another psychiatrist before becoming Dr. Singh's patient. She developed a 'fatal attraction' for the other doctor and he eventually had to get a restraining order to keep her away."

For the remaining four weeks of my rotation, I was harassed by Betty daily. Finally, one day she said, "Mike, I need to talk to you alone."

With trepidation I said, "Uh, sure, just come back to the chart room."

Betty followed me into the chart room and, to my surprise, closed the door behind her. I was now cornered, as there were no windows to jump out of if need be.

"Mike, I need to tell you that I think I am falling in love with you."

My psyche imploded. I was speechless. My psychiatry textbook hadn't prepared me for developments of this sort. My nervousness gave me verbal constipation, but finally I sputtered, "Oh Betty, you have this all wrong. I think you are a nice lady, but I'm not interested in you in that way. Betty, from now on I think it would be better if I didn't work with you."

I was expecting her to turn and leave but she just stood there staring at me—sternly and speechless with her red hair teased out and her eyes open wide—making her look like a giant troll doll. I glanced around the room looking for any sharp objects within her reach. There was a three-hole punch on top of the file cabinet, but with that I imagined she could do no worse than to pierce my ears—or hit me on the noggin.

"Excuse me, Betty," I said as I squeezed carefully between her and the desk and made my way to the door. I couldn't get the door open without making contact with her rear, and that was something I wanted to avoid at all cost. I said a little louder, "Excuse me, Betty."

She took one mouse-step forward, silently. I managed to open the door two inches and slither out of the room like a centipede.

She continued to follow me wherever I went. I was tempted to report her to the police, but I reasoned I would be leaving town soon and just tried to stay calm. Out of embarrassment over the whole situation, I kept quiet.

I had to limit my activities and try to stay closed up in Anna's house to avoid being Betty's object of obsession. This recourse wasn't much better. Anna would talk my ear off, mostly about diet fads and treatments: "I bought this diet powder. It comes from Sweden. You just put it into a bath of really hot water and soak. It melts the fat right off. You can even see the oil in the water when you are done. Did they ever experiment with this powder at the University of Kentucky? It is very rare because it costs $75 per jar. How does it work?" I tried to be kind and avoided telling her how badly she had been taken.

Beth, on the other hand, gave me the creeps. She hardly spoke at all. Yet, when I would be studying in Anna's den, Beth would come down and read in a chair across the coffee table from me. I noticed that she would hold her paperback in an odd way, as if she really wanted me to see the cover. I looked up once and saw it: *The Sensuous Woman*.

I lifted up my huge hardcover book with two hands so she could see what I was reading: *Harrison's Principles of Internal Medicine*, the single volume, unabridged, edition. That maneuver nearly gave me a hernia.

I was looking forward to finishing this rotation and getting back to Lexington as I was entering my home stretch of rotations before graduation. As I pulled out of the small town, I felt a huge weight lift as I wouldn't have to hide from Betty anymore. I would be more than 200 miles away.

When I arrived back in Lexington, I had scheduled during the winter-spring quarter break oral surgery to have my impacted wisdom teeth removed. The teeth were cut out, and my mouth was packed with gauze and still numb. I had been given general sedation plus I had just taken two oxycodone tablets. It was the first time I had ever taken a narcotic. A roommate picked me up from the hospital and took me home to the apartment. All I wanted was to sleep. A few minutes after I had been dropped off, the phone rang. I was just going to let it go, but it rang and rang. Finally I got up, feeling quite dizzy, and staggered down the hall to answer it. "Helwo," I slurred.

I heard a familiar woman's voice on the other end: "Mike, this is Betty. I have left my husband and I want to come to get you. I emptied our bank account of $200,000 and I thought you and I could live in Mexico, where the money would go a long way."

I was in shock hearing her voice, but when she said she had $200,000, I thought, You know, for a sixty-year-old woman, Betty doesn't look half-bad.

I soon came to my senses, though. "Halw did wou find owut my phowne number?"

"Oh, I called the PA program and told them I was Dr. Singh's secretary. I told them that he really needed to talk to you about a patient. They gave me your phone number and address."

"Mwy addwess?" I said. "Wou know where I wive?"

This was the climax of the Stephen King story, like in *Misery*. If it were a film, the dramatic score would start about here, right when she said, "Mike, I am calling from downstairs at your apartment manager's office."

"Wou are in Wexington!"

"Mike, I am coming up to your apartment."

I thought, *Like hell you are.* "Now, Betty, wisten. I wjust had my wisdom teeth cut owut and I am in a wot of wain. I wam woing to get wdressed then weet you across the street at the Burger Wking. But, don't wou dare come up to my apartwent or I am walling the wolice. What part of 'weave me awone' do you not understand?"

I got up and went over to Burger King. There she sat sipping on a big Coke, a big smile on her poor, obsessed face. She bought me some fries—salty fries were the last thing I wanted to put in my sore mouth. I tried to be stern with her. "Betty, you weed welp. This isn't wormal to pursue me like this. Now please weave me awone. Take your money and get back to wyour husband because he wrobably has the wpolice out looking for wou wight now."

Betty continued calling and writing me for several months. It wasn't until I moved to Abu Dhabi for the summer that I was able to lose her. When I came back to Lexington, I changed addresses and no longer had a phone in my name. In the back of my mind, though, I fear she will find me again—some day, some way. I even thought I saw her in Arabia a couple of times. I imagined one of the women dropping her veil to reveal that same obsessed smile. For months, every time I heard the phone ring, I cringed.

I had just a few more rotations left before my three-month preceptorship. After this I would graduate, take my boards, and finally be a PA. I could see the light at the end of the tunnel . . . unless, of course, it was the headlight of an oncoming train.

Chapter Six

The Home Stretch

Amanda was an attractive, thin, very delicate African American woman. I was sitting with her in the exam room, taking her history. She came in complaining: "It looks like I have another urinary tract infection."

As I was writing down her story, I looked up at her and asked, "Why, do you think you have so many infections."

She told me, in a reasonable sounding voice, "I am quite sure it is my prostate."

Prostate? I thought. I was still only a student, but by this point, despite the poorly written textbook, I did know that women–at least the women I knew–didn't have prostates. I was trying to think of how to tell this woman that she was confused without making her feel dumb.

As I contemplated my task, she said, "You don't know about me, do you?"

"What do you mean?" I said kindly.

"You see, I was born in a man's body and had to have corrective surgery a couple of years ago. They didn't remove my prostate, which seems to harbor infections."

Now things started to make more sense. She was my first transsexual.

Amanda was an inmate at the Lexington Federal Prison, where I had set up my one elective rotation. While most of my classmates were setting up their rotations in their hometowns or in some specialty that wasn't offered in our scheduled rotations, I was trying to think ahead to employment. I really loved living in Lexington and wanted desperately to find a job in town. I expected it would be hard given that the PA school was there, plus, Kentucky didn't have legislation for PAs yet and jobs were scarce. The climate for PAs in the state has improved dramatically since.

Around this time, a state representative had even sponsored a couple of bills that would have made practicing in the state almost impossible. For example, one bill required that a physician be in the same room as the PA at all times. Why would any physician want to hire a PA under such conditions? These bills had at least made it to the floor of the state legislation. Our neighbor to the east, West Virginia, had a "Non-Orifice" bill floating around. In this bill, the legislators held that a PA couldn't peer into any bodily orifice. Go figure. Imagine having to tell a patient, "Yes, Mr. Potato Head, I can manage your congestive heart failure, diabetes, gout, and schizophrenia, but don't ask me to look in your mouth–that's illegal."

There was only one large employer of PAs in the Lexington area and that was the federal prison. It was a large co-ed prison that housed its own hospital. I had met a couple of PAs who worked at the prison and seemed to like their jobs very well. Several months in advance, I started trying to set up my elective there. I was the first student to take his rotation at the prison and I encountered a barrage of red tape during the process of getting clearance for my short six-week rotation. However, I figured it would be worth it, because if I could cultivate my contacts it would greatly increase my chances for employment after graduation in the fall.

The prison rotation was a good one. The medical clinic was fully staffed and had a wonderful director (I would find these two things seriously lacking in subsequent experiences with the prison system later in my career).

The medical director was Dr. Sanchez, a very kind and genteel physician from Mexico. He reminded me of Ricardo Montalban. The PAs all were helpful and passed on to me a great deal of invaluable medical knowledge. The prison also gave me many unique experiences that I couldn't have gotten elsewhere. Besides the transsexuals, there were the IV drug users and their special medical problems. This was in the pre-AIDS days, however, and hepatitis was a common problem. Drawing their blood was also a challenge. In fact, many of my chronic IV drug users preferred to draw their own blood. I remember this one Willy Nelson lookalike with tattoos covering his arms and chest. When he rolled up his sleeve so I could draw blood, I found more tracks than Grand Central Station. "Hey doc, I usually draw my own blood." I handed him a syringe. "Arterial or venous?" he said calmly.

"Venous would be fine."

Amazingly, he then dropped his drawers and drew a full syringe of venous blood from the most unlikely place.

The prison system had a hard time housing transsexuals like Amanda. It stood by housing such people with their "new gender" fellow inmates. The real quandary was what to do with those who were cross-dressers but hadn't yet had surgery.

My next interesting encounter with a trans-gender wannabe was very different from Amanda. He was tall, big boned, and heavy, looking a lot like Dick Butkus but with bushy black hair, and went by the name of Katie. This guy was a cross-dresser and had actually put himself on estrogen, which he bought on the street. Katie was trying to save up his (her?) drug money to get a sex change operation, but he got busted for selling cocaine.

Katie considered it psychologically important to go into the clinic once a year for his "annual." Obviously he could not get a pelvic as there was no practical place, well within reason, to stick a speculum. So the staff would do a general exam, including a breast exam.

On this visit, one of the female PAs was looking him over and he really wanted his breasts examined. In working with inmates, you learn to look at everything from a lawyer's perspective. Many inmates love to sue and were just waiting for you to screw up so they could cash in on the legal-lottery. The Bureau of Prisons was very careful to avoid giving them that opportunity. Whenever a provider was seeing a patient of the opposite sex, the door to the exam room had to be left open. Also, we were very careful to have a chaperone in the room during exams that required a patient of the opposite sex to get undressed.

On this occasion, the female PA was preparing to do a breast exam on Katie. She went to Dr. Sanchez. He, wise man that he was, always preferred to err on the side of safety. He suggested that she gets a male chaperone, and she grabbed me.

I followed her down to the exam room. I had never before been asked to chaperone during a breast exam. I entered the room and saw a chubby, broad-shouldered man sitting on the table. He slipped off his blouse and, reaching his hands behind his back, unhooked his A-cup brassiere. He set his bra on the desk and laid down on the examining table, pulling a sheet over himself. He was trying to conceal his considerable 5 o'clock shadow under light make up. He looked like a beached walrus. The PA lifted up the sheet, exposing his obviously shaven chest. She had him place his hand behind his neck and started doing the exam on his normal-sized male breast. He commented in a husky voice, "My breasts were larger when I was on hormones." I am sure they were. As I stood there, I got a load of life's occasional absurdity. Here I was, a male PA, acting as a chaperone while a female PA did a breast exam on a man who wanted to be a woman.

Before I finished my rotation at the prison, I met with the medical director. I said to Dr. Sanchez, "I would really like to work here when I graduate."

"Michael, I have some good news for you. We are losing one PA, Brenda, as she is getting married in September and moving to Tennessee. We have liked your work and will give you the first consideration."

I was very optimistic. Younger PAs might have a hard time relating to this situation—at least those who graduated in the early 1990s, when there were 7-8 positions waiting for each PA. In Kentucky in 1981, jobs were about as rare as fleas on a lizard. So this news of a job opportunity near Lexington was really exciting. However, due to a strange set of circumstances, I eventually missed this opportunity, handing me the first of many professional disappointments.

After my elective, I had an interesting 6-week stay in Loretta Lynn's stomping grounds. My family practice experience was set in a small coal-mining town. It was an interesting clinic. A middle-aged, very determined, divorced woman named Helen had approached the state a decade earlier about bringing a clinic to this under-served area. The state said it couldn't do it because it lacked a facility.

This little fireball of a woman then bought a trailer, parked it in her back yard, moved in, and converted her small, white house into a clinic. Still the state wouldn't help because it couldn't afford axillary staff. Helen then drove herself to Chicago and convinced an order of nuns to staff the clinic with sisters who were nurses. Finally, the state found the funding to bring in a physician and the clinic was opened. Helen was made the official social worker, which she excelled at since she knew the local people so well.

For housing I was given a trailer in a local trailer park. It had seen better days, but I wasn't complaining as it was better than sleeping in my jeep. My six weeks in this town were like a vacation in Hades. I don't mean it was a bad experience, but it had been a very dry winter and the mountains were on fire all around us. At night there were surreal fire ribbons on the mountainsides. There was the constant smell of wood burning, even when you were indoors. During the day, the air was thick with white smoke, reducing the sun to a white circle not much brighter than the surrounding sky. I am sure that folks from LA would have felt right at home.

It was the worst season of forest fires that this area of Kentucky had ever seen. All day long you could hear the buzz of planes dumping chemicals and water on the flames.

I felt very comfortable working with the hillbillies. This was *my* culture. But now I was observing it from a different angle—as a medical provider. One of the first things I noticed was a certain phenomenon when taking medical histories. I wouldn't call it historical drift. I would call it question-answer disassociation (or QAD for short). QAD is when you ask a question and you get a very good answer, but it is an answer that has no relationship to the question asked.

For example: "Mrs. Baxter, do you have diarrhea after the bout of belly cramps?"

Mrs. Baxter looks at you and says, "Oh my Lord, those cramps are so hard they take my breath away. They must go on for ten minutes before they ease up. I think it is from eatin bad creasy greens (a local wild plant that taste like spinach). I pick these out of old man Sam's creek bottom. You know his son Bobby works on his pick-up at his dad's and Iz thinks he lets some of his old motor oil and crap run down into that creek. You know something has killed all the fish . . ."

"That is interesting, Mrs. Baxter, but do those greens cause your bowels to run?"

Mrs, Baxter looks at you and says, "Son, I don't think you even know what creasy greens are, do you? I have eaten them since I was two years old. My grand pappy used to pick them in that same creek. He never had no problem."

Since then I have encountered QAD wherever I worked, even in the Middle East; however, the hillbillies wrote the book on it.

The second medical history phenomena I encountered is something I call quantitative cognition dysfunction (QCD). For some reason, these people couldn't answer questions that required any quantitative measurement, such as time or volume questions.

For example: "Mr. Wilson, how long has this pain been in your leg?"

"Oh, I don't know. I never kept track."

"Can you give me a general idea, was it weeks or months?"

"Oh, for heaven's sake. I've got too much to do to sit and write down when it started."

"OK, Mr. Wilson, I will make this easy for you. Did your leg start hurting five minutes ago or has it been hurting since the day you were born? Which is closest to being right?"

"Hell, boy, I told you I don't know. Now if you can't figure out what's wrong with me, can I see the real doctor?"

You are about ready to pull your hair out when he gives you a false sense of progress. After sitting on the exam table for a few minutes, he says, "Well, I guess it started hurting when Betsy was home."

You finally think you are getting somewhere so you ask, "When was Betsy home?"

"Hell, boy, I don't write that kind of stuff down. I got too much to do. I have a booth at the flea market that I have to get ready each week."

By this time you are ready to scream. Now to finish you off, the patient throws in a little historical drift. You present your case to the attending physician and you tell him how frustrated you are that the patient won't give you a better history. The attending follows you back into the room and says, "Hello Jim, how you doing?"

"Great, Doc. Did you check out that fishing hole I was telling you about?"

"I sure did. My son caught his first fish, a big ol' catfish. Now, I hear you are having some trouble with your leg?"

"Hell yes, Doc. It just started hurting the morning of January 13th at 8:45 in the morning."

Doc says, "Oh, yeah, wasn't that the weekend Betsy was home?"

"Sure was. That is what I was trying to tell this boy here but he just wouldn't listen. The pain has continued to increase since that point, except for three and a half hours on January 22 when I popped one of my mother's 25 mg Indocin."

Now you really look like a fool.

QCD effected volume as well. You ask, "Mrs. Richards, how much blood did you see in your bowel movement?"

"Oh lordy, honey pie, I never stuck my hands down in the toilet and try to measure it."

"Well, could you give me a general idea? Was there a couple of drops on the tissue when you wiped or was it quarts that came gushing out as soon as you sat down?"

"Honey pie, I told you I don't stick my hands in my business in order to measure it. I just flush it down the commode." Then she throws in a little QAD. "I had a friend who had some blood in her bowels. She had blue hair like mine. (This is no punk blue; this is Southern gray-haired-women blue.) Do you think there is some chemical in blue hair dye that makes your bowels bleed?"

About this term, "lordy": some may not be familiar with it. I'm not sure of its origins but I think it is an abbreviated version of "Lord have mercy."

I had a friend who did his Ob residency in eastern Kentucky. He said they were thinking of doing a study of women arriving at labor and delivery. They believed there was a close correlation between a woman's "lordy rate" and the number of centimeters her cervix was dilated. For example, when the woman arrives in tachy-lordy (tachy meaning "fast"), saying, "lordy, lordy, lordy, lordy, lordy," she is more dilated that a woman in brady-lordy (brady meaning "slow"), saying, "lordy . . . lordy . . . lordy." When they looked closer, they found that the number of lordies in ten seconds equaled the number of centimeters dilated. So, nine lordies in ten seconds would mean nine centimeters dilated. Four lordies in ten seconds would mean four centimeters dilated. They didn't even have to glove up until she was at ten lordies per ten seconds. For those of you who are interested, this figure can be charted as "# ldy/ds" (for "number of lordies per deca-second").

The local economy also had an interesting history. Back in the 18th and 19th centuries, when the area was first settled, the rich folks were able to buy the scarce flat, or as they say, "bottom," land. This was the best farmland. The poorer folks were left with the steep mountainsides that were quite rocky and very difficult to cultivate. This pattern continued until the first part of this century. Coal was discovered and the big coal companies came in and bought some of these mountaintop properties from the "Ridge Runners"–a local term given to the folks who lived high up on the mountains and deep in the hollows. Overnight these people went from living in a shack, struggling to grow a little corn to make moonshine, to being millionaires. Jed Clampett was their folk hero. It was interesting what they did with their money.

The TV show "60 Minutes" did a program on this phenomenon. Morley Safer sat in the town's little café one morning and asked, "How many millionaires do we have in here this morning?" About nine men raised their hands. He reported that in this little town, there were more Cadillacs, the car of choice for Ridge Runners, sold per capita than anywhere else in the world.

You could drive through parts of town passing beat-up trailer after beat-up trailer, each with a car or two on blocks in front. Then suddenly you would come upon a house that looked like the White House, or more correctly, Jed Clampett's house. The yard would be populated with plastic flamingos, fake deer, water fountains, big shiny balls on concrete pedestal, and other such yard kitsch. Presumably they felt that if they filled their yards with ornaments then they wouldn't have to mow.

I had a friend at the University of Kentucky named Arnold. His uncle lived in this area and he wanted me to look him up. I gave his uncle a call and he invited me out to his place. He was one of these overnight millionaires. To get to his house you had to go up the mountain. Then you came to a huge wrought iron gate. His house was nice, but not spectacular. We had a hearty dinner of fried chicken, mashed potatoes, creasy greens, and iced tea. Afterwards he said to me, "Hey Mike, do you want to see my Jagdwaar collection?" I wasn't sure what he meant, but it sure sounded interesting. At first I thought he meant the actual cat–a real live jaguar. Then I thought he probably meant Jaguar cars.

We went out to his garage and he started up a golf cart. He put a large tin watering bucket on the back–the kind with the long spout on one side that ends with a round disk full of holes. On the other side was a large loopy handle. He opened four cans of motor oil and filled the watering bucket with them.

We took off, trundling up a dirt road toward a hollow. As we rounded a corner, the mountain formed a huge natural amphitheater. The wall of the mountain was terraced with three or four large slashes, the signposts of strip mining. As we got closer, I could see objects on the terraces. I couldn't believe my eyes, there were rows and rows of real Jaguar cars circling the hollow. I counted thirty! We stopped at every other car and this guy would climb on top and start pouring motor oil all over the car, saying, "I do this to preserve the cars from the weather." He was like a kid with a Matchbox collection, but he had real cars!

I really enjoyed my stay in Eastern Kentucky, but the time had come to move on. I had an uneventful rotation back in Lexington with an older dermatologist who was hard of hearing. All day long you could hear him in the exam rooms screaming, "Stop taking so many hot soapy baths!" He wasn't quite sure what to do with a PA student, so he made me his official zit squeezer, or, as he would say, "acne surgery."

With all my rotations completed, it was time for my elective 3-month preceptorship. It was customary to try to set up one's preceptorship in his area of interest, such as surgery or family practice. Through my involvement with ICO, I had developed a growing interest in mission medicine. My motivation for this was twofold. First, I honestly had a heart to help people in spiritual and physical need. This I thought could best be accomplished in the Third World. Second, and a lessor influence, was the peer pressure of ICO. Many of us in leadership were planning on going into missions. For some Christians, working in missions is at the top of the respectable-occupations food chain.

The ICO leader, Yoda, first planted the idea in my head of going overseas for my preceptorship. I had approached the director of our PA program in early spring about going. After our first year we had a new program director and he was doing a good job of raising its standards to a real class act. The "National Lampoon" medical books were the first to go. The director approached the Dean of the School of Allied Health about my proposal. The report came back: "No way." I believe the school was concerned about its liability should something happen to me overseas.

I remained convinced I should go, so I started applying to different mission boards and relief organizations. This proved very frustrating at first. They had brochures begging for nursing students, medical students, physical therapy students, dietetic students, and even pre-med students. Yet, when I wrote them, I received rejection letter after rejection letter. Here I was, wanting to donate my services to a relief organization for three months. Yet, they all said, "We do not have a need for a Physician Assistant." I would later find out that these letters were generated when my title was cross-matched with their database of requested personnel. The concept of Physician Assistant wasn't even in the vocabulary of these overseas hospitals and clinics.

It wasn't long before I finally received a letter from an organization I will call Medical Alliance or "MA." MA had already received a letter from another PA student named Karen in Nashville, requesting to spend her preceptorship with the organization. She had made phone calls and actually broken the ground for their acceptance of PAs. The organization said it would consider me and enclosed the appropriate application forms. When I examined the list of hospitals and clinics, I saw listed a remote field hospital in Nepal. Being somewhat of a mountain man, I picked Nepal as my first choice. Hospitals in Africa and in the Andes were my second and third choices.

I received a letter of acceptance to the mission organization and later had a phone call. The director of their short-term program asked me, "Mr. Jones, would you consider going to the United Arab Emirates?" I had no idea where U.A.E. was; all I knew was I detested heat and deserts.

I said, "Why U.A.E.? Why can't I go to Nepal?"

"The Nepali hospital is so remote that logistically we can't arrange your visit." That was 20 years ago. Now Nepal probably sports a Wal-Mart at the base camp for Everest. In 20 more years, there will be a McDonald's at the top selling yak burgers to people trying to be the first to reach the top while wearing the San Diego Chicken suit.

All the other hospitals, in Africa and South America, refused to accept a PA. If I had gone as a nursing assistant, they would have welcomed me in a second. But out of ignorance they considered PA too controversial, as though I was some kind of fly-by-night faith healer. A faith healer probably would have been more welcomed.

The MA director went on to say that Karen had requested U.A.E. several months earlier. They had worked with the medical director and finally persuaded him to allow a PA student to come. With the door now open, it would be easier to get him to accept a second student than to get another hospital to accept its first student.

The next time I was back in Lexington, I met with our director, who had had a sudden change of heart. He now saw this as a good thing, and thought it possible the program might even use my experience as a promotional story in the university newspaper. The sail was set. I was off to Abu Dhabi, where my life would soon change forever.

Chapter Seven

Third-World PA

It was in the middle of a dark Arabian night that my phone rang. "Mikeel," came the heavily accented voice, "Dr. Smalley wants you in the OR as soon as possible!"

I jumped out of bed, put on my scrubs, and walked across the dark, sandy compound to the small, cinder-block building that we knew as the hospital. Even at 3:00 in the morning, the air was hot and dry. The outside door led directly into the scrub room. Dr. Smalley was already hard at work scrubbing his nails with a Betadine-soaked scrub brush. He turned off the water to the large sink with his elbows while holding his hands in the air. "Hi Mike," he said with a soft smile.

Dr. Smalley was an American physician in his early forties, with dark hair neatly combed to the side, a mustache, and a kind smile. One of the nurses was helping him tie his green wrap-around cotton OR gown. The Indian nursing anesthetist was already in the OR.

"What is it?" I said.

"We've got an emergency C-section. Can you help?"

"Sure!" I started scrubbing in and gowning up.

Momentarily the nursing anesthetist had the patient sedated with ketamine. Soon, Dr. Smalley had her abdomen opened and the uterus exposed. I was holding a bladder retractor with my left hand and another retractor with the right. The musty smell of human blood was in the air. Dr. Smalley was finding his target at the base of the uterus, being careful to avoid the bladder. Holding the uterus steady with his left

A KERNEL IN THE POD | 87

hand, he gripped the scalpel firmly in his right hand. Just as he was coming down on the uterine landmark, the power suddenly went off, leaving us in total darkness. A collective moan went up. We all stood motionless, hoping it was one of those short-lived electrical pauses in the national power grid. Thirty seconds passed, a minute. Dr. Smalley gave the order: "OK, someone go wake up Abraham (the maintenance man) to start the emergency generator."

We held our positions, hoping and praying the electricity would soon return. I eased up tension in my arms before they started to quiver. Soon I heard the footsteps of someone running across the compound to the generator shed. Dr. Smalley whispered what we all were thinking: "I hope it starts."

In a moment we heard the sound of a diesel engine trying to be started: ror-ror-ror-ror–ror . . . ror-ror-ror-ror-ror, but then silence. Over and over the Pakistani man cranked the engine to no avail.

The nursing anesthetist said, "I am going to need some light to see how the patient is doing."

At this time, Abraham ran into the room. "The generator won't start. I checked the fuel and everything, but it won't start."

Dr. Smalley said, "Forget it. We have to get some light in here now so I can get this baby out!"

The short Pakistani man acted in haste, as if it wasn't the first time the scenario had played itself out. Within minutes he returned from the garage with a car battery, a headlight, and jumper cables. He was a regular MacGyver.

The little man clipped the jumper cables to the head lamp then stood on a stool above the OR table. Finally we could see something again, but not much. The patient's abdomen was brightly lit, the large incision glaring in tones of crimson. The staff, positioned around the table, remained silhouettes at best. The uterus was quickly cut and the baby delivered before the car battery went dead.

Everything was set in place for my adventure as a precepting PA student in Abu Dhabi. On the 5th of June I flew out of Tri-Cities Airport in Tennessee. The first leg of my flight took me to New York City for five days of orientation by Medical Alliance. There I met another forty kids—each with an assignment to some distant village scattered around the Eastern Hemisphere. We spent the days talking about cross-cultural sensitivity and other such issues. To my surprise, I was paired with four girls, all going to U.A.E.. One was a pre-med student, one a dietetic student, and two were nursing students. One of the nursing students carried a backpack—not a sissy book backpack, but a real outdoorsy one. She had very short hair and naturally strawberry colored lips. Her name was Denise. The other PA student, Karen, would be starting her preceptorship in August.

We were flying to Abu Dhabi on PIA—Pakistan International Airways. It was by far the cheapest way to get there. People who flew a lot referred to the airline as "Perhaps I'll Arrive" or "Please Inform Allah." By the time the summer was over, I would understand why—yet I would not hesitate to fly with PIA again.

That night we all loaded onto the plane, taxied out to the runway, then just sat there. We waited fifteen minutes, then twenty-five, then forty-five minutes. The runway was impressively crowded for that time of night—at least that's what I thought. Then after about an hour of loitering, the airplane turned and started heading back to the gate. During this whole ordeal the airlines told us nothing about what was going on.

We were greeted back at the gate by scores of police cars, bomb squad vans, swat teams, and fire trucks. It looked like the set of a Bruce Willis movie. I was starting to gather by this time that something wasn't quite right. Call it male intuition.

The front door of the plane was opened and all 300 of us were told to exit, single-file. A police escort took us to a large room in the terminal. No one was allowed to leave. One by one we were searched and questioned. After several hours it was revealed that just before take-off the NYPD had been informed the plane was either going to be bombed in mid-air or hijacked by a PLO fraction group. Some passengers chose to cancel their trip. Those of us continuing were taken in small groups via police van to an area on the runway covered with opened suitcases. Everyone's bags had been opened and dumped out on the tarmac. We were told to identify our bags, quickly stuff our things back in, and report back to the van.

This ordeal lasted nearly the entire night. Finally we got off the ground, heading for Paris. As we became airborne, the bright yellow sun was peaking over the New York harbor. The dim light was glistening on the choppy sea. The dark silhouette of the Statue of Liberty was set against the pink morning hue. Behind us were the lighted glass and steel structures reflecting on the harbor and the constant flow of white headlights and red taillights in the streets of the city that never sleeps. The tops of the World Trade Center buildings were just catching the first rays of dawn, giving them the appearance of colossal torches–biding us America's farewell. The trans-Atlantic flight was uneventful as I drifted in and out of sleep. Once we left Paris, I felt like I was already in the Third World. The vast majority of passengers were either Arab or Pakistani.

By the time we arrived in Abu Dhabi, we had made up some time, but were still about two hours late. Bob and Tim, two guys who worked for MA, welcomed us outside of customs. They were delightful. Bob was tall, with more hair on his face than his head and a permanently installed ear to ear grin. He had a joke a minute. Tim was my height, five-nine, and had short dark curly hair and a full beard. He walked shuffling the bottoms of his sandals on the concrete or asphalt. We drove sixty miles across the empty desert on a paved highway to a small oasis on the border with Oman, pausing only to dodge camels and the occasional sand drift.

Several barren mountains surrounded the oasis town. The largest one was called "The Whale" because of obvious reasons. Except for clusters of palm trees here and there, it could have been the surface of the moon. It was about as hot as the moon on a sunny summer day. As I stepped out of the air-conditioned car and drew my first breath of the hot air, the fillings in my teeth threatened to melt from the heat.

The hospital had been built prior to the discovery of oil in this part of the world. It was the area's first modern medical facility. By the time I arrived, the oil-rich Emirates had built many modern, well-equipped hospitals. Most of the patients at the mission hospital came from across the border in Oman, where the medical care was still primitive.

The hospital staff was very helpful in helping us get settled. I was assigned to work the women's outpatient clinic. As with strict Moslem cultures, men and women were segregated throughout society. We had to provide not only separate clinics for male and female, but separate waiting rooms, separate lines at the pharmacy, and so forth. The government had requested that the hospital provide a female physician to see the female patient. The hospital had been recruiting for years for a female physician without success.

Dr. Smalley needed help working the women's clinic–a large room with white cinder block walls and a white tiled floor. The plain walls had a couple of pictures of the King of Abu Dhabi, Sheik Zayed, and his family. In the center of the room were two large wooden desks. Behind the desks were "examining rooms" consisting of areas partitioned with mobile curtains on metal frames. The clinic received thirty to forty women every morning, plus children. After a quick lunch, the providers spent the afternoons making rounds in the hospital.

Words can't describe the commitment these missionary doctors and their families made to go there. Although they could be earning $100-200K per year in the states, they were living on about $20-35K per year on the mission hospital compound. Their standard of living was the same as everyone else there. They did what they did for the benefit of the local people.

To my surprise, I was going to see my patients without the benefit of a translator. It was rare to have a patient who spoke English. Dr. Smalley sat at a desk in the same large room, but I couldn't bother him to translate word for word. He was soft-spoken and gentle with everyone, except his wife. He didn't seem to be very fond of her.

We also had a wonderful black-haired Canadian nurse named Nancy, who spoke great Arabic. However, she was often out of the clinic doing other chores.

I quickly made a list of all the important medical history words such as pain, fever, nausea, vomiting, headache, cough, cold, and snot. I also learned to say, "How long have you had this?" Then I learned the words for seconds, minutes, hours, days, weeks, months, and years, as well as the numbers from 1 to 1,000. I crammed these words into my mind over the course of three days.

Things went quite well in the clinic. I could understand enough of what the patients were saying to figure out their problems. They, likewise, seemed to understand me. It is amazing how crucial those few words were.

I lacked the luxury of a physical exam in the women's clinic. I had to go on history alone as men weren't allowed to touch women. Whenever I needed to assess something from an exam, I had Nancy perform the exam behind the curtain and then describe what she had seen and felt. This system seemed to work remarkably well.

One instance when my limited Arabic *was* insufficient comes to mind. The patient came in the door wearing the traditional long black gown and the veil that resembled a goalie's mask called a berka. Her berka was also black, with a dusting of gold color. It covered her face, exposing only her eyes and chin. The palms of her hands were red with henna and she smelled strongly of frankincense. As she sat down in the patient's chair beside my desk, I could see enough of her to realize she must have been in her 70s if not her 80s.

I offered the traditional greeting in Arabic of "How are you?"

She responded, "Great, thanks to Allah."

Then I said, "What is really wrong with you?"

She began jabbering away so fast, waving her hands as she talked, that I couldn't understand a single word.

I asked her to repeat what she had said. This time I identified one word, "Waja," which means "pain."

I said, "Wayne Waja?" which means, "Where is the pain?"

She resumed her speed talking, none of which I understood until she pointed at her back and said, "Waja hina," which means "The pain is here."

Now we are getting somewhere, I thought. Next I got to use my really big sentence, "Min kam yom fe waja?" Which means, "For how many days has there been pain?"

The woman looked at me and began jabbering again. I could only make out the first word, "min," which means "since." I asked her to talk slower.

She did, but it didn't help. I asked her to slow it down even more. Eventually she was saying her words one at a time, very loudly, with a long pause between each one. By this time she must have thought I was a complete idiot. Still, I could only understand the first word. She didn't use any words to indicate time, such as hours, days, or weeks. She also didn't use numbers.

I was growing frustrated. I looked at the frail little old lady and concluded that she must have had a little arthritis in her back since after working so hard her whole life. I gave up on understanding her history and gave her a prescription for an anti-inflammatory drug.

She appeared to be grateful and thanked me. She stood up and walked carefully, with a limp, to the door. As she was exiting through the door, Nancy was coming in.

I quickly shouted, "Nancy, please ask that lady how long she has had her back pain."

Nancy grabbed the woman's shoulder and asked her. The woman gave Nancy the same answer she had been giving me. Nancy turned to me, smiling, and translated: "Since I fell from the top of the palm tree."

I was flabbergasted. I knew these people climbed the tall palm trees to pick dates, but I would never have counted a woman of this age among them. I called her back and got X-rays of her back and hip.

**The author in the women's clinic
with an Arabic "cheat-sheet" on the desk.**

Fortunately we had a very good group of nurses, most of who were from India. They were able to handle all our female exams as well as deliver the babies. The OB department had an alarm button on the wall. If they had trouble, they would pull the alarm and Dr. Smalley would rush in to help. This only happened once while I was there. I followed him into OB hoping for a learning experience–I wasn't disappointed. The patient was on the delivery table with her legs in stirrups. Her little boy was coming out breech and her cervix had clamped down after his shoulders were out, trapping his head.

The room held 4-5 Arab women, who were co-wives (men were allowed four wives) or mothers and mothers in law. It was a mean gauntlet of slapping when the two of us men entered the room. This was a big no-no, to come in with a woman so exposed. We were slapped and hit from all sides by the women as they screamed for us to get out. Still our focus was on getting this baby out before it was too late.

Fortunately, delivery complications were uncommon. Most of the women came in at the last possible minute and were back up cooking dinner for their families within a couple of hours after delivery.

When Karen arrived to start her PA preceptorship I gave her a tour of the hospital. At this point she was a bit overwhelmed, having been in the country only a few hours. As we walked through OB, the outside door flew open and a young bedouin girl fell in, grabbing the footboard of a nearby bed. Immediately, a baby fell to the floor from the bottom of her long dress, dangling by his umbilical cord. It was like the scene from Monty Python's *The Meaning of Life*, in which a Catholic woman in Northern Ireland, who is doing the dishes, downloads her baby onto the floor without so much as a pause in her song.

I immediately turned to Karen and said, "Looks like this lady came in earlier than most."

When Karen started working, I moved from the women's clinic to the men's. There I worked with another American physician named Dr. Jefferson, who also had just arrived. He looked a lot like Dr. Smalley, but without the mustache and with a much louder personality. Dr. Jefferson was a wonderful surgeon who spent most of his time practicing primary care in the outpatient clinic.

I had three major lessons left during my remaining time in Abu Dhabi. The first lesson was how not to run a code on someone having a heart attack. It was a regretfully sad situation.

One afternoon, as Dr. Jefferson and I were finishing up the men's clinic, one of the nurses came and said, "Your friend is waiting for you in the employee lounge." Mr. Shoemacher was a German engineer living and working in Abu Dhabi. He was a very large man, standing about six foot four and weighing over 250 pounds. He was a personal friend of Dr. Jefferson. As we came into the lounge, Mr. Shoemacher greeted us and said, "Eric, I have been having really bad indigestion all morning and wanted to know if I could have some ulcer medicine. I'm sure it was from the steaks I had last night. They were pretty darn greasy." As we spoke, Mr Shoemacher grew increasingly short of breath and clammy. We did an electrocardiogram, which showed evidence (S-T elevation) of a pending heart attack. Dr. Jefferson called the large, well-equipped government hospital. It was brand new and supposedly had a cardiac care unit (CCU). We didn't have so much as a monitor or a defibrillator in our little hospital.

We started an IV, gave Mr. Shoemacher morphine, and put him on oxygen before calling the ambulance service, a recent addition to the local culture. In about twenty minutes, a converted cargo van arrived. It was poorly designed. The drivers sat in the cab, totally separated from the back by a metal wall. It didn't matter that the drivers couldn't reach the patient, as they knew nothing about medicine, just how to drive a van. Dr. Jefferson and I had no choice but to ride with Mr. Shoemacher, who continued to deteriorate.

When we opened up the back of the van, there was more frustration. It had a large metal table welded to the side that placed the patient within 6 inches of the roof of the van. Also, there was no room for passengers in the back. We decided it would be better to put Mr. Shoemacher under the table. There at least the IV would continue to run in. The only place left for us to sit was on top of the table, over our patient.

As soon as we pulled out of the hospital parking lot, Mr. Shoemacher suddenly lost consciousness. There was no respiratory effort or pulse. We tried to start CPR under the fixed table with us sitting above him, which was no easy task. Meanwhile our ambulance drivers were maneuvering like Shriners on go-carts in a 4th of July parade. We were bouncing to the right and left as they made several wrong turns before finding the hospital.

When we arrived, we received no help from the ER staff. Instead, all we had was a crowd of gawkers watching us doing a strange ritual we called CPR. So the two of us strained to carry his stretcher into the building, stopping now and then to do CPR. Finally we made it to the elevator and up to the fourth floor and to the so-called CCU. This was the first patient they had ever had, and he was arriving in full arrest. We carried him into a room and got him onto a bed, still pausing to do CPR. Finally the "Code Team" arrived, made up of a cardiologist, pharmacist, and anesthesiologist. We were exhausted and were excited to have help.

We watched their performance with disbelief. The cardiologist started doing a one-handed CPR that was probably giving the patient about a 1% of his normal cardiac output. Then the he simply stopped and left the room to get the defibrillator and monitor. We jumped back up and resumed CPR.

When the cardiologist returned, he carried the equipment still in its original box. Next, he spent 10-15 long minutes trying to connect the cables and put it together. I could see the desperation in Dr. Jefferson's face, as he knew the situation with his friend was quickly becoming hopeless.

In the meantime, the anesthesiologist had the patient intubated (a breathing tube placed down his windpipe) and was bagging him. The cardiologist still couldn't get the defibrillator to work–the plug was American style while the outlets were European–and had sent a nurse for an adaptor. Judging from how long it took her I think she went to Wal-Mart . . . in Des Moines. The cardiologist then decided to inject epinephrine right into the patient's heart, which didn't make sense because we had a good IV running. He punctured the patient's left lung and he started developing pockets of air under his skin, or subcutaneous emphysema. The anesthesiologist rubbed his hand over the subcutaneous air pockets and then, for reasons unknown, extubated (took the breathing tube out of) the patient.

Dr. Jefferson, usually a very kind man, had been screaming at these physicians throughout the whole code. Now he shouted, "Why are extubating him?"

The anesthesiologist said, "I cannot continue because I am making air pockets under his skin."

"SO WHAT!" Dr. Jefferson shouted. "The guy has to exchange air to survive." By this time, we threw up our hands–the code had been running now for about 45 minutes. We slowly left the room with Laurel and Hardy still monkeying around with their equipment. Tears began to flow down Dr. Jefferson's face. We decided to take the stairs down. On the second floor landing, we ran into, of all people, Mr. Shoemacher's wife, Regina. She was a very cheerful lady and wore a bright yellow sun dress. Regina said to Dr. Jefferson, "Oh hi, Eric. I heard Bill was having some stomach trouble. Must be his ulcer acting up."

We were speechless. We led her to a room on the second floor and broke the bad news. I have only had to tell a family three times in my career that a loved one has died. There is no "proper" way to say those words. Nothing can dampen the blow.

The next important lesson I learned that summer was that the doctor is always right when his diagnosis disagrees with yours, especially when he is wrong. This I expect to experience again and again in my career. I call this phenomena "credentially weighted correctness."

Dr. Jefferson was a wonderful surgeon, but as I mentioned, his skills were needed mostly in the outpatient men's clinic. He did have a surgical case about three times a week. But, the hospital was limited and couldn't offer much more than hernia repairs, vasectomies, and cesarean sections. The men's clinic was quite different than the women's in that 80% of the patients were Pakistani. At the time, the population of U.A.E. consisted of 70% expatriate workers. These men had no access to the national health service, so our hospital was one of their main sources of care.

One morning I saw a man with a "rash" on his penis. When I examined him, I found a large patch of totally depigmented skin on the shaft. On such a dark-skinned person, it was really noticeable. The patient was very worried. It was clear to me that this was vitiligo [a simple loss of pigmentation that is usually not treatable] because it was a non-raised lesion without scaling, and mostly by the fact that it was totally depigmented, not just hypo-pigmented.

With a male, Indian nurse acting as translator, I reassured the patient that it was benign and there was no practical treatment. This part of the country lacked a dermatologist, and I'm sure he would not have been a candidate for a phototherapy trial.

The nurse kept saying, "But he is very worried."

I told him, "I am sorry, but there is nothing I can do."

As I proceeded to the next patient, I saw the nurse leading Dr. Jefferson into the exam area to see my vitiligo patient. Later I asked the nurse, "Why did you take Dr. Jefferson in after me?"

"Oh, I am glad that I did. Dr. Jefferson found the real cause of the rash–a fungus."

"A fungus?" I said.

"Yes, and he started him on griseofulvin and placed him on a cream that will clear it up."

I tried to explain to the nurse, and later to Dr. Jefferson, that I was certain of my diagnosis. First of all, the only fungus I knew of that can cause hypopigmentation is tinea versicolor. This hypo-pigmentation was the result, from my understanding, of the fungus acting as a sun block. This lesion was in an unexposed area, plus it was *total* depigmentation. The nurse looked at me and said, "He is right because he is a doctor, you're not." This statement would always haunt me.

The final major life lesson I learned was that I was in love with Denise. She had come to U.A.E. as a nursing student. I played volleyball with her in New York. One of the other girls quickly pointed out to me that Denise was engaged, so I tried to dispell my interest in her. I did work with her every day in the hospital and we became good friends. But, we really got to know one another in a closet over some dog guts.

An American family who was with MA had a dog they really loved. They had given the dog to Denise and her roommates to watch for a week while they were out of town. While Denise was watching the dog, he went out and somehow got himself disemboweled. It could have been some kind of dog torture inflicted on him by a foreign pack of dogs, like the English did in *Braveheart*. More likely it was one of the locals. The Arab culture despises dogs. His wound was ugly.

Denise came to me looking very worried look and asked if there was anything we could do. I said, "Well, we could try to put Humpty Dumpty back together again."

Since the wounded dog was sleeping in Denise's closet anyway, we decided to do the surgery there. I got a bottle of ketamine from surgery and ended up giving the dog a huge dose before she finally went down. Then she (the dog, not Denise) began to act really weird, twitching, growling, jerking, and drooling—sort of like Michael Jackson with dyskinesia.

Finally I got her subdued enough to clean off her intestines, stuff them back in and close her up, layer by layer. It was a good opportunity to practice my surgical skills.

Throughout the drama, after working so closely with Denise, I knew I was falling in love with her. But, there was nothing I could do about it. My time in Abu Dhabi was drawing to a close and we would go our separate ways. This had been a summer that I would never forget. Little did I know that, in some ways, my Third World adventure was just beginning.

Chapter Eight

PA-K?

"Pakistan?" I asked the travel agent. "I can go to Pakistan for free?"

As we were preparing to head back to the states, I noticed that across my airline ticket was a line with the letters "PAK." I was at a local travel agent's office, trying to confirm my flight home. "What does PAK mean?"

"Your ticket was a round trip ticket from New York to Pakistan. Abu Dhabi was just one stop. The round trip ticket to Pakistan with PIA was cheaper than a direct flight to Abu Dhabi."

"Where in Pakistan?" I asked.

"Anywhere you want to go" he replied with confidence.

I had thought my wild Third World adventure at a close. Now here was an opportunity to prolong it a couple more weeks. Little did I know that those two weeks would change me forever–raising my compassion for my fellow humans to a new level.

I went back to the hospital and spoke with the field director. "Mike, I do have a good friend, Jerry Davidson, who is the field director for one of our hospitals in northern Pakistan. I could check into the possibility of you staying with him."

Northern Pakistan, I thought, this means near the Himalayas, the mother of all mountain ranges. In the meantime, Tim, one of the guys who picked us up when we first arrived, started talking about his upcoming furlough to the states. He was single, in his upper twenties, a career missionary with MA. Tim planted an idea. "Mike, if you go to Pakistan for two weeks, you will be heading home about the same time I'm going there. Are you interested in hitch hiking through Europe on our way home?"

"Europe?" I said, before immediately adding, "Sure!"

It was around that time the field director told me, "Mike, your stay in Pakistan is all set up. The Davidsons will pick you up in Rawalpindi and take good care of you."

Things were starting to mesh. I went to the travel agent and booked a flight for Rawalpindi. I scheduled a two-week layover in Pakistan. Next I scheduled a flight to Paris, where I would meet Tim. I scheduled flights to New York and finally back home to Tennessee two weeks after that. This schedule placed me back in the US the third week in September. My PA class would be graduating in August. I sent a letter to my program director telling him that I would be graduating in absentia.

Early that August morning, we went to the airport in Dubai. I said goodbye to Denise through the security fence. She was flying home to Minnesota later that morning.

The night before we had opened a relationship, you might say, by accident. We had a sick baby in the hospital with severe malnutrition, malaria, and anemia. Since the baby and I both were O-positive, I had given her several transfusions of my own blood. I would go up to the nursery, draw 50cc from my arm, and gave it to the baby. They checked her hemoglobin every hour and would call me for more blood until they reached her target level. This happened several times throughout the evening.

Each time I walked across the sandy compound to the small hospital, I would stop by Denise's house, where she lived with three other American women. I could hear them laughing, yet I could not get their attention. I knocked but no one would come to the door. I wanted to say goodbye to Denise and the others.

Finally I gave up and went to my house and went to bed. As I was lying there, I started thinking about how I was falling in love with Denise, a semi-engaged woman (no date had been set). Surely it would do no harm to get her address. I knew she was studying in Duluth at the time, but I would never be able to find her.

So I got up and got dressed and went over to her house for the fourth time that night. This time the lights were out and all was quiet. I pounded on the door and no one answered. I turned the knob and it was open. I walked into her little kitchen and shouted out, "Anyone home?"

Denise came out in her bathrobe. Obviously she had been sleeping. I felt embarrassed.

"What is it?" she said with alarm. I was speechless. I didn't know what to say. I knew that I was in love with her, and that after this night I would probably never see her again. She would soon be married and starting her new life somewhere in Minnesota. We sat on the couch in silence. She must have thought I was losing my mind, acting like I was. After ten long minutes I blurted out, "I love you," and the next thing I knew we were kissing. Apparently her engagement was the last thing on her mind. We vowed to find each other again back in the states.

It was doubtful whether my plane could leave the ground that morning. Most of the passengers were Pakistani workers, going home for their yearly visit, and they were loaded down with treasures. There were queen-sized mattresses rolled up in huge bundles on their heads, TVs, refrigerators, and all types of appliances. When they got to the airline desk, they simply paid a bribe and got the goods checked through, even though they were well over the airline's limits for size and weight.

My plane took off in the dark and as soon as it reached cruising altitude I witnessed a brilliant sunrise over the mountains of Eastern Iran. The contrast was profound, between the ink-black shadows of the rugged landscape and the radiant red sunrise. It was over these same mountains that the Persian prophet Zoroaster, twenty-six centuries earlier, had seen a sunrise and developed his theory of absolute dualism. This was the idea that the world was divided between two equal forces of dark and light.

I was the only Westerner on the plane. In a few hours, we were approaching Rawalpindi. A steward started passing out disembarkment cards. These had to be completed before arriving in customs. On one side, information was printed in Urdu. On the other side the writing was in English. As soon as I started working on my card, a line of Pakistani men started lining up beside my seat. I was confused. None of them spoke English. Finally the steward passed by and said, "These men don't read or write. They want you to complete their papers for them."

One by one, they handed me their passports and cards. The cards asked for their name and passport numbers. I could handle that. Then it asked questions such as, "What were you doing outside of Pakistan?" and "What is your purpose for coming to Pakistan at this time?" and "How long do you plan on staying in Pakistan?"

At first I was stumped. Then I simply filled them out as best I could. I wrote, "I am coming from Abu Dhabi, where I am working. I am coming to visit my family and I will stay for 30 days." After about the tenth man, I decided to be more creative. I wrote, "I am living in Abu Dhabi and I am coming to Pakistan to visit my aunt Myrtle who is marrying my boss's brother. I will also buy a new cow. I will return to Abu Dhabi after I get my wife pregnant." By the twelfth guy, I was starting to think it would be interesting to see the reaction if I put on this guy's papers, "I have been living in exile in Iran because I am an enemy of the government of Pakistan. I am now returning to organize a revolt and I will stay here until I am made President." Then I remembered the movie, *Midnight Express.* Some of these Third World customs agents might not share my sense of humor. I would feel really bad if they shot the man on the spot! I would feel even worse if they shot both of us.

My arrival in Rawalpindi was very different than it had been in Abu Dhabi. The small dirty airport was in a state of total chaos. After stepping off the plane, I was assaulted by five eager taxi drivers. They all wore baggy pants and matching long tunics that came down to their knees. The colors they wore were pastels–light green, blue, or gray. Most of them also wore a white braided skullcap. One man jerked my carry-on out of my hand and headed to his 1950s-era cab. Another driver grabbed it away from him and headed to his cab. I kept trying to tell them, "I don't need a taxi! Leave me alone!" The only English they knew was "Welcome," "Thank you," "Please come," and "Do you know Bruce Springstein?"

I finally retrieved my big bag from baggage claims and waited almost half an hour with the cluster of taxi drivers around me. I couldn't walk without getting my feet tangled in theirs. The Davidsons were nowhere in sight. I dug their phone number out of my suitcase and started looking for a pay phone. Nothing in sight.

I looked at the taxi drivers, who were following me, and said, "Telephone." I held my fist to the side of my head, like I was holding a phone receiver. Finally one said, "Come." The crowd of us walked several blocks down the dirt street to a telephone/telex office—a small, beige, concrete affair surrounded by a muddy street. The streets were packed with brightly decorated buses, Japanese or old American cars, and ox carts. The air was filled with a blaring of horns and the smell of smoke and garlic.

At the telephone office, I paid to use an old beat-up black rotary telephone. The phone at the other end rang for a while until a man with a strong German accent answered, "Alleo"

"May I speak to Mr. Davidson?"

I was answered with silence, and could hear only the arguing between the taxi drivers behind me. I had to stick my finger in my ear to block out the noise. The voice then said, "The Davidsons are in America."

"America?" I said.

"Yes. They have been in America for eight months and will not return to Pakistan until three more months."

This blew me away. How was I supposed to survive here? I was desperate and begged the man with the heavy accent to pick me up. I concluded the field director in Abu Dhabi had merely sent the Davidsons a letter and had never actually talked to them.

The German man's name was Peter. He was a tall lean man with a weathered, leathery face framed by brown curly hair and a long, equally curly, beard. He was a physician who ran a clinic far up in the Himalayas at a little town called Gilgit. I found this very interesting, because as a lover of mountains I knew that K-2, one of the most famous in the world, was close to Gilgit. That evening he was on his way to Germany and was catching a plane the next morning from Rawalpindi. He was a friend of the Davidsons and had a key to their house.

I asked Peter the directions to the MA mission hospital. I was surprised to learn that it was a 3–to 4-hour bus ride up through the mountains. I couldn't figure how to get there. He agreed to help me catch a bus the next day.

Bright and early the next morning, the kind physician took me to the local bus depot. It was a muddy open square with many vendors selling food, baskets, and trinkets to crowds of bus passengers. I brought only my small yellow day-pack with my toothbrush, a few pairs of clean socks, clean underwear, and one clean shirt. I wanted to travel light, so this would have to get me through two weeks. I left my suitcase at the Davidsons' house.

Peter spoke in Urdu to several people at the depot until he found the bus that ran by the hospital. He had to pay the driver a special "bonus" to look out for me and to find the hospital. Then Peter said to me, "Please be very careful. The bus driver thinks he knows where the hospital is, but isn't sure. If the trip takes longer than four hours, become suspicious." Now I was thinking, *What the heck does that mean?*

The Pakistani buses have style. They are mostly chrome and are outfitted with bells and lights from end to end. They also have tassels hanging across the windshield as well as from the bumpers. Inside they are more like rolling sardine cans with people packed so tightly that a snake couldn't slither between them. The "second class" riders climbed onto the luggage rack on top. The rest of the luggage rack was filled with chickens, baskets, fruit, and all manner of odd objects such as a cardboard cutout of Colonel Sanders and a ship anchor.

The bus took off from the depot at sunrise. Although I had a seat, most of the other riders were standing. The conductor pushed his way from one end to the other yelling at people. I wasn't sure of his intentions, I just hoped he wouldn't yell at me.

I kept my eye on the time. One hour passed, then two, three, and four. We were climbing higher and higher in the Himalayan foothills, in and out of monsoon drizzle. The area reminded me a lot of the Tennessee mountains that I had grown up in, except for the grazing water buffalo and exotic-looking bright green birds. I was starting to become a little worried after six hours. I realized that we must have missed my stop, yet no one on the bus spoke English. After about seven hours, the crowd started thinning as people were disembarking. Finally we pulled into an ancient-looking city crowded with people. The streets were dirt and the buildings were two-story plaster and stone structures. It was like a scene from an Indiana Jones movie. The driver pulled into a busy town square and stopped the bus. The door opened and everyone got off–everyone but me. I sat there for a minute before realizing this was the end of the line.

I grabbed my day-pack and started chasing the driver through the crowd, knowing that he was my only hope. I caught up to him and grabbed his shoulder. He looked at me and jerked away. I figured he never knew where the hospital was to start with; and now that he had his bonus money from Peter he didn't give a damn about me.

I started shouting at him, pointing at my chest, "What about me!" I bugged him to the point he became angry and spun around, grabbing me by the shirt collar and dragging me through the crowd. We arrived back at the square and he went from bus to bus arguing with the drivers. It appeared none of them wanted me. Finally one looked at me and gave me the universal sign, rubbing his first three fingers with his thumb. I gave him several Rupees and he let me on the bus.

It was very crowded, like the previous bus. I found a seat in the back. Soon a frail woman dressed much more seductively than any Moslem female I had ever seen came and sat beside me. She had on bright red lipstick and smelled of strong perfume. I watched out the window as we left town and went back down the mountain the same way we had come up. After about an hour, I started asking out loud, "Does anyone speak English?" Finally a young man pushed his way to my seat. He grabbed the woman by the shoulder, said something to her in a very hateful tone, and pulled her up. Then he sat beside me. "I speak English, how can I help you?"

"Where is this bus going?"

He gave me a "Do you mean you are on a bus and you don't know where it is going?" look. I didn't have time to explain. I asked him if he knew where the MA hospital was. He didn't. Then he motioned for the conductor, with whom he had a short conversation. The conductor looked confused. The young man turned to me and said, "He knows the general area of where the hospital is located. When we go back through it, he will try to let you off where he thinks it is."

During the two-hour ride, the young man filled me in on the local culture and geography. "You know the lady that was sitting here?"

"Yeah." I looked back at her. She was now sitting on the long bench seat that went across the back of the bus. I noticed the men were touching her and putting their hands on her legs. I thought, "Wow, this would never happen in Abu Dhabi."

The steward went on to say, "Well, she sat here in order to seduce you, since you are a Westerner."

"You must be kidding. So she is a prostitute?"

"Yes. And not only that, she isn't a real woman. If a real woman becomes a prostitute, at least in this Moslem country, she would be executed. This is a man dressed as a woman who works as a prostitute. The men pay to touch her. Do you understand?"

"Oh," I said, nodding my head. "We have the same in America, but there, they end up finding a nice man, settling down, having a couple of kids, and then going on a TV talk show 10 years later to reveal their true identity to their totally unsuspecting husbands."

The young man looked really confused, about as confused as I was about it.

At this time, the bus conductor motioned me to the back door. I was thinking the hospital must have been in sight so I worked my way through the crowd toward him. The conductor had me stand against the door and placed his hand in the center of my back. This wasn't a good sign.

The conductor was watching out the window, then he shouted something to the driver. I heard the loud puff of the air breaks and felt a sudden forward jolt. The bus didn't even come to a complete halt when the conductor opened the door and gave me a shove.

I landed in the ditch but was able to run fast enough to stay upright . . . almost. I could hear the bus's diesel engines whine as it picked up speed and vanished around the corner.

I dusted myself off and picked up my day-pack. I looked around, finding no sign of life. I was alone in the middle of nowhere. I had no clue which way to go on the lonely mountain road and I was tired, so I decided to start walking downhill. It was apparent the conductor didn't know where the hospital was either. I could just see the headlines back home in Tennessee: "Jones Man Lost in the Himalayas." My mom on the six o'clock news, in her house coat and curlers, sobbing, "He wasn't a bad boy . . . just a little stupid."

After a couple of miles, I entered the outskirts of a small village. I causally walked down the main street. Since I was wearing jeans, a T-shirt, and running shoes, I attracted about as much attention as Osma Bin Laden in the Pentagon lunch line. Women were grabbing their children. Life in the village came to a screeching halt. I started asking softly, "Does anyone here speak English?" There wasn't one word in response. I kept walking.

Before long I noticed one of the signs in the village had English writing on it. I looked closer and to my great relief, it said, "Bach Christian Hospital." A hand-painted arrow pointed up a dirt road. I took the road, which led straight up a hill. Soon, I arrived at the hospital compound.

A view from the bus window leaving Rawalpindi.

This mission hospital was very different than the one in Abu Dhabi. The most notable difference was that no one spoke English. Although it was operated by an American organization, there were only two Americans present. One was the hospital engineer, Tom Redding. I stayed with him at his house. The other was a very pleasant woman who was the main physician, Dr. Barker. The nurses and other staff were Pakistani and none of them spoke English, except for David. David was the hospital's business manager, and he spoke rustic English. I tried to hang out with him to avoid being totally confused. I couldn't accomplish much in the clinic because I had no one to interpret for me. The physician was very busy, seeing more than 100 patients per day, and I hated to slow her down by tagging along.

This hospital was also very different from its Middle Eastern counterpart in its appearance. It too was on a compound surrounded by a high fence. However, this one was on the side of a lush green hill. Trees were abundant. There were several simple cinder block buildings with tin roofs. These made up the hospital, outpatient clinic, business office, operating room, and the homes and dorms for the staff.

I was able to help by assisting in surgery. The major procedure done at this hospital was skin grafting. The villages had ovens in the ground, and children and young adults often fell into them. Terrible burns were commonplace. Another obstacle to me helping much in the clinic was that I soon became a patient in the hospital myself.

I have a great love for mountains. I liken it to the attraction Richard Dreyfuss's character had for Devil's Tower in *Close Encounters of the Third Kind*. On the morning of my first full day on the hospital compound, I took an early morning walk to get a better view of the towering mountains. It was the middle of monsoon season. Whereas this meant a lot of rain in southern Pakistan, here in the mountains it simply meant a lot of clouds. The day before, when I came in on the bus, the clouds were very low and it had been raining a bit. This morning, the clouds had lifted and the mountains were visible. In the far distance, you could see the gleaming white towers pushing up into the remaining clouds.

On that morning, looking at the mountains I felt a great desire to get closer. I started walking toward them. This took me down the hill back through the village and up the hill on the other side of the highway. I found a footpath and continued walking. I crossed one small mountain. I had planned on stopping at the top, but once I was there I saw the next mountain, which was even higher. I crossed the next valley and up the other side. By the time I reached the top of the second mountain, I realized my little walk, after four hours, was turning into quite a hike. It was then I realized had no water or food with me. It didn't matter. The call of the mountains was overpowering. I kept going on the small clay paths that led higher and higher.

By early afternoon, after a strenuous hike in the hot dry mountain air, I was seriously thirsty. My throat and mouth were like leather, yet I kept going. Before long, all I could think about was my thirst. For the first time in my life, I could begin to understand how those lost at sea approached the point of drinking their own urine. I would have considered it but I was too dehydrated to pee.

All during my hike I kept passing villagers. I was quite an odd attraction. Many of them were driving oxen or carrying bundles of wood or blankets on their heads and backs. I was hoping that just one would have some liquid on him. My eyes began to deceive me. A crate of chickens looked like a cooler of Mt. Dews on crushed ice. When I passed people, instead of seeing their kind smiles, I saw the wet salvia on their teeth and lips. I was tempted to kiss one of the old women right on the lips just so I could suck some spit out of her. I wanted to nurse from an ox, but I believed they were all male. I was growing truly desperate!

So I turned around and start heading back. My thirst was making me delusional, plus I knew that I would be hiking in the dark the way it was. I have a good sense of direction, but darkness could confuse me. If I went too far west, I could end up in the middle of the Soviet-Afghan conflict. If I went too far east, I could end up in the middle of the Indo-Pakistani standoff in Kashmir.

I chose a different path on the way back. It seemed to follow the valleys instead of the crest lines. At dusk I came to a watering hole. There were several people filling large clay or blue plastic jugs. A couple of women were washing their dishes and a few oxen were standing in the water. Although the water was as brown as a Tennessee lake, it looked inviting. I just wanted to look at it for a moment. Then, I thought, if I could just wet my cracked lips, it would give me some relief.

I stooped down to touch my lips to the water and was shocked. I became possessed by the infantile sucking response: I started sucking and sucking the brown water into my mouth and SWALLOWING IT! I couldn't control the reflex. I must have drunk half a gallon before I came to my senses.

As I continued my hike I began to think about what just happened. There I was, Mr. Third World Medicine Guy, trying to bring health care to these people, and I just drank out of a watering hole in Pakistan. I recalled how the previous summer I went on a expedition in the Beartooth Wilderness area in Montana. I wouldn't even drink sparkling water from a remote, pristine-melting glacier without boiling it first. Even then I had giardia by the time I got home. Even a moron wouldn't drink out of a watering hole in Pakistan. I even seem to remember it being mentioned in the famous Jim Croce song: "You don't tug on Superman's cape, you don't spit into the wind, you don't pull the mask off the Lone Ranger, and you don't drink from a watering hole in Pakistan."

I arrived at the village near the hospital at about 10:00 p.m. Now that my thirst had been partially quenched, I was hungry. I bought a water buffalo burger (a half pound piece of ground water buffalo meat with onions on flat bread) and two bottles of Pepsi. I purchased all of this for the equivalent of 50 cents.

I returned to my room and drank pure water all night. However, I was lucky. I didn't become deathly sick from drinking the water—at least not immediately.

The next morning I spoke to Mr. Redding, telling him about my adventure the day before. I think they were all worried about what had happened to me since I had just vanished in the morning. When I described to him my passion for the mountains, he told me, "Well, Mike, I have to take a trip up to the boarding school on Thursday. That is pretty high in the mountains. There is one place you might even get a view of K-2. Do you want to come along?"

"Are you kidding? I would love to come along!" I felt like I had died and gone to heaven. Later that night, I would just feel like I had died.

In the middle of the next night it hit me. The worst abdominal cramping

I have ever had—well, at least since my pediatrics rotation. Soon diarrhea ensued, then, I got to revisit my water buffalo burger again. This continued throughout the night and went from awful to beyond belief. By morning I was running a high fever and was very weak. The hospital physician came up to see me. Beyond this, I don't remember much. She put me in the hospital and pumped me with fluids. It was like a war between my immune system and some germ from hell dug into my digestive tract. I didn't care which one won anymore, but somehow the fighting had to stop. The next couple of days passed in a fog. I do remember Mr. Redding visiting me one evening and telling me that the following morning was his trip across the mountains. As he was leaving I whispered, "Be sure and wake me. One way or the other, I am going with you." Even through the fog I could read the doubt on his face.

The next morning, Mr. Redding came by to wake me. I felt terrible. I tried to sit up and had a close encounter of the syncope kind. I struggled to get one sock on before I fell back into bed, exhausted. My heart was broken. I couldn't go. To be this close to the Himalayas and not get to cross any of them was like Moses stopped at the border of the Promised Land having forgotten his passport.

The beckoning mountains of north-central Pakistan.

It took me a couple of days to get back on my feet. I gave up on seeing the mountains up close. I tried to get my mind off my problems and make myself available to help around the hospital as best I could. I did scrub in for surgery about once every other day. The rest of the time I hung out with David and did anything I could to assist.

I was starting to get a little tired by this point. The fact that I was always in the dark due to the language barrier was getting on my nerves. David stood about five-six. He was very thin, dark skinned, and looked at me from coal black eyes. His haircut was pure early Beatles. He wore a dress shirt, dress pants, and a nylon jacket. He wasn't very forthcoming in keeping me informed about what was going on. Now and then he would say something like, "OK Mike, us go." Then I would just follow him, with no clue as to where we were going. I was experiencing culture shock for the first time since my summer overseas began.

One day the people were running here and there chatting away in Urdu as they normally did. After a few minutes, David came into the clinic office. "Mike, come us go!"

I asked as I followed him across the compound, "Where are we going?" He just ignored me.

David led me to the hospital van. Several other people were already sitting inside, and I climbed into the back. As we were driving away, I assumed we were going to the market. After traveling past all the local markets, heading west, I shouted to the front of the van, "Where are we going, David?"

He was in the middle of a lively conversation with the other Urdu-speaking passengers. Apparently irritated, he said, "Negalabad." The word "abad" is like the English word "ville" meaning a town or home of something.

"Where is Negalabad?" He again ignored me. We continued traveling for hours, through the mountains going west. The road narrowed as we entered an area of steep green mountains beside a river.

Before long, we rounded a bend and encountered a grassy flat field covered with tall, white tents at the base of steep green mountains.

Beside the encampment ran a clear river crossed occasionally by rope footbridges. It was an Afghan refugee camp. I had seen several since arriving in this part of Pakistan. This was during the Afghan-Soviet war, and thousands of refugees were living in the scattered camps inside Pakistan. One of them was near our hospital. We also had several patients in the hospitals that had been wounded in the war.

Now as we approached this refugee camp, I more forcefully addressed David. "Please tell me where we are going and what we are doing here."

He repeated, "Negalabad. We are coming to this camp for clinic. See those hills in front of us? That is Afghanistan."

I said with some concern, "David, what clinic? What are you talking about?"

"Our clinic that we hold here once a month. These refugees come to the border here and have no medical care except what we give them."

I looked at the people in the van. One woman was like a nursing assistant. One woman was like a social worker. One man was a pharmacist, and the other man worked in the hospital business office.

As we pulled over near the camp, I could see mobs of people running in our direction. I jumped out the cargo door and headed around the front of the van to confront David face to face. "David, who is doing the clinic?" My heart was starting to tremble.

David smiled and said, "You, of course, Dr. Mike. We have been talking about this for several days."

"But, in Urdu! This is the first I have heard about it! David, I have nothing, not even a stethoscope!" I looked up as roughly 100 people swarmed around the van and grew quite pushy. Many others were on their way down the hillside. This was a PA student's worst nightmare.

"Don't worry, Dr. Mike," said David, "I will help you." This was NOT very reassuring, coming as it was from the hospital accountant. He dug around in the van and found a very old stethoscope with no earpieces. I tried it on. The small metal threaded tubes were too sharp and painful to use. It felt like a cookie cutter, slicing little round disks from my eardrums. I threw it back under the van seat.

David took me to where the pharmacist was unloading a large tackle box full of drugs. I asked David to translate while I inventoried the drugs with the pharmacist. There was an antibiotic, an anthelmintic, and an anti-inflammatory drug. However, the most interesting one was a tall bottle of a bright red liquid. "What is this red stuff for?" I said.

David translated the answer, "You know, it is for the belly."

"What do you mean it is for the belly? Is it an antacid? Is it for diarrhea or cramps?"

David replied, "You know. It is for everything that ails the belly. It is a belly tonic."

I was getting the message. About this time the office worker showed up with a rubber stamp in his hand and appeared frantic.

I asked David, "What is going on?"

"We need to start seeing patients. We use the clinic stamp to stamp the hands of those who have registered. This prevents people from sneaking into line without getting a file. This worker forgot to bring the inkpad. This is holding everything up."

"I have an idea." I took a bottle of the red tonic and poured it into the lid of the tackle box. I dipped the rubber stamp into the tonic and stamped the back of the worker's hand. It worked as well as ink and that was the only use the magic belly tonic would see that day.

By this time, there were about 200 people crowded around. I stood there in my jeans and T-shirt, no stethoscope, no otoscope, nothing, waiting for the onslaught. And it came. One by one David and I worked the crowd. I felt like a presidential candidate with his campaign manager. I also got a taste of what Jesus must have experienced when the crowds of desperate people were pressing in from all sides. While he gave them miracles, forgiveness, and hope, I had very little to offer my crowd. It was like trying to hold my finger in a dike. However, being totally unprepared for this so-called clinic, it wasn't even my best finger.

That day I saw some terrible things. A little girl with a severely inflamed elbow with several sinus tracts draining green pus will haunt my memory forever. Was it TB, which was widespread throughout the camps?

I saw several little children with thick pus flowing out of their ears and down their necks and huge cervical lymph nodes. I suspected one of having mastoiditis. I will carry those images of their suffering throughout my career. This is especially true when I see kids with mild URIs and slightly pink eardrums and their worried moms and dads demanding that I put their "very sick" child on antibiotics.

One man in his mid-20s was carried in on a wooden bed. His right thigh revealed a very deformed femur. I asked him about the accident. He reported there had been no accident; he had experienced pain in his leg for several weeks then one day his thigh just snapped. I palpated his thigh and felt a large mass–a terrible tumor. Yet the only thing I could do was give him an aspirin.

David would listen to many patients jabbering on and on and pointing here and there. Then he would turn to me and simply say, "They have worms."

I assumed that the patient was telling David that they had seen worms in their stool. After a few of these I asked David directly, "Did these people tell you they had worms because they saw them in their stool?"

"Oh no. They complain of this or that but everyone knows that the main problem in these camps are the worms."

I reflected on the fact that the hospital accountant was diagnosing patients. I then demanded that he tell me exactly what they told him.

He looked at me and said loudly, "Look around. We have more than a hundred patients still to see. I don't have time to tell you all the things they tell me."

Late in the day, we had to stop seeing patients and start packing up. Still people were arriving from other nearby camps. My heart was broken that day. In many cases all I could do was beg them to come to the hospital. Yet, David told me that none would come because they could not afford the bus trip.

On the way back I was exhausted, sleeping most of the way. I hadn't fully recovered from my Pakistani version of Montezuma's revenge. I slept well that night, one of my few remaining ones in Asia.

A couple of days later I began working on finding my way back to Rawalpindi. I was able to catch a ride with one of the workers at the hospital who was making a trip to buy supplies. We swung by the Davidsons' to pick up my suitcase. Little did I know there had been some kind of unrest going on in Pakistan during my two weeks in the mountains, and martial law had been declared. When the hospital worker dropped me off at the airport, it had been occupied by the military. I was searched, as was my luggage, right there on the curb in the pouring rain.

Inside the airport it was chaos. I was the only Westerner present. I finally had my luggage checked through to Paris, although I had to change planes in Karachi. I was anxious, feeling I was on the verge of getting back to the West. I was mistaken. There was a terrible monsoon thunderstorm raging outside, and my flight was repeatedly delayed. Periodic announcements were being made to update the passengers; however, they were in Urdu. Again I was clueless. My connection in Karachi was fast approaching and that was a good two-hour flight away. After four hours of delays, my plane arrived from Lahore. The flight to Karachi was the scariest I have ever been on, with extreme turbulence and bolts of lighting all around during our ascent.

When I arrived in Karachi, I frantically ran into the terminal to see if my connecting flight had indeed left. It had. I made my way to the PIA office and found an English speaker. He was a heavy, short man wearing some kind of PIA uniform and sitting at a gray metal desk. "I missed my connecting flight because your plane from Lahore was late." He flipped through several books and punched some keys on a computer. Then he looked up at me wearing a big smile. "You have good luck today. This same flight next week has an open seat."

"Next week!" I screamed. More than anything, I wanted to get out of Asia. "I must get to Paris as soon as possible. I have a friend who is supposed to meet me there today!"

He returned to his books, punched a few more keys, and looked up again. "I do have one seat to Frankfort in three days."

"I'll take it. But how can I get from Frankfort to Paris?"

He thought for a while. "This is what I will do for you. I will give you a blank airline ticket. When you get to Frankfort, just find an open seat and write the name of the flight on the ticket."

It sounded dicey but I decided to go for it. "Where can I stay for three days? It is PIA's fault that I am in this mess."

He nodded his head. "We will put you in a hotel, either the Hilton, the Marriott, or Mohammed's Inn." After making a phone call he said, "It looks like you must stay at Mohammed's Inn."

Mohammed's Inn wasn't too bad, on par with a Motel 6 that had seen better days. You could call it a Motel 2. Interestingly, there was a group of about fifteen French mountain-climbers staying at the same hotel. The hotel staff made the assumption I was part of that group—always speaking to me in a hybrid French-Urdu dialect. Twice I was mistakenly led to private parties being held by the French, only to be thrown out as soon as I attempted to eat their food.

The three days didn't pass fast enough for me as I had had my fill of Pakistan. I made it to the airport plenty early. The weather was good except for a stiff wind. I was eagerly anticipating heading west. I couldn't imagine anything else going wrong at this point. The call came for my flight. The country was still under martial law so the whole place was crawling with machine-gun-toting soldiers. Three of them escorted us by foot out to the tarmac. Then we had to stand in line to file up the long staircase up to the towering 747. We had our tickets and passports checked twice already. At the top of the staircase was another soldier checking boarding passes. As I stepped up, I pulled my boarding pass out of my back pocket. I was halfway up the stairs when the wind blew it right out of my hand and it sailed out across the runway. Three people stood in line between me and the mean-looking guard checking the passes at the top.

I panicked and took off down the stairs, pushing people out of my way. I could hear the soldier at the top yelling at me but I kept going. When I reached the bottom of the stairs, the soldier there reached out to stop me but I pushed him out of the way. "My boarding pass, my boarding pass!" I ran as hard as I could across the runway, into the path of planes taking off. Finally I caught my boarding pass and turned around. I was jubilant and held it up over my head. As I turned around, there stood two soldiers holding their guns with both hands but fortunately still pointing them at the ground. I held up my pass and, for the first time, they seemed to understand what I was doing.

The plane took off and I was finally airborne, heading in the direction of where the sun sets. I put my seat back, plugged in my earphones, and tuned the dial to the classical track. Pakistan, in two short weeks, had changed me in a profound way. The faces at the refugee camp would haut me forever—eventually drawing me back to the Third World to live.

As I drifted off to sleep, little did I realize that I was within minutes of a major landmark in my PA career.

Chapter Nine

Europe on a Boot String and a Prayer

My seat was reclined and I had the plastic, white earphones securely positioned. I was turned toward the window, facing south just in front of the huge silver wing. Thirty thousand feet below me were deep blue waters, interrupted now and then by arid, beige islands that resembled oblong chocolate chip cookies floating in grape juice. The roar of the huge engines was drowned out by the classical music being piped in through the earphones. The slightly jet-fuel-tinged air inside the plane was quickly taking on the scent of the curry being heated in the kitchenettes. Words cannot describe the peace I felt after our 747 reached cruising altitude and left Pakistani air space. I was exhausted from my two weeks in Asia. I knew that my problems weren't over yet. Somehow I was going to have to find a way to Paris, and in that vast city, I was going to have to find Tim.

Still, I knew enough peace to doze off. My favorite thing in the world is sitting in an airplane seat, high above someplace exotic, listening to classical music. On this day my napping took me in and out of the twilight zone. I remember I was listening to Pachelbel's Canon and suddenly I realized I had no idea what day it was. I had completely lost track of time while in Pakistan as I never wore a watch or saw a calendar.

I started to look around for some clue as to the date. I asked the Libyan gentleman beside me if he knew what day it was. He told me in rather good English, "Today is the twenty-eighth of August." I thanked him and turned back toward the window.

Staring out over the blue waters of the Mediterranean, it hit me: August 28th was PA graduation day back at the University of Kentucky! I was now a bona fide Physician Assistant. My career had just passed a huge milestone—almost unnoticed.

In the following months my immediate future seemed set in stone. I would be taking my boards in October. I believed I stood a really good chance of getting a position at the Lexington Federal Correctional Institution. Things seemed to be falling into place. However, life has taught me that whenever things seem to be "falling into place," they can just as easily end up falling into pieces.

After a few more cat naps and a dumb movie about raising the Titanic, we landed in Frankfort. It was 10:00 a.m. I grabbed my luggage and attacked the task of trying to find a flight to Paris. It must have been "Free Beer and Bratwurst" week in Paris because all the German flights were booked. I stood in line at gate after gate as a standby. After a very long day, I finally had a solid booking on the 10:00 p.m. flight on Lufthansa. I called the MA headquarters in the states, where it was still afternoon. They gave me the name of a staff member in Paris. I then called Paris. It was difficult getting through the German—and French-speaking operators, but finally I connected to an English speaker. "MA-Paris office, may I help you?"

"Yes, do you know if Tim Hatch is in Paris?"

"I think he is. I don't know him personally, but I think I overheard someone saying he had visited them."

"Great! This is Michael Jones and I was supposed to have met him there three days ago. Please tell him that I am coming in tonight on Lufthansa."

"I will try, but I don't know where he is staying. Which airport are you arriving at?"

I felt like an idiot. "Well, I don't actually know which airport. Is there more than one?" With that I heard a sigh on the other end of the line.

The flight from Frankfort to Paris seemed brief. I felt delighted when I came through customs and saw Tim's bearded face in the crowd. I gave him a big hug. We took the bus out to the suburbs, where he was staying with friends. We started to plan our departure for the next day to see Europe by hitching.

Tim was quite flexible, as he had traveled through Europe many times. I had two goals: see the Alps and to try and find one of my University of Kentucky roommates who was studying in Madrid. Tim was agreeable to my agenda. We then inventoried our resources. I had my day-pack. Tim found an over-the-shoulder bag from our French host, who also loaned us two sleeping bags. We pooled our money. I had $65 and no credit cards to fall back on. Tim had almost $85. We prepared to tour Europe for two weeks on $75 each. I had a feeling our trip wasn't going to be filmed for an upcoming episode of "Lifestyles of the Rich and Famous."

We were able to hitchhike to Geneva the first day. We rode most of the way with an English fellow who was on his way to Italy for holiday. He about scared the crap out of us driving on the right side, like in the US, but in a car with the steering wheel mounted on the right (for left-hand driving). He took the scenic route through two-lane mountain roads talking non-stop the entire way. He spoke continuously about "The War" (World War II, I assumed), about how stupid the French are, about how stupid the Swiss are, about how stupid the Italians are, and, sadly, about how stupid his wife was. He kept referring to the United States as "The Colonies" and making fun our president's (Jimmy Carter) accent. While talking, he would swoop out from behind a semi, unable to look out first, and there would be another semi meeting us head on. Tim and I were in the back seat hanging onto the door handles for our dear lives.

Aside from his arrogance, he was a very nice chap. He turned off the main highway and took us into downtown Geneva. After bidding our goodbyes and tallyhos, he sped off toward the Italian boarder.

The city was beautiful at night. The buildings were old limestone and marble structures with large modern windows overlooking ancient cobblestone streets. Tim and I were hungry, having not eaten all day. We did a very American thing and went into a McDonald's, where we bought a Big Mac for about $5. We realized that, at this rate, we would be broke in two days. After the meal, we started to look for a place to sleep. We found our way to a large city park near the shore of Lake Geneva. The lake was calm and beautiful, its surface reflecting the lights of the city.

We were exhausted, still on Asian time, and decided to bed down in the park—in a place where the police wouldn't find us. The last place we wanted to sleep was in jail.

It wasn't long before I found a secluded space beneath heavy vegetation. The accommodations weren't that bad. From my sleeping bag I could see the beautiful lakeshore. We were quickly sound asleep.

Sometime in the middle of the night I heard movement near my head. I was in such deep sleep that it was difficult to bring myself to a level of consciousness where I could open my eyes.

I sat up to see the most dangerous animal I could imagine—a scruffy looking man—going through our belongings. I froze. About this time I caught his eye and he froze, leaving us in a sort of speechless standoff. I think each of us was wondering whether the other was getting ready to cut our throat.

The same sound had awakened Tim; however, he was fiddling around, trying to find his thick glasses. He looked at the direction of the intruder and said, "Get out of here, dog. Come on, shoo, get away from here," as he waved him off with the back of his hand.

Now, by this time, I was thinking Tim had a great deal of courage. This intruder looked really mean. Then, to my surprise, Tim picked up his shoe and threw it at him. The man turned and fled. Tim noticed my upright silhouette against the sky aglow with city lights and said, "Mike, are you awake? There was a big dog in here."

Mr. McGoo had actually thought that the man was a dog.

The next morning I awakened dirty, hungry, and cold. The thick overcast Swiss sky was still blocking our view of the mountains. After a breakfast of sardines and French bread, we washed up in the bus station bathroom.

As Tim and I were coming out of the bus depot, we noticed a sign advertising bus service to Barcelona. The second class "red-eye" cost about $30, which was much more reasonable than we expected. This would leave us very short financially, but it would be a great help in getting to Madrid. So we bought two tickets for the bus, which would depart Geneva in three days, at 5:00 p.m. We were excited to see our plans coming together.

We made it, by foot, back to the main highway departing Geneva. Going around the southwest side of Lake Geneva we headed into the really big mountains. We were lucky and caught a ride within an hour. I told the young Swiss driver that "we just want to get higher in the mountains."

He gave us a big smile and said, "I will go through Chamonix, a ski village at the base of Mt. Blanc." This sounded perfect, as I knew Mt. Blanc was the tallest of the Alps.

We arrived at Chamonix in dreary overcast skies, still without any clear glimpses of the mountains. We were pleasantly surprised with our timing, though. We had missed the official summer "holiday" month by a week. Switzerland had been crawling with tourists. Now, a lot of the shops were closed down for their own holiday. We found a youth hostel that cost an amazing nine dollars per night, including a continental breakfast. We had the whole chalet to ourselves the first night.

The second night we returned to our hostel to find a roommate. He was a thin man of short stature lying on his bunk reading a book. He wore an eccentric getup of a natural-gray cardigan, sweat pants, and a pair of glacier sunglasses hanging from his neck by a strap, while wearing reading glasses on his face. He had a radiant glow of health. Maybe it was his contagious laugh or maybe it was his darkly tanned face. After spending the evening with him, I was ready to change majors again. When I asked him about his profession, he explained, "I have a college degree in recreation. For a living, I bring groups of rich English folks to Switzerland and sometimes even more exotic places like Mt. Kilimanjaro in Tanzania. All I do is put mountaineering equipment on them," pointing at the bundle of harnesses, ropes, crampons, and packs he had neatly stuffed under his bunk. "Next, I hook them to a rope and stick an ice axe in their hand. We ride the tram to the top of Mt. Blanc, get out, and walk around on the glacier and ride it back down. They pay me a handsome fee for my service." He let out a hearty laugh and then added the clincher: "I feel guilty getting paid for this . . . it is too much fun!" I sat in awe as I listened to his stories of travel and adventure. If he had asked me, I would have joined him on the spot, giving up my PA career no questions asked. There were going to be days ahead when I wished that I had.

The next morning I threw back the soft down comforter and jumped out of bed at first light. I rushed to the window and threw open the shutters. From the third floor of our chalet, the view was awesome. In the valley below me was the lovely village of Chamonix. It is made up of rows of two–and three-story chalets with dark brown wooden upper stories and white stone or stucco lower floors. Smoke from a few chimneys drifted lazily over the valley. Through the middle of town ran a roaring mountain stream. To the south was the towering, glacier-clad Mt. Blanc. I was in heaven. Within three weeks, I had experienced the two most thrilling moments of my life. The first was the night Denise and I fell in love, and the second was falling in love with the Alps. I knew at that moment there must be Swiss blood in me, somehow. I also made it to the top of Mt. Blanc during our two-day stay, but I did it the same way as the British aristocrats: via tram.

The day of our bus departure came. Since we faced a two-hour (about 100km) drive to Geneva, Tim and I went out to the highway at 11:00 in the morning. This would give us plenty of time to make our 5:00 o'clock bus . . . or so we thought. After several hours we had covered a few miles on foot, but no ride. We were starting to get nervous as the time approached 3:00 p.m. Our bus tickets were non-refundable and missing it would prevent us from making it to Spain.

Tim and I prayed together, and what followed was one of the few actual miracles I have ever witnessed. As we were finishing praying, we looked up. A little car came down the hill and it pulled over and picked us up. Then the driver told us, "Please fasten your seatbelts. I am very late for work and must drive very, very fast." He peeled out and tore down the twisting mountain highway like a pyrophobic bat out of hell. We were squealing tires around every corner. On a few curves we hit the shoulder gravel and came close to wiping out. Our butts ate a hole in the upholstery. I felt like I was in high school again. Our bus was loaded and getting ready to pull away when we showed up. We hurried on board and waved goodbye to our angelic Swiss driver.

We arrived in Barcelona at sunrise the next morning after grabbing a few winks of sleep on the trip. Tim and I went out to the main highway leading to Madrid and started to hitch. It was worse than our last day in Switzerland. After ten hours in the hot sun, we were blistered and discouraged. No one had even slowed down for us—only shouts of Spanish obscenities, I assumed.

We walked the three miles back into town, almost ready to give up and head back to Paris. We went to the major train station. With considerable effort we finally found a woman who spoke a little English. We asked for the cheapest fare to Madrid. It was $45, well beyond our means. "There are no cheaper fares?"

"No," she said repeatedly, until finally she mentioned, "except for the third class ticket." Our eyes opened wide. "Third class! How much is that?"

"Oh no, you wouldn't want to ride third class. It's not for tourists. It's the night train, and third class is standing room only. Only very poor people ride third class." Tim and I couldn't imagine anyone poorer than us. "How much is it!" we insisted.

Hesitantly she told us the Paso's equivalent of $15. Simultaneously we said, "We'll take it."

We were approaching thirty-six hours since we had been in a bed, but finally we were loading up for an overnight trip to Madrid. To make matters worse, we would be standing the whole way. We were sun burnt, exhausted, and—with all due respect to Snow White's loyal companions—sleepy, stinky, and hungry.

After an hour or two, the people in the passenger compartment near us felt sorry enough for us that they invited us to sit with them. The train made several stops, picking up passengers until our compartment was full. The last couple appeared to be country folks as they were dressed in plain clothes and the woman wore a scarf around her head.

I decided to take a nap. I slipped the hiking boots off my aching feet and made a pillow out of my day-pack. After a couple of hours of unconsciousness a nauseating odor woke me up. It smelled like a blend of rotten cabbage and musty rhino-poop. You could cut the air in the little cabin . . . with a chain saw. Tim was wide awake. "Gross, what smells so bad?" I said.

"I think it is that farming couple. Ever since they got on this place started to stink."

I tried to sit so that I could place my hand over my mouth and nose without being too obvious. Soon enough, I recognized the odor. It was my own feet–smelling about ten times worse than they had ever smelled before! After all, it was the first time my boots had been off in almost 40 hours. I quietly slipped them back on and went out into the hallway, where several of the other passengers from our compartment were standing with their faces stuck out the window, trying to get fresh air.

We rolled into Madrid the next morning. In the main train station I found a telephone. I had called my other roommates in Kentucky before leaving Paris and they had given me the phone number of the Spanish host-family where my roommate David was supposed to be staying. I dialed. Fortunately, a man who taught high school English answered. "I'm sorry, but your friend David never showed up at our house. He must still be in America." This didn't make sense, as my roommates in Lexington told me that David was somewhere in Madrid.

I think this Spanish family figured out that we were in dire straits because they invited us to go to a restaurant for lunch, their treat. It was a meal I will never forget: roasted pork with some kind of tomato sauce. With full bellies, we started contemplating our next move. Our new adopted family invited us to their house that night to sleep. Then we thought we would start hitching toward the French border the next day. I was very disappointed about having missed David.

As we left the restaurant and started walking toward the car, I couldn't believe my eyes. There was David down the street mailing a letter at a mailbox. At six foot two and with blond curly hair, he was easy to spot among the Spaniards. I said, "Hi Dave," and waved but kept walking casually by. He looked up in shock. He had no idea I was in Spain. I had accidentally stumbled onto David in a city of several million.

David took us back to his place, where I took the longest shower of my life, scrubbing my feet for at least ten minutes. Tim and I enjoyed two good nights' sleep. We were now within four days of my departing flight from Paris. We would have to hit the road soon. It was going to be a long four days. We each had about $10 left. After we told David how difficult it had been hitching a ride in Barcelona, he was kind enough to buy us train tickets to the French border.

Tim and I made it to the border and quickly caught a short ride to just north of Bordeaux. Then we got stuck again. We hitched for hours at a divided highway on-ramp but found no takers. I was starting to worry that I wouldn't make Paris in time for my departing flight. Evening was fast approaching, and Tim and I realized that we would be spending the night on the road. It looked like it was about to rain so we decided to seek shelter under an overpass.

As we started toward the overpass, a little French car came backing up the ramp and pulled up beside us. A young dark-haired girl was driving and an older gray-haired woman sat in the front passenger seat. Immediately the older woman started jabbering to me in French, which I hadn't spoken since high school French. My mind racing, I stammered, "Parlez-vous francais?" She gave me a perplexed look because this of course means, "Do you speak French?" Of course she speaks French! I am the one who doesn't speak French. I was trying to say, "Do you speak English?" Then I just said it in English.

The younger girl said in very broken English, "My mother says you come eat sleep at house ours?"

Tim and I said things like, "Oh, that would be too much trouble. We couldn't put you out like that."

The girl looked baffled. "I no understand . . . uh . . . you say what?"

Tim and I just looked at each other and nodded our heads in unison. "Yes."

We got into the back of the little white Renault. The older woman spoke to us continuously in French and smiled. Naturally, we didn't understand a single word. The more confused we looked, the louder she spoke. The younger girl told us her name was Michelle. I asked her in simple terms, "Where do you live?"

She told me, "We live . . . Bordeaux. But this day, we go to farm, family farm in country. You understand?"

"Yes, I understand." I said.

We eventually turned off the freeway onto a small country road lined by huge oak trees. The dirt road led us past beautiful green fields and vineyards and eventually to a cluster of trees with a driveway passing through. In the midst of the trees was one of the most beautiful homes I had ever seen. It was made of stone and had a thatched roof. In front of the house was an old barn made of stone and stucco, also with a thatched roof. The place must have been hundreds of years old. It looked like something out of a child's storybook. We went inside, where it got even more interesting, with a huge stone fireplace in the kitchen, dark brown, hand-hewed supporting beams overhead, and a slate floor. The interior walls were white plaster or stucco.

The older woman immediately started preparing food for us. She brought in loafs of bread, big balls of cheese, sliced meat, and, true to form, several bottles of wine. To hobos like us, this was a king's feast. But now I was faced with a dilemma. My mouth was watering over the wine, but I had promised Tim I wouldn't drink alcohol during the trip.

Tim had been required to take a vow before becoming a career missionary with MA that he would not drink alcohol. This frustrated me because I knew that it had nothing to do with the Bible. The Bible clearly teaches that becoming intoxicated is a bad thing. People do stupid things when they are intoxicated. This lesson is always brought home whenever I watch an episode of "Cops." Those bad boys are usually so bad because they are drunk out of their gourds. However, the Bible never says that drinking alcohol is wrong. As a matter of fact, Jesus loved to party with his friends so much that the religious establishment thought of him as a drunkard. Martin Luther himself, the founder of Protestantism, was known for how much beer he could consume in an evening. My Catholic friends tend to think, *Oh, now that explains things.*

When this woman and her daughter put their wonderful spread

before us, it was hard to say no to the wine. Against my better judgment, I didn't want to offend Tim. It was probably one of their better bottles they had just opened for us. They even poured it in our crystal glasses, but still we refused, smiling, shaking our heads, and saying, "No thank you." Not drinking their wine was one of the most un-Christian things I've ever done.

After eating our fill, Michelle came back into the kitchen said, "You follow me." She took us up a steep staircase to a loft, where we found two beds. She said, "You sleep here." Michelle then left, saying, "I get blankets." While she was gone, Tim and I tried to figure out where the two of them were going to sleep. We hadn't seen another bedroom downstairs and were concerned that they were going to sleep on the couch or floor. We would have been glad to sleep there instead.

Tim made a good traveling companion for me. Where I could be too timid, Tim was more extroverted and confident. Sometimes, though, he got himself into trouble by trying too hard to communicate with the French.

Soon Michelle returned with an armload of comforters. I was sitting on one bed and Tim on the other one. Tim asked her, "If we weren't here, would you normally sleep in this room?"

She responded, "I . . . uh . . . no understand. You say what?"

Tim though for a moment and tried again. "Where do YOU sleep . . . here?"

Michelle gave the same response but had a little more concern in her voice. It began to dawn on me what was going through the girl's mind.

Finally Tim got very basic and started patting the bed beside him and saying, loudly and plainly, "You sleep here?"

Her eyes got as big as wine glasses. "NO!" Then she turned and ran out of the room, leaving Tim looking confused.

I said, "Way to go, Tim. You just asked our host's daughter to sleep with you."

Tim said, "Oh no! I have to straighten this out."

The next morning we enjoyed a wonderful French country breakfast. Michelle didn't speak to Tim or make much eye contact with him. She did explain to us, "My brother, Pierre, is coming from Bordeaux. He goes to 50 kilometer from Paris. He comes here, takes you with him. OK?" Oh, what wonderful hosts!

In about an hour a young thin man pulled up in a blue sports car. We loaded our stuff in his little car and sped off, back to the divided highway. Unfortunately, Pierre spoke no more English than his mother. He delivered us to his exit and let us out. We thanked him as he took off.

We began hitching again, walking in the direction of Paris. As in Barcelona, no one would even slow down for us.

Tim and I never got another ride in France. We eventually walked ten kilometers to a nearby village—a cluster of about thirty stone houses around a very tall cathedral. On the eastern edge of town was a long brick train station with a red tiled roof. A short man with a waxed mustache was sitting inside. He wore a uniform that made it clear he worked for the railroad. He reacted to our presence in the same way as someone in a major American city would react if a bear wandered into town. He nervously rushed here and there trying to explain he didn't speak English. With our few remaining dollars, and using sign language, we purchased commuter train tickets into the main south Paris terminal. We arrived into the station, just missing the last commuter bus out to the suburbs, where we would be staying. We faced one more night on the streets.

The next day we made it back to our American host's apartment. We got cleaned up and shaven, and spent the next couple of days exploring such main area tourist attractions as the Palace of Versailles and the Eiffel Tower. The next morning I said goodbye to Tim as he dropped me off at airport customs. He had been a wonderful traveling companion and a good friend who I would never forget.

I couldn't wait to stand on American soil again. For the first time in my life, I was completely adventured out. Strapping myself into the seat, I felt a jerk as the 747 pulled away from the gate. We had just cleared the gate area when there was another hard jolt. Fortunately, I had a window seat on the right side and could see the problem. We had just crashed into a service truck. I had never heard of a 747-service truck MVA (motor vehicle accident) before. A group of men soon gathered beneath the plane. Some were in coats and ties and some in orange jump suits. The men in ties were taking pictures of the side of the plane. The 300 passengers sat waiting patiently for an hour. Finally, to our great dismay, we were told the flight had been canceled. The plane crash/MVA had damaged the cargo door so it would not close properly. It would take at least 24 hours to replace it. PIA put my group up in the Paris Holiday Inn for the night.

Once back in Tennessee, I loaded up the old jeep and headed for Lexington. It was great to see my roommates again. The next morning I called the Federal Correctional Institution to speak with Dr. Sánchez about my start date. The kind doctor broke the shocking news. "Michael, the position came open just as we had expected. However, when my secretary called your house, someone told her that you no longer lived there, that you had moved to Europe! Therefore, we recently hired an out-of-state PA for the position. We have nothing available for you."

In those days, PA jobs were very hard to come by. This latest development would signal the beginning of a long journey for which I wasn't prepared. But in many ways the two weeks in Europe would provide a good orientation for what was to come. I had a much greater appreciation for transportation–down to my old, rusty jeep. A simple shelter from the rain was a blessing, as was a warm meal. But the best part about beginning my PA career as a homeless bum was knowing there was only one way out, and that was up.

Chapter Ten

Will Practice Medicine for Food

A well dressed, forty-something woman in a cobalt blue wool suit stood glaring at me in the Sears men's department. She had her hands on her hips and was tapping her high heel rapidly on the tiled floor. Near her, trying to keep his distance, was a twelve-year-old boy. He sported a bowl-shaped haircut and wore a red Izod shirt. The woman said, "You mean you work in the men's clothing department and don't even know what the preppie look is? You must live in a cave. It was the rage last summer!"

"Well, ma'am, I wasn't in the states last summer."

Gee whiz, I thought. Was I not even qualified to work at Sears—a position I was taking for the holiday season? I had been ready to go stand on the street corner with a sign stating, "Will Practice Medicine for Food," when someone suggested Sears.

I knew very little about clothing. The last time I had worn a tie was during my PA school interviews. Now I had completely missed the preppie revolution. Of course, Sears was never known for being on the cutting edge of fashion—hardware maybe, but not fashion.

Since I didn't have many dress clothes, friends loaned me some for my position. One guy, Mark, gave me a three-piece green corduroy suit. He was about five inches taller than me, and much heavier. The pant's hem was piled up around my ankles, which was OK, because it helped hide my hiking boots. I cinched the belt extra tight to hold the pants up. This caused the waist of the pants to pucker up in several places. The bottom of the jacket came to about my knees. I often worked with a very stylish guy named Randi. He always looked like he had just stepped out of an issue of *GQ* and had a voice that could have doubled for that of Richard Simmons. The first time I wore my green suit, Randi came over, looked me over from head to toe, and said in a snobbish tone, "Interesting suit . . . Mi-kal." Then he swirled around like a ballet dancer and walked away.

I was always afraid to be seen by a patient from one of my clinical rotations—or worse yet, one of my classmates.

Upon my return from Europe, I had to quickly focus on my national board exams. I had been so distracted over the previous months that I felt in danger of having forgotten my two years of PA school. I could vaguely remember something about an inflamed brick.

I dragged out my old books and spent the time cramming for the exam. The written part was on a Saturday and the practical exam was Tuesday evening the following week. The written exam didn't seem that difficult. The practical exam would be another story. Unfortunately, I had hardly given it a second thought.

When I arrived that evening, several of my classmates were present. To my discouragement, only two out of fifteen had real PA jobs lined up. I was called back and handed a printed history of the patient. The history described two complaints: abdominal pain and a nipple discharge. I quickly considered my plan of action and entered the exam room. Seated on the exam table in a gown was a young coed. In the corner of the same room was a desk with two well-dressed evaluators taking notes.

I introduced myself to the patient: "Hi, my name is Michael Jones and I see that you are Miss Taylor."

She looked nervous and mumbled, "Yes."

I opened up my little black bag. Lesson number one about taking a practical exam: check out your equipment in advance. This is the first time I had looked into the bag since the previous spring. I had not taken it with me overseas. As I looked into the bag, I realized someone had been through it.

I took out my sphygmomanometer and it flew into several pieces. A metal diaphragm rolled across the room and under the desk where the evaluators were sitting. I crammed the springs, dials, and rubber tubing into my hand and pretended to take her blood pressure. As I was pumping up the bulb, I was already thinking about my NEW career—pumping gas at a gas station.

I did a complete abdominal exam, which went well. Then I instructed the young lady, "Miss Taylor, I see that you have been having a nipple discharge. I will need you to take your bra off so I can do a breast exam." She looked horrified, as she had no idea what was written on the history sheet.

"You're not touching my breasts!" She started to sob and then turned to the evaluators. "You lied to me! You told me I wouldn't have to expose my private parts."

There was that old issue again—*touching private body parts*. That was one of the reasons that I did not want a career in medicine. My mind flashed back to the pre-sport physicals that I had to endure a decade earlier. But now, the sneaker was on the other foot—so to speak. How did this happen? Was she imagining that *I* was going to find pleasure in such an exam—afterwards putting my heels up on my desk and lighting up? Good heavens no! That was the last thing on my mind. I just wanted to pass my exam and get the heck out of there.

The evaluators asked me to leave the room. I went into the hallway and they closed the door behind me. I assumed they were going to give me a different history and that I would start over. Instead, after ten minutes one of them came out and told me, "You may resume you exam."

"The same exam?"

"Yes," said the evaluator with an inferred, "Of course."

I returned to the exam room to find Miss Taylor emotionally under control and with her bra off. I wished they had given me a different exam because this one had become extremely awkward. Nonetheless, I completed the exam and the patient kept her composure.

With the exam behind me, I could concentrate on finding a job and earning some money to survive on. I started compiling a list of every family practice physician in the state of Kentucky and sent a letter and CV to each one. I received two responses, both negative. Next I started calling each physician, one by one. The whole process was a daunting enterprise. I knew what it was like to be Bob from AT&T, calling during your grandmother's wake, trying to get you to switch long distance companies. Most physicians wouldn't talk to me.

To say I was professionally discouraged would have been an understatement. One thing I soon discovered was that job hunting didn't pay the bills. I set out to look for a non-PA job so I could afford to eat. I started working for a temporary employment service, where I again found my destiny with the down and out. Most of my co-workers were homeless. Many were working just long enough to purchase their next bottle of Boone's Farm Raspberry . . . fine dinner wine. Actually, for them it was more like an instant breakfast.

The job I hated most was picking up trash. My professional self-esteem couldn't sink any lower. I had completed four years of college, plus two years health care experience followed by 24 months of a tough medical school program only to wind up picking up trash with a bunch of winos. Then to spend my afternoons being told by office after office that "the doctor will not speak with you because he doesn't want no doctor's helper." If I had had health insurance I would have made appointments with the physicians as a patient just so I could speak with them. I could list my chief complaint as depression, which wouldn't have been far from the truth.

I arrived at work early one morning and they told me to report to an industrial site to join a clean-up crew. Soon after I got there, six other guys arrived. I had worked with most of them before. Yet on this morning there was a new face in the crowd—a younger guy, like me. He wore clean clothes and his short blond hair was cleanly cut. We were assigned to pick up slimy papers and other trash along a drainage ditch behind a warehouse. Truly rewarding work. I picked up a wad of crumpled, wet newspaper and a copperhead snake fell from between the pages and slithered off through the grass. I let out a yelp. This new guy walked over, thinking I had been bitten. We began talking. "Yeah, this is my fist day working with the temp service. I actually have a college degree."

"Really?" I said. "So do I. What was your major?" He gave me a little smile and said, "I have a degree in medicine."

"Medicine!" I said.

"You have probably never heard of this, but I am what they call a Physician Assistant."

I began laughing hysterically. The poor guy thought I was laughing at him. It took me a couple of minutes to regain my composure and tell him, "I'm a PA, too!"

Then we both laughed until we cried. We started talking about how funny it would be if the *Physician Assistant Journal* did a cover story about us and our fine work here in the drainage ditch. Graduates from PA programs later, especially in the early '90s when there would be eight offers for every graduate, would think, "I would never stoop so low as to do manual labor after PA school." Well, when you are starving you can find yourself doing some surprising things. I continued working for temporary employment service until I "landed" the Sears job.

Denise and I continued our long-range courtship via letters and phone calls. I saw her again in December when I took a jeepload of college kids to a Christian mission conference in Urbana, Illinois. Within a couple of days, we were talking marriage.

The mission's conference had a computer-based job-matching service for all their guests. On the registration forms I had included information about my education, skills, and profession. Then they cross-matched you with the hundreds of mission and relief agencies who were looking for volunteers. Denise and I went together to pick up our packets. She opened hers first. Inside was a pile of continuous computer paper matching her with more than 300 agencies begging for a nurse. When I got my envelope, my sheets were completely empty. I returned to the office and showed them my sheets. The woman laughed. "Oh, that is a mistake. Let me run your file again." She ran it again and it came back empty. "That is really odd. For the ten years I have been doing this, I have never had a match come up completely negative. What is your degree in anyway?"

"I am a Physician Assistant."

"Oh, Physician's Assistant. I know the problem. The official name for your profession is 'Medical Assistant.' Let me run it through with that title"

"No thanks." I was realizing that I couldn't even give my services away.

The next time I saw Denise was in January in Duluth. I drove up to try out the PA market there. I had sent off letters and CVs to about thirty Twin City physicians.

A winter trip to Duluth was a real eye opener for a southern boy. I was there for five days and the temperature never broke the zero-degree mark. However, I loved the woods and, of course, Lake Superior. Duluth is a beautiful city of 90,000, built on a steep hill overlooking the lake. In the winter, Superior has a personality all its own. Some days, all you can see is white pack ice to the horizon. Then, provided the wind shifts, the next day could see deep blue open water. To the southeast, you could see far over the northern shore of Wisconsin, which sat on a plane 500 feet below the Minnesota side. The shore of Wisconsin was dotted with white birch trees projecting from the deep snow cover. Duluth was like a mini San Francisco, and a heck of a lot colder. Mark Twain said, "The coldest winter I have ever experienced was a summer in San Francisco." Apparently he never spent a real winter in Duluth.

After my week in Duluth, I went down to the Twin Cites for five days. I spent the first few days calling the physicians that I had written beforehand. The response was about the same as in Kentucky, but with one exception. I was able to reach one St. Paul physician named Dr. Hanson. When I suggested an interview, he agreed. Wow, after only six months of being a PA I finally had landed my first interview!

I had left my jeep parked in the heated apartment garage where I was staying. A 50-degree garage seemed luxurious when the outside temp was 10 below. But, such comforts, as I would soon learn, can have a down side.

Dr. Hanson wanted to meet in his office at 5:20 p.m. I dressed up in a borrowed coat and tie and took the elevator down to the garage. I cranked up the jeep and went out the garage door into the frigid air. Within a block I took the ramp up to the eight-lane freeway. It was rush hour and the highway was bumper to bumper screaming metal. I inched my way over to the fast lane because I certainly didn't want to show up late to my first interview.

I was zipping along at 75 mph, cars within inches on all sides. Then the strangest thing happened–pretty little white ice crystals began to bloom on all interior glass surfaces. The jeep had a fiberglass top that leaked terribly around the doors. The carpet was always wet and in fact had remained frozen stiff since I had crossed the Mason-Dixon Line–that is, until I parked it in the heated garage overnight. When I got in that afternoon, I noticed how humid and musty it was. It must have taken 5-10 minutes for the icy temps to pierce the glass of my windows. I quickly used my thumbnail to clear a one-inch hole to see out of. I scraped like mad. I would stop and in a second the little hole would close up. I was shouting at my heater, "Come on, damn you, heat up!" For an evangelical to swear is a sure sign of real fear . . . and that there were no other evangelicals nearby.

I put on my signal and tried to ease to the right. I listened for honking horns. I didn't hear any. Through my peephole I could tell that I was in the center lane now. I tried the maneuver again. This time I heard a honk and jerked it back to the center, one hand was on the steering wheel, the other was scraping frost like mad, this time with my driver's license. I tried it again and finally made it into the right lane. I quickly looked for a piece of shoulder I could pull over on and wait for my defroster to kick in.

I eventually found my way to Dr. Hanson's office but, unfortunately, was ten minutes late due to my little brush with death. It was a terrible way to start out an interview. I went into his waiting room and the lights were out. I said, "Hello," through the receptionist's window. Soon a short chunky man with thick glasses and greasy hair came to the front. He was wearing a brown cardigan and a tie, and looked to be in his mid-30s. He spoke in a very soft voice, so quiet that I barely could hear him above the phone that kept ringing until an answering machine finally kicked in. I had to keep asking him to repeat himself. He mumbled, "Come on back, Mr. Jones."

The front office looked like a tornado had just hit it. Charts were piled high everywhere. We went back to his office. I moved a pile of un-filed lab reports from a chair and took a seat. Dr. Hanson told me, "I went to medical school with the plans of practicing with my dad. After just two years in practice, Dad fell over dead one day, right here in this office." He then pointed across the hall to an open door. "I've been in solo practice for six months now and it's falling apart. My dad was a good businessman and ran the practice for 35 years with no problems. But I don't know a thing about running a practice. My office manager walked out on me three weeks ago because things were in such a mess. I have hundreds of patients who have yet to be billed for the services I performed."

Then he looked at me pitifully. I thought he was about to cry. He asked, "Do you know how to run a practice?"

"Well," I told him. "I've not been trained in running a practice, but I certainly could learn."

He looked at me with some surprise. He took my CV off his messy desk and said, "Here it says you are a Physician Assistant. I thought that meant you would assist me like an executive assistant. Hire people, fire people, take care of billing."

"Well, I'm not saying I couldn't help you with some of those things. I would be willing to learn how to manage an office and even spend half my time doing some of those tasks, but I would like to see patients with my other half." I felt that this was having the flexibility necessary to land a job.

He looked at me funny again. "What do you mean by seeing patients?"

"You know, evaluating and treating patients."

"Oh, good heavens, I couldn't let you do that."

At this point my optimism was waning. "That is what I was trained to do."

"Oh," he said, "so you are like a medical assistant. We have a girl here who is one of those. So you would want to do that, take vital signs, file charts, half of the time, and manage the practice the other half?"

If it had been in an area with more geographic appeal, like Duluth, I might have considered doing something like this. At least it was better than picking up garbage or selling layers of clothes that adhered to the preppy look. I was also thinking that in time I could prove myself and move up the food chain or at least in the direction of clinical practice. However, that was a big "if," so I said, "No, thank you, I'm not interested."

I left Minnesota the next day in the middle of a blizzard and headed back toward Kentucky. I was heading back, discouraged, without a single job lead. What should have been a 24-hour trip turned into a 36-hour mental marathon. It seemed I left in the middle of the storm and traveled with the storm across Wisconsin through Chicago and down through the state of Indiana. I was so tired that I was pulled over in Indianapolis for drunk driving and made to walk a straight line. I finally convinced the officer I was sober, but just barely.

Once back to Kentucky I felt a little lost. I had covered the entire state with a fine-tooth comb without success. Yet I wasn't alone. Most of my classmates still didn't have PA jobs. One of them decided to go on to medical school in the Caribbean. One went into nursing home administration. One went to dental school. A couple took medical jobs around Lexington but not real PA jobs. A couple of guys had jobs lined up before coming to PA school; and, unfortunately, one classmate committed suicide. The rest were in limbo like me.

I had made calls to the Federal Correction Institution on occasion to see whether they anticipated openings. During one such call, in March, Dr. Sanchez asked me, "Mike, would you ever consider leaving Kentucky."

"Why?" I said.

"Well, the Bureau of Prisons has monthly postings for PA openings around the country and I thought you might be interested in seeing one of those."

"Sure. Send me the list and I'll take a look."

After reviewing the list and making a few phone calls, I chose to go for an interview at a facility in Michigan. The surprising thing was that the medical director there, Mr. Ross, acted like he was trying to recruit me—as if he really wanted me to come. Imagine that! Over the phone, he painted a beautiful picture of the position at the prison.

I drove up for the interview. Mr. Ross treated me very nice despite my naivete. I would soon learn, over and over, the principle of "bait and switch" when it comes to job interviewing.

This is like the story in which St. Peter gives an incoming woman the choice between Heaven and Hell. She went to visit Heaven first. It was nice. Everyone was sitting around on clouds playing harps and smiling. Then she went to Hell. When she got off the elevator, a very handsome man in a tux greeted her by name and said, "I will be your guide."

He took her to a concert of her favorite musician. Then he took her to a dinner of her favorite food: Beef Wellington and King Crab legs. They went to an ice cream social with all her old friends whom she loved dearly. She was then taken to a beautiful beach house on a rocky coast. The next day she played golf all day–her favorite sport–with all of the people so admired throughout history. Then they had a huge party in her honor.

When she returned to St. Peter, she said, apologetically, "You know, Heaven is really nice, but I think I prefer Hell."

St. Peter said, "Are you sure because once you are there you can never change your mind?"

"Yes, I am quite sure."

St. Peter led her to the elevator and sadly bid her adieu.

When she arrived in Hell she was horrified to find it dark and filled with smoke. All her friends and heroines were crying out for help as they shoveled coal into the very hot furnace. In the meantime monstrous demons were beating everyone with whips. She recognized the man in the tux, but he now had a very angry and ugly face. She screamed at him, "What happened? Where is the Hell I visited yesterday?"

To this he said, "Oh, this is the same place. But you see, yesterday you were a recruit, today you're staff."

I accepted the position at the prison in Michigan, starting at $14,900 a year. The first thing I did when I received word that I had been hired was to drive to Duluth and ask Denise to be my wife.

From Duluth, I journeyed across Michigan's Upper Peninsula and then down to the town where the prison was located. Crossing the Upper Peninsula left a strong impression on me. It is a beautiful area, totally different from the lower part of the state, where I would be living. It seems very isolated with its forest of birch and evergreens that seem to go on forever. You could drive for thirty minutes on straight two-lane highways without passing another car. The terrain was much different as well. In places where the road passed rocky knobs you had the feeling you were out west. Crystal clear running water crisscrossed the UP, draining the water from the abundant snow. Then, of course, there was the beauty of the white, sandy coast of Lakes Superior and Michigan. I was so impressed that we eventually would settle there for almost ten years. We would still be there if we had had a choice.

The first thing I noticed about my new job was that the other PAs hated their jobs, the inmates, each other, and especially Mr. Ross. This was a huge difference from the "happy" work environment I had found at the Lexington facility.

Soon, I started to understand why morale was so low. Everyone was grossly overworked. The Lexington facility was like any clinic and hospital. It had nice, competent physicians, pharmacists, X-ray technicians, and nursing support. In Michigan, it was a one-man show.

The morning clinic saw 20-30 patients. You had to see them all plus do everything else. You called the patient back and did vitals. If you prescribed a medication, you had to fill it. This meant going to the pharmacy, passing through a couple of locked doors using the mass of keys that hung from a chain on your belt, counting the pills, logging them out, typing up the little label, and dispensing them. If you ordered an X-ray, you had to go through those locked doors, warm up the machine, take the X-ray, develop them in ancient machines, and read them. If you ordered labs, again you were on your own. In the meantime there was a constant "PA Jones" calling from the two-way radio in your hip pocket. The prison was only authorized to hire PAs and we were four PAs short. Even one medical assistant would have been a great help. However, this apparently made too much sense to bureaucrats somewhere.

The physician who backed us up, Dr. Bogan, was a rather odd fellow. He could have doubled for John Belushi in *Animal House*. The other odd thing was that although he had a home with a wife and kids just 14 miles away, he chose to actually live in the prison.

Then, came the daily dealings with the inmates. My mother used to say, "Be kind to people and they will be kind to you in return." As far as I could gather the Detroit crack-dealing society operated from a slightly different perspective. The nicest ones would come into my office and demand treatment for their minor complaints. For example, they might want oral antibiotics and Tylenol 3 for a large zit on the chin. While I was being professional and courteous, trying to accommodate their perceived needs, they would take a piece of the disposable razor blade in their pockets and stick it with chewing gum under the edge of my desk hoping I might lacerate myself. Why? I don't have a clue. Maybe they were bored. I'm glad that the prospect of me bleeding to death could provide them with a little entertainment. The lovely inmates would also affectionately refer to us as "muther" as in, "Hey muther, where are my *&%^$&* pills?"

Within a few months, the situation at the prison went from bad to worse. One day, one of the other PAs got into an argument with Mr. Ross, which wasn't unusual. However, this time it almost came to blows. In the end, the PA threw his stethoscope at him and walked out the door, never to be seen again. About the same time, we had orders from the Bureau of Prisons to increase our coverage to 24 hours and seven days a week, up from the previous 16 hours and five days a week. This was like Pharaoh telling the Israelites to make more bricks and to start getting their own straw. The workload was growing unbearable. We were all stressed out. To make matters worse, Mr. Ross chose to handle the stress by becoming chemically impaired.

Being low man on the totem pole, I was assigned to what they called the "shit shift." I had to come in at 5:45 a.m. and set up a little booth in the prison yard to take sick call appointments. This would take about an hour as one dorm was released at a time. Next, I would have to return to the clinic and run the seven o'clock pill line. Any drug with the potential for abuse in the prison economy had to be hand-fed to the inmates, one pill at a time.

After the pill line was complete, I would start seeing sick call appointments at 7:30 a.m. When the next PA arrived at eight o'clock, I would then do rounds at the D Block.

D Block, for Detention Block, was the prison within the prison. This was where they housed the really bad inmates, those who had killed fellow inmates or raped staff. These bad boys were locked up alone in individual cells for 23 hours a day. D Block had six locked sections. Each section had one inmate whose door was left ajar so he could move about the catwalk as the "orderly."

After dealing with the D Block boys, I felt hopeless for many of them. I could see why the Brits sent their inmates to Australia during the last century. Paradoxically, however, I still believed in my heart that they too were created in God's image and had intrinsic value and thus some hope.

As I walked down the catwalk it would be a barrage of insults. I was coming here to help them, to attend to their medical needs. I had to stay away from the bars to keep from being assaulted. Cups of urine in the face were a common threat. It amazed me to see such hostility. I always wondered where this intense anger came from. Were they simply standing in line at the car rental place one day and blew their top when the car they reserved was not available? From that point on, did they become piles of angry protoplasm? I don't think so. They must have been abused as children . . . or perhaps the abuse was self-inflicted.

I was told about one laid-back physician who did my same job back in the '70s. One day an inmate threw a cup of urine in his face. Naturally we were required to act professionally at all times to avoid lawsuits. This physician calmly licked his lips and said, "Hum, that tasted a little sweet. You may have diabetes." Then he ordered a blood draw for glucose every two hours, around the clock for two days. It took four guards to restrain the inmate for each blood draw. This drastically reduced the inmate's urine-flinging tendencies.

Dr. Bogan wasn't the only odd employee in the place. A man from New York called "Boots" was hired as a guard at the same time I started. He was 27 years old and had never been outside the city limits of the Big Apple. During orientation, PAs were required to go through the same training as guards. Boots and I were paired up together.

Boots got his name because as soon as he was hired, he went to a uniform store on the East Side of New York and bought a fireman's coat and boots and a policeman's uniform. The boots came up to his knees and had huge chrome buckles. He wore these at all times, that is, until he was issued his official BOP uniform.

I couldn't believe that Boots was from NYC and had never held a gun before. I had to show him how to hold and fire it. He was very dangerous. He took six loaded pistols from the firing range and stuffed them into his pants, pretending to be some kind of Old West marshall. Then he took a loaded pistol with the safety off and tried to twirl it like a gunslinger. His last act was aiming a loaded shotgun at his classmates. He was driving the firearms instructor crazy.

Boots only lasted two weeks as a guard before he was fired. He refused to leave the prison where he shared a room with Dr. Bogan. The personnel director had to throw his stuff out on the curb. Next thing, Boots took one of the guns and held up the bank across the street. He wanted to get caught. He said as they were hauling him away, "I'm not going back to New York City. If I can't stay in the prison as a guard, then I want to stay as an inmate." When I saw them arresting him on TV after shooting up the bank, I thought, Hey, I taught that guy how to use a gun.

After just five months, I was approaching an emotional meltdown. I wasn't cut out for this line of work. I'm too kind and soft-spoken. I tend to internalize things. To be a good prison PA in this situation, you need the personality of Robert De Niro in *Raging Bull*.

One morning, later that summer, I was working the early shift again. After signing guys up for sick call I returned to start the morning clinic. I was the only person in the clinic when they released the first wave of inmates with appointments.

At this time, unknown to us, an inmate in one dorm wanted to kill an inmate in a different dorm. He had waited for months for his target to sign up for sick call. Then he, likewise, signed up for sick call and got a time slot near his intended victim's appointment. When they were dropped off at the clinic, they came into my office. There were about six of them. The assailant pulled out a homemade knife and jumped on the other guy. I could see the hate in his eyes as he stabbed the man's chest and abdomen over and over.

Fortunately the homemade knife wasn't very sharp. It hit several ribs without penetrating the chest and only one wound penetrated the victim's abdomen, which required a trip to the local hospital and to the OR to repair a nicked bowel. This event, however, increased my anxiety. The inmates' frustration with the medical department was growing and threats on my life were increasing. I felt very little support from the security end of things.

The final blow came when I had to testify against one of the inmates as a witness of his attempted escape. I had tended to his wounds after he got caught in the razor wire. He was put in D Block, but for some absurd reason was made the section's orderly. I was locked in alone with him every morning while I rounded on his section, and he knew I was the main witness against him. He was in my face the entire time. Each morning, I half-expected, to get a broken off broom-handle rammed into me.

Denise saw me coming apart at the seams. She was the first to suggest I find a new job, but I couldn't imagine leaving my first job in less than a year, especially when it had taken eight months to find it! However, the medical department was going to hell in a hand basket.

One day, I did see an ad in the *Detroit Free Press* for a Physician Assistant. It was a little like a Big Foot sighting. Before then I didn't believe PA want-ads existed. I called the number and set up an interview.

I was surprised to find the clinic located in a very rough part of Detroit, with several burned out, abandoned cars in the street outside. Downstairs was a pharmacy with bars on the window. I went upstairs and waited for Dr. Alexander, the director. When he was finished seeing the morning patients, he called me in. He took his bag lunch and we went into a back room.

He was a small man, in his forties, with long coal-black, slicked back hair. He spoke with an accent that I vaguely identified as either Russian or from some other Slavic country. He was a very smooth talker and came across like a Mafia boss. After describing the practice, he laid down his sandwich, got up, and closed the door. He returned to his seat and took another bite, washing it down with a Diet Coke, and gave a soft belch. When his mouth was clear he looked up at me and smiled. "Mr. Jones, this is a very lucrative practice, you would be a . . . mazed. I deal exclusively with medicaid customers." Then he took another bite and winked at me with a big smile on his face.

I have to admit that I was pretty naive about medicaid fraud. But, I would leave that day with very negative feelings about the whole scam. I never even called him back.

Less than a week later a friend of ours, an RN named Linda, called about a PA job. She was sitting at the desk on the floor of the hospital when she heard this neurologist say, "I really need to hire a PA." This neurologist was Joel Saper, one of the world's leading authorities on headache disorders and the director of one of the largest headache centers in the U.S.

I sent Dr. Saper a cover letter and CV. Within a week I had a call from his office manager wanting to set up an interview. I arrived at the interview eager with anticipation. I had to wait for quite a while as Dr. Saper was still busy with morning patients. I was given a tour of the pleasant but hectic office. I was impressed but I couldn't imagine a big clinic like this devoted entirely to treating headaches.

I met with the nursing supervisor first. She had been in academia at the University of Michigan nursing program prior to joining Dr. Saper. I tried to be nice, but I could tell she was uptight about something. While we were waiting in silence, finally she leveled with me. "I've been fighting the idea of a Physician's Assistant being hired here. I don't want my nurses taking orders from a PA; that would be very belittling to them."

When Dr. Saper came in, he gave me a very different impression. He was glad I was there. I can't remember his questions, but however I answered them, I must have impressed him. Although he had interviewed a couple of other PAs, he offered me the position on the spot and offered me a great deal more money than I was making at the prison.

I was excited about the offer, but I was also feeling a lot of guilt. I didn't take the job at the prison, intending to leave in 6-7 months. I hated to start my career that way. Also, I hated to drop the number of

PAs there down to three. This would make the place a little more like hell for the rest of them, and they were my friends.

I called Mr. Ross. "Hi, this is Mike Jones. I know that you will be gone by the time I come to work this afternoon, but I need to talk to you. Will you be there at three?"

"What the hell is it?" came his unfriendly reply.

"I will tell you when I come in." I left it at that.

I had Dr. Saper's office manager promise that she would give me time to break the news to the prison. Unfortunately, she didn't. She called them for a reference right after I left the interview. By the time I got to work that afternoon, as they might have said in the Middle Ages, "the dung had hit the windmill."

As I walked into the building, I thought about my "first impression" interview. This was during the "bait" phase. At the time Mr. Ross was telling me how great it was to work there. He shared a long and somewhat bizarre list of perks such as providing me with low-cost housing, free pilot ground and air school if I wanted, etc. None of them panned out.

Then I thought about his promise to me. I knew that I wasn't allowed to take vacation time until I had worked there for 12 months. However, I was getting married in three months. I asked him if I could have one week off, without pay, for my honeymoon. He promised me that I could.

My wedding was on July 31, a Saturday morning. About two weeks before my wedding, Mr. Ross posted the August calendar. On it I was scheduled to work on Monday, August the 2nd. I took the calendar to him and calmly said, "I think you made a mistake on the schedule. You have me working on the second. I am on my honeymoon that week."

"Like hell. I made no mistake. We're too short to let you have that time off. You have to earn your damn vacation days like everyone else around here." At that, I lost a lot of my guilt that afternoon.

Mr. Ross was not happy. I was willing to put in my 30-day notice, as required by my contract. In his anger, however, he wanted me out immediately, screaming, "Well if you don't like it here then get the hell out. We don't need you!" Great! I was a free man.

Now I had a chance to work at a nice professional place. To best appreciate the experience you should read C. S. Lewis' book, *The Great Divorce*. It is a wonderful story about a bus trip from Hell to Heaven and paints an accurate description of this job change.

My experience at the headache clinic was very positive. Dr. Saper had great confidence in me, which really helped me get on my professional feet. He was as supportive as a supervising physician could be. Extremely bright and gifted in his bedside manner, he made each patient feel like they were special. Working there was a little intimidating at first, with patients coming to see us from coast to coast, and sometimes even from overseas.

During the first two years it was just the two of us seeing patients. After my second year, he suddenly hired three neurologists to see patients and I moved into research.

One might ask, if this job was so good why would I ever want to leave? I have asked myself that question over the years. After I moved into research, I started to doubt my professional direction. The pharmacological studies paid the practice very well. Dr. Saper was very generous and rewarded me accordingly. I was now at the higher end of the PA pay scale. But I just couldn't get those Afghan faces out of my memory. I knew that the world was covered with countless other faces of individuals created in God's image, people whose lives were filled with suffering–suffering I might be able to ease. Although developing better treatments for migraines is important–even life-changing for some–I just didn't feel my full-time research capacity was fulfilling my original dream.

Denise and I both had been moved by our experience overseas. We started thinking about going back to the Third World and trying to find a place where we could make a bigger difference in the lives of our patients. After almost five years working with headaches, we decided it was time for a change.

We spent more than a year looking at different serving opportunities abroad. Initially I wanted to find an organization where I could go as a hired employee. These opportunities were few and far between. The couple of opportunities I did find were for single-status only. Not only was I married, but we had our first son, Bryan, by this point and soon found ourselves pregnant again.

The other route, rather than being salaried, was to go on donor support. This is how most church and other Christian missions work. I hated the thought of raising our own financial support from donors, but, in the end, to fulfill this dream we would have little choice.

The next challenge was choosing a mission agency to go with. We looked at opportunities in the Philippines, Africa, and even Iceland. We were leaning toward one in Paris.

I know that Paris is far from Third World. As a matter of fact, some of the French probably consider the U.S. a Third World country, especially with how so many free-spirited American youths went to live like hobos on their soil. This opportunity was with MA, the same agency Denise and I worked with in Abu Dhabi. Our experience with MA had been very positive. The organization was interested in us coming and working with a large Arabic-speaking immigrant population living outside of Paris.

Although we did love the Arab people and culture, I didn't care much for the Middle East. That's not as much of a contradiction as it might sound. The truth is I didn't care for the Middle East geographically. Although I was a lover of mountains, that had to do with mountains with some greenery on them rather than those that looked like they had been imported from the moon. Denise and I both loved cool weather and snow. So when MA spoke to us about France, it caught our attention. Paris was only a day's drive from the Alps—indeed, the language school that we would be required to attend was actually in the French Alps.

Denise and I decided to make a fact-finding trip to France to visit the MA field office. About three weeks prior to our departure from the states, I received a strange call in the middle of the night from an ICO missionary in the Middle East named Chuck. We had corresponded on occasion and I had mentioned to him in a letter that I was making this trip to France.

The ICO Middle East office had been in Beirut during the zenith of the Lebanese civil war. There were only a few American men left in Beirut who weren't hostages of one clan or another. The U.S. embassy had evacuated American citizens from the bombed out city a year earlier. Chuck put his family on a helicopter to Cyprus at that time, telling them, "I will join you later." But he decided to stay behind alone and continue working with the Lebanese. He certainly deserved a lot of respect for his courage and love for the people. But, he never communicated with his own family for many months and had been feared dead. His family eventually relocated back to the US until six months later, when they heard from Chuck. He became something of a cult hero among the ICO staff people. He was their Rambo missionary guy.

On the phone, Chuck said, "Michael, since you are heading to France in a couple of weeks, I would like for you to come on down to Cyprus."

"Come to Cyprus? For what reason?"

"Mike, I need to talk to you about something very important . . . . but I can't discuss it on the phone."

"OK," I said with hesitation. "But, where do I go in Cyprus?"

"Just buy a ticket to Larnaca. Let me know your arrival time and I will meet you at the airport."

It sounds odd to me now, but back then this was the type of aura that ICO cultivated around their staff people. Leaders were elevated to the point of being practically infallible. This was the cultic side of the group. When an ICO staff told you to "Jump," on the way down you said, "Thank you sir." Their model of leadership, or the abuse thereof, derived from the military, certainly not from anything that Christ taught.

I quietly crawled back in bed that night, trying not to wake Denise. In her half-asleep voice she asked, "Who was that?"

"Chuck . . . with ICO in Cyprus."

"What did he want?"

"Well, I guess I will be making a detour to Cyprus while we are in France. There is something very important he needs to talk to me about."

Denise, who was a little less familiar with the ICO leadership style, suddenly sat up in bed. "You are leaving Bryan and me alone in Paris while you run down to Cyprus, just because Chuck has something important to tell you?"

"Yeah, that's right. Good night honey-pie." Then I rolled over and closed my eyes, trying to escape further conversation and my somewhat shallow explanations.

After a brief layover in Iceland, we enjoyed a well-planned visit in Paris. Again, MA had treated us very well and appeared to be extremely organized. Denise and I played tourist for the first couple of days. I was able to show her the sights, including the park benches where Tim and I had slept six years earlier.

Denise and Bryan hiking along an Icelandic fjord.

On the third day we had a long meeting with Mr. Boswell, MA's field director for central France. His wife had prepared a wonderful seven-course French dinner. Afterwards, we moved out to his parlor to sip coffee while he gave us the discouraging news. "Mike and Denise, we would be excited and honored to have you join us here in Paris. I will notify MA's home office. But I can offer you this position only on the condition that both of you complete two years of Bible college. Then, when you arrive here, I will send you for two years of French language study, immediately followed by two years of North African Arabic studies. I have learned during my fifteen years here that if you don't get a good grip on the language up front, you never fully assimilate." He paused to sip coffee and to take a bite of his decorative sherbet. Meanwhile, I was using my fingers to count up the years: two . . . four . . . six. I couldn't comprehend six more years of school prior to doing the work that I wanted to do. To a 28-year-old, six years seemed like an eternity.

In the midst of this mood of discouragement, the next evening I had to leave Denise for my trip to Cyprus. Little did I know that this mysterious island meeting would start our family down a very difficult path that would profoundly change us forevermore. Once Pandora's box was opened, it could never again be closed.

Chapter Eleven

A Mission, Impossible

Around midnight a woman in her late 70s came quietly walking down the French train car aisle. She was wearing a brown floral print dress and had a large white leather purse hanging from her left arm. She also wore a very worried look on her face. Pausing at each seat, she asked the passenger in her southern American accent, "Does anyone here speak English?" She worked her way toward me, her question being ignored at each juncture. I cowardly decided to do likewise and pretend I was asleep. Despite the fact I spoke English, I was just as baffled as she was. The train was being taken apart, one car at a time, and I didn't know what was going on either. As she arrived at my seat, I ignored her as the French had, yet I hoped someone would eventually respond. Finally a French man answered her in broken English, "Yas."

She said with concern, "Why are they taking our train apart?"

The thin man, with a silk blazer draped over his shoulders, said, "Da front of de train is going to London. Da reer of de train is going to Belgium." She turned and started to walk fast toward the front of the train, pausing at her seat to grab her carry-on bag. I waited until she was out of sight before doing the same.

My journey to Cyprus had just started and already was running into complications. I left Denise and Bryan at the MA missionary's apartment in the Parisian suburb for my overnight trip to London. For the first leg, I took a commuter bus to the westernmost stop of the

Metro, which is the Parisian subway. From there I took the subway to the Garde de Nor, or the northern train station. I kept searching the tracks for my train as my departure time was fast approaching. At the last minute I saw a train with the words "London/Belgium" on it. I jumped on the last car with my backpack just before it pulled out of the station.

The train departed at 10:30 p.m. and was due to arrive in London at 6:00 a.m. My flight to Cyprus left London Heathrow at 7:30 a.m., which meant I would be cutting it very close. It was an interesting overnight journey. I learned that just being on the right train isn't enough. You must also be in the right cars.

The London sunrise was a beautiful sight. We came out of a long stone tunnel to see rows and rows of old red-brick buildings with tall chimneys. Narrow cobblestone streets divided the buildings, giving me the sense that I had been transported back to the time of Dickens. The train pulled into the busy station and I made it quickly through the underground out to Heathrow, where I found my British Airways flight to Larnaca, Cyprus.

Upon arriving in Cyprus, I suddenly had the feeling I was back in the Middle East, although most Cypriots would prefer to think of themselves as European. Cyprus is a fascinating island country that, at times, has been almost torn to pieces by East-West tensions. I had started this trip with a visit to an island nation, Iceland, a fascinating place in its own right. I noticed many parallels between the two.

Iceland sits on top of the mid-Atlantic ridge, where the two major tectonic plates upon which the European and Western plates rest are separating. Iceland was formed from the volcanic action associated with this separation. The island itself is constantly being pressured apart and then built up with lava flows.

Cyprus straddles the rift between two giant "political and cultural" tectonic plates–one being the Western Christian culture and the other being the Eastern Moslem culture. This island has been on the verge of being torn apart several times throughout history. Indeed, at the time of my visit, and to this day, it has been torn apart, north to south, by political lines between the Greek Orthodox and the Turkish Moslem cultures. This tension led to an all-out war with a Turkish invasion in July 1974. Since that time, the island has been divided between the northern and eastern Turkish areas and southern and western Greek areas. The line is a 50-foot-wide "no man's land" controlled by the UN. The major city, Nicosia, is divided in half. Rumor has it homes caught in the middle of this strip are like a moment frozen in time at the instant of the Turkish invasion. Uneaten food still sits on the tables, certainly long-decayed by now.

The Turkish north controls the Nicosia airport so I had to fly into Larnaca. This was the major airport on the southern Greek-controlled side of the island. As I came through customs, I felt the modern tensions as machine-gun-toting solders surrounded the whole airport. The custom agents were very thorough. Every pocket of my backpack had to be emptied. Then I was searched from head to toe.

After I finished with customs, Chuck greeted me. He was stocky, six feet tall, in his late thirties, and with a freshly burned face. He had a goatee and short grayish-brown hair, thinning in the front. He greeted me with a very Middle Eastern-style kiss on the cheeks. This was revealing of his great desire to relate to and adapt to the local ways. We walked across the blistering hot parking lot to his van. We took a seat inside and he handed me a 15-page syllabus. Centered on the front page in large letters was, "Mike Jones' visit to Cyprus, June 1985." He turned to me and said, "I have you here for 48 hours, therefore, I am going to start my debriefing immediately." We pulled from the parking lot and started our 75-mile trek toward the city of Nicosia. At any moment I was expecting to hear the theme from "Mission Impossible."

Chuck had been on staff with ICO for at least ten years. He held a Ph D degree in Public Health. He told me that he was also a veterinarian but I was never sure if he actually had a degree in veterinarian medicine or just specialized in animal issues in public health in obtaining his original degree. He was a very bright man nonetheless. I quickly learned during the trip to Nicosia that I would have a very difficult time understanding him. I have searched for the words to describe the communication problems between us. It certainly wasn't his accent as he was originally from North Carolina—in fact, not far from my home in Tennessee. He, too, was a Midwest transplant. A small part of the problem was his vocabulary. He certainly had a diverse vocabulary and used it well. He also used common words in atypical ways. But the best way I can describe his communication style was tangential and allegorical–giving no warning when he was about to depart from the literal.

The whole trip to Cyprus had been veiled in mystery when it didn't have to be. Most people would have been direct and told me what was so important that it required my immediate trip halfway around the world. However, he would later tell me this shroud of mystery was one of his "tests" of me, to see if I was trusting. These kinds of games were rather common in ICO. All of us "Jedis" wanted to be faithful, available, and teachable, which might best be abbreviated by the initials G.U.L.L.I.B.L.E. To express doubt about coming halfway around the world in response to an ICO leader's request wouldn't be consistent with the Jedi way. I ended up learning the hard way how human and fallible we all are. Therefore, blind trust in a stranger, just because he was ICO staff, was a serious mistake.

By the time I arrived at Chuck's house in Nicosia, I was as confused as when I had landed in Larnaca. During the 1-1/2 hour drive across the arid Cypriot countryside, Chuck kept talking about "building laboratories in Cyprus." I still didn't know what he was talking about. I kept thinking in literal terms and asking him, "What kind of laboratories? Are you talking about building a medical lab?" He wouldn't give me a direct answer but remained tangential: "Mike, what do you think I mean by laboratories?" I went to bed that night exhausted but excited about being in Cyprus.

The next morning bright and early Chuck and I resumed our marathon conversation. To break the monotony and heat, we went to a sports club and sat by their shaded swimming pool sipping fresh-squeezed lemonade. I was still trying to make sense of what Chuck was saying, but to no avail.

From there we went to the ICO Middle East office in downtown Nicosia, where we met with Bill, the Middle East director of the organization. Bill was a tall, thin, olive-skinned Italian American in his mid forties. He was wearing a dark sports jacket with some type of gold crest embroidered on the pocket. He wore a cotton dress shirt opened at the collar, apparently to help dissipate the Cypriot heat. Bill was soft spoken, and thankfully much more direct than Chuck. He had a nice office on the seventh floor with large windows overlooking downtown Nicosia. From that vantage point you could see well into the Turkish-controlled northern part of the city and the distant dry mountains to the north and west.

Bill explained to me in common, non-metaphorical English what Chuck was talking about. "Mike, ICO is offering you a position here in Cyprus, working among the Lebanese refugees." I was very surprised. ICO, prior to this point, had never offered new staff overseas positions. It had been against their policy. Bill went on to translate what Chuck had been trying to convey. "These so-called laboratories were Chuck's way of saying that we would be 'experimenting' with ways to serve the Lebanese refugees." I took advantage of the opportunity to flood Bill with questions.

I learned that ICO was inviting another American couple and a Lebanese couple from Beirut. We would form a team of four families, including Chuck, his wife, and two daughters.

The plan was for us to live in Nicosia, a beautiful Greek city with palm trees and modern concrete buildings lying in a circle like a large wheel. The hub of the wheel is an intriguing medieval, walled city. Outside the walled city, the streets are orderly and well planned along the British model, which ruled here for many years. Inside the walls is a maze of narrow ancient streets. I could get intentionally lost there for hours. Intersecting the center of the large wheel was the "no man's land" that separated the Greeks from the Turks.

I was becoming increasingly excited about the opportunity, especially the chance to live in a beautiful island country like Cyprus, where the mountains even had a little snow in the winter. Also, Cyprus was enough like Europe to make daily life much easier. Unlike Paris, Nicosia was a charming small city, which was much more appealing to me. Additionally it was in the heart of the Middle East. Lastly, in Cyprus, at least we were told, we would be part of a close-knit team. Being part of a team was very important to us. Things were starting to come together like a dream coming true.

The view of Nicosia from Bill's office.

As Chuck drove me back to Larnaca to catch my plane, he injected one last mysterious twist. "Mike," he said, "you have one week to decide to accept this invitation or the invitation will be permanently withdrawn."

Feeling freshly confused, I said, "Now why the timetable?" It wasn't like there were several applicants for the position.

"Mike, that is the way I operate. I have learned to force an answer with a timetable; otherwise things never get done."

Here was another major lesson I was slow in learning. Anytime you are offered an opportunity that requires immediate action, or forever will be lost, it is usually better to lose it.

By the time I got back to Denise in Paris, she was becoming convinced that a huge European city wasn't where she wanted to live. My enthusiasm about Cyprus quickly started rubbing off on her. It is impossible to ever share accurately the experience of visiting a place that someone else has never seen. However, I think she too was becoming excited about the opportunity.

Serving in Cyprus with ICO was starting to look like the perfect situation. It was as if God was opening all the right doors for us. The following Sunday I called Chuck to inform him of our decision to accept his offer.

I knew the tough road that lay ahead of us. It wasn't like accepting a regular job, where you just show up and go through orientation. The process of raising our financial support would be a very grueling and sometimes humiliating process of asking individuals and churches to give monthly financial support to sustain us during our time overseas. ICO would take 10–25 % of the money for administrative expenses, including health and life insurance, and deposit the remaining amount in our account for our salary and ministry expenses.

Strangely, after I told Chuck that we were coming, he and the whole Middle East operation seemed to vanish–like it was Brigadoon. It didn't take a hundred years to reappear, but it did take twelve long months for Chuck to do his paperwork so we could get started raising our support–this was despite our frequent prodding letters and phone calls. During these twelve months our second son, Daniel, our strong-willed child, was born.

In my great zeal, I had figured that I would have all of our financial support raised within six months. Maybe I acted a tad impulsively, but to move things along I decided to quit my job, give up our apartment, sell all our possessions, and move into our Volkswagen van so I could focus on fund raising. We said goodbye to our duplex on September 17, 1986. We didn't actually sleep in the van that often, but it was going to be our only home for a while. I was determined to be moving to Cyprus by January 1987. The three months soon grew to ten tedious months. Still, I was constantly amazed by the generosity of some people.

The most humiliating part of fundraising is the negative perception by some. Within Christendom there are basically two types of financial giving. One is the support of full-time Christian workers, such as pastors and missionaries. It is the same as a salary. Pastoring or working among the Third World poor is non-profit. The Lebanese refugees were certainly not in any position to pay for our help, so the money had to come from somewhere. The second type of financial giving is benevolence. This is the act of giving money to the really down and out—such as beggars on the street.

The problem was that many people thought of us as in the latter category. They expected us to be in rags and hungry. OK, maybe a few years earlier I would have met their criteria. If we wore decent clothes, some people seemed surprised. One church had a clothes closet for missionaries. They invited us to come and "shop." We went into this Sunday school classroom and there were tables piled high with clothes. It soon became clear that the clothes were garage sale leftovers. There were three-inch-wide polyester lime green ties and double-knit dirt-brown pants. The pants came with those micro Dacron fuzz balls that form at worn areas such as the knees, belt line, and crotch. There were a couple of leisure suits, one white with yellow armpit stains and one navy with white threads on the seams. It was hard to walk through and not take anything. A woman said, "Now don't be shy. Take anything that you want." I know that they were kind folks with good intentions.

I think our most difficult experience was the Lutheran church in Minnesota where Denise attended while she was growing up. This concept of raising support was very new to them. I became accustomed to it as I had been around people raising support for mission projects for more than 10 years. I didn't realize that Lutherans don't do things the same way. Lutherans do send out relief workers and missionaries to the Third World, but they support them out of a general fund rather than requiring the missionaries themselves to raise their support.

I contacted the pastor and he seemed interested in what we were doing, but I had some difficulty communicating to him the whole concept of raising support. I wouldn't know just how much difficulty until I arrived at his church. Usually when we visited churches, we were asked to address the congregation about what we were going to be doing. During our visit to this church, the pastor conducted the service as usual, following the order of service script to the letter. Toward the end of the service, he acknowledged our presence, though I could tell he was very uncomfortable with the whole situation. He then did the bizarre thing of walking up and down the aisles passing out a copy of my CV to the whole congregation. Next he stated, "Mike Jones is unemployed right now because they will be moving overseas. He and Denise need financial help to make ends meet. If you have any money to spare, they could use it." I wanted to crawl under the pew. He then asked us to stand at the back of the church as the whole congregation filed past us. They were shaking our hands and saying things like, "I hope you find work soon." Or, "Can you use any canned beans? I have extra in my pantry."

To add insult to injury, these were Denise's people. It is something to have one of their own marry this Tennessee boy, only to come back in a few years poor and having to beg strangers for money. Two older women put a couple of dollars in my pocket. All I needed was a tin cup and some pencils or a monkey on a tether. We did have a passion to serve the Third World and this, unfortunately, was the means to that end. At least that is what I kept telling myself. It wasn't a totally wasted trip. Some of Denise's relatives did seem to appreciate what we were doing and decided to, generously, give us their support

During the first few weeks of fund raising, we were consumed with speaking engagements at churches across the Midwest and South. After Christmas with our families, we were facing a real dilemma. We had no more speaking engagements scheduled and nowhere to go. I was expecting to be packing up for Cyprus by this time. Instead, we had only about a quarter of our needed support raised. The support from individuals was coming in on schedule. However, it was the long delay by the churches that I hadn't counted on. Committees and subcommittees take a long time to reach their decisions.

Denise and I started to consider options. Her sister's mother-in-law had a cabin on a lake near La Salle in Michigan's Upper Peninsula. There was only one problem. It was a summer cabin, without heat or insulation. If you know anything about the weather in the UP of Michigan, you can see why this presented such a problem. The owners were obviously very hesitant, but agreed to let us use it. They were hesitant because the cabin had been closed up and winterized–meaning all the pipes had been drained and antifreeze put in the toilet and drains to keep them from freezing and breaking. No one had ever tried to stay there in the winter before. I felt even more awkward in the face of their hesitation; on the other hand, I was starting to get a little desperate.

La Salle gets a tremendous amount of lake effect snow via Lake Superior. We made it to the cabin in the middle of the night, driving down a long two-tacked, unplowed road. We were able to wade through the knee-deep snow and get the door unlocked. Once inside, we piled the boys inside our down sleeping bags and built a fire in the fireplace. Because the cabin had no insulation, the heat seeped right out through the walls and ceiling.

We took the term "living room" to new heights as we literally lived in that one room. Denise would put on her winter coat to go out into the kitchen to cook. Since the bathroom was on the other side of the kitchen, no heat made it there. I was always careful to make sure my butt was dry before I sat down on the icy seat because I was afraid it would stick.

We had to heat water on the stove and take sponge baths. Despite these pioneer-style hardships, it was a really special winter for our family. The cabin sat on a beautiful inland lake surrounded by pines and white birch trees. On days it wasn't snowing, the sky was a brilliant blue and set against the green pines and blinding white snow. The quietness was deafening. There would be many noisy days in the Middle East when our hearts would drift back to and long for this solitude.

Over the following months we encountered many acts of extreme kindness. Friends of ours owned a couple of beautiful vacation homes in northern Michigan. They called us one day and said, "Mike, do you need a home to live in? You are welcome to one of ours in Petosky." It was the nicest place we have ever lived and it was situated right on a gorgeous lake.

Toward the end of spring, ICO contacted us, wanting us to attend a special orientation for new missionaries in a western state. The orientation would last a week. The other couple, the Scotts, who were preparing to move to Cyprus, would also be there. Even Chuck and his wife Marlene were going to make an appearance. It would be a good chance for Denise to finally meet all of them.

The week out west started to go awry as soon as Chuck arrived. He had sent word that he wanted to meet us in the lobby of the lodge we were staying in the second day after his arrival. The Scotts were also invited. They had served with Chuck and his family in Beirut and knew them well.

When we entered the lounge that second night, Chuck was in Arab attire, sitting in an overstuffed chair with Marlene sitting at his feet. Marlene was a very thin, quiet woman with coal-black short hair. She could easily pass for Arab, but I think her ancestry was Eastern Europe. The Scotts were seated in an overstuffed love seat. Denise and I took our seats on the floor as there were no more chairs. I introduced Denise to the group.

Once introductions were over, Chuck began downloading some rather powerful things on us. "Mike and Denise, I just came from a meeting with the other ICO Middle Eastern staff in Jordan. We made a decision to send you to Cairo, Egypt instead of Cyprus. We think you should be 'baptized by fire' into the Arab culture and language—something you can't do living in Cyprus."

I sighed. "But, Chuck, we have Arabic classes set up in Cyprus. There are 75,000 Lebanese refugees living in Cyprus. We don't need to go to Egypt to learn about the Arab culture."

"Mike, you should be thanking us, not complaining. We are giving you a unique opportunity to study Arabic in an Arab country."

"But Chuck, we don't know a single person in Egypt. Are we going to live there alone?"

"Mike, you worry too much. I will be down to help you guys about once a week. Also, Mike, there is another issue. We have come to realize over the past seven years that single men do much better than married men in the Middle East."

OK, Chuck was losing me at this point. "What does this mean?" I said.

"We think that you should come as a single man."

I was waiting for someone to burst out laughing, but no one did. Now I was thinking, is he suggesting that Denise and I get a divorce?

"We want you to go to Egypt alone." He added, in a conciliatory way, "Only for the first three-year term. After that, Denise and the boys could join you."

Denise, in her own state of shock, said, "And where I am I supposed to be during this time, living with my mother?"

"Sure, if that works out for you. Otherwise you could live alone in Cyprus, but it would be much more difficult for you there." I could sense in his tone that he wanted Denise to stay in the states.

Denise and I returned to our room that night still in recovery from our shock. I had never said "no" to any ICO staff before—a real ICO Jedi would never say "no" to a leader—yet my soul was in real turmoil.

Denise and I had a unique relationship. Some marriages are close and some are very close. Denise and I felt like Siamese twins. I knew her heart inside and out, and she knew me the same way. We were inseparable. We had spent only two nights apart and those had been very hard. Chuck was asking us not see each other for three years. It seemed nothing for him to be away from his family for weeks or months.

I didn't sleep much that night. In Chuck's usual fashion, he gave me a timeline for our decision—twelve hours.

The next morning I saw Chuck at breakfast, in the buffet line. Weighted down by guilt (false guilt, of course), I told him, "Chuck, Denise and I have decided that we can't live apart for three years. Wherever we go, we are going together!" Chuck gave me a cold stare, immense disappointment in his eyes. He sighed, then took a large scoop of scrambled eggs and put them on his plate. He looked up at me and said, "You can only do as you have the faith to do. Those of little faith do little things." He, like many in ICO, were masters of guilt manipulation. Telling an evangelical, especially a Jedi, that he lacked faith was the deepest of insults. It was like telling a Navy Seal that he lacked courage.

Weeks later, I argued with Chuck on the phone about going to Cairo. It represented the last place on earth we would ever want to live: a huge, hot, dirty Third World city. I had already described how Cyprus had been on my heart and how it was the fulfillment of what we wanted in our mission experience–the geography, the close-knit team for support. At this, Chuck said, "It's not negotiable. The Middle East team had made its decision." We had already taken the bait, investing two years of our lives in this process, so now it was time for the old switcheroo.

The next little bomb Chuck dropped on us was that he wanted us to show up in Egypt with only the "shirts on our backs."

"What do you mean?" I said, thinking he must be speaking metaphorically again.

He repeated, "I mean what I say. No shipping of personal belongings, no suitcases, nothing! Burn everything before you leave the states. I wish I had done that before I moved to the Middle East." This left us dazed and confused.

Marlene was in Michigan later that summer visiting her sister. Fortunately, she stopped by our house for a couple of days. During her stay, Denise brought up the topic. She was much more reasonable than her husband. She gave Denise a list of essential things to bring to Cairo.

The Scotts, who were leaving for Cyprus within a couple of weeks, told me they had shipped 1,000 pounds of personal effects. Rather than listening to Chuck, I decided, for a family of four, reducing our total worldly possessions down to 900 pounds would be more than reasonable. Besides, we had just found out that Denise was pregnant again. So we would be needing the baby supplies. I built four crates and we carefully picked out only the essential things to pack.

It was like people at Mt. St. Helens just before she blew. They were allowed into their houses to get only what they could carry in a pickup truck. We selected a few clothes each, plus kitchen wares, the kids' toys, and bed clothing. Scrap books and special wall hangings also made the cut. Everything else we sold, gave a way, or threw in the garbage. We were burning all bridges with the expectations of being in the Middle East for the rest of our lives.

As we approached our departure, Chuck found out about our crates and called me. "Mike, you can't ship your crates to Egypt. The Egyptian government won't allow you to bring them into the country. You'll have to ship them to me in Cyprus."

That made no sense to me. But Chuck had lived more than a decade in the Middle East and should have known what he was talking about. "But Chuck, how are we going to get our belongings if they are in Cyprus?"

"Oh, don't worry about it. I will hand-carry your belongings down to you. Like I said, I will be coming down to Egypt every week to help you get on your feet. On each trip I will bring a hundred pounds of your things."

The finances were finally raised and we said our goodbyes and headed off to the Middle East. We would fly to Cyprus for a three-week layover to meet with the ICO staff. Chuck and his family were supposed to be in the states during this time and the plan was for us to stay in their duplex. Their home was very comfortable and cool. It didn't have air conditioning, but it was on the ground floor and surrounded by a park-like court of lemon and lime shade trees.

When our plane arrived in Cyprus, we started our convoluted passage through customs. Outside the door, I could see a crowd of faces. I was hoping to see someone from ICO. I was very surprised at the familiar face that I did find. It was none other than Chuck's. Once we got through our interrogation and pat-down search I approached him. "Hey, what in the world are you doing in Cyprus? I thought you were in the States."

He smiled. "There have been some developments; I will tell you about it on our way to Limassol."

"Limassol?" (a town on the southern coast of Cyprus), I said.

"Yes, you will be staying in Limassol as there has been a change of plans."

As we made the 80-kilometer drive, Chuck began telling us his shocking news. "I have decided to accept a job with the Syrian

Government. We are moving to Damascus in three days so we came back to Cyprus to get our belongings."

This development had huge ramifications in our lives. Chuck was going to help us settle in Egypt and bring our things down to us. We just traveled halfway around the world to contribute to mission work that Chuck was starting.

"What about our belongings—who is going to bring them down to us?"

"Don't worry about it. Bill will bring them to you."

"I thought you were going to be the one to help us settle in Cairo. Does this mean we are completely on our own now?"

"Oh no. Bill will be down there every few weeks to check on you guys and to help you."

In Limassol, Chuck took us to an apartment that he had picked out—a two-bedroom apartment on the top floor of an eight-story building. The apartment was filthy and not typical of Cypriot homes at all. It was also very hot, functioning something like a solar collector on top of the building. The other big problem was the large windows came down to within two feet of the floor and had no glass in them, just wooden shutters on the outside that didn't lock. If you barely touched the shutters they would swing open. The concrete sidewalk was 80 feet straight down. It was late at night and we were exhausted from an 18-hour flight and eight time-zone changes. However, it was a terror to try and house two toddlers in this place.

When Chuck dropped us off he had a warning for us: "Mike, the windows are a death trap. If I were you, I would find a hardware store and cover them with chicken wire." Then he sped off to Nicosia.

Now where in the hell would I find a hardware store in a strange country at ten o'clock at night? I didn't want to arrive only to start complaining and whining immediately. Denise and I were both very disappointed in how things were working out. It was a huge departure from when we'd arrived in Abu Dhabi with MA. Whether or not it was the right thing to do, we decided to keep quiet about our disappointments and not be whiners, with the expectation that these setbacks would be temporary.

That night and the remaining three weeks in Cyprus we slept up on the roof of the building. The apartment was too hot and the windows were too dangerous. At least the roof had a wall around it. The only problems were the huge flying cockroaches that would climb up your leg while you were trying to fall asleep.

In three days, Chuck and his family were gone. He had debriefed me with some hard news. He was very concerned with security, having something of a James Bond complex. Of course, most Moslem countries didn't favor Christian missionaries living in them. Chuck told me, "Mike, once you get to Cairo, you can't give your address or phone number out to anyone, not even your own family in the states. I don't want you to receive or send mail from Cairo. All of your mail must be addressed to Cyprus and then get hand carried down to you. And when you send mail, it must be carried out to Cyprus and sent to me in Syria. I will need to review it for security reasons. We don't want you getting in trouble with the Egyptian government. Additionally, as part of your training in Egypt I want you to have no contact with other Americans. You can only relate to Egyptian Moslems."

After Chuck left Cyprus, Denise and I met with Bill a few times before he left for the US. In preparation for this move to a slum-like area of Cairo, we were to meet with Bill at a five-star hotel. He was trying to prepare us for life in an Egyptian slum, yet it was plain he knew very little about it. He had only visited Egypt as a tourist. Life in Cyprus was light years from that in Cairo. Months later I would be feeling like a solider in Vietnam. (This solider had gone though orientation at a plush officer's club in Guam. Then he boarded a Lear Jet with his orientating commanding officers (COs). As the jet crossed over the jungles of Vietnam the COs filled up a glass of champagne and gave a toast as they pushed the young naive recruit out the door with nothing but a parachute and a rifle. The COs waved as the jet turned and headed back to the comforts of Guam. The recruit never hears from them again but finds himself alone in the brutality of the jungle.)

Now things were starting to get really interesting. I said to Bill, "Chuck said you would be coming down to Cairo to help us get settled."

"No, I have no plans of coming to Cairo. I have arranged to have Habib (a Lebanese acquaintance of ICO, who lived in Cairo) help you guys get settled. Now give my secretary your travel agenda and flight numbers and I will make sure it is telexed to Habib."

Bill, left for a trip to the states and Denise and I found ourselves alone in this strange country for the first time. In the middle of the night, Bryan, our four-year-old, awakened screaming in pain. We could not console him for an hour. The night before he had run a slight fever and thrown up a time or two. It appeared to be a viral intestinal infection. In the middle of the night he developed severe right lower abdominal pain. I checked him out and found he had extreme guarding and rebound over his appendix (McBurney's Point). It was the clearest case of appendicitis I had seen in a long time. I knew nothing about health care in Cyprus. I hadn't even seen a hospital or anything of the sort. It was a parent's worse nightmare.

I called a single American guy, named Tom, who worked for Bill. He was the last ICO person in the country except for Bill's wife, Barbara. Barbara was staying somewhere in Larnaca, where she had dropped Bill off for a flight to the US, but no one knew how to reach her.

Tom wasn't very reassuring. "Mike, everyone in Cyprus has their own personal physician. Personal physicians won't see patients they haven't established care with him."

"But what do people like us do in this situation?" I said.

"Well, there are the government hospitals. They are very small and staffed by new graduates. Chuck and Bill always referred to them as butchers."

"We are at a loss." I pleaded. "What should we do?"

He seemed more lost than we did in this situation. In the background, Bryan was continuing to cry.

I got off the phone. Here we were, feeling very alone in a crisis, with no car or anyone to help us. Denise and I held Bryan tight and prayed in desperation. As we prayed, Bryan soon fell asleep. I stayed up with him for the rest of the night. If he awakened in pain again, I would have to take him to a government hospital and take our chances with a poorly trained surgeon.

The next morning, Bryan awakened without a fever and appeared to be feeling much better. There was no trace of abdominal tenderness.

Barbara stopped by on her way back from Larnaca the next morning. She was a very pleasant, attractive woman who reminded me of 1950s TV mom, such as Donna Reed or June Cleaver. "Good morning," she said with a bit of cheer and a smile. "I was going to stop by and say goodbye. I called the ICO office this morning and Tom told me that Bryan had been sick. Is he all right?"

"Yep, he is doing better," I said. During her visit I asked, "Barbara, we will take some of our things from our crates to Cairo with us, but most of them will be left behind. When will Bill be bringing the first load?"

A wrinkle formed above the rim of her glasses as her face tightened into a perplexed frown. "What do you mean, bring your first load?"

"Chuck told us he was going to bring our belongings to Egypt."

"Oh, I don't think so," she said. "First of all, he will be in the states for three months. When he does return, I know that he has no plans of coming to Cairo. Mike, why didn't you have your things shipped there from the states? Why would you ship them there first?" (With an implied, "duh?")

Good question. Now I look like a real idiot. "Chuck told me to ship them here and that he would bring them down to us in Cairo. He told me Egyptian customs would never let me bring our things in."

"That doesn't make sense," she said. "Habib shipped his whole household plus a car to Cairo from Lebanon with no problems."

"Well it didn't make a whole lot of sense to me either. Yet, Chuck seemed to know what he was talking about," I said, trying to retain my composure.

We had been hoping that our crates would arrive in Cyprus before our departure. Our goal was to retrieve a few essentials such as a cooking pot, some clothes, and a few toys.

We were excited when the customs agent reported, literally, that our ship had come in. We had two days to get our things through customs and sorted before our departure to Cairo. Then the unexpected happened. The dockworkers went on strike. We weren't allowed to cross the picket line to get our stuff. This was a good initiation to the Middle East, where the "unexpected" is to be expected.

The day of our departure came. Denise, the boys, and I boarded our plane for Egypt. We had sent a message to an American girl in Cairo named Luci. She was referred to us by friends six months earlier. Her husband was doing an international business rotation with a bank in Cairo. Already, Luci had been very helpful in our preparation for Egypt. At least she was living in Cairo and knew what life was really like. She was also instrumental in helping us secure an apartment. So at least we would have a roof over our heads.

On the day I departed for Egypt, I sensed a huge relief. After two grueling years, we were finally getting on with our lives and our impossible mission. I finally felt that a normal life, including our own place to live, was at hand. This must have been something like the naive stupidity that a lobster senses when he looks down and sees the boiling water in the pot: "Hurray, soon I will be back in the water and free again!" If I had any clue as to what lay ahead, I would have opened the emergency exit of the plane over the Mediterranean Sea and jumped out. A quick death is always preferable to a slow, tedious one.

Chapter Twelve

Walk Like an Egyptian

To speak of Cairo is truly a tale of two cities. I have met some people who had visited Cairo as a tourist and they described it in a way that sounded one universe removed from the Cairo that we learned to love and hate. If it weren't for a few landmarks, such as the Pyramids and the Nile Hilton, I would have sworn they were speaking of somewhere entirely different.

Tourists usually arrive at the modern Cairo International Airport. For them, a trip through customs is a breeze, often being escorted through by their guide. Then they journey downtown to the main square via the most beautiful boulevard in Cairo. It is lined with palm trees and two story villas that give you the sense that you are in southern California. They stay in the little Western oasis downtown, either the Hilton or Sheraton. Quaint little shops surround these, run by Egyptians who cater to Westerners. Most of them speak English, German, and French. A few of them even know a little Japanese.

Modern air-conditioned buses, always accompanied by bilingual guides, then escort these tourists to the museum and pyramids. The tourists gaze out the windows at the chaotic masses below in beat-up little cars, black taxis with white fenders, motorcycles, bicycles, donkey carts, and people on foot. It is as if the bus window was a TV screen and they're watching a National Geographic special. We, however, lived in the realm of that street crowd. But we didn't land in Egypt as a conquerors–more like beached jellyfish. It took some time to get on our feet.

Traffic near our flat.

Our arrival in Cairo was very different from that of a tourist. We arrived at the small, old regional airport. It must have been the same one that the Pharaohs used. We had no information about the convoluted process of customs. Here I was with two little boys, a seven-month pregnant wife, and ten suitcases.

Things started out smooth as the people from the airplane walked slowly across the tarmac toward the airport door. It was like a calm, slow-moving stream. Once we were inside, the slow-moving stream became a torrent rapid. The signs were written in Arabic and I was quickly becoming disoriented.

The first official rite-of-passage was a visit to a bank teller. We soon learned that Westerners aren't allowed through customs unless they first prove that they have exchanged at least $300 US to Egyptian pounds. Egypt was starved for hard currency. They needed it, especially U.S. dollars, to purchase things on world markets. Of course, they received several billion dollars of aid from the US every year (second only to Israel), but they still needed more. When I exchanged dollars to pounds, the hard currency became theirs forever. You can't exchange pounds for dollars.

Luci, our one reliable source on living in Cairo, had warned us not to claim our electronics if we wanted to take them back out of the country. Egypt is also hungry for technology. If you claim electronics, video cameras, computers, etc. and if you are going to be a resident, you have to turn those items over to the government prior to leaving. They don't buy it from you. You give it to them! Now that sounded a lot like stealing to me, but later on my Egyptian friends would try to convince me that it made sense. Why? Because there are more high tech items in the US than in Egypt, therefore it is only right that we give our items to them when we leave.

While we were in the process of raising our support, I had purchased one of the first laptop computers on the market. It was a Kaypro 2000. It had a whopping 768 k of RAM (random access memory)–less than 1 MEG–and no hard drive! A modern wristwatch probably has more memory. Yet, at the time, it was state of the art. The computer was very handy for doing the 300-400 newsletters I had to produce each month to keep our supporters informed of what we were doing. I decided not to declare the computer to customs. The name "2000" indicated the price, not that it was Y2K compliant, which I am sure it wasn't. I couldn't imagine giving it to the Egyptian government when I left. I decided instead to hide it and take my chances with customs. If it was found, then they could take it, or I could get in trouble with the police and end up spending my first few nights in a dirty Egyptian jail–a thought that frightened me. However, after a couple of years in Cairo, I grew accustomed to being in trouble with the police.

As I approached customs the agent spotted us, the only Western looking people on the plane. He motioned us to the side, saying, "You come. You come."

I had the laptop in our most beat-up suitcase. It also was near the bottom of the stack. The customs agent was a lean, dark-skinned Egyptian man wearing some type of blue uniform. He walked around the stack, looking intently at them and rubbing his chin. Then he pointed to the very suitcase where I was hiding the laptop. Beads of sweat started to breakout on my forehead. He said in broken English, "Open please." I complied.

Amazingly, the agent lifted up the clothes and went directly to the laptop. I started to wonder if I had an informer within my own family! Maybe I was just very unlucky, or he was very smart.

The agent kneeled beside the suitcase and took the laptop. He said, "Show me how to open." I opened it up and he grew very intrigued. He started playing with the keyboard. He had never seen a laptop before. He looked at me and asked, "What this is?"

I knew if I used the word "computer," it would be gone forever and I could end up in a heap of trouble. As well, I was determined to speak the truth. I looked at him, took the laptop, and pretended to type, praying silently that the computer wouldn't wake up, beep, and start coming on. Fortunately, you would need a flashlight and magnifying glass to read the tiny black and white LCD screen, which was before the days of back-lighted or super-twisted screens.

I said to the agent, "I type letters on this."

He looked puzzled and began to look at the laptop from all angles. "This a typewriter? Where do paper goes?"

Again I say, "I type letters on this." He went to get his boss. I considered making a run for it, but the guards outside were carrying loaded machine guns.

The two men soon returned. The boss looked like a dark-skinned Carroll O'Connor with a cigarette hanging from the left side of his mouth. He looked at the machine and me. Then he said, "Why you come to Egypt?" He took one last drag off his cigarette, pulled the butt from his lips, dropped it on the concrete floor, and stepped on it as if it were a cockroach. He looked intensely at me, waiting for my response, while slowly releasing smoke from his nostrils like a dragon.

"I am a student at the American University."

"What do you study?"

"Arabic."

"Arabic?" He laughed and said, "OK, you speak Arabic to me."

I had been working on the Arabic alphabet. I also remembered a few words from my experience in Abu Dhabi. I gave him my best try, "Sabbah el Hxaer" (for good morning).

The man smiled and turned to the agent and confidently said to him in English, "Yes, this is a typewriter. He needs it for school."

Once we got through customs, and the sweat on my brow had just started to dry in the blazing heat, we were met with a chaotic crowd. Taxi drivers and others began fighting over us like we were Amazonian monkeys in a school of piranha. One man grabbed a handful of suitcases, saying "Where your hotel? You go to pyramids?" While I was trying to wrestle our suitcases out of his hands, a cleaning lady, wearing a long black skirt and a head scarf, dropped her broom and grabbed the cart holding the rest of our suitcases and headed out the door. I caught up with her outside. She began to say, "I poor woman." Obviously she wanted a tip for pushing our suitcases twenty feet through the door.

I reached into my pocket where there was the bundle of recently exchanged Egyptian pounds. Although I had read two books on life in Cairo, I knew nothing about the currency. All of their money came in paper denominations and coins were rarely used. I had in my hand paper money that was worth anywhere from 7 cents to 14 dollars. I didn't know my Arabic numbers well enough to tell which was which.

I handed the woman a couple of the bills. Judging from the look on her amazed face I clearly had made a mistake. Later, I figured out that I paid her a half-month's salary, 28 dollars, for a tip. At the appearance of the bills, the piranhas collapsed around me again and another tug of war over suitcases commenced. The taxi drivers took turns putting our suitcases in the trunks of their taxis or on the chrome luggage racks on top. I kept saying "NO! I have a friend coming to pick me up."

I kept hoping Habib would appear from the crowd to rescue us. We had no idea where this apartment was that we had rented. But there was no Habib. Actually we never heard a word from Habib until we had been in Cairo for over two months. There was a mystery to his elusiveness that took us two years to solve.

However, pushing her way through the crowd was a very thin, curly-haired blond woman with a baby cradled in a front pouch like a marsupial. It was Luci, our angel of mercy. She greeted us and gave us a hug, quickly taking charge of the situation like a regular Joan of Arc.

Luci had us loaded up in a taxi and then said something to the driver in Arabic. I was impressed. We sped away from the chaotic airport and entered the stream of screaming pandemonium that they call traffic. Our suitcases were tied, precariously, with white cotton twine on the chrome luggage rack over our heads.

It is hard to describe my first impressions of Cairo. In the months after learning of our assignment, I spoke to everyone I met who had ever visited Egypt. Some would describe it as a modern, almost European city. Others would tell me it was a very dirty, crowded, broken down, Third World city. The disparity could be accounted for by the-old-five-blind-men-and-the-elephant parable. The tourists were seeing the trunk and others had seen the tail of the city. Unfortunately we were going to be living in the tail. Later, I would be working just beneath the base of the tail, if you know what I mean.

Our hearts sank as we drove through the section of the city that we would be calling home. The concrete buildings were in poor repair. Every vacant lot and alleyway had piles of trash. Blue plastic shopping bags were blown around like tumbleweeds in a western ghost town.

But this was no ghost town. Everywhere you looked were scores of people crammed together in tight living spaces. The buildings, few trees, and cars were coated with a thick layer of brown Sahara dusts. But the main thing I noticed was the gross lack of space.

Under the direction of Luci, the taxi pulled in front of one of the buildings and came to a halt. It was an older, rough-looking, three-story concrete structure made up of seven apartments. Each one had a balcony in the Mediterranean tradition. The windows and balcony doors were framed with dark brown working shutters. The staircase ran up the center of the building, open to the outside elements.

After getting out of the taxi, the driver quickly recruited a couple of men off the street to act as porters. I could just read their thoughts: Hmm . . . *Rich Americans, a chance for a juicy tip.*

Luci led our entourage up the stairs to the third floor. Soon a short man who looked like one of the Marx brothers came running up the steps. In his broken English, accented with nervousness, he said, "Welcome." He then unlocked the door. We walked into the spacious front room and set our things on the coarse parquet floor. I tipped the porters, this time with a more reasonable amount. Within a few minutes the Groucho-looking fellow returned with his wife and two daughters. She was carrying a silver serving tray of small clear glasses of pink fluid. It was a traditional rose petal drink that tasted like sweet perfume.

He introduced himself as Mr. Fakry and informed us that he was the landlord. He and his family lived in the apartment just beneath us. Although his English was poor and difficult to understand, his daughters, especially the younger one, spoke English as well as most Americans. They helped to clarify or translate whatever their father was trying to tell me. He gave me two important pieces of information. First he told me that he was planning a trip to downtown Cairo the next day and I could go with him. I needed to get to A.U.C. in order to register, as classes would begin in just a couple of days.

The other important information was a warning about the family on the first floor, just below his apartment. He told me with a strange intensity in his voice, "Avoid those people. They are evil! They are militant

Moslems and very dangerous! You must never even make eye contact with them, let alone speak to them." The Fakry family was Coptic Christian, a minority at extreme odds with the Moslem majority.

The Fakry family left and we started to explore the apartment. This was the first place we could call home in over a year. As Denise and I went from room to room the boys stayed in the front room playing. Daniel, our 2-year-old, was somewhat addicted to his bottle. Denise had just weaned him the week before we left the states. We finally got him to switch to a bottle, and he became more attached to it than a dehydrated wino.

As Denise and I were inspecting the bedrooms, Daniel walked over to the window, and for some reason, threw his bottle onto the balcony of the first floor apartment. This apartment was the headquarters of the neighborhood terrorist family, at least according to Mr. Fakry.

When I discovered what had happened I said, "Denise, I am sorry, but that bottle is lost forever." Denise looked and me with pitiful eyes and said, "We must get that bottle or Daniel will be very hard to deal with at nap or bed time. I don't have another one. The others are in the crates!"

I have a theory about children. They are on a mission to destroy their fathers. I'm not sure who sent them on this mission—it could've been aliens who want to take over the earth. By killing all the dads, or at lease driving them insane, the aliens plan to achieve a foothold on their conquest, reasoning that the dads will eventually be hauled off in wooden paddy wagons to funny farms. There, in a zombie-like state, they will graze like cattle on the hillsides while the aliens rule the world. On the other hand, it might be the Devil himself who is behind the whole plot.

For example, if a kid finds a paper clip on the floor, what does he do? Does he throw it in the huge round garbage can? No, he sticks it up his nose and loses it, at ten o'clock, in a cabin 70 miles from nowhere. Or, he sticks in the tiny holes of an electric outlet.

Now, right off the bat, I have to face these dangerous neighbors. I went down the stairs and knocked on the door. In a moment, someone yelled, through the door, ")$ ^ #*(#(#_@&." Ever the optimist, I figured that must mean, "Who's there?" I had no idea if he spoke English so I just shouted back, "This is Michael Jones, I live upstairs."

The wooden door slowly opened and there stood a tall older man with bushy white hair. He looked like a dark-skinned Doc from *Back to the Future* and was wearing a long white robe and a knit skull cap. I was expecting him to scream, "Death to the American" and run me through with one of those curved swords, like on *Raiders of the Lost Ark*. But that was OK if he killed me. That is part of a father's job description, giving your life in pursuit of a baby bottle.

Well, the kind man didn't run me through. Instead, a big smile came on his face and he said in rather good English, "Please come in." He was very happy to meet me. It turned out he had completed his Ph.D. in plant pathology at the University of Minnesota. He still had the tip of one finger missing to prove it. He lost it to frostbite as he tried to walk home from campus with ungloved hands and a temperature of 20-below.

This was the beginning of a long and beautiful relationship between the terrorist family and ours. They felt sorry for us and adopted us as in-laws. The older gentleman had two grown children living at home. His son, Mohammed, was about my age and soon became my best friend. I think our friendship with the Moslem family really angered our Coptic landlord.

The next morning, I left Denise and the kids and journeyed to the heart of Cairo with our landlord, Groucho, in his little Fiat. As all the streets converged toward the city center, the pandemonium expediently multiplied. It was like taking a ride on a huge river of humanity.

Every few miles you would come to a British-style roundabout, where traffic spun in a whirlpool of confusion and fender benders. These roundabouts were called "medans" and each one had a proper name. For example, we lived near Medan Hegaz. We would soon learn that it was key to map out the order of medans in your mind to find your way home. The main boulevards run like twisted spokes on a wheel. The hub of the wheel was a huge medan called Tahreer. Tahreer was Mr. Fakery's destination on that day.

When we arrived at Tahreer it took a while to find a small space to squeeze in the little Fiat. The medan was bustling to say the least. On the north side was the famous National Museum, the home of King

Tut's treasure plus countless other Egyptian artifacts. On the western side of the medan, along the banks of the Nile, was a complex of hotels and tourist shops with the large, blue Nile Hilton at its center. Standing south of this was the huge beige government building called the Mugumma. This was where the bulk of the Egyptian people worked, or in some sense, didn't work. In the coming months I would spend many hours in the halls of this building, pleading for help to get me out of the trouble I would find myself in with the Egyptian government.

Mr. Fakry and I parted ways as I headed south, into the labyrinth of narrow streets looking for the American University in Cairo. Although I had a map, it was no easy task.

My first impressions of downtown were striking. Some of the buildings were new, with modern designs. Most were vintage early 20th century, adorned with iron-railed balconies and wooden shutters. Some were even much older, going back hundreds if not a thousand years. You could spend a lifetime studying the buildings alone. With every turn, the curious and the contrasts startled me. On one street corner men were screaming at one another, on another a paralyzed beggar was crawling in the dust beside the street begging for money. Next to a fence men were urinating on the sidewalk. In the street, overladen donkeys were being led while a shiny new Mercedes sports car was honking and passing by. And of course, there were the masses of humanity on foot walking the streets. Rarely, you would even find a human body, usually covered with newspaper to keep the flies off.

The stores were tiny by U.S. standards. It appeared that each block had at least one coffee shop or juice bar. The cafes and some of the shops had large roll-up metal doors. When the doors were open, the interior space merged onto the sidewalk. The cafes had small round wooden tables and decorative wooden chairs that spilled outside. Several men sat at these tables drinking hot tea in small clear glasses, smoking water pipes, and playing backgammon.

There was a very obvious lack of variety on the store shelves. Each one had the same box of tea, the same detergent, the same brand of toilet paper.

A few of the men were dressed in Western style while most wore the pastel green and gray gallabaya (long nightgown looking robes). They usually had either the small, lace, white skullcaps called a kufis or a turban-type head wrap.

The women usually were well dressed with dark colors and a lot of jewelry. They wore highly decorated, stylish shoes and usually had their heads covered, though only a few actually wore veils. Even the head coverings had been reintroduced in the past twenty years. I was surprised to see Egyptian TV shows from the 1960s. The women dressed much more like American women of that period, with not only their heads showing, but dresses short enough to show the bottom of the knee.

In general, the Egyptians dress up much more than their American counterparts. If jeans were worn, they wouldn't be faded but rather new looking and worn with dress shirts and sweaters. The lower class, which made up the majority, wore more traditional clothes such as the gallabayas.

Cairo is a city of over 12 million people. It is walled in on all sides by the inhospitable Sahara desert. The density of the population is about three times that of major Western cities such as New York or London. Due to the winds off the desert and the lack of rain for eleven months out of the year, the thing I noticed most was the omnipresent beige that covered everything with a dust camouflage. Even the palm trees had lost their green to the layer of dust. Once a year when the rains washed off the dust, everything bloomed into color, for about two days.

One after another shop owner would come up to me, trying to get me to come into their stores. For example, a young man walked up beside me and started to speak to me in English. "Welcome to Egypt. Where are you from?"

"America," I mumbled.

"You American! Hey, have you ever met Arnold Schwarzenegger? I like Michael Jackson. OK, you come inside for tea?"

Eventually I found myself walking along a high black iron fence that led to a well-guarded gate. Above the gate was a sign that read, "The American University in Cairo." I entered the beautiful sandstone building, which was the administration building. Inside, I was surprised to find the hall packed with young Egyptians wearing the latest Western fashions and speaking perfect English. They were all standing in line to register.

The Egyptian system offers free higher education. For a student to pay $5,000–$10,000 tuition to go to A.U.C., they must be from a rich family, especially when you consider the average income was $60–$75 a month.

I found the registration office and met the dean of the Arabic program. I took care of my paperwork and returned to our apartment with a sense of accomplishment, having survived my first journey to the center of Cairo.

I started Arabic classes the following week. It was far more difficult than even PA school. The problem was that almost everyone in my class had studied Arabic before. They were all single, except one other man, and they lived on campus. For me it was a 1-3 hour commute each way, depending on the mood of the traffic. When our classes ended at 3:00 p.m., the other students went to the library to study. I would start my grueling commute.

I rode a city bus back and forth. Coming into town wasn't much of a problem because I lived so far out, the bus actually started at our medan. I rode a mini-bus that was considered first class because it was a requirement that everyone have a seat. It cost 28 cents each way. The problem was coming home. There weren't nearly enough buses for the amount of people who wanted one. Each bus could seat about 25 people, however, about 75 desperately wanted on. It was a literal free-for-all. This took a lot of getting used to. At first I would wait for rush hour to calm down and catch a late bus. This wouldn't get me home till 7:00 or 8:00 p.m. at a time when Denise really needed me home to help her. I finally learned the "survival of the fittest" technique for getting on a bus. This meant pushing people out of the way, out-running them down the street and jumping through the open windows of a moving bus. Some of the people were brutal, stepping on others, pushing, ripping clothes, etc.

During my commutes I was as a deaf mute. I didn't understand what was happening around me. Once the driver yelled out something and suddenly everyone jumped off the bus in the middle of town and took off running. Till this day, I have no idea what it was all about, but it meant that I had to find another way home. Another time I paid my fare with a torn bill. I didn't think much about it. As the driver drove through traffic, he counted his money, holding the dirty bills in his mouth. When he came to my torn bill, he slammed on the brakes right in the middle of traffic. Then he jumped up from his seat. He started screaming at each customer, pushing my torn bill in their faces as he walked up the aisle. I knew I was in trouble. When he came to me, I took the bill and handed him a new one. The whole bus stared at me like I was a crook. I didn't know at the time, but it was very insulting to give someone a torn bill because a torn bill has no value. If you take the same bill home and tape it, the full value is restored. Go figure.

My other option was riding the metro, which consisted of a beat-up, old, faded-green electric commuter-train. Most of them listed seriously to one side from years of being grossly overloaded. They made a loud grinding noise with sparks flying around them as they ran. Every time I got on a train, the hour-long ride had more thrills than Space Mountain. People were packed on the train so tightly that you could not even expand your lungs enough to take a full breath. You couldn't talk without your mouth filling up with the hair from the back of another passenger's head. The chain of moving sardine cans rocked violently on the worn-out springs, pushing me to the edge of regurgitation. It never happened to me, but a friend had projectile vomited on such a train. It wasn't pretty.

During the first few months, I arrived home each evening to find Denise in distress. Her days were very hard, almost impossible if it hadn't been for Luci. Even shopping for food was a full-time job.

It is hard for Americans to comprehend giving up the freedom of car ownership and relying instead on your two feet. Denise was seven months pregnant and had two small children. Daniel would ride in a stroller and Bryan would walk closely at her side. The problem was the distances she had to cover each day. The largest store in our neighborhood was called, ironically enough, "The Greenhouse Supermarket." It was about a mile away and was the size of a gas station quick market. But most of our daily substances came from small stands.

To buy bread, she would walk to the bread stand. To buy milk or yogurt, she would walk to the milk store. Then there was the fish store. Several miles away, was the butcher shop, which was easy to spot because it was the place with half a cow hanging from a meat hook in front, in the hot sun. We were advised to only buy beef that was covered with flies. Some of the butchers had taken to spraying the carcasses with bug spray, so one devoid of insects was not a good sign.

To buy fruit, Denise would have to walk a block or two to the fruit and vegetable stand. In addition to walking in the hot sun, in the dusty smoggy air she had to push the stroller with a cluster of blue plastic grocery bags hanging from each handle. The sidewalks were in such poor repair that she would have to take her chances walking in the street, in the midst of the ongoing demolition derby.

It was during my first week in Egypt that I came home from my long commute one night to find out that the stove didn't work, the plumbing was backed up, and several other household crises. I believed I could fix the problems, however our belongings, including my tools, were in Cyprus. I approached our landlord. "Mr Fakry, do you have any tools I can borrow?"

He looked at me like I was from Mars. "Tools? Why would I have tools? Only plumbers and carpenters have tools." Then I learned that I couldn't get a plumber. In Cairo, due to the extreme shortage of skilled workers, you inherit your plumber like an heirloom. Your grandfather's plumber (or your grandfather's plumber's son) becomes your father's plumber, who becomes your plumber. Therefore, the chances of me hiring any kind of skilled worker were next to nil.

I decided to go out and try to buy tools for myself. I asked several people before I found out where I could even buy them. It was about six medans away. They insisted, "Mike you must take the metro for twenty-five piasters (about nine cents) rather than a taxi for three pounds (about $1.25).

I knew very little Arabic by this time. Each metro train had its name written in Arabic on the front. The name of the train that ran by our house was Nusha. My first floor neighbor convinced me that "catching the metro is easy, Michael. Just look for the train with red writing. It is simple. All the other trains had their names written in green, black, or other colors." Before the night was over, I would learn the hard way that he was wrong.

I asked Bryan, "Do you want to go with dad on a little adventure?" Little did I know that would be an extreme understatement. We boarded the metro near our house and headed toward the city center. I counted six medans and then got off. According to the directions I had been given, I walked toward what I thought was the hardware district. I felt very pleased that I was able to find and buy the basic tools that I needed: a pipe wrench, screw drivers, toilet plunger, hammer, and pliers. I thought I was starting to get the hang of this Cairo living.

Denise shopping in Cairo with Daniel.

I made Bryan's day by buying a small rabbit from a butcher. The customers would walk up to his stand, and pick out a live rabbit in the same way we pick a lobster at a restaurant. The butcher would then chop his little head off with a meat cleaver and wrap the limp body in newspaper. On the street was a basket of rabbit heads. I bought the little bunny then had to wrestle with the butcher to get it out of his hands before it met its demise. I kept shouting, "He's a pet, he's a pet!" Bryan cuddled the lucky fur ball all the way home.

When Bryan and I journeyed back to the medan, we found things had changed over the two hours we had been shopping. The medan was now packed with people.

Cairo runs on a different schedule than the US. Most of it, I am sure, has to do with the heat. Shops open in the morning while it is still cool. Then, when the afternoon starts to heat up, everything starts to shut down. Most of the Egyptians return home, eat a large meal, put on their pajamas, and go back to bed for a few hours. Then, at 6:00 or 7:00 p.m., as things start to cool down, the city comes to life. All the stores stay open until about 10:00 p.m. When Bryan and I came to the medan it was about 10:00 p.m. and everyone was heading home.

We waited among the crowd as the first metro came by. It had green writing on the front. The next train luckily had red writing. This train, however, was more than packed; people were hanging on the outside. A policeman who was a passenger on the train reached out the window to take Bryan and his bunny, who was hiding under his shirt. I handed Bryan to the policeman through the window and jumped on the side of the train, holding on to the window frame with one hand and holding my hardware treasures with the other. My feet were planted on a quarter-inch metal ridge that protruded from the side of the train car. I certainly wasn't alone as many others were hanging on here and there. The scariest ones were kids, some almost as young as Bryan, sitting on the front bumper of the train unsupervised. Just one slip and they would fall on the tracks and be run over.

As we passed the first few medans, more people climbed aboard. Then, the crowd started decreasing. I began to grow concerned because I didn't recognize any of the landmarks that I had tried to remember. I counted six medans and realized that I was nowhere near my area of the city. We were completely lost.

Soon the train emptied enough that I could move inside and sit with Bryan. He had a smile on his face, as he seemed to be having a splendid time snuggling with his new pet.

The passengers continued to thin out as the buildings got newer and smaller. Finally, the streets around us turned to dirt and we were now ten medans from where we got on. The train came to a halt with all the remaining passengers getting off, except for Bryan and me. End of the line. I was expecting the train to start going back into town. But it didn't. The conductor turned off the lights and mumbled something to us in Arabic and got off himself. We sat there in the dark. Around us were cinderblock and tin shacks, people, goats, and donkeys. Some of the people stood around bonfires of burning garbage in the streets. I felt like I was in some futuristic *Mad Max* movie, but unfortunately, I was no Mel Gibson.

A crowd, first of children, then adults, began to gather around our window. The stranded tourist with his offspring was the greatest entertainment they had seen for a long time. It was like a traveling zoo. They gathered outside and shouted Arabic words at us and laughed. I felt like a monkey in a cage. I was expecting them to start throwing peanuts at us next while they waited for me to start picking lice out of Bryan's head and eating them. I refrained from grooming my son. I hoped to bore them to the point that they would simply leave. It didn't work. I was expecting to spend the night on the train with the gawkers crowded around, watching and mocking until sunrise.

After I dozed off for a while with Bryan curled up in my lap, another train conductor climbed aboard. He turned on the lights and glanced back at us, not saying a word. I think he had heard about the lost tourists on board. In a matter of minutes, he started up the train and it started to move. Bryan waved goodbye to our spectator friends as the train started making its way back toward the city center. I envy children's innocence. I counted the medans until we came to the stop where we got on, and we quickly exited. After more than a two-hour journey, we were back where we started. Later I found out that TWO trains had red writing. One was our train. The other train went in a very different direction.

This time, I was able to flag down a taxi in the deserted streets. At this time of night, the taxi I flagged down was empty.

Soon we were back at our apartment (or flat, as it is called in Egypt) to find a very worried Denise. But, now I had my tools to fix some of the problems. The next challenge was trying to get a few winks of sleep in a bedroom whose temperature hovered around 95 degrees from March until November. The fact that our apartment was on the top floor made it like something of a solar collector, as if the Sahara sun needed collecting.

But, through it all, we were getting on our feet and starting to walk like an Egyptian. Six months later, looking back, we would describe it more as crawling than walking. Yet, ahead of us lay challenges of a different sort.

Chapter Thirteen

The Curse of the Mummy's . . . Toe

The second floor classroom always carried an atmosphere of trepidation. Just outside the huge double-hung windows stood the tops of dusty palm and mango trees. Inside the room, Dr. Nabila was intimidating in the Egyptian educational tradition. She equated poor performance in her Arabic class with a deep moral failing. The months of strain were reaching a point of impasse. The fact that my nights were consumed by a long commute, taking care of a family, and fixing a broken-down apartment, while my single counterparts were in the campus library studying their Arabic assignments, gave me no favors. Dr. Nabila constantly hounded me and told the class, "Michael is a very lazy man."

Denise's due date was fast approaching and we were faced with a problem. She would really need my help when she went into labor. Her previous labors had been quite short, lasting a couple of hours at the most. If I were in school, a two-hour commute away, I couldn't make it home in time to get her to the hospital. The phone system was unreliable. It could take an hour to reach me, then two more to get home. We decided that I would stay home until the baby was born. I tried to explain that to Dr. Nabila, who wasn't the least persuaded.

A week or two passed with no sign of labor. Then, in the middle of the night, Denise awakened me to say, "This is it." I had learned to never doubt her. A day or two before, our landlord had offered to drive us to the hospital. I rushed downstairs to awaken him. Then I awakened another neighbor and asked her to watch our boys.

We arrived at Cleopatra Hospital at 1:00 in the morning. I was told, "Mr. Jones, we must first call in the accountant. Once the dollars are counted, then we can call in the doctor." As soon as the accountant had given us his blessing, the nurses led Denise off to change clothes. I had to stay with the accountant to get all our documents in order.

Egyptian husbands never went into the labor room with their wives. They usually didn't even go to the hospital with them. We had an arrangement with the British-trained physician to allow me in the delivery room. I couldn't explain that to the nurses, so I took off running upstairs until I found her. She was in the worse scenario she could think of for having a baby. Denise was into natural childbirth, yet they had her on a stainless steel table in the midst of a huge, tiled, clinical operating room with bright lights shining down on her. She had an IV in her arm. They wanted to give her enemas but she pleaded with the physician to change the orders. She was very happy to see me.

The physician was in dress clothes but wearing a long lab coat. After checking Denise, he said, "You are fully dilated. Do you feel like pushing?"

Denise calmly replied, "No, not at all."

"OK, Mrs. Jones. I will be back to check you in 30 minutes." He left the room with his entourage of nurses. As soon as the doors to the OR closed, Denise reached down, grabbed her thighs, pulled them up as far as possible, and started pushing with all of her might.

I said, "Uh Denise . . . what are you doing?"

"I want you to deliver this baby. I don't want them in here when he is born."

It had been six years since I delivered a baby. "Let me go and get the physician," I said.

"No! I don't want them in here when I have this baby!" Denise can get a little grouchy whenever she is in labor. Don't ask me why.

Denise left the hospital in a couple of days with our wonderful third son, Tyler. Our complex life would become even more complex.

My first day back at class, Dr. Nabila called on me to come up to the front. "Michael, please cite the Arabic paragraph that I gave the class yesterday to memorize."

"I can't," I told her. "I never saw that paragraph before now." When I couldn't do it, she said in a perturbed voice, "Please sit down." Next she called on her star student. He was an American kid named Brad Thomas, and had already completed a year of Arabic in the states. He quoted the paragraph perfectly. The teacher smiled and said, "Mr. Thomas is a wonderful man. He works very hard and is very bright. Mr. Jones, on the other hand, is very lazy . . ."

As soon as the word "lazy" came out of her mouth, I exploded. I screamed at her, "I don't care who you are, I'm not taking these insults anymore. I told you why I had to miss class for a week. Of course I didn't have that paragraph memorized because I wasn't here when you handed it out. Don't you ever call me lazy again!" I sat down and looked around me. The class sat in silence. Later some of the other students came up to me and gave me a slap on the back and said, "Mike, it is time someone put her in her place."

I wish I could say she changed her ways and started giving me more respect. However, she used my outburst as fodder for more of her criticisms, but these new criticisms were more indirect. She would say, "Mr Thomas is very smart, a hard working student, and gives the teachers much respect. He is a wonderful man! Not like others in the class." Then her evil eyes would roll in my direction.

With our new baby, it soon became crystal clear we would need to retrieve some of our things from the crates in Cyprus. We had been in Egypt for over two months without one word from anyone in ICO. I decided to fly over and bring home a suitcase full. When I got to Chuck's garage, I saw so many things that we needed I couldn't pick out just a hand full. I felt like a member of the Swiss Family Robinson on his last supply run out to their sinking ship. I ended up filling up a steamer trunk with winter clothes, baby things, a couple of pots, and some toys. These I shipped to Cairo.

When I flew back to Cairo, immigrations became a problem again. I was in line with those getting their passports checked. Everyone else went right through. Then I came up to the desk. The man studied my passport for a while and said, "You have a very big problem." He threw my passport into a drawer and locked it up. He motioned me out of the way.

After all the other passengers had been processed, I was taken into a small office. The man looked at me and said, "Mr. Jones, you have lived in Egypt for almost three months and you don't have a visa."

"Yes I do. I wrote the Egyptian consulate in Chicago and got one before I left the states."

"All you have is an entry visa, not a residence visa. You don't have permission to live in Egypt. We could deport you."

Wow, I thought, if only I could be so lucky.

"Also, Mr. Jones, you never registered with the police."

"What do you mean?" I said.

"All foreigners must register with their local police station whenever they enter the country."

"OK, I didn't know this. What do I do now?"

"You must go to jail" . . . (long pause) . . ."or pay about $1,000 in fines."

"You must be kidding? I can't register with the police now and get a residence visa to fix things."

"Well, Mr Jones, there is one other way. You could get a letter of apology from the U.S. Ambassador to Egypt, bring it to the government building downtown, and they might forgive you."

I was thinking, how on earth am I going to get a letter of apology from the ambassador? I had never even been to the U.S. Embassy. I didn't even know where it was.

The man placed a stamp in my passport that would make it impossible for me to leave Egypt without forgiveness or paying my fines or going to jail.

I missed class for the next two days as I stood in long hot lines, first at the U.S. Embassy then at the Egyptian government building. In the U.S. Embassy, I had to go upstairs to a room for U.S. citizens. Then I stood in line in front of a small, very thick (obviously bulletproof) glass window. The Egyptian worker behind the window spoke through a microphone, sounding like the order monkey at a burger joint, but

with a strong accent. I was wondering how in the world to explain
what I needed.

When my turn came, I bent over and started speaking in the little
microphone to the woman, whose outline I could barely make out
behind the thick glass. "Yes . . . ma'am, I need a letter of apology from
the ambassador . . ."

Before I had said many words, she interrupted me. "Which letter
of apology do you need? For not having a visa or not registering with
the police?"

"Er . . . both," I said with a bit of surprise in my voice.

She immediately spun around and opened a tall filing cabinet, taking
out two form letters and handing them to me through the slide-out
drawer. One letter started out, "Dear President Mubarak, I am so sorry
that this U.S. citizen was living in Egypt without a resident visa . . ." The
second letter started out, "I am so sorry that this U.S. citizen did not
register with the police . . ." The ambassador had signed both. I thought
how silly this whole thing was. Apparently I wasn't the first American
to be caught in this dilemma.

After we had been in Egypt for four months, we had a surprise
visit from Chuck. He was in Egypt on business and decided to give us
a call. We had him over for dinner. Chuck brought us a mail drop, for
which we were quite hungry. He commented that he had heard through
Bill that Habib was taking very good care of us. "Chuck," I said, "Does
Habib really exist? We have never seen him." Chuck looked a little
confused but didn't say anything. I wasn't sure where Bill was getting
his information. We hadn't heard from Bill either.

It is hard to describe the emotional toil our short months in Cairo had
had on us. Chuck asked, "Well, are you getting through the culture shock?"

"Chuck, the real issue isn't cultural shock. It is what I define as
situation shock." I elaborated. "Suddenly we were thrust into a situation
where we don't know anyone, where we don't even have a car to go
where we want to go. We are like prisoners in this extremely crowded
slum. You told us that we couldn't have contact with Americans or the
outside world. I have to get in a brawl every day just to get a bus ride
home."

I went on. "Chuck, on top of this, we have the relentless heat making it impossible to sleep. Our windows have no screens and it is far too hot to close them. Therefore, we have huge black flies constantly zooming around the room and trying to land on our eyes and mouth. The windows also let in the smog from the city, not to mention the constant smell of rotting garbage and rotten animal flesh. I understand that cultural shock is where cultural behavior puts a strain on you. But we would have the same stress if we had moved from small town living to a hot dirty slum in New York City, where we couldn't communicate and had no friends. Do you understand?"

Chuck, trying to be helpful, took the Rambo approach to my whining. He began to criticize us, saying, "You really don't know what suffering is like. I lived in Beirut during the war. Now that was suffering. Compared to what I've experienced, you guys have it made. If you think things are bad now, just wait. Things are going to get a heck of a lot worse." Then a big smile crossed his face and he laughed.

I didn't want to get into a pissing match over who had suffered the most. I just wanted a little compassion, and for him to be less hard-nosed. Chuck left immediately after dinner, and Denise felt quite depressed.

For the first time, we were beginning to wonder if it was worth it. We just wanted to help people in need. This wasn't like a job you could just walk away from when things didn't go right. It was more like an expedition to the South Pole—something that you had been preparing for—for years. As soon as you get halfway across the Ross Ice Shelf and realize your expedition leader is a lunatic, you don't just quit and go home. There is too much invested—too much at stake—and it isn't like there is another expedition just over the ice flow that you could join. In this situation, you press onward, tolerating the lunacy, trying to focus on the goal—in our case, the people we were trying to help.

That night in bed, Denise turned to me in tears and said, "Can we go home?" Leaving my pride intact, how could I face all of the people and churches I had persuaded to support our cause? If she had insisted I would've taken her home, but when her mood lifted in a few days she decided she would stick it out.

But, Chuck was right–things did get a lot worse. Once we were standing on our own two feet, the next problem was our health. From our first week in Cairo, someone in the family was always sick, usually with diarrhea and/or fever. We tried desperately hard to watch what we ate. We boiled all of our water. We bleached all of the vegetables, but it still couldn't fend off intestinal infections. I suffered from chronic giardiasis, as did the boys. We all also had Ascaris and who knows what other parasites.

As we survived our first winter in Egypt, Denise and I both were feeling that we were going to make it. Although Luci was now gone, Denise could fly on her own wings. Her shopping Arabic was coming along rather well.

My own Arabic was starting to gel. I finished dead last in my class during the first semester under Professor Nabila. However, I kept working hard. The second semester, we had a new teacher. He was as good as Nabila was bad. He was extremely nice and encouraging, relying on praise rather than ridicule. I started to excel and finished near the top of the class by the end of the term.

Our next challenge was the pack of wild dogs that had moved into our neighborhood. The U.S. Embassy had put out warnings that 40% of Cairo's wild dogs carried rabies. After several close calls with attacks, I decided to give the two older boys the rabies vaccine. There was no post-exposure treatment available in our area, so if the boys were bit they could die. The only pre-exposure vaccine was on the black market. Within a couple of days of receiving the vaccine, Daniel started running a fever. That wasn't unusual, but it seemed to get worse by the day. He also stopped eating. He complained of a bad sore throat so I started him on penicillin. I didn't have the luxury of a lab for a strep culture.

A hundred things were racing through my mind. Was it a reaction to the vaccine or even a contaminated vial? Was it a strep infection? In a couple of days, he broke out in a terrible rash from head to toe. It is hard being a parent and a PA. One thing worse than being a parent of a sick child and a PA is being a PA who had just spent four years exposed to headaches and your kid is really sick, but doesn't have a headache. I couldn't figure out if the rash was an allergic reaction to the penicillin or part of the disease itself. In Egypt, it could be anything—there hoof beats could mean zebras or camels as easily as horses.

The other cloud hanging over my head was something Mark, Luci's husband, had said to me before he left Egypt: "Mike, the local pediatrician is OK for well baby checks; however, if you ever have a serious illness, never take your child to them—they're dangerous."

I wanted so much to care for Daniel myself. However, we finally got the Egyptian pediatrician involved. Still Daniel went downhill fast. We had no rescue plan. ICO had no evacuation plan for sick employees. As a matter of fact, we had strict orders from Chuck to rely on the Egyptian system for all health care needs. It was insane.

One evening Daniel started to become non-responsive. There were no ERs, pediatric wards, or ICUs. We were treating him in our flat. Denise and I were doing everything we could, trying to keep him hydrated. Yet, in that context, it appeared we were losing him. We were alone and without resources. Our best medicines were prayer and oral antibiotics.

In the midst of this crisis we had a surprising call. It was Chuck's secretary, Mona, calling from Cyprus. This is the first time we had heard from anyone in almost six months. She said, "Chuck is arriving in Cairo from Syria tomorrow on business. I want to make sure he is well taken care of by someone. Mike, please get a nice taxi and meet him at the airport. Take Chuck to your house for a meal and please see that he gets to all of his appointments."

I told her, "Mona, we are in the middle of a crisis here. Daniel is very sick."

Mona said, "Well, then it is good timing to have Chuck there to help you, considering his background in public health."

I knew too much about Chuck and wasn't convinced his visit would be all that helpful. In the midst of what was going on, Denise started preparing dinner for Chuck. I got a taxi and went to the airport. I waited at the gate for Chuck's late-arriving plane. When he disembarked he greeted me and said, "Here is your mail," handling me a bundle of letters with string tied around it. I was surprised when he added, "I am in a big hurry because I have some friends meeting me in luggage claim."

"Well, Mona called and told us we are to have dinner waiting for you and I am to be your host."

"Oh, maybe that was her plan. But, I met an old friend on the plane and he has invited me to go with him to Minia." (Minia was a town about two or three hours away.)

I tried explaining to him as we walked through the terminal what was going on with Daniel. He appeared distracted and uninterested but said, "Sounds like typhoid to me." Then he jumped into a Mercedes with the other men, waved, and sped off. When I got back to the flat, the whole family had been waiting for over two hours for the guest. I showed up empty-handed, except for the mail.

In a couple of days, Dan started a very slow recovery. It was a month before he could get up to play again. I still didn't know his diagnosis. The pediatrician thought it was scarlet fever, but that didn't make a lot of sense to me, especially considering I had him on antibiotics from the start of his sore throat.

That week was a critical week for many reasons. We had another call from Mona. "Mike, Chuck is coming back from Minia on Thursday night by train. Habib will pick him up and bring him to your apartment. Please have good accommodations for him."

Thursday came and we waited up until two in the morning, but no Chuck. I called Habib's flat and woke him up. "Hello," he said. "Yes Habib, where is Chuck? I understood that he supposed to stay with us tonight."

"Well, I went to the train station. When the train from Minia came in, he wasn't on it. I don't know or care where he is." I detected a familiar frustration in his tone.

On Saturday, Mona called again. "Mike, Chuck got delayed in Minia. He will be coming to Cairo on Sunday. Please have lunch for him and get him to the airport for his five o'clock flight back to Syria."

We prepared lunch for him on Sunday and waited for several hours, but still no Chuck. Around 4:45 he called from the airport. "Hello, Michael. I'm just letting you know that I got busy in Cairo today and didn't have time to stop by."

Dan had enjoyed about two good weeks of health before we were faced with our next medical crisis. He started developing a strange rash that would haunt us for the next 12 months. The rash was extremely pruritic and appeared on his arms, legs, and the sides of his face. It started with deep blisters filled with clear thick liquid. Not like herpes with superficial blisters. It was as uncomfortable as a severe case of chicken pox. Night after night we were up with him. He was miserable and Denise and I were becoming severely sleep deprived.

Yet, unlike chicken pox, this rash didn't go away. From early April through the end of May, it continued. Dan was so irritable during the day that he was hard to cope with. At night he whimpered, crying over and over, "I've got blood." He always had bleeding sores from his fingers picking and digging at them. He had dug huge craters in his arms and face. The big ulcers would then get infected and start impetigo. We had him wrapped up in gauze like a mummy just to protect his skin from his own scratching.

Denise and I were about to go off the deep end. Dan was crying day and night. The pediatrician had no clues as to what was wrong. I had been treating him already for everything I could think of, including secondary bacterial infections. I went to other doctors, yet they didn't have a clue either. The gawkers multiplied. We couldn't take Daniel outside without a crowd of kids following us and staring and laughing at him. The relentless heat didn't help matters, but only managed to drain what little energy we did have.

One day I was in the main shopping area of town and a stranger came up to me. "You should be ashamed having a son that looks like that. Why don't you take him to a doctor?"

I screamed at him. "I am a doctor! Plus I have taken him to every Egyptian doctor I know!"

"Have you taken him to Dr. Shfik?"

"Who is Dr. Shfik?"

"Oh, Dr. Shfik is the greatest skin doctor in all of Egypt."

"Give me his address!" I demanded.

I immediately lifted Daniel up, turned, and ran out into the street to flag down a taxi. I handed the driver the paper, saying, "Take me there!"

When I got to Dr. Shfik's office, the waiting room was empty but the door was unlocked. There was no receptionist. I wandered through the office and the only person there was Dr. Shfik himself. The first thing I noticed was that he only spoke Arabic. Medical school training in Egypt is in English and Egyptian doctors pride themselves in speaking English, usually very good English, to foreigners. Even though I spoke to Dr. Shfik in English, he answered me in Arabic. So we continued in Arabic.

Dr. Shfik never removed Daniel's gauze or even touched him. It was like he was afraid to. Then he wrote out eight prescriptions. Topical fluorinated steroids, oral steroids, oral antibiotics, oral antihistamines, topical antibiotics, topical antifungal creams, oral antifungals, and topical anti scabies creams. I realized, as he was writing out the scripts, that he didn't know what the hell he was doing.

The next day, Denise's parents called and expressed interest in coming to visit us in Egypt. They thought they could be of some help during those hard days. I speculated they were actually coming to rescue their daughter and take her away.

I was tired of being out of medical practice. My purpose was to use my medical skills to help the poor. Cairo had some of the world's poorest people. They were called the people of garbage because they actually lived in a huge garbage dump.

I knew a Canadian woman who worked in the garbage village, assisting a French nun. Diane Sawyer had just been to Egypt to do a story about her for 60 minutes. Sister Immanuel was a remarkable woman–a regular Mother Teresa. To the shock of some of my Protestant friends, I have to admit she was one of the greatest Christians I've ever met. She has done a tremendous amount of good for the village, such as building them a school and a rug weaver's factory. She was even able to market their rugs in the chic markets of Paris and New York. With the income, she built a school and a small clinic.

I started to work in the garbage village clinic one or two days a week, while keeping up on my Arabic studies. Words can't describe what life was like in this place, where filth and poverty ran to the extreme. It was a maze of shacks built of stone, cinder blocks, tin, and just plain garbage. The smell of rotting offal would take your breath away. The little children were filthy. I mostly worked with them on a social level, but ran an adult medical clinic.

In the clinic I had a desk, one examining table, and a metal locker of donated expired medications. If I couldn't treat them from what was in the locker, they would go untreated.

One of the biggest problems with the kids was that they were always barefooted. They occasionally found shoes in the garbage, but couldn't get used to wearing them. Living in a garbage dump poses many dangers to the barefooted. Glass, jagged metal, even old syringes and needles were everywhere. The streets and alleys were filled with the stench of burning garbage and rotting animal carcasses. It was a hellish place.

The kids wore rags but it didn't seem to bother them. They had fun playing soccer with a pop bottle or roll of rags. I joined them in many of their games. We played on a flat spot at the base of a 150-foot cliff. On top of the cliff was Maquattum, one of the wealthier Egyptian neighborhoods built up high, where the air was a little cleaner and cooler.

The first time I went out to play soccer with the kids, their playing field looked nice, with a small waterfall coming off the cliff forming a small pond where the kids would go wading. When I got closer, I realized that the waterfall was actually raw sewage coming from a pipe beneath the expensive apartment buildings at the top.

The week before my in-laws were due to arrive in Egypt, the nuns planned a week-long camp for the garbage village children on the Suez Canal. There the Nuns owned a three-floor cinder-block dormitory. I went as the medical director and took Bryan. The few days I spent there would be the worst days of my life.

The power was off when we arrived, therefore there was no water. It was above 100 degrees and, being this close to the Red Sea, very humid. Air conditioning remained a distant dream. These kids had never lived inside or used indoor plumbing. Soon after our arrival they began to defecate up and down the halls. What made it worse was that the younger kids began walking barefoot through it and tracking it around. I spent all day shoveling poop and picking lice out of kids' hair. With no running water, there was no way to wash down the halls. It smelled like an outhouse after a Fourth of July barbecue.

The Eastern-style toilet (ceramic hole in the floor) was filled to overflowing. Someone ran into town and bought a case of bottled water but it had to be rationed–one cup per person about every two hours. I reflected back on my previous life, seeing headache patients in a plush office in the US. Most of my patients in Michigan were professional people of the up-and-in variety. But, this was what it was all about. This was why I came into medicine in the first place; well, not necessarily to shovel poop.

Bryan and I had to catch a bus back to Cairo early to be there when my in-laws arrived. Thank goodness we could leave early. I arrived home to find that Daniel's rash had taken a turn for the worse despite me eventually putting him on oral steroids. This meant more sleepless nights for the three of us.

The day of my in-laws' arrival I awoke with a headache, which was unusual. The headache built in intensity as the morning progressed. Denise needed help to get ready for her parents, but I could hardly move. As the time approached to go to the airport, my head was really pounding and my neck was sore. It was clearly the worse headache I'd ever had. I hated not being able to help Denise get to the airport, especially with three small children, but I took my temperature and it was 102 F. I just couldn't go. During the two hours that Denise was picking up her folks, I went downhill very fast. I felt horrible–so horrible I was afraid I was going to die. Then I felt so horrible I was afraid I wasn't going to die. I was burning up and couldn't move my neck or head. I tried to get up to go vomit but collapsed on the floor. Every time I even raised my head up, I would feel very faint and loose my vision. I was lying on the floor in our boy's room until Denise got home and found me. She took my temperature and it was 104 F and she could barely wake me.

Camp "Hell" on the Suez Canal
(With Bryan in the bold-striped shirt sitting on the woman's lap).

Denise quickly filled up the bathtub with cool water and dragged me into it. She ran and called Habib's wife, who sent over their family doctor to our apartment. I spent the next week on a foam pad, on the boy's bedroom floor with daily visits from the older Egyptian physician. Denise's folks were sleeping in our bed. I don't remember much for the next few days, but apparently I had viral meningitis. In the states I would have been in ICU. It was ten days before I could get up and move around. Denise was exhausted, being the single parent and nurse to both Daniel and me over the previous couple of weeks, as well as entertaining her folks. Fortunately her mother was there to help with some of the household chores.

During my in-law's remaining few days, we wanted to do some tourist things. I was still feeling quite weak, plus I had a sequel to the meningitis: a painful outbreak of shingles on the left side of my face. We took them to the pyramids and then downtown to the National

Museum. As we were walking down the halls, still feeling quite weak, I thought about the first time I had visited the museum.

It had occurred soon after our arrival to Egypt, when we were still healthy and full of energy. After viewing King Tut's golden treasures, I was walking down an upstairs hall. As I walked by one of the security guards, he said, "Psssssst . . . U C 2, 5 pounds. U C 2, 5 pounds . . . OK?" I had no idea what he was talking about except that he wanted five pounds to show me something. All behaviors in Egypt are lubricated by bribes or "tips" called bucsheesh. After my experience at the airport a few days earlier, I was much more careful and handed the guard two pounds. With great anticipation, I waited to see what my two pounds bought me.

The guard led me to an employees only area where, to my amazement, were racks of thirty or forty mummies. He took me to one of the mummies and pulled back the sheet. The wrapping was coming off the mummy's foot and you could see his toe. Now I got it. He was saying, "You see toe, five pounds." He then took my hand, saying, "Touch." With hesitation, I felt the hard, leathery toe of the mummy.

Later some of the Egyptians told me that we would have bad luck because I had the "evil-eye" on our family, a curse from the pharaohs for touching the mummy's toe. I rejected that theory and laughed. Now, a year later, I was beginning to reevaluate my skepticism.

We played tourist for two more days, then it was time for my in-laws to go back to the US. They were catching a very early TWA flight on Thursday morning. Wednesday night, we got them all packed up and tried to go to bed early. I was almost asleep when I heard a thump in the hall outside our door and then my mother-in-law screamed my name, "Michael . . . Michael!"

I was startled and jumped out of bed. As I came out of our bedroom, I found my father-in-law laying face down in the floor, not moving, and a very worried mother-in-law stooped at his side. I kneeled down beside them. My father-in-law wasn't breathing and I couldn't find a pulse. I rolled him over onto his back to start CPR. As soon as I did, his airway opened and he gasped for air. I could then feel his pulse but it was very faint and erratic. He remained unconscious for a couple of minutes before starting to come around.

We carried him to bed with him in a stupor. His pulse was still very erratic and he was apparently not getting much blood to his brain. Yet another nightmare about Cairo is that there is no 911 to call, no ambulance, and really no ER. In these situations, it comes down to you and Allah to work these things out. Certainly I prayed.

Then I thought about an American PA I had met in Cairo named Bob. He was working for an American company and lived a very different lifestyle than us down in Maadi, which was an hour or more away. I knew that Bob had some medical resources as well as a background in cardiology.

I hated to impose, but I was desperate. He was very helpful in our time of need. He awakened his Egyptian driver and they brought the ambulance on the 90-minute trek. Once they arrived, he had oxygen, IV supplies, and an ECG machine. We started an IV and hung a bag of fluids. The ECG showed that my father-in-law was in atrial fibrillation with somewhat erratic ventricular response. Bob convinced me that we should get him admitted to a hospital, which wouldn't be easy.

My father-in-law was a patient for the first time in his 65 years. He had even been born at home. He hated being in a hospital where no one spoke English. It was finally determined that his potassium was extremely low. He was on a diuretic in the states for hypertension. I didn't know it at the time, but his potassium was borderline low to start with. When he got to Cairo, he caught "Pharaoh's Revenge" the first day there and had been having diarrhea every day since. This is what depleted his potassium and exacerbated his arrhythmia.

After spending several days in the hospital, he and my mother-in-law were very happy to get back on American soil. Denise and I felt stunned by all that had been happening in our lives. We were beyond exhaustion. Still, we were back to baseline—Daniel up all night digging at his sores and the endless heat. About this time, Barb, Habib's wife, called Denise. "Habib and I can't understand why you don't get Daniel to an American doctor."

I thought it was a wonderful idea but I knew that Ghandi, er . . . I mean Chuck, wouldn't allow that. I was starting to come to my senses as I grew fed up with him and the whole ICO outfit. The other issue was that we would have to come up with funding for the trip somehow.

I called our church in Michigan and explained what had been going on. The next day the pastor called me back "Mike, we will provide round trip airfare for the whole family and have a place for you to stay. We also have an appointment set up with the Department of Pediatric Dermatology at the University of Michigan." We were overwhelmed with their kindness. I made reservations at TWA. I sent a telex to Mona in Cyprus, not intending to ask anyone's permission, but just to let them know what we were doing. As it turned out that was a big mistake.

Within two days I had a call from Mona. She said, "I called Chuck in Syria when I got your telex. He says that you don't have permission to go to the states." The comment that he passed on through her was very condescending: "We don't go off to America every time we have some kind of problem." Chuck had been totally out of touch for months and didn't know the first thing about why we wanted to leave.

Mona added, "Chuck has orders for you to be in Cyprus in two weeks. ICO is having a business conference in the mountains and he wants you there." I think the most Christian thing I could have said at this time was, "Tell Chuck to kiss my lilly-white Jedi butt." But, I am ashamed to say that I didn't. Now, it is very hard for even me to understand why I didn't. I can only say I had been brainwashed by ICO into a cultic view of leadership. Like a good Jedi, I followed orders from ICO one more time. I thought, too, maybe I could find help for Daniel in Cyprus.

I told Mona, "OK, the last time we came to Cyprus we were put in a dirty, hot apartment. Mona, we are exhausted. I want to know, if we come, where we are going to stay."

"Oh Mike, you can have my flat. It is quite cool and very clean."

"OK, regarding this so-called business meeting, I'm not attending a business meeting. Our family has been through a lot and needs rest badly."

"Mike, I don't think Chuck really wants you to attend the meetings;

he just wants you guys to be near the rest of the team since you have been alone for a year."

I hesitantly agreed to go to Cyprus. However, since my orders were that I couldn't go to the US, instead I went to the Swiss Air office. I made our reservations to Cyprus, but then from there I got reservations on to Zurich. I then made a return reservation to Egypt one month later. We had no idea what we would do in Zurich or where we would stay, but anything was better than staying in the situation we were in. I had a two-man pup tent and threw it in a suitcase. We gathered up our three boys and headed to Cyprus. We had survived six months of poor family health and more than one close brush with death. We had high hopes that things would get better. As I thought about Switzerland, I was hoping for another "bus trip" from Hell to Heaven, like the one I had experience when I left my first job at the prison. Maybe this time I would be right . . . just maybe.

Chapter Fourteen

Where's Moses When You Need Him?

The two engines on the little Egypt Air jet roared and the acceleration nudged me back into my seat. Bryan and Daniel were sitting beside me. Denise and baby Tyler sat in the row ahead of me. We lifted off from the Cairo airport and were sky-bound. The huge congested city soon faded into an impressionistic blur of grayish browns beneath the smoggy and dusty air. A short flight across the deep blue waters of the eastern Mediterranean and we would be at our destination.

We certainly had mixed feelings about this trip to Cyprus. The thoughts of being with the ICO people brought feeling of dread. It was like a runaway teenager who, after finding living in the streets unkind and lonely, tries to return home to a dysfunctional, abusive family. The prospect of home doesn't give the sense of returning to a harbor of safety that it otherwise should.

When we arrived at the Larnaca airport, Chuck was there to meet us. He did seem to be out of character in his compassion: "Mona said you are having some kind of trouble. You have my attention for 30 minutes, so speak to me! Here is your chance. Talk!"

Denise and I were speechless and we just sat in the van in silence, still in a state of shock. I think it was the overwhelming feeling that Chuck (to borrow a phrase from *Gone With the Wind*), "frankly, did not give a damn."

Chuck then started doing the talking since we weren't. "The meetings are really going good. I hope you will join us soon."

We continued up the mountain in silence. Finally I said to him, "Chuck, we are in no mood to participate in an ICO business conference." In his authoritarian way Chuck said, "I will give you 48 hours, then you will be expected to attend the conference meetings."

I just looked out the window of the VW van as we drove up the ancient serpentine mountain road. Stone fences lined the fields where sheep grazed on brownish grass. I have to admit, the mountains looked wonderful. Although the place was arid, compared to Egypt the few olive trees made it look positively verdant. Once we climbed above 3,000 feet, the wind was actually cool. The hotel was a charming Greek getaway. Once we were out of the van, Denise and I immediately felt the tension of Cairo draining out of us like dirty water out of a bathtub. We checked in and went to the restaurant to have dinner. As we walked in, another Western-looking couple came in right behind us. The woman said, "Are you Mike and Denise Jones?"

"Yes," we said with surprise.

"My name is Mary and this is my husband Tim. We are with ICO in Jordan."

We had heard of them many times, but this was the first time we had met them in person. Tim had been an excellent college athlete and even had the chance to be a major league baseball pitcher. He had passed on the opportunity to come and work in the Third World. Both were tall and slim and appeared to be tan and fit.

As we worked our way through the buffet, Mary turned to us and said, in a tender voice, "How is it going? I hear Cairo is a very tough place to live."

Our eyes filled up with tears. No one in ICO had treated us with this much respect. We both had had verbal constipation coming up the mountain with Chuck. Here was a woman we just met, but knew, by the inflection in her voice, the look in her eye, that she really meant it when she asked how we were. We ate with Tim and Mary that evening and told them our story. It was like finding the beautiful, sane cousin Marilyn in the midst of the Munster Family.

By the second day in the mountains, Daniel started making a dramatic improvement in his health. I don't know if it was being in the cool air or just being away from something in Cairo that was causing an allergic reaction.

I will never forget the peaceable hours of lying in the hotel pool, feeling the cool mountain breezes and the silence. We hadn't experienced a moment of silence in almost a year. You could actually hear birds singing. We became intoxicated on the simple pleasures, like swinging our kids on a swing or taking a long walk, things we could never do in Cairo. Unfortunately, our 48 hours of tranquility would be coming to an abrupt end. Chuck wanted us, or at least me, to attend the ICO business meetings the next morning.

I got up early and enjoyed breakfast alone and joined the meeting. My mind was far away. I just couldn't relate to the trivial gripes and whining that were being discussed by these people living in very different circumstances from us. Someone wanted the company's van to go to the beach but someone else was using it. The food at the conference hotel was too hot or too cold, etc. Compared to where we had been, Denise and I felt like we were living in bliss.

When lunch came, Denise joined me. To our good fortune, Tim and Mary also joined us at the table. They weren't participating in the conference but just happened to be staying at the hotel for a vacation.

Chuck was always able to surprise me, no matter how prepared I tried to make myself. "Mike and Denise, you aren't allowed to return to Egypt."

I was trying to eat my delicious Greek Salad and stuffed grape leaves in peace when I had to sigh, dropping my fork, and ask, "Now Chuck, where did this come from? What on earth are you talking about?"

He searched for a response that would account for his authoritarian command. Finally he came up with, "Habib says that you aren't allowed back in Egypt because you have a sick child and that he is fed up with taking care of you."

Denise and I both started laughing. What he was saying was

ridiculous. "Chuck," I said, "that makes no sense. I have only seen Habib a few times. He knows almost nothing about Daniel." Chuck was lying to us again and I was getting angry. I took another bite of my food, cleared my throat, and looked up at him. "OK Chuck, if we aren't allowed to go back to Cairo, and we aren't allowed to take Daniel to America, then what are we supposed to do, live on a barge in the Mediterranean like the man in *A Man Without a Country?*"

Denise and I tried to take a few bites of food before Chuck dropped his other big bombshell. "Mike, I want you to move to Cyprus in two months and take over the medical directorship of my company, Medical Consults LTD."

The job of medical director of his little company wasn't as promising as it seemed. Chuck had created Medical Consults LTD a year earlier. It was a sinking ship, sinking under the load of mismanagement and interpersonal conflicts.

"Chuck," I said, "I was promised that we would be given a few days to rest here. We have been through hell. When we get here and you demand I attend this business meeting, and now you are laying on us these heavy changes. Can't you just leave us alone?"

"I will give you 48 hours to make up your minds about the move."

Tim and Mary had been observing the conversation quietly when Mary spoke up. "Chuck, why 48 hours? Is there some good reason for that?"

"Yes," he exclaimed. "I am going to Syria in 48 hours. If he doesn't give me an answer before I leave, he will be required to report to my house in Damascus within one week."

"Great! The last thing I need right now is to leave my family and make a trip to Syria." I tried to inject sanity in this situation. "Chuck, what is the big deal if we think things over for a few weeks and give you a call on the phone. Abruptly moving to Cyprus at this point is a major decision. You just told me to raise another $6,000 from our donors and enroll in A.U.C. next fall. That money has now been raised and paid to A.U.C., and is non-refundable."

"I never accept a response over the telephone. You must come and speak to me face to face, either here within 48 hours or in Damascus within one week. That is my final decision." Then Chuck pushed his chair away from the table and got up and walked away.

After another day in the mountains, we caught a taxi with Mona, heading back down to Nicosia. Halfway down the mountain I asked Mona, "So, we are going directly to your apartment?"

She hedged. "Uh, Mike, there has been a change of plans. Chuck has a friend coming to Cyprus and he told her that she could have my apartment to herself tonight."

Now here was an interesting development. "So where are we staying?"

"Chuck says that is your problem. You are adults and can find your own hotel."

"Hotel? We have to find a hotel?"

"Uh . . . I guess so."

We did find a hotel. It was cost us $125 a night and the air conditioner was broken, but it was the only room in town at that late notice.

The next day, I took Daniel to a Cypriot dermatologist. He, like his Egyptian counterpart, never even touched him, but wrote out a prescription for a steroid cream. He diagnosed him as having atopic dermatitis. I wasn't convinced, considering the way his rash started with deep vesicles, which is certainly not typical for atopic dermatitis. However, Dan was 80% better since leaving Egypt so we were happy about it.

That evening, after we got the kids to sleep in the hotel room, Denise and I sat on the 8th floor balcony with glasses of fresh squeezed lemonade. The hot breeze was starting to cool and there was a sent of jasmine in the air. We had a long conversation about moving to Cyprus. Denise had a host of concerns about planning a major move at this time. It took until the stars were brightly overhead in the Mediterranean sky before we reached our decision. The following day was Chuck's departure so I would have to meet with him early.

After breakfast I took a taxi to Medical Consults LTD's downtown office. It was a small, glass storefront with the words, "Med Consults, LTD." stenciled on the glass door in bold white letters, in English, Greek, and Arabic. You entered the office by walking down a couple of steps below the sidewalk level. Inside the office, on the first floor, were three desks, a couple of office machines, and a table. Another desk was on a loft level, which was accessible via a spiral metal staircase. Chuck was just finishing a meeting with his four office staff at the table, so I pulled up a seat and joined them. Chuck looked up at me and said, "Well Mike, I am catching my plane in two hours, so what is the verdict? Are you coming to Cyprus?"

"Yes Chuck, we are, but conditionally. Denise needs some time to wrap up loose ends in Cairo and move in a non-rushed way. We are willing to make the move only if we can have until Christmas in Egypt."

Chuck smiled and said, "Uh, Mike, someday YOU need to wear the pants in your family."

The word "jerk" popped into my head as if on a Las Vegas marquee. "Chuck," I said hatefully, "I care very much about what Denise thinks and feels. That doesn't mean she 'wears the pants!' We are partners in the decisions we make." The rest of the staff sat in silence.

Chuck responded to my tone by saying, "Mike, you sound a little stressed. You better learn to relax if you are going to survive over here." Then he laughed.

Chuck returned to his desk on the loft. I stayed downstairs for a few minutes to visit with Mona and the other staff, who were really nice people. Tom, who worked for ICO's main office, came in the door. He looked like he had just stepped off a tennis court, wearing sunglasses, white shorts, and a white short-sleeve knit shirt. He was the one I had called during the night when I thought Bryan had appendicitis. We exchanged greetings and then Chuck called from the loft railing upstairs, "Hey Tom, come up here a minute, I want to talk to you."

I was just getting ready to leave when Tom came slowly down the spiral staircase from Chuck's office. Chuck, standing at the top, said to me, "Hey Mike, Tom here is going to take you to lunch and show you how to relax."

I didn't have a clue what this was all about. Was Chuck just being kind?

"Come on, Mike," Tom said, "This won't take long."

Tom and I walked into the old medieval city until we found his favorite café. We took a seat at an outside table, shaded by webs of grape vines strung overhead. We ordered kebab sandwiches and Tom ordered himself a pint of beer and a quart for me. He took off his sunglasses and looked at me. "Chuck says you drink beer and this café has some of the best beer on the island."

"Well, I'm not a big beer drinker, only on rare occasions. A quart is quite a bit for me."

Once the beer was on the table, Tom insisted, "Mike, you have to drink all the beer in the mug or the owner will be offended." Just as I finished it off, Tom ordered me a second quart, this time a stout ale.

"Tom, are you crazy? I can't drink another quart."

"Oh, Mike, you've got to taste this ale, they import it from England. It's expensive, so you can't let it go to waste."

I was just going to taste it, but then he lifted up the bottom of my mug and started coaching me, like a freshman recruit at a fraternity binge-drinking party. "Come on, Mike, drink up."

"Tom, stop it. I can't drink anymore. I am already starting to feel the effects."

"Mike, keep drinking, I've just ordered you a quart of the owner's own brew. You've still got to drink that."

Even in my woozy state, I was starting figure out that Chuck had sent Tom to get me drunk. It frustrated me that Chuck, in his manipulative, simplistic mind, thought that getting me drunk would erase all the hard experiences we had been through and magically make it all better. I certainly had a personal conviction about being under the influence of alcohol. I am sure that Chuck had the same conviction, but somehow believed, in this case at least, the end justified the means.

I called a taxi. When I stood up to get in, my legs felt like rubber. Still Tom was insisting that I drink more. I told the driver, "Take me to the Swiss Air office, please." As we came down the street, I could see an office with a square red flag hanging in front. My eyes were too blurred to make out the Swiss cross in the middle of it. Once inside, I rescheduled our flight to Zurich for the following day. This would cut a week off our stay in Cyprus and I was ready to get out of there. I was a little nervous the next day to even look at our plane tickets. I never told Denise that I was half drunk when I rescheduled the flight. Fortunately I got it right.

Before we left Cyprus, we took our boys on a journey to Chuck's garage to see their toys. It was like a time capsule. They had been away from them for over a year, but could remember them well–their favorite truck, a little gas station and parking garage. It was heartbreaking for us, but we had to eventually put them back into the crates and leave them behind. We switched our suitcases for backpacks, which were in the crates, and soon were en route to Zurich.

The experience of arriving in Switzerland was like starving kids arriving in a candy factory. We were euphoric. The green hills and mountains were so bright that it hurt our eyes, which had grown accustomed to nothing but shades of brown. We looked on a map and decided we wanted to go to the highest place that we could within the shortest distance. We boarded the train with our three little boys and a couple of backpacks. The crimson-colored train sped by beautiful villages, lakes, and rivers in the low lands until we came to Luzern. There we switched trains and headed straight up into the mountains. As the train climbed higher and higher, we entered a forest of evergreens and steep banks, which were surrounded by sheer walls of gray, and sometimes pink, granite. The train passed over bridges above gorges so deep that it took our breath away. Soon we came to the cog track, where the incline is so steep that the tracks have special gears that allow the train to get traction and not slip backward. You could feel the clank-clank as the cog engaged with each turn. After a couple of miles, we started to feel the altitude. A mist covered the hills around us and the air was very cool.

Before long, we came to a beautiful alpine village nestled in the bottom of a steep valley floor. The village was called Engelberg, which means "Village of Angels." My understanding was the village was so named because it grew up around a very old convent.

The village itself was quaint, with a population of 2,000 people. At the west end of the valley, the direction in which we were arriving, sat the train station. The village was laid out on a relatively flat valley floor running east and west. The valley was divided on the south side by a roaring mountain stream and small lake. From the standpoint of the train station the valley seemed to narrow before climbing to a huge wall of granite and ice mountains ten miles directly ahead to the east. To the south, the viewer's right, was the towering, glacier-laden mountain called Titlis. A line of bright red tram cars left the village, going high toward Titlis and disappearing over the first evergreen-covered mountain ridge. To the north, the viewer's left, the mountains rose more gently and are not as high. On that side of the valley, the green meadows were dotted with chalets and old barns. At the bottom of these green grassy hills stood the old stone fortress, which was the convent. In the center of the convent was the bell tower, from which the sounds of high chimes and low bongs rang out every hour. A quieter chiming, or tinkling, was heard from both sides of the valley as cows lazily grazed on the high hills. A tall granite cliff was formed where the smaller hills on the north met the taller mountains ahead to the east. From the top of this cliff tumbled and roared a waterfall for hundreds of feet.

The village itself was made up of two–to four-story buildings. Some appeared very old, made of huge hand-hued beams and stones. Others were more modern, but tastefully built in the alpine esthetic. Compared to Cairo, the town was amazingly quiet. Except for the sounds of the bells, all you could hear was the sound of nature, falling water, birds, barking dogs, and an occasional human voice. Words can't describe what this experience was like. It is the closest I have ever experienced to being in Heaven. It was a wonderfully shocking contrast to where we had been living for the past year.

My attention quickly switched from admiration to contemplation as I needed to find a place for us to stay. We got our backpacks and left the train station. We found out that the village had one campground and it was on the other–east–end of town, about four miles away. I flagged down a taxi. I had never gone camping in a taxi before. Admittedly, that was a little weird.

The campground was beside a roaring mountain river, the same one that divided the town downstream. Glaciered mountains surrounded the campground on three sides as we were in the narrow end of the valley. We put up our little pup tent and moved in.

Camping in Switzerland is different than the US. The Europeans camp in style. They eat gourmet food on fine china sipping wine from tall crystal glasses. They have fine outdoor furniture, as campsites don't come with picnic tables like they do in the states. They camp in Westphala VW campers and large cabin-type tents. All we had was an aluminum mess kit, a pup tent, and no table.

On our second day I hiked down to the village and purchased a small folding table, two chairs, a pot, and dishes. I also filled up my backpack with food. You could get a hundred dollars of food in my backpack–not because it was so huge, but because the food was so expensive in Switzerland. That was one long trek back to the campground. With a table, chairs, and an icebox on my back, I looked like Jethro Bodine from the "Beverly Hillbillies," on foot. I could see the parade of VW vans slowing down to look at the tacky American as they trudged up the mountain road to the campground.

Our three weeks in the tent were some of the greatest days of my life, at least so far. For one three-day span, it rained continuously. Talk about quality family time. We were pent up in a two-man pup tent with three kids for three days and one of them was in diapers. Pew! We had a deck of Old Maid cards and made up stories and songs about the character on each card. Even with the rain, it was a glorious time!

Our boys had some great experiences, such as being yelled at everyday in German by the campground maintenance man. We never knew why. We must have been doing something terribly wrong. After a week a British family came into the campground so our boys finally had someone they could communicate with. They spent the afternoons playing cricket with the British kids, frequently running over to me an asking me about specific rules of the game. I must have responded a hundred times with, "I haven't a clue."

During our stay, we hiked a lot of trails through the mountains. The Alps are different than the Rockies. For one thing, they are different geologically. The valleys are much deeper, going down to lower than 1,000 feet above sea level. At the same time, the mountains' summits are higher than the Rockies by 1,000 feet. These mountains have also experienced Western civilization for a very long time. You might climb a mountain thinking you were way out in the boonies only to come upon another farm with a field of cows wearing giant bells. Higher and higher I would climb, but still another farm and even more cows.

About every other day I would put on my backpack, take Denise's shopping list, and hike the two miles into town. The trail followed the river crisscrossing on footbridges. With precision, every hour the convent bells would ring out, echoing against the distant mountainsides. The endless blaring of the Cairo car horns was swiftly and softly erased from my ears and soul by the seductive mountain sounds.

Once in town, I would buy a copy of *USA Today* and a German beer and find a seat on the second story balcony of the café. There I sat, reading my paper and sipping my beer. Now and then I would look up to study the dance of the sunlight across the bright mountain glaciers. It was a dream that I never wanted to wake up from. Before leaving town, I would go to the market and fill up the backpack with groceries before heading back to camp.

The most notable thing that happened was that we got a long needed rest. Dan's health was restored and I came to my right mind. It is funny how, when you are in the midst of a crazy situation, you lose track of which way is up. Then, when you get some perspective, get some rest, the picture becomes so much clearer. Looking back, I think it was denial. We wanted so badly to work among the poor in the Third World. ICO and Chuck presented the means to that end. I knew now that we couldn't continue under Chuck's leadership and that I had to do something about it when we got back to Egypt. As bad as we wanted to spend our lives in the Third World, I knew that it would all be in jeopardy if I confronted Chuck.

Dan and Mike hiking near Engelberg
(Dan with just a few bandages left on his arms).

The problem with dreams is that you eventually have to wake up. I began to wake up as we were walking down the gate ramp at Cairo International Airport. Bryan voiced what Denise and I were feeling. He sat down in the middle of the ramp and started screaming, "I'm not going back to Cairo." We had to drag him to customs, kicking and crying. Naturally, at customs, everyone was waved through but us. Again our passports were thrown in a drawer and locked up. The agent looked at me and said, "Fe muskilla kabeer" ("There is a big problem").

"Now what?"

Again I was taken aside into an office and questioned. "Why are you here, Where did you go?"

"What is the problem this time?" I would learn that if you leave the country for any reason, and you are in Egypt on a residence visa, your visa becomes void. Therefore, I was trying to enter Egypt without a visa . . . again. I was told I had the option of paying a huge fine, going to jail, or getting a letter of apology from the ambassador. I agreed to the apology.

On our first day back in the country I found myself in the middle of a riot at the U.S. Embassy. A mob of several hundred people was pushing and screaming in front of the building as a group of Egyptian soldiers tried to keep the crowd back.

I started pushing my way through the crowd. My daily bus commute had given me a lot of practice in crowd penetration. This crowd was becoming more violent and I ended up getting my glasses broken in the mayhem. I finally made it to the front and shouted to the soldiers, "I'm an American citizen!" He motioned me toward the large, bombproof door.

As the door came open, a mad rush of Egyptians tried to force their way through with me. A wrestling match broke out between the Egyptian solders and the people who had breached their defense. I got up the stairs to the "drive-up window" woman. I said into the little microphone, "What is going on around here?"

The lady explained to me, amid the commotion, "The U.S. government announced today that a new program for obtaining U.S. citizenship has been started. Rather than the usual process, where only a few qualify, and they have to spend years doing it, a percentage of applicants was going to be offered citizenship by a lottery."

So, I thought, this was what had sparked the riot that almost swept me away. Before I was finished at the window, I heard a crash downstairs. The guards hadn't been able to close the door behind me and a flood of Egyptians came pouring in. A line of U.S. Marine guard in full dress uniforms came running past the open door of the little room. This was the first time I had seen real live Americans at the embassy.

I got my letter and the next day I finished the process of getting our visa. Denise and I started making plans to move to Cyprus. I was making headway in Arabic so I needed to set up classes to finish on a strong note. Last, I made plans to visit Chuck in Damascus to confront him about his leadership style.

To our dismay, by our second day back in Egypt Daniel started coming down with his awful skin rash. It was deja vu all over again, as Yogi Berra would say. The figurative bathtub started to fill with dirty water again.

Early in September we had a surprising phone call one day from Chuck. "Hello. I just called to tell you that I have been in Cairo for a few days. I am willing to meet with you if I get a break in my schedule. I want the two of you to stay near your phone for the next few days. If I get a break, I will let you know and you can come downtown and see me. Please don't bring the children; I want to meet with you alone."

Finding a baby sitter in Cairo was next to impossible. During our first year, we did meet an Italian woman, Madam Mary, who appeared to be about a hundred and four. She had married an Egyptian man, I think, during the Roman conquest of Egypt, about 100 B.C., and had lived there ever since. She was recommended as a babysitter. Denise and I hadn't had time alone for many months and decided to go for it. The first problem was that she didn't have a phone. I had to walk a couple of blocks to the main freeway, stand in the middle of traffic, and scream in Arabic at passing taxis. Once I found a taxi that was willing to pick me up, it was a 20-minute ride to her flat. Since the taxi was full of other passengers, I would have to give it up when I got out. I would arrange the time for the babysitting assignment and then reverse the process. The night of the babysitting, I had to repeat the process to get her and bring her back to our flat and afterwards take her home.

Madam Mary wore a heavy, wool, full-length, dirty black coat and walked bent over at the waist. Our boys were convinced she was a witch. As soon as she came into the apartment, she plopped down in the living room chair closest to the door and said in a very crabby voice, "I want some food. You have to feed me if you want me to watch your babies." She looked and sounded like a thin version of the mother from, *Throw Momma From the Train*. Denise brought her food and she ate it right there at the chair with her coat still on. She acted like she hadn't seen food in a month.

We had some uneasiness, but we were desperate for time alone so we left on our "date." When we returned in two hours, there she sat, in the same chair, with her dirty overcoat still on. The boys told us she had never moved and at times they wondered if she was dead. As soon as we got out the door, she had snarled to the boys, "You got to sit here in front of me till you mama and papa come home." At first they obeyed her because they were so afraid she would turn them into a toad. Later, they realized she was almost blind anyway and occasionally they would slip into the other room. Once there, they could do things like building a small campfire in the bathroom floor. Fortunately the only things they could find for fuel were a couple of old toilet paper tubes and wads of snot-filled toilet paper in the trash can. The matches came from a little Egyptian neighbor boy. All of this, you'll remember, was part of the alien plot to destroy dads.

We used Madam Mary only on very special occasions. Going to meet with Chuck wasn't an occasion worthy of such a sacrifice. Besides, Denise knew that I wanted to have it out with Chuck, and she didn't want to be there when it happened.

Finally the phone rang one day about noon. Chuck said, "I have an opening in my schedule tonight, be at my hotel at 5:00 p.m." I took the metro into the city center, thinking it would be easy traveling that time of day. By the time I arrived at Tahreer, it was going on five. It took me a while to find Chuck's hotel as it was not on a main street and was a one-star (out of five) establishment. When I got to his door, it was already ten after the hour. In my head I had been practicing my speech all the way into town. I felt about as prepared as I would ever be.

I pounded on his door and there was no response. I pounded again, still no response. I pulled the directions out of my pocket to make sure I was at the right place. I could barely read them in the dim hall light, but it appeared that I was where I was supposed to be. I thought I would hang out in the dark deadly hall until he came home.

Within minutes, the door opened an inch and there was Chuck's sleepy face poking out of a dark room. When he saw that it was me, he let me in. There was also an Egyptian man sleeping in the room.

Chuck grabbed his watch off the nightstand and said, "What time is it?" Now, I was expecting him to say, "Mike, I am sorry I was asleep, I didn't know it was so late." But what he said was, "Ahmed, wake up. It is after five o'clock and we are late."

As he was putting on his shirt he told me, "I was supposed to be at a meeting at 5:00 p.m." Then he darted off to the bathroom as Ahmed started getting dressed.

I yelled at him through the bathroom door, "What meeting?"

"Oh, I have a meeting tonight with Egyptian business men," he mumbled through the door.

Now I was confused again. "Didn't you tell me to come downtown to meet you at five?"

"Yeah, I guess I did, but then this came up this afternoon. I have your mail if that is what you want." He came out of the bathroom and took a small bundle of mail off the dresser and gave it to me, obviously expecting me to simply turn around and leave.

"Chuck, was there a textbook on dermatology in my mail?"

"Oh yeah. I really liked the pictures in it so I took it home to Syria a couple of months ago."

"I really needed that book, Chuck. I thought it would help me figure out what was wrong with Daniel. A physician friend in the states bought it for me and sent it as a gift."

"Don't worry about it. I will send you a check for it."

"That's not the issue. I was hoping that it would give me some leads on Daniel's problems."

I took the bundle of mail and waited while the two of them continued getting dressed. I was feeling a huge wave of disappointment coming over me again. "Chuck, I really need to talk to you about something."

"OK, you can walk out with us. The meeting is about two blocks away."

Chuck and Ahmed were dressed and headed down the stairs. I had to walk fast to keep up with them. They were deeply involved in an Arabic conversation. I could only understand about half of what was said, but I couldn't get a word in edgewise. He was acting quite odd, like he was trying to avoid giving me the chance to talk. Before long, we were at his destination. Chuck was trying tell me goodbye, when I said, "Chuck, like I said, I still need to talk to you."

"What's up?"

"It is a long story. How long will your meeting last?"

"About an hour."

"Can I wait for you?"

Chuck paused and then cautiously added, "I guess you can come inside and wait."

We entered what appeared to be someone's flat. There were two men inside wearing white gallabayas and smoking a water pipe. Chuck introduced me and asked me to sit in the living room while they went into another room for their meeting. It was a slow hour but finally they came out and offered me some tea. We sipped tea together and made small talk.

Chuck and Ahmed said goodbye to the men and we headed back out to the street. I was hoping to quickly shake Ahmed, but Chuck announced, "I've got to go to another meeting." I followed him to another flat where we repeated the same scenario with a couple of other men.

When Chuck and Ahmed emerged from that meeting, I was hoping, after going on three hours, to have his undivided attention. Then Ahmed said to Chuck, "I would like to go out to dinner with you." Now I was getting really frustrated. I was hoping that as soon we were done eating, we could shake Ahmed because I definitely couldn't speak in front of him. Chuck was in Egypt on official Syrian business. I wanted to talk to him about our situation with ICO. Chuck was always in his cloak and dagger mindset and would panic if I brought up ICO in front of Ahmed.

We went to a Chinese restaurant near Tahreer. I was really trying to be patient. Then Ahmed said to Chuck, in English, so I would be sure to understand, "Chuck, I want to talk with you alone." Chuck, surprisingly, turned to him and said, "Sure, Mike will leave soon."

I had about had it with him. I had spent the last four hours trying to speak to Chuck, now he was giving me the brush-off. My temper was starting to build. Then, Chuck did something that set off the pressure cooker that had been simmering for two years.

He looked over at me. "Before you leave I wanted to tell you that the Middle East ICO team met a few weeks ago and have decided that you won't be staying in Cyprus. You will come over for only a couple of months and then be moving to Sana, Yemen. Now don't tell Denise. Make her think you are moving permanently to Cyprus." He paused to take a sip of his Chinese tea. "I have learned that women are too weak to handle these changes and it is better to lie to them and then surprise them with your plans." I came close to leaping across the table and throttling him. I wanted to perform a frontal lobotomy on him with my chopsticks. For better or for worse, I was able to control my physical behavior, which became one of the deepest regrets of my life. If there is a place within Christendom, for punching someone's lights out, this was just such a situation.

I didn't refrain from yelling, though. "We're not taking orders from you any more Chuck! We are fed up with this crap!"

He in response started yelling at me, "I am fed up with wimps like you who only care about your own damn families. Come on Ahmed, let's go."

"Chuck, I have more to say to you."

"Write me a letter." He took Ahmed and left.

It was a long, cold ride back to Medan Hegaz on the almost empty metro. When I got to our flat at around midnight, Denise was already sleeping. She heard me arrive and got up, slipped on her bathrobe, and come into the living room. It was a reenactment of the night we fell in love in Abu Dhabi, but this time, instead of one of the highest points in my life, it was one of the lowest. She said, "How did it go with Chuck?" I told her the whole story. Both of us sat up the whole night contemplating our future. I felt a rage that ate at me from the inside out.

I take interpersonal conflicts very hard. I think most of this comes from my mother's soft heart and her philosophy that it is always better to be hurt than to hurt others–like some dysfunctional take on the golden rule. But, I hate to be mad at someone as much as I hate for someone to be mad at me. It picks at my soul. Yet, the frustrating aspect of this situation was Chuck's elusiveness. I couldn't sit down and talk things out. I did begin a letter that night–finishing it by six o'clock the next morning. It was 15 pages long. I quickly mailed it before I had second thoughts.

That same week, I had a call from Bill. He and Barbara were on their way back from the states and had a few days' layover in Egypt and were staying with Habib. They wanted to come over for dinner.

Bill and Barbara were nice people; however, they were about as in touch with what was going on with us as Marie Antoinette was with her subjects when she uttered, "Let them eat cake."

Bill and Barbara had spent much of their time during our first year in Egypt in the US. While in the Middle East, they lived in a very comfortable house in Cyprus, with air conditioning and heat, which was similar to many American middle class homes. They had barbecues on their back patio as they overlooked the surrounding lemon orchards and mountains. They had a car to go wherever they wanted in addition to having ICO employees at their beck and call to give them lifts and run errands for them.

I am sure they had their share of hard times during their many years in the Middle East. However, I couldn't imagine that Bill was spending every day chasing buses, being pushed and hit, and having his shirt ripped off his back only to get home two hours later to find a mountain of other problems to be dealt with. I am sure he never had a boss who was as insane as ours.

When Bill and Barbara came over, I told them about the difficulty we were having with Chuck. He wanted to see the letter. It had been written in a very angry tone. I ended it by saying, "Hell no, we aren't going to Sana."

Bill became very disturbed, not by the content or the issues we had raised, but by my anger. The anger seemed very "un-Christian." He had hoped I hadn't sent the letter yet. When I told him I had, he was worried that Chuck might feel sad when he read it. He had no comment about our ordeal. No apologies were given, although I did hear his wife sigh in disgust at one point.

Some evangelicals are terrified to look into the eyes of the horrible dragons that inhabit the dark corners of their souls. They pretend such beasts had been immediately exterminated at the moment they embraced the Christian faith. For a distraction, some of them focus on the trivial surface issues, such as saying swear words, drinking alcohol, or being angry. It is much easier to catch the butterflies in the belfry than to slay the dragons in the dungeon. My experience in Egypt would not only bring me face to face with some of Chuck's dragons, but with some of my own as well.

As much as our hearts were bent on working in the Middle East, it was becoming obvious we needed to be delivered from Egypt . . . and quickly. Where is Moses when you really need him?

Chapter Fifteen

Disconnected

My Aunt Helen has just one haunting black and white picture of my grandfather Jones sitting in vigilance beside the simple wrought iron bed of his dying daughter. She looks like a victim of the Nazi holocaust. Her wasting away was so severe that you could see the outline of both the ulna and radius bones in her forearm as it lay across the white, crocheted bedspread. Her face was so thin that with just a slight squinting of the eyes, it appeared to be a skull. She was dying from consumption–tuberculosis to us moderners.

My grandpa was a tall slim man with dark hair and sunken dark eyes. He wore overalls and held his 1920s-era wide-brimmed hat on his lap with both hands. He was a quiet man, which I could tell from the photo because I never got the opportunity to meet him in person.

As a small boy, my father painfully watched first his mother, then his three sisters, succumb to tuberculosis. My grandfather was devoted to each one during their wearisome passage to the grave. He acted as breadwinner and nurse to each of the dying family members.

When my dad was a teenager, my grandfather suddenly died in church from a heart attack. Maybe it was a broken heart. All of these losses surely took their toll. But dad had no time to mourn as he soon enlisted in the army to go and help save Europe from the Germans.

My dad immediately went into training for the Normandy Invasion. He was always hesitant to talk about Normandy, but as a college student

I began to prod him for more details. He ended up telling me step by step what it was like to land on the beach that day. I wish he had lived to see *Saving Private Ryan*. The movie portrayed the beach landing exactly as my father had described it. It put flesh on the skeleton of the horrible images that my dad's stories had introduced to my imagination.

While Bill and Barbara were in our apartment that afternoon, I had a call from my mother in the states. She tried calling at least once a week. I interrupted my conversation with Bill to go and talk with her.

During our chat, she mentioned that my dad had stopped drinking. He had been a very good father—not perfect, but very good. Long after I left home and he retired, he began to self-medicate his painful soul with alcohol. Being a product of the late 1920s, his pain had to be buried as deeply as possible.

I had never seen my dad drink. In my entire life, he never laid a hand on me in anger. I can only remember him raising his voice a couple of times, and I certainly deserved it much more than that. Although I am sure his pain affected the way he related to others, his alcoholism had very little overt effect on my life.

When I returned to the living room, Denise said, "So how's your mom?"

"She is doing OK. She was excited because dad said he was going to stop drinking . . . again."

Bill's ears perked up. "Mike, is your dad an alcoholic?"

"Yes, he is." I really wanted to get back to our conversation about our problems with Chuck rather than talk about my dad. When Bill finished reading the letter I had written to Chuck, he was surprisingly quiet. His response was, "I don't want you to move to Cyprus in three months. Chuck is moving back in a few weeks and he has too much to deal with trying to save his medical consulting company to deal with you right now." Before Bill left, he said that someone would communicate with us about what we should do next.

For the next four weeks, we again felt like we were on the backside of the moon with no communication from Bill or Chuck. I sent a letter to Bill. I told him I would be willing to go any place at any time to meet with Chuck and him to resolve this and to reach some agreement about our future. After two more months, still silence from Cyprus. I was about ready to go off the deep end. Daniel was now as bad as he had been the previous year; huge ulcers covered his face and arms. He couldn't sleep from the itching—neither could his mom and dad.

I decided to go and visit my ex-roommate from Kentucky, Antonio, who now lived in northern Spain and worked with ICO there. I schedule a flight on Iberian Airlines. Antonio met me at the Madrid airport at six in the morning. He was a dark-skinned stocky man of my height. His hair could not be any blacker. In his familiar face, I saw the blood of the Arabs. The genetic influence of the Moors on Spain was much greater than I had imagined. It was good to finally be with a true friend.

Antonio lived four hours north of Madrid and had driven all night to get to the airport. We stayed in Madrid that day, waiting until his girlfriend, Helena, got off from work. He only got to see her once a month. He didn't want to waste this trip to Madrid. While we were waiting, we took a short nap on a park bench and then I did my Christmas shopping for Denise and the boys.

It was so much fun to be there and proved the perfect distraction. Tony and I were close and I could share my heart with him. After dinner with Helena and some other friends, we went to some bars. There you go from bar to bar, drinking a little at each and eating pig ears. It was a riot. Then we returned to Helena's unbelievably tiny apartment. I'm sure it would violate many codes in the US. It was a very small attic that had been turned into a living space. You could only stand up at the very center. So we spent the evening crawling around on our hands and knees. Then we took off for Antonio's place. It was a wonderful time. We did nothing special, simply sat around and talked. Talking to a friend was more rejuvenating and meaningful than anything I could do as a tourist.

Toward the end of my two-week stay in Spain, I called Denise. "Mike, you got a response from ICO and it was very different than what you expected. You'll have to wait to get home to read it." This got my curiosity up.

As I arrived back in Cairo, the man at customs, true to form, told me I was in violation of the law and needed yet another letter of apology. I can't remember what the problem was this time. Who knows, maybe it was because I didn't have my boxer shorts registered with the boxer short commission. I was surprised, arriving in Cairo at 3:00 a.m., to find Mohammed there to greet me. That really said a lot about the friendship of the "terrorist" family.

Denise was up waiting on me. She tried to persuade me to wait until morning to read the letter from Chuck. She was rightfully concerned about the impact it would have on my sleep. She caved to my pressure and handed it over. I felt like I was in an Alfred Hitchcock movie. The letter from Chuck began, "Bill and I have met and discussed your situation. It is clear to us that you are really angry with your father who is an alcoholic and probably has abused you. We may have to dismiss you from ICO staff because you need counseling and we are not sure if we can arrange that kind of help here in the Middle East."

I felt myself drifting into a chaotic swirl of emotion and confusion. My initial reaction was, "Could they be right? Am I just a bitter man for no reason?" When you are alone facing a situation like this, it is as if you have no reference point, no handle to grab on to by which you anchor yourself so you can make sense out of things.

My insomnia intensified. If I did doze off, Daniel's crying with his itchy sores would soon wake me. Once awakened, I would ruminate over the issues and conversations in my mind. I would have several nights of soul searching. I started to look for the dragons in my own dungeon. Was I really angry with my dad? I had no reason to be angry with him.

No, the dragon I found in my dungeon was of a different color. I began to realize that my problem was my naivete. I tended to let people walk on me, deceiving myself the entire while-that they were acting out of good intentions. My mom's version of the golden rule wasn't working. The evangelical's masquerade wasn't working either-pretending that we all love one another with big smiles on our faces. The world is a cruel place where some people only feel secure when they are controlling or hurting other people. This dragon of mine was ugly and well entrenched. As a man, a husband, father and protector, it was hard to acknowledge my weakness. My family had been hurt and they were hurt on my watch. I had to change but I knew this dragon would not go down easy.

I also knew that I couldn't continue with ICO, yet we didn't want to give up our dream of serving the medical needy in the Third World. I wrote the hospital in Abu Dhabi where Denise and I had met. They were very interested in us coming and considered us "good people." That statement meant a lot to us coming when it did. However, the problem was the rules for going to this hospital. We would be required to complete two years of Bible college in the states and one or two years of Arabic study in Jordan. That didn't appeal to us at all. We had already spent three and a half years trying to reach a point where we could start helping people.

I sent a letter to Bill and Chuck telling them that I didn't want to associate with ICO anymore. I bothered to add, "Would we be allowed to stay in Cairo for another year as ICO staff, but without any contact from ICO?" I was expecting them to make us resign and go home but Bill came through and grant our request.

It was like a breath of fresh air, being out of ICO's control. Free at last, free at last, Lord have mercy, free at last! We sent out our Egyptian address to friends and family so we could start receiving mail directly. We made the most of our remaining months in Cairo. I continued working on my Arabic, thinking that some day I would return. Life for Denise was improving as well. Shopping was becoming much easier. I also continued my work at the village of garbage. The only down side was Daniel's skin disease. It just wouldn't let up. The little guy just couldn't get a decent night's sleep.

To help deal with the stress I decided to resume my jogging program, after a two year hiatus. The block around our building measured roughly a half-mile–I reasoned that four laps would be a good start.

One morning I got up, put on my running suit and shoes and made my way down the stairs. After stretching out, I took off on my imaginary track. As I passed the bread stand, I waved and shouted "Sabbah el Hxaer" (good morning) to Mohammed, who was seated inside.

Mohammed shouted back, in his limited English, "Mr. Mike, why you run?"

Not wanting to break my stride, I ignored his question. I soon heard the door to the bread stand open and slam shut. The next thing I know Mohammed was jogging right behind me—running in his polyester pants, button-up shirt, dress shoes and with a lit cigarette dangling from the left side of his mouth. He repeated, "Mr. Mike why you run?"

My mind did a quick inventory of Mohammed's limited English vocabulary and my limited Arabic vocabulary. I explained to him in Arabic, "I am running to make me strong."

About this time, we were passing in front of the yogurt stand. Mohammed—the bread stand Mohammed—yelled to Mohammed—the yogurt stand Mohammed, "Yaullah" (meaning to come). Now there were three of us. After we took the first turn around the block, we passed the fish stand. Hisham was likewise summoned by his fellow merchants to join our running party. Hisham came out the back door of the fish stand, wearing his white apron—an apron covered in fish scales and blood—and being followed by two stray cats that stood with vigilance nearby. I heard Hisham ask bread-stand Mohammed (in Arabic), "Why is Mr. Mike running?"

"Because he is weak," came his reply.

By the time I finished the first lap, I had five men running behind me—two wearing dress slacks and shoes and three wearing gallabayas and sandals. Two of them were also smoking. Our group was starting to look like a scene from an Egyptian remake of Forrest Gump.

About this time, I noticed the families on the balconies above us. They were just sitting down to a breakfast of olive bread, fool (cooked beans) and tea. The men were putting down their newspapers to observe our strange group. I imagined them asking their wives, "Why are the street merchants chasing the American?"

"He must have done something bad, like stealing something from them."

Then the husbands add, "Hmm . . . maybe he did something even worse. Look the American is still in his pajamas."

It was not a good commentary on my running abilities, the fact that I wasn't able to lose them–in the same way I was able to out-run Betty in her spandex, at the Kentucky YMCA. I soon gave up my running program because of all the commotion I was causing.

I had been considering taking a job with Bob's (the PA who was our angel of mercy) company. We were ready to stay in Egypt. The only thing that kept me from doing so was Dan's misery.

We finished up the year strong. We enjoyed a bus trip to Israel. By late spring I wanted to make a trip to Cyprus to crate up our belongings. I hadn't heard from ICO for months and was thinking they might have had a change of heart.

When I left for Cyprus, Denise and I had just found out we were pregnant again. I decided to give Chuck one more chance. I would tell him about the pregnancy. His reaction would decide if we moved to Cyprus and stayed with ICO.

I spent the day repacking our crates and nailing them shut. I clearly recalled the day I had originally nailed the crates shut in Michigan.

That evening, when I was almost done, Chuck and his wife invited me in for a glass of wine. While I was sitting with them, we had a few minutes of superficial small talk and then I broke the news. "Denise and I are pregnant." I could see the great disappointment on Chuck's face.

He said soberly, "You are medical people, you should have known how to prevent that. If you were planning on having a bunch of kids, you should have stayed in America or found yourself a nice comfortable home in Europe but certainly not the Middle East."

I looked at him and said, "And why not?"

"The Middle East is full of wars and terrorists, not a place for children," he said.

"Chuck," I said, "the only terrorist we have come across here is . . . you. You are the one who sent us to Egypt and wouldn't allow us to have our belongings. You are the one who gives us orders saying you must live here or there with no input from us. The so-called Moslem terrorists have been extremely nice to us. They love our kids. When we told them we were pregnant, they said 'Congratulations.'"

As I returned to his garage to pound the last nail into our crates, I knew that conversation was the last nail in the coffin for our career with ICO.

When I got back to Egypt, I started looking for a PA job back in the states. After cooking in the Egyptian sun for two years, we decided we wanted to live in a cool place. I had fallen in love with Duluth, Minnesota when I went to visit Denise in nursing school. It is called the naturally air-conditioned city because the breezes off Lake Superior stave off the summer heat.

I took the AAPA directory and looked up the names of the PAs living there and wrote each of them a letter. It turned out that all of them worked for the same hospital. The hospital had a contract with a federal prison to supply outpatient care for the inmates. I thought, *Inmates! No! Never again!*

I was determined to live in Duluth and decided that if I applied for this clinic, I could find another job in Duluth after I got my foot in the door. From what I had read, the PA market was really starting to open up in the states.

Before leaving Egypt, I also spoke to Habib, person to person. Then he gave me insight into why he had been avoiding us. "You see, Mike, a few weeks before you came Chuck was in Cairo. Chuck and I got into an argument. I became very angry with him and decided that when you and Denise arrived, I was going to avoid you because you work for Chuck."

"Why did you tell Chuck that you didn't want us back in Egypt because of Daniel's illness?"

Habib said, "That is total nonsense. I haven't communicated with Chuck since before you guys came. The night I was supposed to pick him up at the train station would have been the first time I had even seen him in two years. But, as you know, he never showed up. I never told him I didn't want you back in Cairo."

By the spring of our second year, the loose ends were wrapped up and we were heading home. I purchased one last treatment for our Ascaris and Giardiasis. America had enough of both and didn't need any of our intestinal hitchhikers. We said goodbye to all our dear Egyptian friends and boarded a KLM flight for Chicago. As the sun was rising, our plane lifted off from Cairo International Airport. I looked out of the window far to the west over the desert and to the south where the huge pyramids rose like a series of small bumps. The Nile was like a long green cobra fanning out into a rich triangle until it opened into the deep blue of the Mediterranean. I felt a lump in my throat, seeing my mission fading in the dusty red horizon behind me. Denise's disappointment was soon replaced by the anticipation of being back on American soil. I was feeling the loss of a dream, a loss I feared would be a mortal wound to my immortal soul.

Chapter Sixteen

Reentry

I have read stories about Russian cosmonauts who, upon returning from long missions aboard the space station Mir, are temporarily unable to stand once back in the grip of Earth's gravity. Upon landing, they must be picked up and placed on a stretcher that is locked in the sitting position. Despite great attempts to exercise on treadmills onboard Mir, being held down by bungee cords to imitate gravity, their lower extremity muscles atrophy.

Another feature of being in micro gravity is the loss of orientation. I have heard cosmonauts and astronauts alike comment on how they become disorientated without the effects of gravity on their bodies. They have to remember, for example, "Today the top of the shuttle is facing Earth," otherwise they would have no clue and keep looking out the wrong window.

When you are socially isolated in an exotic culture, it is easy to become similarly disoriented. For us, there was a loss of moral gravity to act as a reference point. If we decided to resign from ICO were we being wimps and quitters? Was it our own fault? Were we being unfaithful to God and the people we had come to serve? We decided to put off making the final decision about our future until we were back in the grips of our own culture and friends.

Like the cosmonauts, we needed to take things slow on reentry. There is no way I can describe accurately what it is like to meet your own culture again, but as a stranger. All the things that were taken for granted as bedrock, now seemed as only the progeny of culture–culture itself seeming to be built on the shifting sands of history and circumstances.

Our first impression of America was its social ugliness, especially the gross excesses and waste. The first time Denise ventured into an American grocery store, she was overwhelmed and broke into tears; she had to leave. In Cairo, there is only one kind of soap. Cornflakes was the only kind of breakfast cereal available. Walking through an American supermarket, you feel like a child lost at a huge state fair. Everywhere bright signs flash product endorsements. The cereal aisle alone had more items than an entire store in Egypt.

We had to stick to convenience stores for a while. What made it even easier was that in southeastern Michigan, for some reason, most of the convenience stores were owned by Arabs. You could even shop using Arabic. We felt a closer kinship with them than with the Americans, at least for the first few months.

Even in Cairo, most Americans working there had other Americans to relate to, U.S. TV links, U.S. newspapers, even their own U.S. grocery store. We visited the U.S. commissary in Cairo once with American friends who, out of the kindness of their hearts, took us shopping. The purpose of the commissary was to support U.S. government staff working in Egypt. I couldn't believe what I saw. Behind four walls in Maadi it was like an American, middle-class microcosm. Egyptian bag boys were wearing white, Kroger-style aprons and pushing shopping carts out to American-made mini-vans. It was bizarre. The store carried only American goods. Even Chiquita bananas, were flown in by taxpayer dollars to Cairo, whereas Egyptian bananas sold on the street for 1/10 the price. Denise and I set our priorities. She bought a couple cases of Campbell's Cream of Mushroom Soup to help in cooking. I took two cases of Mt. Dew. These were our treasures.

Mt. Dew wasn't sold in Egypt, but I thought I kept seeing empty cans laying in the ditch down in Maadi. It was like seeing little UFOs. I would be speeding by in a taxi or train and see something green and white flash from the ditch out of the corner of my eye. We Mt. Dew addicts can spot a green and white label a mile away. When our friends showed us the commissary, I found the source of the mythological sighting–the Dew mother lode. Once back in the states, I could lay curled up in a ditch drinking Mt. Dew out of a brown paper bag all day long.

Like returning cosmonauts, our ground crew supported us; in this case, friends at our home church. The last leg of our homebound flight took us from O'Hare to Detroit Metro. As we came down the exit tunnel to the gate, we could see a crowd of wonderful people punctuated with balloons, flowers, and welcome home signs. We felt we were among friends.

To further assist with our reentry, one of the couples took us home with them. They had set up their basement as temporary living quarters for us–sort of a reentry hospital.

Once we were back on our feet, the next hurdle was figuring out our future. I had an interview with the hospital in Duluth the first week home. The following week, I was scheduled to go to the American Academy of Physician Assistants (AAPA) conference in Washington, D.C., where I would take my national re-certification exam. To remain a certified physician assistant we had to take a national board exam every six years. The exam, I thought, would prove a challenge for me. I spent my first four years in headaches, and the remaining three years in non-clinical roles, such as raising support and studying the Arabic language. My experience in the garbage village was more in the realm of public health than a real PA role. I was sure there would be no questions on the exam about the best technique for shoveling poop or how to hand-pick lice out of kid's hair when you have no drugs to treat them, and certainly no questions about conjugating Arabic verbs.

Just before I flew to Duluth for my job interview, Bryan came down with a bad case of a stomach virus. He had been up vomiting all night before my morning flight. I was somewhat distracted by my upcoming interview. I wanted to be very careful to ask the right questions. I wanted to avoid repeating my previous ordeal with the prison system.

The bliss I felt upon arriving in Duluth rivaled that felt upon first setting eyes on Zurich a year earlier. I sat at a window seat with great anticipation as the metal bird cut through the thick cloud cover over the rough landscape of the north land. The deep blue of Lake Superior and the beauty of the white birch and evergreen trees were beckoning me to stay–from the first sight.

My main goal with the interview was to talk to the staff and not just to the clinic director. I wanted to hear the truth, not the image that the employer would present. That was the great lesson I learned from my first experience with a prison clinic.

The interview went quite well. The clinic supervisor, Sandra, was a very nice woman. She reminded me of the actor Sandy Duncan, when she was in her thirties.

I took one of the Nurse Practitioners, Ann, to the local Perkins restaurant for lunch. I was very impressed with her. After small talk, I said, "OK, what's the real scoop here. Does everyone get along?"

"Oh, we all get along very well. We always pitch in to help each other out. Besides that, we are all best friends even outside of work."

"How does everyone get along with Sandra?"

"Oh, she's a doll. Bret, one of the PAs, says she is the best supervisor he has had in his ten-year career. Mike, if you are worried about working here, I can tell you that it is a great place to work." She then took a sip of her Coke and tore into her salad.

The salary offered me was slightly less than double my last PA salary three years earlier–thanks to the rapid growth in the average PA income. I left Duluth feeling very positive. If I accepted the position, I would be their sixth midlevel provider. Seven would bring them up to an ideal staffing situation. I met with a realtor and started to look at homes.

I arrived back in Michigan late at night. Early the next morning we took off for Tennessee in my recently purchased minivan. I was eager to get going since I hadn't seen my folks in over two years. My son, Tyler, had never met his grandparents.

To break up the long trip, we were planning a stop at a friend's house, the Larsons, in Bloomington, Indiana. Ken and Tina had been dear friends and mentors. They worked with ICO as well, but were a breath of fresh air. They led by example, not by control. Their genuine caring attitude was never questioned. It was going to be great seeing them again.

Soon after we were on the road and Denise was wide awake, she said, "Mike, Bryan has had the stomach flu for almost five days now. He still doesn't feel any better now than before you went to Duluth."

"Wow, that is a long time for the a gastroenteritis. I suspect it is a combination of a viral illness, jet lag, and readjustment to the states."

Just before reaching our friends' house, we moved Bryan to the front seat of the van as he had just vomited again all over his brother. I thought sitting in front would help him—believing it might just be a simple case of car sickness. He sat very quietly during the seven-hour drive through Indiana.

We pulled into the Larsons' driveway and they came out to meet us. I was talking to Ken, and walked slowly around to the passenger side to give Bryan a lift down. When I opened the van door, I looked at Bryan directly in the eyes—they were as yellow as a canary. He had hepatitis this whole time! I felt so bad arriving on our friends' doorstep with a son sick with hepatitis. I couldn't believe that as a PA I missed such a diagnosis . . . and on one of my own kids! But I had been too distracted with all the goings on in our lives.

The next day all of us, including the Larsons and their three kids, journeyed to the local health department, lined up, dropped our drawers, and bent over for gamma globin injections. What a way to bring good cheer to long lost friends!

With Bryan's illness we now faced a dilemma. Bryan would need a long recovery time. We were planning on going on to Tennessee the next morning. My parents were in their 70s. My mom was in good health but my dad's health was becoming frail. I didn't want to show up on their doorstep and expose them to hepatitis. This could be tragic for dad. Once again, it appeared we were going to be homeless.

Ken knew of a woman in French Lick, Indiana who owned a trailer park. She rented the trailers to missionary families by the week. She considered this her ministry. Ken called her, "Mrs. Hobert, hi, I have some friends who have just returned from being missionaries in Egypt and they need a place to stay. Any chance you could help them out?"

"I would be glad to help them," said Mrs. Hobert. "I have several trailers available right now." Ken never mentioned Bryan's illness. I decided to let sleeping dogs lie. I didn't want her to panic. Besides, I would keep Bryan quarantined in the trailer. When it came time for us to leave, I would disinfect everything.

When I arrived in French Lick I stopped at a gas station and asked a woman there for directions. "Ma'am, do you know the way to Mrs. Hobert's missionary trailer park?"

"I sure do. You go to the stop sign and turn left on the blacktop road. It goes right by Larry Bird's folks' house. You know Larry, the NBA star? Her trailer park is another two miles on the right."

I turned on the blacktop road and had driven only a few miles when on the left appeared a nice brick home. What made it unusual was a full-size basketball court next to the swimming pool. Two men were riding lawn tractors, one near the pool and the other one coming right at us along the edge of the road. As we got within a couple of feet when I realized that it was none other than Larry Bird himself mowing his dad's grass.

"Hey boys, see that man on the riding mower? That's the world's greatest basketball player."

The boys quietly looked out the window and then returned to their coloring books.

On our third day at the trailer park, my mom wanted to reach us to find out how Bryan was doing. The only phone in the park was at Mrs. Hobert's trailer. When my mom called, she said, "How is that little boy with the hepatitis doing?"

Mrs. Hobert pulled up in front of our trailer in her maroon Cutlass Supreme. She was a short, dark-haired woman in her fifties, who, until this point, was quite pleasant. She always spoke with a high-pitched nervous kind of voice, like Edith Bunker, but with a southern rather than a Brooklyn accent. She honked her horn and motioned for me to come down to the road. I was changing the oil in our van, and put down the tools and walked down to her car–she would barely crack her window.

Mrs. Hobert appeared to be upset. "Why didn't you tell me you had a kid with hepatitis? I rent these trailers out to other people." (There was only one other family in the park at that time and they were on the other side).

I tried to reassure her. "Mrs. Hobert, I am keeping Bryan away from everyone else. I am going to sanitize the trailer when we move out."

"Well, I think I would feel a lot better if you moved out now. I've got other families to think of here." I could tell she was mad. We didn't feel a whole lot of compassion at that time. If one of our kids had had AIDS, she probably would have wanted to burn down the whole trailer park and start over in another state.

We started packing up the van, but we didn't know where we were going. We still had the pup tent that we had taken to Switzerland and were thinking about settling down in a state park somewhere. There it would be even more difficult to keep Bryan in isolation, having to use public toilets and all.

I returned my mom's call. She was chomping at the bit to see her grandchildren. She finally persuaded me to come to Tennessee, promising to keep Bryan far away from dad. I was uneasy about it, but we went.

After becoming reacquainted with my folks we started heading to Minnesota to visit Denise's family. Once I had them settled in back on Grandpa's farm, I flew out of the Twin Cities to DC. Through all the commotion, I never had time to study for the national board exam. It didn't matter whether or not I had time because my medical books were still in our crates in Chuck's garage in Cyprus.

I sat in on as much continuing medical education (CME) as I could during the conference leading up to the exam. I wanted to keep somewhat to myself. I especially wanted to avoid those PA friends who had been receiving our newsletter from Egypt. I just could not talk about the experience yet–the wounds were still too fresh. One day, I was sitting in the hotel lobby, resting comfortably in an overstuffed chair facing a coffee table and a love seat. I was sipping my coffee and eating a pastry when a large gentleman sat on the love seat. He had long, gray hair and a Fu Manchu mustache-looking a lot like David Crosby. He was wearing jeans and an olive drab coat. He looked up and smiled as he placed his coffee on the table across from mine, using his AAPA nametag as a coaster. Beneath his name it had his city, "Jackson, Michigan." I looked up and said, "Hi, I see you are from Jackson. I am from Ann Arbor, sort of."

He spoke softly. "I've never seen you around any of our local PA meetings."

I went on to explain about living in Egypt. He was intrigued and full of questions about our experience. He went on to tell me about himself. He was a Vietnam vet and recovered alcoholic. He was refreshingly real and non-judgmental. For the first time I understood what some Vietnam vets when through when they returned home. I related, at least in part, to giving your heart and soul—and almost your life—for a cause, only to return home as a failure, rather than a hero. This kind man raised the question, "Mike, do you think you are suffering from post-traumatic stress disorder?" He seemed to speak from experience. It was food for thought. We hung out together for the following few days and I deeply appreciated his friendship. I've never seen him since.

The day of the exam came. I felt nervous and harbored severe doubts as to whether or not I could pass it. The worst case scenario passed through my mind: failing the board exam and eventually losing my certification. I imagined working in a McDonald's drive-thru window for the rest of my life, trying to support a family of five.

The 200-300 PAs were seated in the exam room and test booklets were passed out. When the time came, I broke the seal and started my endeavor in ignorance. To my surprise, it became obvious that I remembered more medicine than I had expected. I left the exam that day with a good feeling that I might have passed.

On the flight back to Minnesota, I wrote out my letter of resignation to ICO on my beat-up old Kaypro 2000 laptop. At the same time, I wrote out my letter of acceptance for the Duluth position.

Upon arriving back in Minnesota, we made a trip up to Duluth to look at houses. From the first time we started working with the realtor, Jack, it seemed that he was speaking a different language. He would say things like, "Now, Mike, if you plan on buying 'points' and securing an ARM we will need to set up an escrow and do an FRM and WXYZs." Over and over I had to ask, "What does that mean?" Prior to this point, we had never so much as taken out a loan. We paid cash for our cars. We had never even carried a balance on a credit card. It made us feel like idiots.

When the day of the closing finally came, we were presented with what seemed like a hundred legal-size pages in small-font type. Here and there were blanks for our names tagged with tiny, yellow sticky notes. The banker said, "Here, Mike, you and Denise sign all of these places." This experience greatly increased my sensitivity to patients and how our medical terminology and behavior may confuse them.

The medical terms that I use so carelessly–"etiology," "hepatic function," "sub-therapeutic," and "sub q"–may sound like Greek to them. I think those of us in medical professions would be very surprised by the low level of comprehension of what we tell patients. It's our fault, expecting patients to speak the language that we spent years familiarizing ourselves with.

I have hung out at a barbershop, pharmacy, even a family reunion and listened to what people say when they talk about their medical conditions:

"Yeah, Bert, the good doctor told me that I had a cancer sore in my mouth. I don't know if it will spread or not. He didn't say."

"Well, Clyde, my doctor told me that my blood was too high. He says that it's high because my chest is squeezing my heart so hard that it is like an ACE wrap. He put me on a pill that inhibits the ACE wrap. But I'll save money and only take it if I feel tightness in my chest."

Denise and I settled on a small, ten-acre farm west of Duluth. We made an offer and it was quickly accepted. The relator started the paperwork just before leaving Duluth, but warned us, "It might take about 30 days to close. The closing might have some problems, but I wouldn't worry about it."

I raised my eyebrows and looked carefully at him. "Like . . . what kind of problems?"

"First of all, the couple selling the house is divorcing. The husband is an alcoholic and is rarely sober enough to carry on a conversation. He lost his job and the wife couldn't take it anymore. She was selling the farm to pay off debts. She tells us that often her husband is out of circulation for days and no one knows where he is."

The banker called us a week later and began our conversation with, "Mr. Jones, I have some bad news."

"Now what?" I said.

"Mike and Denise, your credit check is blank. Haven't you ever taken out a loan before?"

"Nope," I proudly said.

"Don't you use credit cards?"

"Nope."

Well, I am afraid that you have no credit rating–it's absolutely blank! The problem is, we depend on credit ratings for setting up loans." Denise and I couldn't believe that our being frugal in our finances was working against us.

What compounded the problem was the down payment. We had literally given up our life savings to go overseas. We recently inherited stock, but even that wouldn't quite meet the requirements for a loan since we had no credit. Yet, the banker was optimistic that he could, somehow, "work things out."

As we were finishing up business in Duluth, we were again facing the problem of having no place to live. It was now mid-June and my start date at the hospital was one month away.

About this time, Paul, our friend who had given us the place to live in Petosky, contacted us from Indiana. "Hey, Mike, Susie and I were wondering if you would like to use our house in Fort Wayne this summer. We are going to Nepal on a short-term mission assignment."

"You know, Paul, again you and Susie are a godsend for us. We were just talking about having no place to live."

We drove down to Fort Wayne, and it was truly a blessing. For the first time in months, except for the two days in the trailer court, we could live as a family–alone. We were delighted.

I had sent my letter to ICO the week before and was waiting for the dung to hit the windmill. I had as yet heard nothing. Then I called the ICO accounting department to close out our account.

"Hello, this is Linda, ICO accounting, how may I help you?"

"Hi, Linda. This is Michael Jones. I don't know if you remember me, but you helped us set up our account when we first went on staff with ICO three years ago."

"Of course I remember. You were living in Egypt. Are you in the states?"

"Uh . . . yes we are. You see, Linda, we are resigning and need to close out our account."

There was a brief moment of silence. "OK, sure. Let me look up your account, and I will send you a check for the balance."

Not even two hours had passed when the phone rang, "Mike, this is Linda at ICO accounting. Well, I pulled up your account and it looks like you will need to send ICO a check for $17,000, then I can close out the account."

If I had been a denture wearer, they would have fallen out.

"What on earth are you talking about? How do I owe ICO $17,000?"

"Mr. Jones, you had that amount of ministry money unaccounted for."

I was horrified! I couldn't understand what she was talking about– at least not at first. It took a few days for things to sink in. When we raised our support the money went to ICO. They took off their 10-25% for overhead and then paid us the rest, divided between salary and ministry expenses. These numbers should have reflected the real-life situation. For example, if we spent on average $500 a month for ministry expenses, our budget should be set up so that $500 is designated as ministry, and the rest, say, $2,000, as salary. Ministry expenses included such items as books, supplies, and ICO-related travel. Chuck had set up our account. He told me that he designated 75% of our income as ministry expenses. I questioned that unusual amount, but he told me to "trust him." He said, "Mike, it really doesn't matter. While you are in the US, you have to keep receipts to prove that money was used for ministry because ICO doesn't withhold income tax on the ministry portion. However, once overseas, you don't pay U.S. income taxes anyway so it doesn't matter which portion we call ministry. When you move to Cyprus, they will tax you on the salary portion so I want to keep that amount low." It sounded a little flaky, but I trusted him, which at this point appeared to have been a very big mistake.

Linda said, "Because ICO had given you $17,000 toward ministry that wasn't accounted for by your receipts, you must now pay back that money to ICO."

I said, "I don't have $17,000. We are trying to scrape together enough money to make a down payment on a house. We just want a place to live."

Linda, with a bit of alarm in her voice, said, "Mr. Jones, you didn't spend ministry money on personal items did you?"

I felt a wave of guilt, like I was a child molester or a cheesy TV evangelist who cries and begs for money. (He gets money from people like Bertha, a little old lady who sends in $2,000. Bertha had been saving part of her social security money for five years to purchase a hip replacement. The evangelist then turns around and buys an exotic lizard skin golf bag or designer vinyl boxer shorts with the money—Bertha's money.)

I tried to tell Linda, "We just bought food and paid rent with the money. We lived well below the U.S. poverty level. Chuck had set up our salary only to be a few hundred dollars a month. Even in Egypt a family of five couldn't live on this amount. Is the issue about taxes? If so, let us pay income taxes on the amount that is unaccounted for."

The obvious thing was that we didn't need to pay income tax because we weren't U.S. residents during the time. She confirmed that the issue wasn't taxes.

"Well," I said, "what's the real issue?"

"You took the money from ICO to spend on personal effects. If you don't have the money now, then you will have to take out a loan to pay it back."

The reentry process seemed like it would never end. Our Egyptian ICO nightmare just wouldn't go away. It was like a horror movie where the vulnerable female is running from the terrible monster, keeping you on the edge of your seat. She finally reaches the house and slams the door shut and turns several dead bolts. She thinks she is safe, but she didn't see the monster slip in through the window.

When Linda implied that the money belonged to ICO, I said, "How is this ICO's money? We went out and worked our butts off for two years raising this support. It wasn't ICO sleeping in a van out in the middle of nowhere. This money was given monthly by our friends and family to support the work we were hoping to do. Part of it was our own savings. Why is this now ICO's money?"

Linda tried to explain: "Mr. Jones, donors didn't give that money to you. They gave their money to ICO. It is ICO that gives the money to you."

I thought, *Right. Ninety percent of our donors had never heard of ICO before we told them.* I said, "Just because Chuck set up our budget where most of it was designated as ministry, now we must give that money to ICO? The budget, in Chuck's eyes, was arbitrary. He could just have easily made 100% of it salary. Would ICO then owe us money for the ministry receipts that I did turn in?

"Of course not," she said.

"Now, if I were to find $17,000 in receipts, would we still owe this amount to you?"

She paused. "Uh, no, I guess not."

I spent the next week writing out receipts. These were real figures based on money that we actually spent, but it took eight hours of work per day for several days. I would write out, "Bus ticket to Arabic class 45 cents." It took a huge bag full to reach $17,000. Then I sent the hundreds of receipts to Linda. I never heard from her again.

I was expecting to hear from someone in the mission's department at ICO after we resigned. But there was just silence. Finally I called the director of overseas missions. He knew we had resigned and had already talked to Bill and Chuck about it. This director seemed unusually uncomfortable talking to me. I just had to ask: "What is your final understanding of why we resigned?"

"I think ICO didn't do a good job . . . (At this point, I was hopeful that he was about to admit their mistake and tell me he was sorry. But, I would be disappointed.) . . . in screening you. I don't think you were overseas staff material. Now, for the sake of the Kingdom of God, don't talk to anyone about your experience." The dragon roared in my dungeon. I felt so much rage that I was speechless. But life had to go on and, somehow, I had to deal with it.

The closing on our house was scheduled for July 5th. Three days later, I was to start my new job. When we drove across the long scenic bridge across the Duluth harbor, I said to the kids, "Guys, see that beautiful city on the hill? That will be our home for a very long time." The reentry process had run its course. We were ready to settle down and try to find normalcy in our lives. Little did I know how foolish that thought was. Reentry would eventually be defined in years, not months.

Chapter Seventeen

Dalooth

Somehow, I found myself at the end of a long canvas firehose, holding the brass nozzle with both gloved hands. I was in the middle of an outdoor ice arena covered in a foot of ice. Fifty feet behind me stood another fellow at a red hydrant, recessed into a tall snow bank. The guy attached a long wrench to the top of the fire hydrant and screamed, "Are you ready?"

I was starting to wonder, *Ready for what?* I didn't like the situation I found myself in. It was ten below zero. I had no winter boots. Instead, I had on about five pairs of socks inside rubber boots I bought at a yard sale. The boots weren't the Sorel brand, with lugged, soft-rubber soles, which everyone else was wearing. My boots were slick-bottom waders. Something seemed wrong with this picture, yet the other fellow seemed to know what he was doing.

I yelled back to the guy at the hydrant, with some evident hesitation, "I'm ready," while mumbling "I guess," softly to myself. He pulled on the wrench and the proximal end of the hose came to life. The section of engorgement moved rapidly toward me. I felt my feet slowly starting to slide on the ice. The water came gushing out of the brass nozzle. Suddenly I was being whipped to the left and the right. I spread my feet to create a wider base to keep me upright. It was the ride of my life. Finally a couple of other men shimmied down the hose and helped me tame the water beast before it beat me to death with the heavy nozzle.

Upon our arrival in Duluth, or as the locals say, Dalooth, we pulled into a Holiday gas station to fill up the minivan. Daniel looked over and said, "Hey dad, there's some camels." He was pointing from his booster seat to the trailer beside us. I looked over and saw two horses. At that point I realized that the boys' readjustment to American life might be more problematic than I had expected. To help them blend with the new culture, we signed Bryan up for hockey. Part of the deal was that one parent had to help coach, do drills, or make ice. Being a southern boy, I had never donned ice skates before, so I was assigned to ice making duty. To keep the rinks smooth, we had to flood them once a week. That is where the fire hose idea came into play.

I did have to put skates on once—at the end of the season when the parents played the kids. During the game, I came down the ice with my stick against the puck, doing the splits, my ankles at a strict 45-degree angle in borrowed, too-small figure skates. I had no clue about how to stop. I took five heavily padded, waist-high future NHLers with me, passing through the net and crashing against the wall. As we lay in a pile on the ice, one little boy on the bottom of the pile—his helmet pushed down over his eyes—said, "Do you know how to skate or what?" They had never witnessed an adult who didn't know his way around the ice. It was about as strange to them as a grown-up who'd never learned to talk.

When we first arrived in town, we checked into a hotel for the night before we were to move into our house. The next morning, the real estate agent called me early. "Uh, Mike, I have some bad news. We just found a major lien against the house and you won't be able to close. This lien must be settled or you could be left holding a debt for thousands of dollars. It may take a month to clear up."

I thought, now what are we going to do? We couldn't stay in a hotel forever. As a last resort I called Ann Rivers in the hospital's human resources department. "We have a problem, Ann. We have no place to live and we can't get into our house for a month and I start work on Monday."

She had no ideas but gave me a confident, "I will check into it."

The next day Mrs. Rivers called me back. "Mike, I have asked around and the only idea that we came up with is the Salvation Army Homeless Shelter. Here is their phone number." Hmm, Salvation Army Homeless shelter, I pondered. Is this the best they can do?

I started to look around town and asked strangers if they had any ideas for rentals by the week. Someone suggested the University of Minnesota at Duluth. I called them and found out that they did rent out married student housing to outsiders during the summer. Our temporary home was parked in a trailer park, but it was less per week than the hotel was per night.

We were a family of five starting all over again. We didn't have a single household item. Not a fork, not a spoon, not even a broom. We didn't own a single piece of furniture. Even our bed clothing and books were still in the crates in Chuck's garage.

Just like the wedding shower and the baby shower, someone needed to think about starting a tradition of "Just sold everything and moved to the Third World had a terrible experience and now we're back home without a material possession to our name" shower. Hallmark could jump on the bandwagon with JSEMTWTENWBHWMPTON cards. They could always shorten it to a tidy sound bite: "Returning Missionary Failure Shower."

A few people, including some of our donors, did communicate disappointment in our return. They blamed us for "Not trusting God," or "Not being able to handle culture shock," or just plain "Disobedience to God." In truth, these people were a minority. I took their comments very hard and magnified them in my mind to the point that they overshadowed any positive comments, such as one by my Michigan pastor: "I am glad you are back among people who love you."

The job started with no surprises, at least at first. The PAs and NPs were a very competent and nice group of people. The site administrator, Sandra, was perfectly pleasant and professional, as the staff had told me. This was a minimal security prison, so the inmates were a bit easier to deal with than at my previous prison job.

For the first time, I had the opportunity to work with nurse practitioners. At first I thought it would be like an interracial marriage in Georgia in the 1960s. Not that I had problems with NPs, but, I was afraid they would be hostile toward PAs and therefore difficult to work with. However, it turned out to be a very positive experience. I think PAs and NPs should be blended in every practice. We had a mutual respect. Although I prefer to avoid stereotypes, I saw how we complemented one another. The PAs, coming out of the medical model, like to do minor surgeries and orthopedic practice. The NPs, coming from a nursing model, liked doing the long-term care of diabetic and hypertensive patients. Certainly our practices did overlap in about 90% of our functions.

Soon, however, I saw a dark cloud on the horizon. One of the PAs was accepted to medical school starting that fall. I began a slight panic remembering the previous prison experience and being extremely short of staff.

I walked into Sandra's office. "You know, with Brett going to medical school, we are going to be down to five. I haven't seen any candidates coming through the door. That concerns me."

"Oh, Mike, don't worry about it. I'm on top of things," she said with her perpetual smile. "We are thinking about sweetening our package to get more recruits. If we don't have an applicant within a month or two, we will hire a headhunter"

Over the next few weeks I still didn't see any candidates pass through, but something interesting did happen.

One Monday morning Sandra called a meeting. As soon as we were through our morning chores, we assembled in the large office that the clinicians used. It was a long room with eight gray metal desks neatly lined up in pairs. The prison had–in a previous life–been an Air Force base. The layout and furnishings were remnants of those days. We each took a seat at our own desk as Sandra pulled in a large wooden chair on wheels from her own office. She had a larger smile than usual on her face. It was like she was going to tell us she was getting married. With a bright glow and a chipper voice she announced, "I have some exciting news. I have just accepted a position as an area administrator down at the hospital." Several quickly responded with, "Congratulations!" Selfishly, I couldn't smile, fearing what may lie ahead.

The hospital made a move that didn't help matters. In Sandra's place, they promoted one of the NPs, Jeff, to the clinic's administrator position. I thought that was a serious mistake, a real shortsighted act. Sure, Jeff would make a good administrator, but an office administrator (non-clinical) would have been much easier to recruit from the outside than trying to fill a clinician's shoes. We were now down to four medical care providers. Work was starting to become much more difficult.

Soon after Jeff took his new position, he called me into his office one day. "Mike, I just wanted to tell you that Mary (another NP) has decided to take a part-time position nearer her home. Therefore she is going part-time here. I know that you have been concerned about staff shortages, so I will make recruitment my highest priority. Having been a practitioner here, I know how difficult things can be when we are short staffed."

Work was quickly becoming very interesting. It was beginning to resemble my first prison experience in Michigan. The chain of jailer keys and a noisy radio hung from our belts. We had no axillary staff, except for three inmate orderlies.

The X-ray machine was from the last century. In the beginning, I often had to repeat the X-rays once or twice because I didn't have the settings right. I took some chest X-rays that probably cured the patient's cancer by sheer virtue of the radiation emitted. The film would be almost completely black with a shadow of one vertebra peeking through.

I approached Jeff. "If we can't hire another midlevel at this time, then why don't we hire a pharmacy tech or a nursing assistant or a med tech–someone to take the load off."

My request was met with a blank stare. "We can't do that, Mike. According to the contract, we can't hire anyone except PAs or NPs."

"Well, change the contract!"

"We can't."

Those were words that I have grown to hate: "I can't." Sometimes, I believe rules are the sticks that people use to build their houses when they have no imagination or creativity bricks.

I was reminded of this a few years later when I was sea kayaking with a kayak club on Lake Superior. It was a windy day with 3–to 5-

foot waves. We were doing a crossing from Munsing to Grand Island and were going to circumnavigate the island. We took off directly into the wind. I was paddling my old yellow Eddyline Sea Star kayak. I was going up the sides of the waves and then crashing down on the other side. When I would come crashing down, the front of my 21-foot kayak would completely submerge and water would come up to my spray skirt. I was having a marvelous time! Suddenly, from the side, I saw a woman racing at me from about 50 yards downwind. She looked frantic, like there was a tsunami coming. She came up beside me and shouted, "Don't do that! That is called porpoise-ing and it wastes kinetic energy!"

Give me a break! I thought. This poor woman had been to one kayak class too many. Now do we need kayaking police to enforce the kayaking rules?

The season of Christmas was quickly upon us. The prison was having its annual Christmas party at the officer's clubhouse just outside the front gate. Our clinic inmate-orderlies, because of their excellent work record, were granted the job of parking cars. That night, all three orderlies got busted breaking into the cars they were parking. They were stealing information out of the glove compartments, such as names and addresses, so they could use them in a credit card scam, which they were running from inside the prison. Next thing I knew, the clinic was losing their orderlies to the trivial, non-patient contact duties such as making coffee, sweeping floors, and unloading supplies.

At the party I heard two other horrible bits of news from Jeff. I went over to his table and took a seat to visit for a minute. He seemed especially distracted for someone at a Christmas party. "Uh Mike, Nathan (the other PA) told me today that he was taking a long leave of absence to go on a National Guard assignment in Norway." He paused to take another sip of his beer. "Also, Tammy (the other NP) is pregnant and she told me today she was taking a year leave to have the baby. She will return when the baby is old enough for daycare." Then he looked at me and said, "Now Mike, don't worry. I know that this means that you will be our only provider, but things will work out. Trust me."

I just stared at Jeff with glossed-over eyes across the table of half-empty beer mugs. He quietly sipped his beer and turned away from me to watch the rockabilly band across the room play "Jingle Bells." I was quickly losing my Christmas spirit. I couldn't believe it: my worst fears were coming true . . . again. The clinic had enjoyed three stable years of bliss. Then, as soon as I was on board, it became like rats diving off a sinking ship. A clinic requiring seven providers would soon be down to one: ME! The contract also required 24-hour coverage, seven days a week. Now, what exactly is the rationale for not worrying?

Work became terrible once I was alone. I would arrive at 6:30 in the morning to open sick call and run the pill line for unit dose medications. One PA's capacity during the morning clinic, with all the other responsibilities, was a maximum of twelve patients. As I signed inmates up for appointments, I would soon fill up all the slots and then start double booking, triple booking and quadruple booking. It was insane. There was no way I could care for the needs of this many patients plus do all the other chores.

This is where the word "can't" came in again. I approached Jeff, saying, "Well, we are still underpricing PAs and NPs because we haven't had a single inquiry regarding the position and we have been running ads for a year."

"But Mike," he said, "we are already offering near our salary cap."

"Then increase the damn cap!"

"We can't raise the cap," he said.

"And why not? It can't be that you don't have the money. The clinic was budgeted for seven or eight clinicians and now there's only one. This money has to be somewhere, Jeff. If the clinic was budgeted for $35,000 per year for seven providers, that would be a budget of $245,000 per year. Since I am alone, either pay me this amount and I will stop complaining, or offer $75,000 a year for three more providers and none of us will complain." Jeff looked at me as if I was speaking an ancient, lost language. It made perfect sense to me.

Inmates aren't known for being the world's most gracious and understanding clients. They were becoming very angry that I couldn't meet their needs–and they were right: I couldn't. I had tremendous pressure to cut corners in the quality of care I was giving.

One morning, during a very busy sick call, an older gentleman came in complaining that he had fallen on the ice. He walked in with a slight limp and was complaining of ankle pain. Normally I would have X-rayed his ankle. However, an X-ray would mean 45 minutes to warm up the machine, take the films, then develop and read them. The lobby was full of angry inmates wanting to be seen. I examined this man's ankle carefully. It was sore–clearly sprained–but I had seen worse. Under the pressure, I made a decision not to X-ray. Three days later the man returned to the clinic still in pain. That time I did X-ray it and found him to have a fracture that required surgery and pinning. He had been walking on it the whole time. I felt terrible. I knew I was being forced to practice a quality of medicine that was below my personal standards and I hated that situation.

The other pressure was I couldn't get away from work. I had to be on call every night and every weekend. The hospital persuaded a few of their nurse supervisors to come to the clinic to do evening pill lines so that was helpful. During the night we had no one actually at the clinic although the contract required 24-hour coverage. I guess my beeper met that requirement. Several times I had calls from the guards in the middle of the night saying, "We've got a man down."

"Now, please tell me, what does that mean?" I would ask.

"We have an inmate lying on the ground?"

"Why? Can you give me a little more information? Is he facing Mecca and praying?"

"Don't know. Might be his heart."

"Does he have a pulse?"

"Don't know."

Even though all the guards had been through CPR, in these situations they would often panic and run for the phone and page me. I lived close, but it was still 3-4 miles a way. I would say to them, "If they don't have a pulse, call 911 and start CPR. The ambulance can get there before I can!"

"We aren't authorized to call 911 until you see them first. That is the RULE."

Fortunately, none of them arrested during this time. It was usually a seizure or simple fainting.

Once I was called in at 1:00 a.m. and given the assignment of breaking the news to an inmate that his wife, who was just 28 years old, had been killed in a car accident on the way to visit him. She dodged a deer and hit a tree doing sixty. I'm not sure why breaking this news was considered to be a medical problem. A compassionate guard or warden could have done just as well. I ended up sitting in the dark clinic, holding the inmate's calloused, tattooed hand while he cried his heart out for the rest of the night. I took him over to sit with the chaplain when it was time for me to start the morning pill line. With no sleep, I was facing an overwhelming day.

On top of having a lousy job, I was experiencing a clinical depression of my own. I had experienced periods of melancholy—which I consider natural—several times in my life, but never severe. I knew, after that terrible night with Chuck in the Chinese restaurant in Cairo, that I was struggling emotionally. At first I had an opium to deaden some of the pain in my soul: it was the anticipation of coming home.

For the first few months, the business of trying to get settled and the thrill of living in Duluth kept me afloat. However, after the newness of Duluth began to wear off, the pain began to work its way up through my being like sap in a maple on an early spring day.

It was difficult to know exactly when melancholy gave way to clinical depression. It was gradual. It was like sinking in an abyss, a cold black abyss, slowly, like a penny sinking in an urn of honey. Steadily I was going down until one day I noticed the lighted rim of the abyss becoming more distant above me. I could see Denise leaning over the side and grasping for me with all her might, yet her hand was now far out of reach. Echoing in the distance, I could hear her cry, "Mike, are you OK?"

I have heard that Eskimos have ten different words for snow. I think the English language has far too few words to describe the feelings that one experiences upon entering a major depression. Clinical depression is to sadness as melanoma is to a freckle. The two are disjointed, and don't simply reside on two different points on a continuous scale.

In the middle of the abyss was a vortex of my own pain. I couldn't resist its pull. I became consumed with my own pain in a very selfish way. It is like the dog I sewed up at Denise's house in Abu Dhabi. I thought I had done a swell job putting his abdomen back together. Later the dog became obsessed with his own wound. He licked it day after day until he had pulled all the sutures out. That is why they make those huge cones that go around dogs' necks. With clinical depression they should fashion a cone that goes around your neck to keep you from becoming obsessed with your own emotional wounds.

The purpose of my life had been wrapped up in us going to the Third World and spending the rest of our lives there. Now that dream was in an ash heap and, ICO at least, saw me as a failure.

I had rage at Chuck, at ICO, and at God himself—that is, if He was really there after all. I was drifting in space with no purpose, just earning money to buy food and shelter for a pregnant wife and three kids. I felt like the same need could've been met by my life insurance policy if I were gone.

I have heard when someone wins the lottery, they have long-lost friends coming out of the woodwork. People will just call up and say, "Hey Buddy, remember me? We went to school together. I have been a little down on my luck and I was wondering . . ." When you lose your soul, the opposite seems to happen. The phone sits dead. No calls, no letters, as if the world has ended, leaving you alone. This is partly real because I think people feel awkward around someone in depression. Most of us want to hang around happy people. The rest is just the perception of the depressed person's mind. You *really* want someone to call. Not that they would have any answers, but to stand in contradiction to a world that seems to be shouting, "I don't give a damn."

I didn't know where to put the poison of my anger. I needed a lead-lined safe to put it in, as if it were kryptonite . . . and it was wasting away my bones and taking away my strength. Wise people have said, "No one is bad enough to ruin my life by making me hate them."

I used to enjoy going for long walks at night and praying as I walked. In Duluth, I took a long walk in our fields and looked up at the heavens. Were they really empty? Was God a myth?

As a believer in God, the contemplation of the vastness of the heavens was wonderfully reassuring. A God that powerful and big is there and considers me of value, as His created likeness. When He isn't there, this contemplation brings the opposite effect. The billions and billions of stars (as the late Carl Sagan would put it) gave me a great sense of insignificance. A pile of molecules arranged by accident into this carbon-based machine, having no more value than a rock, a pile of dirt, or even a dog pile for that matter. It was just like in Monty Python's *The Meaning of Life*, where the man sings the "Universe Song." The tune gives you the same feeling that I had: insignificance, and with a small "i."

During those days, I remember walking and looking up with tears in my eyes, screaming, "Where the hell are you, God!" There was just the awful silence.

As a PA, I had always thought that depression was a treatable disease. On the other side of depression, looking back, the problem didn't seem like a mood disorder, but a disorder of the world or life itself, and that isn't treatable. All the medications in a psychiatry ward's cupboards couldn't fix the screwed-up world around me. No pill could give me back the opportunity to serve overseas under a good leader instead of Chuck. No mode of therapy could restore my reputation. Nothing couldn't erase this terrible experience. At least that is what I thought.

Depression becomes self-perpetuating. When there's no desire for life anymore, there's no desire to get better. It is like the start of a black hole. Once a critical mass—or, in the case of a black hole, a critical density—is reached, it can't be reversed. The point of no return near a black hole is called the Event Horizon. It seemed everything in my life was inside this boundary.

Although I didn't know where I was heading spiritually, I didn't want to make the decision for my wife and kids, so I agreed to take them to church. We visited church after church. It looked totally different than ever before—with neatly dressed people carrying neatly strung smiles and giving neat little answers. It seemed so superficial. I had decided in my heart to seek the truth and to be real, no matter how much pressure they would put on me to fake it. With each church, the same conversation would ensue.

"Did you just move here?"

"Yes."

"Where did you move from?"

"Egypt."

"Egypt? Were you with the military?"

"No, we were missionaries."

"Missionaries, well praise God. That must have been a blessing."

"It was hell."

Then would follow a long, very long silence, and a change of tone. "God is always faithful. If you had a bad experience, you must not have trusted Him."

It seemed curious to me that people living in comfortable, middle class homes could diagnose our problem so quickly, "We had not trusted God."

Just prior to leaving for Egypt, the U.S. had bombed Libya. The State Department had posted warnings about travel to the Middle East. These weren't abstract concerns for me. Tom, my Cypriot beer-drinking buddy, almost lost his life a few years earlier when the TWA plane he was on was bombed over Athens. Three people were sucked out of the plane at 25,000 feet after the bomb blew a hole in the fuselage. Tom missed his demise by four rows. Before leaving for Egypt, I had to come to terms that our mission endeavors could cost us—or even worse—our children's life. I had to trust God that we were doing the right thing.

If the church people didn't give that diagnosis, they would simply walk away and start talking to someone else, someone who would make them feel more comfortable. What made this most painful was knowing that this was the same way that I had related to people prior to going to Egypt.

We did visit one church where I found a very different reaction. In the vestibule a man named Dave Peterson, a newspaper man, started the same conversation, however he had a different twist. When I said, "It was hell," I could see the honest concern in his face. He said, in a very genuine way, "I want to hear all about it. Can we go out to eat this week? Do you mind if I bring the pastor?"

Later that week, I hesitantly met with Dave and Gary, the pastor, at a Hardees. They wanted to hear the whole story and never flinched when I was brutally honest. They weren't afraid of my anger as Bill had been. In the midst of the telling, I looked up and saw a tear forming in the corner of Dave's eye. This caught me off guard and the dam burst in my own eyes. I knew beyond a shadow of a doubt that these two men really did care. That is all we wanted, someone to listen to us— someone who honestly cared. We didn't want great advice, instructions, orders, or condemnations. We didn't want assignments such as read this book or watch that video. We certainly didn't want simplistic clichés or one simple Bible verse. This might have been the point that the momentum of falling in the abyss began to slow down.

I reached rock bottom during that winter of my discontent. The terrible stress of work may have made things worse or may have been a good distraction. I will never know. It was during this time I started seriously considered taking my own life.

My serious contemplation of suicide lasted for about two months. Two images kept me from doing it. One was my mother's face. I knew that she loved me dearly and such an act would rob her of all the life that lay ahead of her. I could do it to myself, but I couldn't do it to her. It takes an incredible amount of selfishness to take your own life. The second image was of my wife. She too loved me very much. She wanted to help me with all her heart, but I was far out of her reach by this time. I falsely believed that my kids would recover quickly from losing me.

It is hard to know what turned the corner on the depression. I did notice that when I focused on others, the slide would halt and start to lift. For example, if one of the boys had a problem, I could spend an hour or two focusing on his sadness and helping him solve his problem, and it would provide a brief reprieve from my own pain. There certainly were moments of true joy, especially the birth of my daughter Amy. I also tried to force myself to go outside and start to enjoy nature again, which I used to love.

As my depression began to lift, I started on a personal crusade to find the true meaning of life. I was fed up with the Christianity that I had known, but didn't want to throw the baby out with the bath water. The late theologian, Dr. Francis Schaeffer, had started an organization called LA'bri, whose motto was, "Honest answers for honest questions." It was the antithesis of a cult. The organization had no authority structure that I observed, and questioning and healthy doubts were encouraged. I began to devour books and listen to lectures about philosophy and history, searching for the truth. I read *The Complete Works of Francis Schaeffer*. I couldn't escape the notion that brought me to God in the first place, the haunting knowledge of self-awareness. Inside, I am a person and I cannot escape that. Some would call this consciousness. It is far more than just a very intricate network of memories and logic neurons. No computer could ever obtain this.

As an atheist, I realized that I–the person–am merely software loaded on a carbon-based motherboard called the brain. That's all–but worse than that–I'm not even software. Real software reflects the ingenuity and creativity of the programer in the same way that a canvas reflects the soul of the artist. But, without God, I–the person am software without a programer, just a sum of billions of accidents–freaks of nature if you will. To somehow put value or meaning on my life (within this framework) would have taken an existential leap that I just couldn't make. I knew on the inside that I am a person and couldn't be the artifact of an impersonal universe. My journey eventually would lead me back to God and to the historical Jesus–the Jesus who left footprints on Galilee's beach–who left wood shavings that are now soil near the site of his father's carpenter's shop, but forever away from the Jesus created by some American evangelicals

As a footnote, we did see reconciliation with ICO five years later. I made a trip to their headquarters, where I presented our case to their leadership, including Bill. Chuck had been fired two years earlier due to financial "indiscretions" committed by him. After I presented my case, the ICO mission director looked honestly at us and said, "Mike and Denise, we are very sorry for what happened. Would you please forgive us?" We did. At that point, we sensed a long needed closure to the whole Egyptian ordeal.

During my time of depression, Denise was able to do much better than me. For her, ICO wasn't her family. She hadn't spent years around them as I had. She also didn't have a deep conviction about working overseas. Her adjustment back to the states would have been uneventful if it hadn't been for my depression. My whirlpool was attempting to suck her in as well. She wanted her husband back, but there wasn't much she could do. I felt negative about everything and was constantly irritable. She was able to cope through the friendships she developed with several other women.

The kids did remarkably well. Bryan entered public school for the first time. He and Daniel loved their newfound space. They had forts in the woods, in the swamps, in the barn, and in the rock piles.

I hated the thought of starting to look for another job after just one year, but the prison position didn't pay enough for the misery it brought me. This feeling was confirmed when a temporary PA was recruited. He was a well-seasoned PA who worked as an independent contractor. He was hired to come in and help me for six months. He lasted a little over a week. He said it was the worst job he had ever worked at, and then he resigned.

I sent letters of introduction to every family practice and neurologist in town. Only one practice would talk to me. A physician told me on the phone, "Mr. Jones, we are all overworked and our appointment openings are out about a month. I believe the practice could support two or three more full-time providers. Why don't you come over for a lunch interview with the other four physicians?"

The day of my interview came. I put on a new suit and practiced the interview in my head. This would be my one chance of staying in the beautiful city they call Dalooth. The office sat on a hill overlooking the city and the deep blue waters of Lake Superior. I waited for the physicians in their downstairs break room. Finally the physician I had spoken to on the phone made an appearance. "Hi, Mike. I am sorry I kept you waiting, but we have a problem. When I told one of my partners that you were coming for a visit, she became quite upset and said she wouldn't attend the interview. As a matter of fact, she said, 'If a position is offered to a PA, I will immediately resign. I will not work in the same practice as a midlevel clinician.' Mr. Jones, as much as I would like to offer you a position, my hands are now tied so an interview would be a mute point."

About this time, I felt like an African-American trying to join a private, white men's club in Birmingham in the 1960s (or maybe even the '90s). My rejection had nothing to do with reality or nothing to do with my abilities. I could have been the greatest family practice provider in the history of the world and it wouldn't have changed her attitude. Her opinion wasn't based on my performance, but my title. As bad as that experience was, it was the only door that was even cracked open.

I made the reluctant decision to begin looking for a position outside of Duluth. I called a headhunter named Barb and told her what I was looking for.

One day Barb called, "Mike, are you sitting down?"

"Uh . . . yes."

"I am going to tell you about the world's most perfect PA job. Can you imagine running your own clinic in a beautiful area of Wisconsin?"

Denise and I eventually went for an interview for the position. The first strange thing that happened was that the hospital administrator, Mr. Dawson, canceled our hotel room and decided to save money by putting us up on his pull-out couch in his basement. That couldn't be a good sign.

The next weird thing was my visit to the hospital. Mr. Dawson started to explain: "We are looking for a PA to operate a rural clinic in a town about 15 miles away." As we toured the hospital, he started telling me, "The outpatient clinic administrator, Joe, is a real jerk, but he will be the one that pays your salary. Joe's physicians will be your supervisors so your salary will have to come out of his budget."

Mr. Dawson took me on a drive to the house that had been turned into a clinic. At the time it was being rented out to a dentist. When we pulled up in front of the frame house, a balding man in a blue smock came out the door and began screaming at Mr. Dawson. "When the hell are you going to fix my roof! You have been promising this for three months and I am fed up with you bunch of assholes."

Mr. Dawson spoke to him in a somewhat calmer tone, with some obvious embarrassment. "Well, I am looking into it. We hope to have a contractor come out and look at it this week."

"Right. That is what you have been promising me for months. I'm not paying you another penny of rent until this is done. Our contract said you would keep the place in good repair. Now, every time it rains we have buckets everywhere. This is no way to run a dental practice."

For some reason, Mr. Dawson lost his enthusiasm for showing me around the clinic. "Well, we really don't need to look inside because we will be remodeling before you start." Then he smiled.

I thought, *Likely story*. About this time, I was starting to get, as you would say in the '60s, some really bad vibes about this place. Yet the icing on the cake was still to come.

When I got back to the hospital, Mr. Dawson let me get away to have lunch with Denise, who was being entertained, in more ways than one, by Mr. Dawson's apparently emotionally unstable wife. When I arrived back he turned me over to Joe, the clinic administrator. The clinic was attached to the hospital and was a short walk from Mr. Dawson's office.

As soon as Joe started showing me around he began bad-mouthing Mr. Dawson: "That Mr. Dawson is an idiot. He doesn't know one thing about running a hospital. He got the position because his uncle was chairman of the board." Later he added, "Mr. Dawson is the one hiring you, we aren't. He thinks there is money to be made in that run-down house he calls a clinic. Our doctors will be supervising you, but the hospital will be paying your salary, NOT us."

By this time, I had formed just one question: "Which road leads out of town?" This so-called perfect PA job was proving to be one wasted trip.

I asked Denise where would she live if she had a choice. We both agreed that if we had to move from Duluth, La Salle, Michigan would be our first choice. So I directed my efforts toward finding a position there.

I wrote letters to every PA in La Salle but couldn't establish a positive lead. About this time I was attending a regional CME conference.

As I was walking through the display room, sipping coffee, the Air Force recruiter started talking with me. I was a little naive to realize I was the fly caught in his web. He asked me, "Where do you work?"

"I work in Duluth, but I am looking for a position in La Salle."

A soft smile came on his face and he said, almost in a whisper, "I can get you to La Salle."

Apparently I was too dumb to figure it out, so I asked, "What do you mean?"

He went on to explain, "If you come into the Air Force, I could guarantee you an assignment to the Air Force base near La Salle."

"Air Force? You want me to go into the Air Force? I am almost 35 years old!"

"How close are you to 35?"

"I will be 35 in four months."

"Yep, we can make it."

I had never given the military a moment's thought since receiving my draft notice at age 18. Soon after I received it, the draft was abolished. I never imagined myself in a uniform. However, the more I thought about it, the more appealing the idea became. For one, Denise and I still loved living overseas. The Air Force would be one door to overseas living that we could use down the road.

Second, we had friends in the Air Force and they seemed to really enjoy it. The drawback was that it would take a lot of trust. The recruiter had said, "You'll have to trust me on this one, Mike." This was regarding my assignment to La Salle as well as being made captain my second day on duty. The recruiter told me, "Mike, you will go in as a captain." When I got my papers they referred to me as "Lt. Jones." Now, this made me nervous, but the recruiter said, "Mike, just trust me." After my experience with Chuck, I wasn't so sure I could trust anyone again.

"You see," he said, "the Air Force is only allowed to bring in so many captains per year. In order not to violate this quota, you will come in as a lieutenant for only one day. The next day you will be automatically promoted to captain." Knowing how the government tended to work, it did have a ring of truth to it.

Denise and I thought and prayed about it for a few weeks. We took our annual trip down to visit my mom and dad and we reached our decision while we were in Tennessee. I had a deadline to make before I turned 35. I remember my mother arguing with me, as a worried mother would, "I am so afraid you will go to war. After your brother served in Vietnam, I just knew you would never have to fight."

I thought mom was out of her mind and tried to reassure her: "Mom, give me a break! You are worried for nothing. With the fall of communism, the threat of war is the lowest it has been in the history of America."

On Friday, I signed the papers and sent them in via Federal Express. On Monday, I awakened to the news: Iraq had invaded Kuwait and the U.S. military was on alert. I called my recruiter to inform him that I had signed on the dotted line. I could sense concern in his voice. "I don't want to alarm you, Mike, however, I need to know exactly where I can reach you until you return to Duluth. The military is on a state of alert and there is a chance you could be deployed directly overseas."

We had experienced a peacetime military for 20 years. The day after I signed up, on top of assuring my dear mom how safe it was, we go to war! With my luck Saddam intentionally had waited until I had signed the stupid forms before giving the orders to invade Kuwait. It was really all my fault! OK, maybe this was getting a little paranoid. After the bad experiences in Egypt, then Duluth, now this, I was starting to have the feeling a dark cloud was hanging over my life. I had the anti-Midas touch. Everything I touched turned to crap.

The next problem was I still had another week with mom, the same dear person I so arrogantly had persuaded the previous week that going into the military carried no risk. She watched CNN all day, turning our living room into the war room.

I made it back to Duluth without hearing from the recruiter. I dropped by his office for my swearing in. I still have the photo of me standing there, weaning my jeans and hair down to my collar. Life would never be the same. We were going to find out in a hurry if I had made the next biggest mistake of my life. Regardless of the outcome, Dalooth, our new "permanent home," was, unfortunately, going to be just another milestone in our lives.

Chapter Eighteen

Shangri-La Found?

Early one Thursday morning in August, Jack the Re-Max guy pounded a for-sale sign in our yard down by the road. Within minutes, a white SUV drove by. It was the prison warden, Mr. Wolf, behind the wheel. As soon as he got to the office, he marched down to see Jeff. "Hey, Jeff. Doesn't PA Jones live in that yellow farm house on Arrowhead Road?"

"Yes he does."

"Well, I just saw a for-sale in his yard. Surely you aren't losing him, too?"

Jeff mumbled a little and said, "Well, maybe."

With that the warden marched back down to his office and in no happy mood. The grossly understaffed medical department was one of his biggest frustrations. Unfortunately, this was the beginning of the end of the hospital's contract with the prison.

As I left, resigning my position, I felt like the last American out of Nam. I could see Saigon burning behind me. Actually it was the prison system revoking the contract with the hospital because they weren't living up to their end of the deal by supplying appropriate staffing. Again I sensed the sheer waste. This could have been prevented by even modest foresight.

It took three long months to finally close on our little yellow farmhouse. The realtor told us that because of the liens it was the most difficult closing in his twenty years. Now, before even a year was up, we were putting it back on the market again.

The problems with the house hadn't ended with the closing. The previous owner, in a desperate attempt to raise cash, had done some shady things. For one, he had turned the back two acres into a sprawling refrigerator landfill. I would have to get rid of the junk before putting it on the market. I hired a man to haul the refrigerators away. He showed up in a beat-up old truck. He was quite heavy and had a cigarette hanging from his mouth. His wife was 8-1/2 months pregnant. Somehow, the two of them managed to remove it all. I don't know how they did it. I tried to lift one refrigerator and couldn't do it. Besides their empty weight, the soggy insulation in the doors and walls made them much heavier than normal. I considered leaving a crash cart and an emergency c-section tray with Denise before I went to work.

As a homeowner of an older house, I came face to face with the money-pit syndrome. I had my paycheck direct deposited . . . to Menards (building supply). We became regular godparents to their delivery man's children.

Our first remodeling job was to bring it back from the early '70s decor. The main living room and dinning room had shag orange carpet. The kitchen had all orange cabinets. The rest of the rooms had plaid orange and black carpet. The best way to describe it? Groovy!

The other problem was that the previous owner had four Siamese cats that she dearly loved. During our first tour of the house, you could smell the very strong scent of air freshener. This was a bad sign, someone owning cats and using air freshener by the gallon.

Once we had moved in, the stench of cat urine became horrible. We ripped up the carpet in the vain hope of solving the problem. The solid oak floors beneath the carpet were soggy black in the corners. After sanding about an inch of wood off and putting gallons of polyurethane on the floor, you could still do a precise urinalysis on each of the cats purely through your sense of smell. (One of them had a little protein in its urine.)

The house was sided with dreary, faded yellow aluminum siding. I think the name of the factory color was Tobacco Tar Teeth Yellow. The trim was a flat brown, named Burnt Dog-Turd Brown.

I decided to paint the trim in a more '80s spirit: Country Blue. I avoided the '90s color–Forest Green–because every house on our street already had Forest Green somewhere. When I placed my ladder against the side of the house, the siding buckled. I climbed up the ladder to check things out. I peeked between the siding and the soffit to find the real reason someone had installed siding in the '70s: the original walls were gone. They had simply rotted away. The aluminum siding was like one of those cicada hulls you find in the summer stuck on bushes or trees. The bug long gone, but his skin still present.

I replaced the rotten porch with a pressure-treated deck, one that would never rot. I can just see, in the year 3000 AD, archeologist return to earth to dig up the thousand-year-old ruins of American suburbs. The houses would all have rotted away, leaving only green and brown pressure-treated decks, in pristine shape, randomly scattered across the countryside. The anthropologists would then conclude, the Americans of that era all lived outside on wooden decks and porches, spaced, for some strange reason, about 30 feet apart.

The remodeling was done, and the house quickly sold. Soon the movers were scheduled and I flew off to MEMSO–the medical officers training and indoctrination program.

The cultural adjustments of going into the Air Force were more severe than those of entering Egyptian society. I felt like Hawkeye Pierce in the military realm. Once my hair was cut and I was fitted for double-knit polyester uniform and a bus driver's hat, I had the feeling my soul had been transported into someone else's body. Next my moustache was trimmed on both ends. It was a challenge trying to suddenly adapt to being inside the body of a trans-mutation between Jackie Gleason and Hitler.

It seemed like yesterday we had crossed the bridge coming into "Dalooth." Now we were crossing that same bridge–Blatnik Bridge– heading east, our dream of having a small sheep farm never realized. The beautiful city on the hill was gently fading behind us–beneath the morning mist coming off the greatest of lakes.

Our first night in La Salle was like a homecoming. We had permission to stay at the same cabin we stayed in before going to Egypt. This time we drove through the woods right up to the door of the cabin, rather than wading through snow. The little house sat in the midst of a forest of pine and birch trees. It had exterior walls of white shingles with bright red trim and a screened porch facing the small lake. The interior looked more like a cabin, with tongue-and-groove knotty pine in each room. In that part of world, houses in the woods or on a lake are called "camps," not cabins. We were going to stay at this camp until we could move into a house all our own.

A month earlier Denise and I had found a house on five acres. It was a traditional white two-story farmhouse with a small red barn. It sat on the top of a large hill about six miles south of La Salle. From the upstairs window, you could see the bright blue waters of Lake Superior to the north. To the south and east were forests of birch, aspen, and evergreens sloping off to distant mountains. It felt like home our first day there.

Bryan and Daniel remembered the cabin with the cold kitchen well, especially the frosty toilet seat. However, here in early September, the cabin was very comfortable. A fireplace took the chill out of the night air. Paddling a canoe across the lake during the evenings was spectacular.

The first night in the cabin did come with an abrupt surprise. At about two in the morning, bright lights suddenly shone in every window. This was especially strange because the cabin was set deeply in the woods, with the next cabin half a mile away. I felt like I was having a *Close Encounters of the Third Kind* experience. I couldn't see a thing. I jumped up looking for my pants, but it was impossible with the blinding light in the unfamiliar bedroom.

A voice from a loud speaker said, "Please come out of the house. Come out of the house now!" Someone started knocking on the back door rather aggressively. I still couldn't find my pants in the blinding light. I don't know what made me think that aliens would want me to have pants on. After all, they could do their famous experiments on me much easier if I came out in the buff.

Finally I found a pair of jeans on the floor and slipped them on. From the way they fit, I knew they were Denise's. I unlocked the back door and there stood what appeared to be the silhouette of a policeman. I couldn't see well because he was holding one of those 36" heavy duty black Mag Lite flashlights, shining it right in my face. The ones they use to beat you in the head if you piss them off. He said, "You're being arrested for unauthorized entry into this cabin."

"What? No, we DO have permission to be here."

"Who gave you this permission?"

"The owners."

"The owners just called and said you didn't have the authority to enter."

"The owners live in South Dakota and they did give us their permission. You can call them."

Then he said, "What's your name?"

Still holding my arm up to shield my eyes from the bright light, I said, "Uh . . . Mike Jones."

"What are you doing here?"

"I start active duty at the Air Force Base tomorrow."

"So you are in the Air Force. What is your rank and who is your commander."

"I am a lieutenant," I said before looking at my watch, and saw that it was past midnight. "Er, I mean I am a captain and I can't remember my commander's name (I never was a stickler for details). I am a PA and I'll be working in the hospital." Some people aren't very good liars. I'm not a very good truth teller.

The cop looked me up and down. There I stood with my skin-tight Chic jeans unbuttoned at the top and unzipped so they would fit. Now I looked like a cross between Hitler and Cindy Crawford. Judging from his facial expression, I imagined him thinking, *So this guy is an Air Force captain?* Then he said, "Do you have ID?"

"Yes, just a minute." I ran back into the bedroom, where Denise was now sitting on the edge of the bed.

"What's going on?" she said.

"It's the police. I need some ID." We were finally able to find a lamp to turn on. I located my real jeans and billfold. I slipped on a shirt and took the nice officer my billfold.

The policeman took my billfold out to his squad car. I could hear him on his radio. It took him 15 long minutes to do his check. "It looks like someone across the lake called when they saw lights on in this cabin. They assumed you had broken in. We have had a lot of break-ins around here lately. We assumed the ones who called were the owners." He gave no apologies and simply left.

Early that morning I got up to start my new life. As I drove through the base, I was in awe. It was heavily forested with the beautiful Silver Lead Creek running through the middle. I felt like I was in Shangri-La. The whole area was picturesque. The base water tower had a rainbow painted on the side with the words, "Some Place Special," which it was.

When I arrived to the family practice clinic—my new station—I was taken back to the break room by an airman from personnel. There sat the two PAs and three physicians drinking coffee. As soon as the airman introduced me and left, the senior PA, Rick, said, "You know . . . you are a complete idiot!"

Now there was an interesting Air Force greeting.

"Why in the hell would a civilian PA want to come in the Air Force? Most of us are trying to get out." Then he gave a boisterous laugh. One of the physicians, Dr. England, chimed in, with a smirk on his face: "This is the armpit of the universe, you fool."

After my two previous horrible job experiences, my heart began to sink. If this were going to be number three, first of all I would be stuck with it for three years, then I would leave the PA profession altogether. I would go into secondary science education or cabaret singing and dancing—something . . . ANYTHING . . . else!

Despite my initial impression, I found life as the Air Force PA to be a wonderful experience. It was by far the easiest job I had ever had. One week I would be in the family practice clinic, seeing 14-15 patients per day. The next week I would man the ER during the day. Except during the Gulf War, the ER had a very manageable caseload.

The war had an impact on the patient load because a few of our providers, including Rick, got deployed to other bases. Only one, Dr.

England, went overseas. The others went to cover the positions of some of the physicians who did go to the gulf.

When the cold season hit, the ER reminded me of the Duluth Prison days. The load was becoming unmanageable. One two-week period was particularly hard. It entailed the eclipse of the four factors: the cold and flu season, and the time when three different providers were simultaneously gone. I started to get stressed out, trying to see 40-plus patients per day in the ER, which resulted in me developing insomnia. I simply couldn't turn off my brain at night. I kept going over drug doses, symptoms, etc. Then I did something stupid. I had prescribed amitriptyline for patients for many years. It is a good headache medicine. The report I heard back often was how well it helped the patient sleep. I decided to try one tiny 10mg tablet. I would usually start my patients on 10-25mg per night and work up from there.

Indeed, I did have a hard time falling asleep again. At about 1:00 a.m. I took the tiny tablet. In 30 minutes, I didn't go asleep . . . I fell into a coma. When the alarm went off the next morning, I slept right through it. Denise had to shake me to bring me back to the real world, for just a brief visit. Again I fell asleep. Over and over she tried to wake me.

Finally I was able to plant two feet on the floor and make my way to the shower. Again I fell asleep in the shower, leaning against the wall.

Even standing out in the zero-degree weather in front of our farmhouse didn't wake me. I caught the county bus to work every morning for the 14-mile commute to the base hospital. The bus picked me up as the last stop coming out of La Salle. The next stop after me was the base hospital 20 minutes later.

This morning, I went into deep sleep on the bus and slept the whole way. The ride seemed more like 2 minutes.

Once I got to the ER, the lobby was already full. All clinic appointments had long been booked. I couldn't get my eyes open, no matter how hard I tried. When I did, everything was blurred. I couldn't believe that 10 measly milligrams of amitriptyline could have such an impact. I know that if I were a good PA, according to our ethical code, I would report that I was mentally impaired that day and go home. However, the hospital shortage was so bad I felt I just couldn't let them down. I also had the feeling that I would wake up at any time. So many times I had instructed my patients that "you might be a little drowsy in the morning, but it will soon burn off."

The day continued in chaos. I moved from patient to patient like a drunk hummingbird from flower to flower. I was slapping my face trying very hard to wake up. I desperately didn't want to make a mistake. I read each record over and over. I checked and rechecked allergies and co-morbidities before prescribing a drug. The technicians had to practically lead me by the hand from room to room.

By lunch, the lobby was so packed that there were no seats left and the halls were full of families sitting in the floor—all engulfed by the sounds of crying children. Four treatment rooms were kept full. I didn't even have time to pee until early afternoon.

In the midst of this, the hardest day of my PA career (except for my experience as a student at the Afghan refugee camp), I had my greatest test. This was the closest I had ever come to a career-ending choice.

As the ER provider, I was also responsible for any emergency within the hospital. If a patient keeled over in the lobby, it was the ER PA who had to respond. I had such an in-house emergency about once a week. Usually it was a fainter, typically in lab area.

On this day, in the midst of all the madness, I had a call from the sergeant who directed the X-ray department. He was referred to as Napoleon. He was roughly four feet tall and had the personality of Mussolini, but not quite as sweet. He was screaming, "I had a lady faint in MY X-ray department and she can't be moved until YOU come and clear her. You got to come now because I am a very busy man."

I arrived at X-ray and found a heavy woman in her 60s lying on the floor screaming at the wise X-ray tech, Sergeant Moore. He had her immobilized. "Let me up NOW, you idiot, this damn floor is hurting my back."

I stooped down beside them. "What happened?"

"I was doing a mammogram and she just fainted. She fell backwards, striking the back of her neck and head on the X-ray table behind her."

"Where do you hurt?" I said to the patient.

"My damn back hurts, what do you think! I've got chronic back pain and I can never lie flat like this. Now tell this idiot to let me up."

"Yes ma'am, I know your back hurts, but what about your head and neck?"

"Of course they hurt! Wouldn't your neck and head hurt if you just hit it on a damn table."

Napoleon walked in and screamed at Sergeant Moore in a hateful voice, "Would you hurry up and get her out of here, we are behind schedule and I've got patients waiting!"

Even in the midst of all of this, every cell in my body was demanding sleep. I could have easily cuddled up beside the woman and gone directly into stage four. I looked up at Sergeant Moore and he smiled and said, "Can I let her up so you can take her down to the ER and examine her. That way, I can keep the schedule moving."

Napoleon had been trying to drive Sergeant Moore to the brink of insanity for the past two years. Sergeant Moore had learned if he didn't keep things running smoothly, life would be hell for him.

I had the word "yes" on the tip of my tongue. I just wanted get back to the ER myself. Instead, some voice within me said, "No. Let me examine her here."

Napoleon left in disgust. I started to palpate her neck again, more carefully this time. Between her screaming about her back it became clear that she was having a great deal of pain in her neck as well. She didn't want to admit it because she knew that might mean she would have to lay on the cold floor a little longer.

I continued with a neurological exam. It was perfect, except for a slight numbness and tingling in her right pinky. I repositioned her elbow and arm and re-examined her. She still had the tingling in her hand.

The small instinct was speaking caution. I broke the news to Sergeant Moore. "I want full cervical neck precautions and cervical films taken."

This was a huge deal. It meant getting a backboard, neck collar, and sandbags. Even getting her on the table and the films taken would take 30 minutes–30 more minutes that X-ray would be shut down.

When the cervical films were done, I had a call from Sergeant Moore. I finished up my patient in the ER and returned to X-ray. As I walked through, the patient was taped down on the backboard, on the table. She was certainly in no better spirits. She shouted, "Get me off this damn board, you bunch of idiots!"

"Ma'am, I need to look at the films. If they are OK, I will let you get up and get dressed."

Sergeant Moore stuck the films on the view box. He was really hot under the collar as apparently he and his boss were going at it again. "Please get her out of here. I am ready to either kill her or my boss or both." He was able to bring back the next patient and start catching up.

I looked at the cervical films and started realizing how little experience I had reading neck films. I had never seen a cervical fracture, at least since I was in school. The vertebra appeared intact, but I wasn't sure. I thought there might be an irregularity, but I also thought it could be my imagination.

I walked in and examined the patient. She still had the numbness of her pinky, but now it seemed to have spread into the side of her hand. Yet, I knew there was a good chance that this reflected more nerve impingement in her arm.

Sergeant Moore walked in and said, "OK, can I let her up?" Again, I was at an important crossroads. I knew in my heart that I couldn't say for sure she that didn't have a fracture.

I told Sergeant Moore, "No, I'm not going to clear her. You will have to get one of the physicians to look at it."

When Sergeant Moore called Dr Bantle he said, "I'm not going to come and look at it and clear her if PA Jones wasn't willing to." He felt that if there was enough concern to make me doubtful, then he was doubtful. This complicated things but showed the kind of support and trust the Air Force physicians, at least those in family practice, had in the PAs.

The very unhappy lady was admitted to our hospital with neck precautions. An airman was called to run the films down to the radiologist in La Salle. It took over two hours to get a reading. I was near the end of my very difficult shift when Dr. Bantle called me and told me that the radiologist just called him and told him that the woman had an unstable cervical fracture. She was being transferred via ambulance to the neurosurgery service in town. I saw her in the hospital a few weeks later donning a halo cast. She had no expression of gratitude and, in fact, was trying to sue the hospital for letting her fall. Even her new halo couldn't impart an angelic demeanor.

I sat in the ER call room that afternoon and felt a chill. I was exhausted, having seen more patients in one 8-hour shift than I would for the rest of my career: 56. I was thinking how tempted I was to let the crabby woman get up. I had tremendous pressure from all sides, including from myself. I was within half a millimeter of letting her get up and go home. If she had, she probably would've had some permanent spinal cord damage. How could I have lived with myself?

This was certainly the most difficult of my Air Force days and these days were brief. Soon Rick came back from his TDY (temporary duty) and I started to rotate back into family practice. The physicians started returning soon as well. I think I could have survived even the terrible job in Duluth had there been a light at the end of the tunnel. The tough Air Force days were more of an underpass than a tunnel.

I actually spent most of the Gulf War in the bathroom, and it had nothing to do with oat bran. Our new, old house was in need of remodeling, giving us another opportunity at the money-pit syndrome. We had a little money left in savings after the Duluth house, so we figured, why not finish it off with another fixer upper?

The downstairs bathroom was the worst part. It had cheap, dark, almost black, paneling and a goofy drop ceiling, the kind you might find in a low-end business. In fact, I believe they had been recycled from a closed business. The most undesirable element was the green shag carpet. Anyone with little boys knows that carpet in a bathroom is never a good idea. Women don't seem to understand how hard it is to hit such a big toilet with such a small stream. It gets especially tricky when you have to stand on your tiptoes and hold the lid up with one hand and aim with the other.

I decided to gut the whole bathroom and start over. It took me about two months. I started the project about the same time President Bush (senior) launched Desert Storm. I was intensely interested in the war because I knew that at a moment's notice I could be going. I also had at least one good friend on the front lines. He was with the Army Intelligence Office.

I'm no pacifist, but I hate war. Maybe it stems from my mother's soft heart. When I was a little boy, I was fascinated with war. It seemed that all baby boomer boys were because of the positive effect of WWII on America. The TV and movies glorified war. As a kid, you had this innocence that made you believe that wars had some sophisticated purpose, something that only adults could understand.

I remember reading how Roosevelt sensed a deep glory about war. Part of it went back to his childhood and the shame he felt when his father had refused to fight for the Union Army. I read that when he headed the war department, he felt a war, any war, would be good for America. When we finally did get into it with the Spanish, he resigned to lead his Rough Riders up San Juan Hill in Cuba. It is recorded that when he came upon each of his Rough Riders laying in the dirt dying, Roosevelt would shout to them with a big smile on his face, "Isn't war glorious!" I think the man was insane. However, he was a strong leader and the country may have benefited from his strong leadership when he later became president.

As an adult, I realized that war held no great mystery. It is the same psychological dynamics that make two little boys get into a fist fight on the playground, boiling down to issues of self-centeredness, deep personal insecurities, and greed. Maybe their mommies weaned them a bit early. Rather than dealing with it, they take it out on the world–men like Hitler and Saddam, who want to play the game of Risk but using real land and causing the horrible deaths of real people, many of them innocent women and children. Short of redemption, I believe they will have box seats in Hell, right next to the furnace.

Each night in the bathroom, I listened intently to Public Radio International. It was the CNN of radio land, and it kept me spellbound.

I never had a reassignment during the war and for that I was grateful. Our base sent many military police to the gulf and I had to help many of their families deal with the separation. It seemed unfair that I got to stay home with mine. Twice our hospital commander called me to his office to interrogate me about my ability to speak Arabic and relate to Arabs.

Our commander, a physician, was the one person in the hospital who was military to the core. He was like a skinny, tall, Texan version of Major Burns from the TV show "MASH." He would welcome me into his huge plush office. There he would sit with his lanky six–foot-four frame leaning back in his chair, his heels on the desk. I was expecting him to be wearing spurs.

"Jones, have a seat. Do you want some coffee?"

"No thanks, sir." I had no idea why his secretary had called me to report to the commander's office.

"Jones, I see here in your records that you have a degree in Arabic. Is that true?"

"Yes, sir."

He sat up and leaned across his desk and looked me in the eye. "Jones, let me hear you say in Arabic, What's your mission? Which town are you from? What company were you with?"

I had to think about it. My Arabic was rusty and my class didn't include a section for military interrogation. "Well, I can ask which town you are from . . . Inta min ay madeena? For the other questions I would have to look up a couple of words."

For the next few weeks I was expecting to get orders to go to Saudi. But I guess in the end my Arabic abilities didn't impress anyone, thank goodness. I had no fear of the war itself and would have been the first to volunteer if had been single. However, my long absence would have been hard on my family.

Soon the war was over, although in reality it still continues. Life in the Air Force quickly returned to normal. I finally finished my bathroom, although not without some frustration.

I was never able to do a good job of drywalling. This time, however, I was determined to drywall the new bathroom ceiling to perfection. I worked for a week, countersinking the screws, applying mud, sanding, and applying more mud. I wanted a perfect ceiling. Finally, I had it looking great. I primed it, painted it, and put in the new ceiling light. I finished late one Saturday night. The wind was a howling and we were in the midst of a snowstorm with temps drooping to twenty below zero, wind chills of minus fifty.

The next morning, Denise got up and went down to the new bathroom to shower. When she was finished, she came back up stairs. "Mike, the globe light you put in looks like a fish bowl."

I was face down on the pillow, but raised my head and opened one eye. "Fish bowl? What do you mean?"

"Oh, the light comes on OK, but the globe is full of water like a fish bowl. What would cause that?"

"Oh no! Oh no! Please tell me you are joking!"

"No I'm not joking, why is that so bad?"

I went crazy. I ran downstairs in my undershorts. Just as I poke my head in, the bulb popped, the water level in the globe having risen above the hot bulb. "Shoot, I can't believe this! Oh no!"

Denise was watching in ignorance—which sometimes truly is bliss.

Then I grabbed a hammer and started pounding my perfect ceiling. Plaster was flying everywhere.

The problem, which I had figured out as soon as Denise had said the phrase "fish bowl," was that the pipes in the ceiling had frozen and broken. The cheesy drop ceilings had let enough heat into the ceiling space to prevent them from freezing; the new, perfect ceiling blocked the heat so the pipes froze. The only way to get to the pipes would be to tear out the ceiling.

I don't know what my problem is. As I type this, I am faced with my fourth major house-remodeling project. It is about to drive me mad. The next time I buy such a house, my family should just tie me up inside and set the whole thing on fire as some fitting human sacrifice to the fixer-upper gods. Then I would be out of my misery and the fixer-upper gods would be appeased, once and for all.

The most difficult days of my Air Force career were behind me. However, ahead of me lay some challenges that would prove to be a turning point in my PA career and my life. The hard lessons, which I had learned in Egypt, would come home to roost. I would go up against some of the dragons in my own dungeon. Yet, through it all, La Salle would remain our Shangri-La.

Chapter Nineteen

A Rite of PAssage

Mr. Robertson was the sickest man I had ever seen in my little Air Force ER, yet Dr. Foley was releasing him to go home with just a muscle relaxant. I couldn't figure it out.

Dr. Foley was new to our family practice department. He was about six foot three, with a slightly heavy build and curly brown hair. He was a very nice man and I considered him a personal friend, but I learned to never trust his medical judgment. Judgment is something that can't be taught in medical or PA school. It is instinctive. Dr. Foley's heart was clearly in alternative medicine and wanted to pursue a career in that avenue when his commitment to the Air Force was over.

One day, during the hard ER days of the Gulf War period, Dr. Foley came down during his lunch hour to help me out. This reflected how nice a person he actually was. He just walked into the ER and said, "Mike, go get some rest and lunch. I'll take care of things here until you get back."

When I returned from lunch Dr. Foley was standing at the desk, completing a chart note. He looked up at me and smiled. "Mike, I've got a gentleman back in the trauma room. He was complaining of neck pain. I've examined him and given him a prescription for a muscle relaxant for a strain. However, I did order X-rays of his neck and chest—which aren't back yet. Would you mind going over the X-ray with him? I'm sure it's normal."

"Oh, sure. I'll be glad to. Thanks so much for your help."

Between patients, the ER technicians told me that the gentleman's films were back. I made the mistake of grabbing the envelope of films and walking into the room where the Mr. Robertson and his family were waiting.

Mr. Robertson was a rough-looking stocky man in his sixties with a gray flattop. Even if this were not a military ER, you would immediately conclude he was a military retiree. He looked like a burnt-out Navy Seal and was a splitting image of Rudy from the first "Survivor" TV show. He had already put his sheep-shear's coat on and was standing up, pacing the floor, ready to leave. His son and daughter-in-law sat on a stretcher on the other side of the large trauma room. I introduced myself, expecting to quickly go through the films and send him on his way.

I walked over to the view box and pulled the film from the envelope. As soon as I separated the top film–the chest X-ray–from the stack, I could see a baseball-size tumor in his right lung field plus several satellite lesions and a large pleural effusion, which is water on the lung. I didn't even put the film on the view box, instead simply sliding them back into the envelope.

"Before I look at these, Mr. Robertson, I would like to hear more about what has been going on with you." Dr. Foley's patient presentation to me had been brief.

"Well, like I was telling the other doctor, for two months I have had some chest pain and I have been winded. I cut all my own firewood, but this year I could split only a few logs before I had to sit down and rest a spell. I also have a pinched nerve in my neck and my chiropractor thinks that's what causing my chest pain. I have been seeing her twice a week for the past two months. She is quite confident that she can eventually get my neck bones back in place and get rid of the pain. She didn't want me to see a regular doctor because she said that a regular doctor would just prescribe a bunch of harmful drugs. When my son here, uh . . . Derrick, came home from Idaho for Christmas, he insisted that I come here for another opinion."

I asked Mr. Robertson to remove his coat. I couldn't believe my eyes. The poor man had extreme muscle wasting of his right arm, and he was right-handed. He could barely move the arm. In shock and confusion, I asked, "What happened to your arm?"

"My chiropractor says the pinched nerve in my neck is doing this."

"Do you mean that your arm just started to shrivel up like this recently?"

"Yeah, about two or three months ago, when I couldn't move it any longer."

Then I noticed a significant deformity of the right clavicle. "When did you break your collar bone?" I said.

"Break my collar bone? Oh, do mean these bones here (pointing to the obvious deformity)?"

I nodded.

"I went to put my coat on a couple of days ago and heard a pop when I tried to lift my arm up. I think it is probably related to my vertebra being out. The chiropractor thought she could fix it as well."

Next I listened to his chest and found his lungs very congested. I left and went to my call room and stuck up his films. Besides his lung tumors, it looked like he had metastasis in his cervical spine, clavicle, and ribs. It was horrible. To make a long story short, I had Mr. Robertson admitted downtown that afternoon. Within two weeks he was a quadriplegic and on a ventilator. Within four weeks he was dead.

I would have been dumbfounded if a PA student had seen this patient and wasn't extremely alarmed by his history, tremendous muscle wasting, and crappy lungs. If I had overlooked such a blatant finding, I would never have heard the end of it. Yet, no one was reviewing the physicians' records.

In our family practice section, we had two other physicians. Dr. Bantle, my supervisor, was an outstanding doctor. He was bright and cared deeply for his patients and had great judgment. He also had the humility to ask me questions, especially about headaches. He would also ask Rick orthopedic questions—this being Rick's area of expertise. He wasn't threatened by the fact we weren't physicians.

Dr. England was also a nice guy and I am sure he could have made a great physician, but he had one minor downfall: he hated patients—all of them. I'm not sure why he went into medicine. He would tell me, "Mike, your problem is that you touch the patients." Dr. England's attitude was that each patient had a hidden agenda, such as getting a sick slip for work, a work restriction, pain medicine, or antibiotic. He resented them "wasting his time." He would just cut to the chase and ask the patient, "OK, why are you REALLY here? What do you REALLY want?"

The patient might say something like, "Well, I was thinking that little Susie might have an ear infection and . . ."

"OK, that is all I want to hear." Then he would write out a prescription for amoxicillin and move on to the next one.

He also hated the Air Force. As the time of his commitment shortened, he became more radical in his approach to patients. One example was his behavior during sick call. All of us medical providers would gather in the clinic prior to our first morning appointments. Active duty personnel would show up and check in. We would take them first come, first served. By the time the thirty minutes of sick call were up, we each would have seen four or five patients.

Dr. England started coming into the front office and grabbing an arm full of charts. He would head to the lobby and call out seven or eight names. The patients would follow him back to his office as a group. There he would line them up and, one by one, ask them, "What do you want?"

They didn't know how take him at first. "Excuse me, sir?"

"I said, what do you WANT!"

If they started describing their symptoms, Dr. England would interrupt: "No! No! I don't want to hear all your complaints–just tell me why you are really here."

The first one in line would figure it out and the others followed suit. "Sir, I don't feel like working today."

Dr. England's response: "OK, one work excuse for you. Will you feel like working tomorrow?"

The next patient might say, "Sir, I think I need a work restriction so I won't have to work outside until it warms up."

"OK, one work restriction for you." Then he writes, "Patient cannot work outside until May." Then he says, "Next."

"Sir, I need something for my cold."

"Do you mean antibiotics?"

"Yes sir, something to knock it out."

Then he hands them a prescription for "vitamin Am," which is amoxicillin.

Dr. England considered his patients a captive audience. It's not like they were going to get mad and go to the clinic down the street. Also, he wasn't going to get fired. If he could've been fired, he would have been the first one wearing a nightie and a fuzzy boa like Klinger. There is nothing he wanted more than to get fired.

I took advantage of my captive audience as well. I used it as a forum from which to practice the medicine that you should practice, not the medicine that the customer demands. You could say I moved in the opposite direction of Dr. England. I only prescribed antibiotics when they were warranted. This made for a lot of unhappy customers. But I did try to instruct them in the proper use of antibiotics, which was of little help.

My most notorious case was a woman who came into the ER around Easter time. She was in her late forties, with brown dyed hair and wearing a spring-like flowered cotton dress. "I have a sinus infection. My nose has been running for two days. I really need something strong to knock this out."

I reviewed her history carefully and did a full ear, nose, and throat exam. She had no evidence of anything more that a cold. I gave her my spiel about the difference between viral and bacterial infections. I went on to describe the difference between the symptoms of a common viral cold and acute sinusitis. When I was done, she said, "Do you understand that I have family coming in for Easter? I must cook and entertain a house full of guests. I don't care if it is a cold, I NEED SOMETHING to knock it out."

"Ma'am, I am sorry you feel that way, but like I said, I'm not going to give you antibiotics."

She then looked at me and smiled. "Captain Jones, I don't think you know who I am. I'm the base commander's wife."

Well whoop de doo . . . so what! I thought to myself. "Ma'am, who you are married to doesn't influence my medical decisions. It doesn't turn a viral infection into one that will respond to antibiotics."

She went home angry. I ran into her a few weeks later in the vegetable aisle of the commissary. She appeared to gloat: "Jim, my husband, called your hospital commander, who was very apologetic. He told Jim, 'I am so sorry that your wife saw just a PA. Please call me the next time someone in your family is ill and either I or one of my flight surgeons will see them directly.' Then he called the pharmacy and prescribed Augmentin for me."

Another issue that made the military a good learning experience was socialized medicine–in other words, medical care was completely free. No money changed hands. There were no insurance papers to complete. You just walked in every time you had a problem without having to give a second thought as to the cost of health care. Prescriptions were totally free as well.

One of my most interesting experiences came one very slow morning. I was back in the call room watching the war on CNN. I hadn't had a patient for over an hour. I heard the automatic doors open and close. After about 15 minutes, Sergeant Hanson came back to the call room. He stuck his head in the door and said, "Got one for you."

I looked up. "What is it?"

Hanson rolled his eyes. "A guy with a splinter."

I stood up and stretched and grabbed my stethoscope out of habit and stuck it in my lab coat pocket. Now a splinter in the ER could mean just about anything. A month earlier I had a construction worker fall off a roof and ram a one-inch diameter, foot-long piece of wood through the lateral side of his arm. It had an entrance and exit wound, with the foreign body going through the subcutaneous space, nicking the triceps muscle. I called the orthopedic surgeon in town and he convinced me to take it out in the ER. He told me just to irrigate it out, and sew it up, leaving in a surgical (Penrose) drain. I followed his advice with some reluctance, but it turned out fine.

As I got to the treatment room, a very tall, thin airman was sitting on the end of the examining table wearing BDUs. "Hello, I am Captain Jones, the ER PA. What can I do for you today?"

He showed me his right index finger. "I've got a splinter." There was a tiny sliver under his nail.

I couldn't help but say, "You came in here for that!"

"I tried to pull it out with my pocket knife, but I couldn't." I had the feeling, if he had been at home, he would have gone to his mommy.

"OK, I'll get it out."

I turned around and took a 21-gauge hypodermic needle from the drawer. Immediately the young airman asked, "Whatcha gonna do with that?"

"I am going to take your splinter out," I said and gave him a look as if to say, "What else would I be doing with it?"

He was starting to act nervous. I bent over and took his index finger with my left hand and started to touch his finger with the needle. He jerked his hand away and put it behind his back.

I looked up at him with frustration and he said to me, "Aren't you gonna numb it up first?"

"Numb it up? Oh, that would hurt a heck of lot more than me just taking it out."

He kept playing hide and seek with his hand. "I really want you to numb it up."

"Do you know what is involved in numbing up your finger? I need to do a digital block. That means, I need to do a couple of injections at the base of your finger."

Amazingly, he said, "I still want you to numb it up."

I would never have considered it, but the ER was very quiet and I like doing procedures. I had been doing a lot of toenail resections for ingrown nails and was trying to improve on my digital blocks.

"OK," I said and started drawing up 2% lidocaine into a large syringe. I scrubbed off my landmarks at the base of his finger with iodine soap, still thinking to myself how ridiculous this whole thing was. I returned with my syringe. I created a clean field on the patient's knee and stabilized his hand there. I bent over to get a good close-up view and raised my needle to the base of his finger. As soon as the needle touched his skin, I immediately felt this huge weight land on my back, forcing my forehead down to the end of the table, between the patient's legs. For a second, I was shocked and confused. My first thought was that a wheel off one of the B-52s—which were constantly flying overhead—had come crashing through the ceiling. Then I looked down at my crotch to see the very pale face of a man. It took me a second to realize it was the very pale face of my patient. For a second I thought it was anaphylaxis. Then I remembered that I hadn't even injected him yet! He had passed out, stone cold. Being so tall, towering over me on the high table, when he passed out, he had fallen forward right over my back.

I tried to stand up, but the patient was so limp that he began to slide toward the hard, tiled floor. I bent back over and reached my arms around his thighs to catch him, with the syringe and uncovered needle still in my right hand. I pulled down hard to try and pull him back up. Now my head was sticking up between his legs. Again I tried to stand up and he started to slide down.

Now if I had the agility of a 12-year-old Olympic gymnast—the only people in the world I knew who could actually see their own butt (except for Mel Brooks in *Spaceballs*)—I could have gotten myself out of this predicament. But every time I moved, he started sliding toward the hard floor. Out of desperation I shouted, "I need some help in here!"

This wasn't the first time I had to shout out for help like this in the ER. However, the other times I was in back with a chest-painer who was arresting. I am sure the techs had heard me but just weren't responding. They couldn't take me seriously, considering all I was doing was removing a splinter.

After no one came to my rescue, I shouted out again, a little louder this time: "I said I need a little help in here!"

In a moment, Sergeant Hanson came strolling back with his hands in the pockets of his BDUs. As he reached my open door he looked in to see me bent over in a squat with the patient on my back. The "splinter man" was still out cold with his head dangling between my knees.

Hanson calmly said, "Uh . . . what are you guys doing?"

I kept my composure. "What does it look like I am doing? I am helping this young man get his splinter out. Now will you help me before I drop him on his head and break his neck?" Another broken neck is the last thing I wanted.

The airman quickly came to and I told him, "Just keep your splinter. It will fester up and eventually come out on its own."

The ER experience also brought home the professional injustice that non-physician clinicians must sometimes face. I can't imagine any other profession in the world that has as much scrutiny as ours. In the ER, the PAs had supervision, including 100% chart review. It was the responsibility of the evening shift MD to review the daytime PA's charts. This meant that on a rotating basis we were being reviewed by the three MDs from family practice, the two from internal medicine, the two pediatricians, the three flight surgeons, and even the general surgeon.

Our own colleagues in family practice rarely found an error because they knew us and trusted us. They assumed the best from our notes. However, it was impossible to meet the requirement of so many different providers in other departments. One of them, a flight surgeon, Dr. Straight, was especially difficult for me to deal with.

Dr. Straight was a cocky man and very confrontational. He was in his early thirties, just out of his residency. He was quite athletic, being a competitive runner. He had made it clear on several occasions that he had a low opinion of PAs. Even the other physicians didn't like his arrogance.

Dr. Straight was merciless in his quest to prove that PAs were idiots. Errors on records during reviews were called dings. I remember one such ding, which was typical for him. I had failed to address the patient's "fever." It was a man who came in with a twisted ankle. The techs had taken his vital signs on admission to the ER. This man's temp was 98.9. Frankly, I wasn't looking for an infectious cause to his twisted ankle. I knew from his history what the cause was. It was caused from an inversion injury after coming down on another basketball player's foot after going up for a rebound. It is a common injury in basketball. I don't think I even looked at his temp, and if I had, I couldn't have cared less that it was 98.9. After all, he had just been playing in a strenuous game of basketball, which could have accounted for his slightly elevated temperature.

After this flight surgeon reviewed my 15 records from the day, he might find ten dings. He would start speaking to me like I was a 6-year-old. The next day, Dr. Bantle would follow me and he too would review 15 records. Dr. Bantle would tell me, "Mike, you did a great job," and give me no dings. The flight surgeon and I locked horns on more than one occasion and I was getting tired of it. I was determined not to walk the same path as I had done in Egypt, where, for the sake of keeping the peace, I had allowed Chuck to walk on my family and me for almost two years. I had reached a turning point in my career and my life. I was ready to slay that dragon and put up personal—and professional—boundaries.

I went into the ER one morning after this flight surgeon had worked. I reviewed HIS twenty charts from the previous 12 hours by the same (or even slightly more forgiving) standards than he judged my work by. I discovered 15-20 errors. Some of his errors were much worse than mine. As he was packing up to go home for the day, I confronted him with his dings. "Dr. Straight, there are some errors I found in your charts from last night I want to talk to you about."

"What the hell are you talking about?" he said as he stuffed the last of his belongings into his duffel bag. To say the least, he wasn't amused.

"My charting is none of your damn business!"

"Well, I see here, Dr. Straight, you never commented on this patient's systolic pressure of 180. You dinged my chart the other day because I hadn't commented on a gentleman's pressure of 152. So, what is the difference?"

"The difference is that I am a physician and you are just a PA! When I don't comment on something, there is a medical reason I don't. When you don't, it is a mistake because you don't know any better because you are just a PA."

"I think you lost me there, Dr. Straight. Isn't a systolic pressure of 180 higher than 152?"

"A physician's knowledge is so vastly higher than a PA's that you can't evaluate an MD by the same standard. A physician has so much insight that he doesn't have to comment on such findings. I knew that the systolic BP of 180 was of no clinical significance because I understood the state of the patient's general health much better than a PA possibly could. Why am I even talking to you? Get the hell out of my way."

With that, he turned, threw his duffel bag over his shoulder, and marched out the automatic ER doors to his jeep warming up in the doctor's on-call parking spot.

I soon had another experience that put me to the test. One Monday morning in sick call I had an active-duty man come in for a work release slip. A moonlighting civilian family practice resident had seen him in the ER the previous night.

The patient told me, "Last night I went to the ER because I was having anal pain. The civilian MD diagnosed me as having hemorrhoids and an anal fissure and gave me some cream. The doctor last night told me I could take a couple of days off from work since I have to sit all day driving a runway snow plow. The doc last night told me he could not give me a work release because he is a civilian, and that I had to come to sick call to get one. You don't have to examine me, do you? That scope he used last night hurt like hell."

The patient's medical records were still in the ER, so all the information I had was based on what he was telling me. This was common practice in these situations since the civilian physicians were not allowed to change active-duty work orders.

"No, if you are here just to get a work release slip and you don't want me to examine you, I won't." I gave him a work release slip for two days.

Two days later the patient was still having pain, so he went back to the ER. Rick saw him there and didn't examine him but extended his work release slip for another two days.

Two days later, the patient showed up again in the ER with serious pain and fever. He had a perirectal abscess and was taken immediately to surgery.

The base surgeon was a personal friend of mine. We had gone fishing together. Our families went boating together and we attended the same church. Without my knowledge, he wrote up a major reprimand against me for committing an act of "mal-practice." He didn't write up the ER physician and he didn't write up Rick, but he wrote me up because my name was on the original work release form.

One day the medical staff director, Dr. Carson, came to my office to present the reprimand. Dr. Carson was a gentleman in his early 60s. He was mostly bald and of a short statue. He wore gold wire-rimmed glasses and spoke softly. He had been in a civilian gynecology practice for 30 years before deciding to semi-retire by going into the Air Force as a full colonel. He was always easy to spot because his two cars had the vanity license plates, "Gyno 1" and "Gyno 2."

"Mike, let me explain how this works. This is will be part of your permanent record. Also, for the next three months you will be placed on probation, where all of your charts, even in the family practice clinic, will have to be reviewed."

"What can I do to fight this?" I said.

"Oh, not much. Don't let it bother you, Mike. Don't take it so personally. You just have to sign this reprimand. It's not a big deal. It is just an Air Force formality."

I looked the papers over. Signing it would mean that I agreed with the conclusion of the medical staff. I handed it back to him and said,

"I'm not signing this because it isn't true. I did nothing wrong so I'm not signing this paper."

"Captain Jones, you are making too much out of this." He then left my office. Later he called me and said, "Mike, I have checked into the policy. If you refuse to sign this, we will have to schedule a special meeting of the executive medical staff."

"Well then, do it," I asserted.

After the medical director left my office that morning, I was feeling crushed. It was one of the lowest points in my medical career. But, I sensed a deep injustice was afoot. If this had happened to any other provider in sick call that morning, I was convinced they would have done the same thing as I had done. If I had MD after my name, no one would have questioned it.

The day of the special medical board meeting soon arrived. This board was chaired by Dr. Carson and was attended by each departmental head, the head of Nursing, Pharmacy, Dentistry, Psychology, Optometry, Family Practice, Internal Medicine, and Peds, and of course, the surgeon. PA s couldn't be represented because we didn't have department status.

I wasn't allowed in the room as the surgeon presented his case against me. Then I was called in to take the stand. I presented my case as thoughtfully as I could. I was dismissed to sit in the hall again. The surgeon was allowed to stay inside and continue with the deliberation.

After about 15 minutes, Dr. Carson brought me back into the room. He read the verdict. The vote in my favor was 12 to 1. Only the surgeon had voted against me. I was vindicated as the staff read their verdict that I had done nothing wrong and, indeed, it had been the ER physician's fault for not making the proper diagnosis to start with. The ER physician had overlooked a temperature reading on the patient of 101. When I had seen the patient, I had no vitals and no records from the ER visit. This became one of the highlights of my career and gave me renewed confidence as a clinician. The dragon had been slain—or at least mortally wounded.

The frosting on the cake of my wonderful Air Force years came at this time with the birth of my son Ramsey. An Air Force midwife delivered him. It was a very positive experience. Our family had grown to seven hungry mouths to feed. Now Amy had a living, moving doll to play with.

Rick was a great jokester, which was one of my own weaknesses. He would slip over to my office and paint the earpiece to my phone with a black Magic Marker while I was in the adjacent exam room. Then he would dial my number. When I answered the phone he would have something trivial to tell me and then leave me with a black ear for the rest of the morning. Throughout the clinic there would be Dr. Bantle with a black ear and Dr. England with a black ear. Instead of ashes on our forehead as on Ash Wednesday, it looked like we had ash on our ears. I wondered if the patients thought this was some kind of satanic ritual.

One time, I picked up the phone and found it covered in Rick's trademark black ink. I looked across the hall and he wasn't in his office. I quickly unscrewed the earpiece on my phone and switched it with Rick's. In a few minutes Rick went into his office and closed the door. Then my phone rang. After our brief conversation, he strolled over to look at me with his coffee mug in hand. There he stood, looking like the cock of the walk, hoping to make fun of my black ear, but this time it was his ear stained with the self-inflicted black ink.

We had another PA join our department just as Rick was retiring. Chris was a really nice guy and this was his first assignment after completing the Air Force's PA program. He too was a family man, with five boys. Between the three PAs, we had sixteen children.

Chris took Rick's office, which was a mistake. After working with Rick for two years, I was deep into practical joke mode by the time Chris came around.

Chris, being a new graduate, moved deliberately while attending to patients. One day I came down the hall and there were three charts of patients whom had checked in to see him. We would then take the chart and call in our own patient from the lobby.

The techs at the front desk frequently put little yellow sticky-notes on the front of the chart to give us a heads up. A note might say, for example, "The patient was seen in the ER last night; however, we don't have his ER note yet."

I noticed that two of the charts in Chris's box had sticky notes on them. Apparently both of his next two patients were retirees. The note on the first chart read, "Please finish your note quickly, the patient is traveling and hand-carries his records."

Now the note on the second chart read, "Speak very loudly, patient is almost deaf." A sudden impulse came over me—maybe it was the devil. I switched the sticky notes.

I was caught up, so I just sat in my office and listened. I could see Chris reading the sticky note as he walked to the lobby. Then he screamed, "Mr. FRED BROWN!" I heard the two go into Chris's office and he shut his door. I got up from my desk and went across the hall to listen. I didn't even have to leave my office because you could Chris from anywhere in the building. "NOW TELL ME, MR. BROWN, HOW LONG HAVE YOU HAD THIS NASTY BOIL!"

You could hear a very low mumble as the patient responded. The, Chris replied, "YOU SAY IT HAS BEEN DRAINING ON YOUR UNDERSHIRT?"

Next the low mumble.

Then Chris: "OH, SO YOU HAD A BUMP THERE LONG BEFORE IT GOT SORE AND SWELLED UP?"

Mumble mumble.

Chris: "IT LOOKS LIKE IT IS WHAT WE CALL A SEBACEOUS CYST AND NOW IT IS INFECTED!"

Next I heard Mr. Brown say in a louder mumble, but with some tone of pity, "Son, why the hell are you yelling at me?" When Chris showed the patient the sticky note, they both got a big chuckle out of it.

From that point on, we were often putting sticky notes on each other's charts. We would write things like, "Speak very loudly, patient is almost blind," or "Speak very loudly, the patient is quite constipated," or "Speak very, very loudly, wife is waiting out in the motor home and wants to hear."

Soon after Rick's departure, something strange started to happen.

It was the dark clouds starting to accumulate in our crystal blue skies. I was in denial at first to think that these great days could ever end.

We suddenly had a new PA recruit come to the base. Like me, he requested La Salle and the recruiter was able to promise him the position. Next, we had a PA transfer from Homestead Air Force Base. After Hurricane Andrew destroyed the base, he was given his choices of destinations and he picked our base. Next we had another PA come who was promised our base after completing a remote assignment in Korea. He wanted to retire out of our base because he owned a cabin in the area.

With this new brood of PAs I soon realized that our profession has its bad apples as well. One PA, Captain Fish, was a quiet man in his late thirties–approaching Air Force retirement. His trademark was a coffee cup that he always carried in his right hand that bore the words, "Old Fart." I will never forget our first conversation of substance. He was in the break room, sitting quietly at the table in his BDUs and lab coat, sipping stout coffee from Old Fart. I said, "So, what are your plans after retirement?"

He seemed to ignore me at first, just sipping coffee and sloshing it around in his mouth, like he was trying to appreciate the flavor of each bitter bean. Then Fish said, "Oh, I think I will move back to the small town in Ohio where I grew up and join a practice there."

Just to make further conversation, I added, "I think it would be hard to go back to the town where I grew up–that is, except for seeing my folks more often."

Fish seemed to collapse into his own internal virtual reality as he stared off into space, softly whispering, "There is nothing I would like better than to do pelvics on all the girls that wouldn't go out with me in high school." With a smile still on his face, he leisurely slurped another mouthful from Old Fart.

My skin began to crawl. I started to have the feeling that if the high school girls thought he was too creepy to ask to the prom, then they certainly would consider him too creepy to ask for a pap.

Our little hospital had only two slots for PAs and now we were up to five. I was experiencing the opposite problem as I did in Duluth–a sudden oversupply of manpower–and since I was the senior PA, I started to feel that my days were numbered. The dark clouds reached their culmination with the announcement that our base was on the closure list. One by one our friends started to disappear over the edge of the earth through reassignments.

The only thing the recruiter told me that didn't develop just as he said was that I could expect to stay in La Salle for at least 10 years.

At about this time, the Air Force Assignments office in Texas began calling, telling me, "Captain Jones, your base is over-manned and you need to transfer." This was heartbreaking because we loved La Salle. My 3-year commitment had ended three months earlier. I had just signed up to stay on active duty indefinitely when the latrine mud hit the propeller. I started getting calls from a colonel at a small medic station in the Nevada desert. They wanted me and they wanted me now!

I discussed the matter with Denise and the family. The desert station, with the closest town–Las Vegas–about 50 miles away, was the last place we wanted to live. I offered to go to exotic places like Crete, Turkey, Korea, or North Dakota. Still, Assignments told me that the medic station in the desert was my only choice.

It was a tough decision, but we decided to jump ship and separate from the Air Force. It had been a very enjoyable three and a half years. I believe military people are some of the nicest people I have ever met. Part of the reason is everyone is so used to moving and having new people move in, they have refined the skill of making friends to a high art. If the Air Force would just get rid of the dress code, haircuts, saluting, and war games, it would have been the perfect job.

With my short career with the Air Force drawing to a close, I started job hunting. I couldn't believe the turnaround in the job market since looking for my first job a decade earlier. I had hospitals, recruiters, and doctors calling my house constantly. I felt like a 600-pound hemophiliac in a school of sharks. I was soon to learn that some of the perspective employers were shark-like in more ways than one.

But, the Air Force experience had changed all of us. We wish we could have suspended those three and half years indefinitely, but reality would not permit that. However, I had a newfound confidence and was prepared to leave someplace special and take on the real world.

Chapter Twenty

The Real World

Early one Friday morning, the beige phone on the farmhouse kitchen wall began to ring. I had just finished my shower in the downstairs, remodeled bathroom and was standing barefoot in front of the mirror, wearing my BDU pants and brown T-shirt, combing my hair. I couldn't imagine who would be calling at 6:00 in the morning.

I quickly grabbed the phone, trying not to wake the rest of the house. I could tell by the clicks and long pauses that the woman on the other end of the phone was calling from overseas. "Michael Jones? Is this Michael Jones?"

"Yes it is."

"My name is Dr. Linda Weaver and I am the medical director of Medi-Co in Cairo, Egypt. I was told by a previous PA, Bob, that you might be interested in a job here."

"Cairo! Yes, I think I might be interested. What is the scoop?"

"Well, in this position you would be taking care of American staff. Your patient load would only be 4-5 patients per day, but we need you to be available on the compound 24 hours a day for emergencies."

"Can I bring my family? I have a wife and five children."

"I will have to check into that. Right now we offer a two-bedroom duplex and we don't furnish education for the children. However, I think I could get both sides of a duplex for you and your family if you would be responsible for their education."

"Education isn't a problem for us, as we can always home-school the two who are old enough."

I was very excited about this possibility and couldn't keep my mind off of it all day. It seemed like God was opening a door just when I was leaving the Air Force. There was nothing we would rather do more than return to Egypt, but under different circumstances than before. I was 90% sure this would be our choice, when life revealed a sudden new development.

During the winter, prior to my separation from the Air Force, my dad had a case of pneumonia. Within two months he developed another case, in the same lung, which started to raise my suspicions. Within a few weeks of the second episode, he developed a fever again. I told mom to take him to the ER. Later that day, mom called me in tears. I already knew what she was going to say: dad had lung cancer.

Dad had received his first pack of cigarettes in his rations from the Army at age nineteen. He became a smoker during the war, like so many others. It was a small sense of pleasure in the midst of hell on earth. I probably would have done the same.

The news of his lung cancer came within a couple of days of getting the job offer in Egypt. I was really torn. I didn't know the future, but I knew that dad didn't have very long. On the other hand, it didn't matter if I were in La Salle or Cairo. The drive to Tennessee from La Salle was about the same as the flight from Cairo.

I spent the morning on the basketball court alone. We really wanted to go back to Egypt. I had Denise's full support. It would be my chance to finish learning Arabic and for us to succeed at living there.

One thing I had learned during my Air Force battle training was when a solider went into battle shock, it was best to give him a short recovery on the field and send him back to the front lines than to send him home mentally defeated. Denise and I both wanted to go back to the Egyptian "front lines." Yet, I knew my mother and siblings wouldn't see things the same way. As I worked on slam-dunks in my imaginary NBA game (on an eight-foot goal), the choice became obvious. I would have to turn down the Egyptian offer. It was one of the most painful choices I have ever made. Over the years I would try to go back to Egypt with the same company, but the job offer had been withdrawn and I never could get them to respond to my letters or calls.

If we weren't going to Egypt, our next preference would be to stay in the La Salle area. I had my hand on the pulse of the medical community and I knew there were no PA jobs in town. Therefore, I was going to have to create a job.

Since I had an interest in headache disorders, I wanted to create a headache position. There was one neurologist, Dr. Lessen, who had a special interest in headache. We had already shared several patients.

I had been on the ground level of one of the premier, comprehensive headache centers in the country while I was in Ann Arbor. I put together a plan of developing a comprehensive headache treatment center in La Salle. The hospital there was trying to become the regional medical treatment center and this would fit with their goals.

I mailed my package to Dr. Lessen and sent a copy to Mr. Baker, the CEO of LaSalle General Hospital, which employed her. Soon I called them and got the ball rolling. Dr. Lessen told me in a sweet voice over the phone, "I am quite interested in this idea. I would love to talk to you about it. Why don't you come by my office on Thursday about 5:30, when I am done seeing patients."

On Thursday I rushed home from work and switched into civilian clothes and headed down the hill to LaSalle. Dr. Lessen was in a group practice of four neurologists on the ground floor of a large four-story medical complex. I was taken back to her office, where I only had to wait a few minutes before she joined me.

Dr. Lessen bounced through the door with more energy than you would expect at the end of a grueling day. She was a young thin woman with medium-length crinkled hair, and quite pleasant. "Mike, I have wanted to branch into headache treatment for a long time. Your letter was quite timely. I really think I could get this off the ground with your help." We ended the meeting with her saying, "I will set up a meeting with Mr. Baker within the next two weeks."

The meeting with Mr. Baker was very productive and it seemed this thing was going to fly. I was getting excited. For the next several weeks I continued dialoguing with the two of them, then something strange happened. Suddenly, neither of them would return my calls or letters. Three weeks later, I got the surprise of my life. In the local newspaper was LaSalle General Hospital's ad announcing the opening of Dr. Lessen's headache clinic.

After several additional attempts to reach her, finally we connected. "Mike, I am sorry, but there is no place for your services in our headache clinic."

I didn't want to beg, but I offered to make a deal. "Give me three months to prove myself and I could be laid off if I'm not worth much more than my cost."

She responded with, "Well, it is our feeling, Mr. Baker's and mine, that, PAs can't work in specialties, only general areas of medicine such as family practice."

"Really?" I said. "Someone better tell the thousands of PAs who presently work in specialties and are excellent at what they do." It was hopeless to reason with them.

The time of my separation from the Air Force was fast approaching. I had invested several months in the hopes of the headache clinic. Now, I had to start over looking for a job. I was about to give up on La Salle when I had a call from Rick. He had taken the plunge into the civilian world a year earlier and was working in a family practice clinic in the basement of the same building as Dr. Lessen's practice.

"Mike, the internal medicine practice in my building just lost their PA. The people up there are really nice and I think you would love to work for them. Do you mind if I give them your name?"

"Sure," I responded.

The next day, the rheumatologist in the internal medicine group called me and set up an interview.

I met with the practice administrator, Jim, the rheumatologist, and the two nephrologists. They did appear to be very nice people. By the end of the interview, the three physicians told Jim, "Let's start the process of hiring him."

They called my references within three days and were ready to draw up a contract. I met with Jim as we were putting things together.

When we got to the point of discussing compensation, I was offered a base salary that was less than what new graduates were making. Jim pointed out, "Mike, you see this salary is just a base. If you are willing to work hard, our incentive package would greatly increase your income. Beth, the previous PA, was quite slow but she was still able to earn $10,000 a year extra."

I had never worked under an incentive program and approached the arrangement with great caution. Rick was working under an incentive agreement and was doing quite well. He was earning over $20,000 per year in additional income.

Jim then showed me the formula they used to calculate the bonus. It looked like an equation written by Stephen Hawking. It made no sense to me since I wasn't familiar with their collectibles, billables, and expenses, each of which was a variable in the formula. This would have been an excellent time for me to introduce a lawyer of my own into the process. Unfortunately I didn't. I preferred working on trust. I was young—well, not that young—and foolish. If I had involved a lawyer, I would probably be working in that practice to this day. I did ask to see the incentive payment records of the previous PA. The records were consistent with what Jim had told me.

In a couple of weeks, Jim sent me the final contract to sign. I certainly hadn't memorized the original incentive formula, but the formula written in the final contract did seem different to me. I called Jim and said, "Jim, this formula looks different than the one that was in Beth's contract. Are you sure it's the same?"

"Oh, yes Mike, it's exactly the same."

I accepted the position and soon started to work. I was excited to continue on with our lives after the past few months of uncertainty.

We were now looking forward to a long life in La Salle. Everything seemed to be coming together for us. We had our farm and our sheep. During our four years in La Salle we had made some of the best friends of our lives. We loved the forest, the mountains, Nordic skiing, and of course Lake Superior. I had become an avid sea kayaker and thoroughly enjoyed paddling on the big lake year round.

The sheep were a blast. We started with two ewes. Our first lambing season was a crash course in shepherding. The previous fall I took my two ewes on a date to a large sheep farm about 75 miles away. There were about four rams. Each of them, to borrow a line from Mae West, were "very happy to see" our ewes. In the end, however, only one of our ewes conceived.

With Easter approaching, I started reading several books on lambing. Unfortunately there was not a *Lambing for Dummies* book out at the time (although there probably is now). One book I read made the point that lambing was natural and the best thing for the shepherd was to just leave the ewes alone.

Well, I did leave my ewe alone. She started labor. After a few hours of moaning, I walked out to the field to check her out. There was something black hanging out of her rear. From a distance I thought it was mucous or blood. When I got close, I recognized the hair on the tip of it. It was a tail! This lamb was full breech.

I pulled on the lamb for half an hour. I had my arms inside her up to my elbows, but still I couldn't get the lamb's rear legs out. Denise, who at least grew up on a farm, started pulling. I went in the house to get our brilliant book about lambing. I read the directions while Denise continued pushing and pulling. Between the three of us, the lamb was finally born. He was a cute little black lamb with Apgars (a scale for evaluating newborns) of about negative 2. His eyes were crossed, as were his legs. He acted like he had just finished off two quarts of cheap liquor. We named him Bam Bam. His sister, Pebbles, came bouncing out, head first, as easy as a greased egg out of a turkey. Pebbles was up on her feet within minutes. Bam Bam, unfortunately, didn't survive the night.

The next events unfolded like we were following the book's list of lambing tragedies item by item. In a couple of hours, our ewe collapsed and started having seizures. While she was having her seizure, she pushed her uterus completely inside-out. From the book I gathered she was having seizures from a condition they called "milk fever." This is a metabolic problem caused by a sudden shifting of calcium out of her serum into her mammary glands. This happened to be Easter Sunday and the veterinarians in town weren't reachable. I did leave a message on the answering machine at one vet's office.

I was able to find a local market open and I bought a large bottle of Tums. All they had were mint flavor. While I was gone, the vet called and said she was on her way.

I force-fed the ewe a whole bottle of the chalky tablets while she continued having seizure after seizure. She about bit my index finger off during one spasm. In between the seizures, she was belching mint-flavor belches.

When the vet arrived, she started an IV of calcium glutamate. Within minutes, the ewe started coming around and was on her feet and eating. The next problem was putting her uterus back in. This was a lesson in the difference of animal and human medicine.

The vet washed the uterus off and crammed it back in with her fist. The uterus kept sliding out so we had a problem. "You know," said the vet, "normally we would put a ewe down in this situation. But, I understand she is a pet. So I'll do my best to save her."

The vet looked around the barn trying to decide what to do. She still had her right hand in the ewe's vagina, holding her uterus in. She looked toward her backpack and said, "Hey, hand me that bottle of Coke." It was a large 20-oz size.

I handed her the bottle, thinking she was thirsty. She finished drinking the cola, screwed the cap back on, and then stuck it into the ewe's vagina to hold in the uterus. Then she sutured the vagina closed. For the next two weeks the ewe walked around with the white bottle cap sticking out of her vagina with "Always Coca Cola" written on it. I don't think I had seen this particular technique in human medicine before, but I saw no reason why it wouldn't work.

It did work for our ewe and she lived to lamb again the next season. During that next season, all three ewes conceived and two had healthy triplets. Our flock went from three to ten overnight.

I enjoyed my new position in internal medicine. The staff was made up of some of the nicest people I had ever met. The first time I stopped by to drop off my books, the medical technologist asked, "What's your favorite kind of cookies?"

"Uh, oatmeal raisin, why do you ask?"

"I was just wondering."

My first morning at work, to my surprise, there was a large plate of freshly made oatmeal raisin cookies.

Out of the seven physicians, all were very smart and six were very nice. The seventh one, Dr. Holcomb, was very anti-PA. He was a young physician who was the son of a physician. When I first started, I was warned, "Mike, never see one of Dr. Holcomb's patients, or he will be very angry." I couldn't understand why. I was told, "Dr Holcomb hates all non-physician clinicians."

Until my Air Force experience, I had an almost subconscious mental framework that physicians held the deed to "Medical Practice Land." Maybe it was from my upbringing and the larger-than-life mystique physicians held in our eyes then. I had the sense that I was in this land as a guest of theirs, and I didn't have a "birthright" as a citizen—having been allowed into Medical Practice Land out of the kindness of the physicians' hearts.

It reminded me of our first few months in Egypt. When I had first arrived in Cairo, all the merchants took advantage of us. A cab ride for my neighbor would cost them two pounds. The same ride for us would cost five-ten pounds. It was the same with food and other products. One of the first things I learned to say in Arabic was, "I'm not a tourist—I live here!" We were dependent on the local economy because we were locals. In Medical Practice Land, PAs are not tourists, we are "locals." Practicing medicine is what we do.

Dr. Holcomb did hate all PAs and NPs. As far as I know, it wasn't traceable to a single bad experience. After 15 years in practice, it was finally coming clear to me. He hated them for the same reason that white supremacists hate African-Americans: blind bigotry and prejudice. Just like butchers, bakers and candle stick makers—in all walks of life some people are insecure. Physicians who are insecure feel threatened by non-physicians who are doing some of the things they are trained to do. Sometimes this insecurity is expressed as bigotry.

I could only imagine a world in which quality of care was REALLY the concern; in which all providers were on the same team, playing on a level ball field–where the patient wins. A world in which you were not measured by the letters after your name, but on such parameters as your listening ability, medical judgment, empathy, bedside manner, as well as medical skills and knowledge.

Those physicians who are bigots fortunately constitute a relative few. But for several years to come, as I tried to make a beachhead in the real world, physician bigots became like land mines in my fields of dreams.

After working in the internal medicine practice for six months I was becoming quite busy. The first quarter, things had been slow, and I didn't receive an incentive check. I wasn't too surprised. With the second quarter over I was expecting a generous bonus, but none came. One afternoon, I went to Jim's office and took a seat. "It has been 45 days since the end of the quarter. When do I get my incentive check?"

Jim, who kept the books and knew where all the money went, said, "You have not broken the threshold for earning incentive yet." I was perplexed. It had been a very busy quarter.

Something wasn't making a whole lot of sense to me. Now that I knew more about the nature of the practice, I sat down with a calculator and started working with the formula, running different numbers through it. I was shocked to see that even if I greatly out-performed the physicians, I could never earn incentive. Was something wrong with my math?

Jim had hedged every time I brought up the subject. Finally I went into his office again and was insistent. "Jim, something doesn't make sense here. I am working harder than Beth, but not earning the incentive that she did. What's going on?"

He got up and closed his door. "Mike, you see, after your interview (and before I had signed the contract) the physicians had their monthly staff meeting. When we announced that you were joining the practice, Dr. Holcomb said that PAs don't deserve to earn the kind of incentive that we were paying Beth. The other physicians agreed. Therefore

THEY changed your formula. That is why Beth was able to earn incentive and you aren't."

I reflected back on the phone call I had made to Jim from the Air Force base–when he told me the contract had not changed.

I don't consider myself materialistic. Being the sole provider for seven changes your perspective on money. I had turned down other positions that had paid much better because I was counting on the incentive money. With my kids' futures in mind, I knew I needed to be in a situation where I could work my buns off and get paid accordingly. Now, I would be earning less than a new graduate–no matter how hard I worked, I couldn't change my income.

I left Jim's office and went directly to find the rheumatologist. She was busy seeing patients. As she walked out of a room, I grabbed her and took her into an examining room. "Dr. Pierre, we have a major problem."

After I told her the story, she said, "It was Jim's idea to change the incentive formula to save the practice money."

I hated being lied to; it was starting to taint what had seemed like a very good job.

The physicians I worked with were very smart, and their patients often were very sick. I was on another steep learning curve. With time, I started getting my greatest support from one of the nephrologists, Dr. Pollock. Through my persistence, he eventually got my contract changed back to the original one that Jim had shown me. Dr. Pollock grew to appreciate my contribution to the practice most and gave me the most professional respect. After the incentive issue had been resolved, there appeared to be smooth sailing ahead until another infamous dark cloud started developing on the horizon. This time the disturbance had to do with a major dispute developing between Drs. Pollock and Holcomb.

The two physicians had been partners for ten years, but due to personal problems, their professional marriage began falling apart. Dr. Holcomb went on vacation for almost two months. While he was gone, the other physicians led a crusade to sell the practice from beneath his feet. Secret meetings ensued; however, these were MD-only meetings.

I was left in the dark and had to rely on the same rumors the secretaries and other office staff heard.

When Dr. Holcomb returned in the fall, things were tense. He too was in the dark. Then the physicians had a practice-wide meeting and announced the practice had been sold to LaSalle General Hospital. There was no question that was a declaration of war. Dr. Holcomb eventually resigned, as did another physician.

You would think that life would have improved for me in the practice with Dr. Holcomb gone. Yet, the clouds were still building. In the aftermath of the practice war, peace was not a simple assumption. The office climate underwent a dramatic change. What had been a happy "mom and pop" type of practice soon became a corporate machine. What had been a family was now a factory. I am sure the physicians were well compensated during the buyout, but the nursing and clerical staff watched helplessly as their status deteriorates from colleagues to cogs in the machine.

One day, precisely at 5:00, I watched in amazement as the nurses lined up at the time clock, clocked out, and returned to work without missing a beat. I asked Ruth, the head nurse, "Why did everyone just do that?"

"It is mandatory by LaSalle General. Everyone has to clock out at five because they don't pay overtime. Anyone working over forty hours a week can get into trouble."

"But Ruth, you are still working. There're still patients in the lobby."

"The hospital tells us it is our fault if we can't get our work done by five."

"But Ruth, it's not your fault. You can't just walk out while the physicians are still seeing patients, can you?"

"Well, no. But you see, Mike, we have talked to the hospital about this. Their response is that they have a filing cabinet full of applicants. If we don't like the way they do things, they can always find someone else."

During the buyout, I attempted several times to get an audience with LaSalle General because I needed to iron out my own contract. Finally I met with none other than Mr. Baker.

"Well, Mr. Jones, I hear you are worried that you will not have a job. You don't need to worry because the physicians want you to stay."

"I wasn't worried about that; what I am concerned with is my contract."

"We will extend to you the same conditions of the contract you started with last year."

"Yes, but we changed that contract. The original incentive plan was just smoke and mirrors—it would never have earned me a dime."

"Mr. Jones, we are offering you a fine contract, now take it or leave it."

The great twentieth century philosopher, Maria Van Trapp (from the *Sound of Music*), once said, "Whenever God closes a door He always opens a window." About this time, a physician in town, Dr. Bohjanen, wanted to take me out to dinner to discuss an idea he'd had. He had a reputation for being one of the nicest, most laid-back physicians around. He was a heavy man, in his forties, with sandy blond hair and glasses—looking something like a middle-aged beach-boy.

Denise and I met Dr. Bohjanen and his wife, May, on the corner of Main and Front streets in downtown LaSalle. The old storefronts behind piles of snow always gave me the feeling of being somewhere in the Yukon rather than Michigan. We walked up the sidewalk sharing small talk, each breath turning opaque in the cold December air. We ducked inside the Italian restaurant favored by all the locals.

Dr. Bohjanen shared with me what he had on his heart.

"Mike, I have heard through the grapevine that you are a good PA and I know there has been a lot of turmoil over at the Internal Medicine practice. I own the Superior Medical office in Haines. When I first had it built, I anticipated it being a busy medical center. I started out doing family practice, but now of course I spend all my time in OB. I am only in my building two days a week. I spend the rest of the time at one of the other clinics owned by Mason Memorial.

I've been thinking that you could come over to Superior Medical and start a family practice clinic—under my supervision, of course. What do you think?"

The concept of working for someone like Dr Bohjanen and having the freedom to start my own practice was every PA's dream. "I think I might be very interested in this."

I soon set up a meeting with the CEO of Mason Memorial, Mr. Jansen. He was a recent transplant from Ohio and knew the value of PAs and NPs. He too was excited about the concept. I would be the first PA employed by his hospital.

I shared my financial requirements. Mr. Jansen was much more accommodating than his counterpart at LaSalle General.

I decided to give the Internal Medicine practice another chance. I returned for a few weeks only to see that the turmoil had snowballed. Now there was a very soap opera-type saga being played out in the office that was affecting the practice. This time two real marriages (rather than professional marriages) were the causalities. The last chapter of the saga ended with an impaired physician, and me in the awkward position of covering for their spontaneous absences. The happy family environment seemed lost forever. Maybe I am too idealistic. Maybe I only see the glass as half full, even when it is as full as everyone knows it's ever going to be. But I decided there must be a better place to settle down in the real professional world.

I accepted the offer with Dr. Bohjanen's hospital, Mason Memorial. I started meeting with Mr. Jansen in the weeks leading up to starting the new practice. I developed a marketing strategy and put together an inventory of needed supplies. I had determined in my heart to make this practice succeed. I was confident that, given the freedom, I could do it.

My father was taking a turn for the worse in Tennessee. I had all the plans set into motion for the new clinic and decided to take a four-week break between jobs. We went to Tennessee and spent Christmas with my dad, who was at home in a hospital bed. I knew it would be the last of 39 Christmases with him.

The one Christmas with dad that I will always remember was our fifth one together. Earlier that year, he had taken a job in a small town in Florida called Orlando. No one had heard of it at the time. Dad left the rest of us in Tennessee until the house sold. Since he was 550 miles away, we only saw him once every few months.

Dad was going to have four days off for Christmas and was planning on getting home Christmas Eve. Two weeks earlier, dad had asked me over the phone, "Mike, what do you want Santa to bring you this year?

"What I really want is a toy electric razor, like one I saw on TV."

Christmas Eve came and Tennessee was receiving one of its rare snowstorms. My siblings and I watched out the windows all day as the snow accumulated, first on the mountain tops and then in the yard. Dad never showed. Mom grew nervous. While she ran a frantic pace in the kitchen, making Christmas cakes and pies, I would catch her looking out the glass door at every opportunity.

Late that evening, the phone rang. The operator said, "Will you accept long distance charges from a Bill Jones?"

"Yes," I said and quickly handed the phone to mom. Her head just moved up and down as she listened intently. "OK, just be careful. Sure they will be disappointed, but I don't want you to take any chances. I love you, too."

I quickly walked into the living room, trying to somehow put distance between the bad news and me.

Mom walked in with her apron still on, her hands covered in flour, and her eyes filled with tears.

"Your dad ran into snow in northern Georgia and is going to spend the night there. If he can't get through tomorrow, he'll have to turn around and go back to Orlando for work." She started to cry and said, "Santa might not make it either." She had to turn around and almost run back into the kitchen.

Mom didn't know what to do since dad had all the presents. On Christmas morning, we woke up to an empty tree. The snow was about ten inches deep by then. It was the most beautiful, but oddly the saddest, Christmas morning I can remember. Just as we were sitting down to one of mom's famous biscuits and gravy breakfasts, dad pulled in the driveway. We couldn't believe it. He came in the front door carrying two large brown paper bags. He told us that he had checked into a motel, but couldn't sleep because he was thinking about us. He got up and decided to drive on, all night in the snow, to reach us by Christmas morning.

After our hugs and kisses, he handed me a box. He said, "I ran into a chubby man in a sleigh during the night. He told me this was for you."

My eyes were huge as I opened the box to find a battery-operated, teal-colored, toy razor. The next day dad returned to Orlando. We weren't able to sell the house and dad eventually moved back to Tennessee.

Ironically, during our trip to Tennessee to see my dying father, we made the 550-mile journey to Orlando. It was my kids' first trip to Disney. We had a great time and it was a good distraction. Then we returned to spend more time with dad. Our time together passed much too quickly, though. As I kissed dad goodbye, I knew I would never see him alive again. As I kissed mom goodbye, my heart broke. She had stood by dad day and night through his illnesses. Most families would have had their father in a nursing home or a hospice. But mom was determined to be his sole provider to the bitter end. You could criticize her for this choice, and sometimes I did, but you owed her your respect at the same time. This was her interpretation of her wedding vows. And dad hadn't been the easiest person to take care during the previous ten years.

We backed out of the driveway and drove up the large hill that led away from my mom's house–the same hill on which I learned to ride a bike. My mom and Aunt Helen (who was like my second mom) stood at the end of the driveway waving, as they always did, saying "Goodbye, sweety. Goodbye, honey-pie." The hill is named Painter Hill after one of the first residents on our street. We should have renamed it the "Crying Hill" after all the sobbing goodbyes that had taken place there. Each of my mom's four children had moved far away. Not having her grandchildren nearby was something else I felt bad about.

**Mom and Dad saying goodbye to their grandchildren
at the base of the "crying hill."**

We made the two-day drive back to La Salle. The next morning I drove down to my new clinic. I was excited to get things going. Finally I had found a home for my soul. La Salle was a beautiful place to live and this clinic was going to provide a wonderful work situation. If I could've created my perfect job, this would have been it! So far, the taste of the real world had been bittersweet. But, I was hopeful we had finally found a resting place and that the best was yet to come. But dreams can have a way of slipping through your fingers just as you are clenching your fist around them.

Chapter Twenty-one

Invasion of the Clinic Snatchers

About two blocks from the new clinic, out on Highway 41, sat the Traveler's Motel. It was a cheap reproduction of a Bavarian-style building with a fake brick façade and imitation brown beams. Ten-foot mountains of plowed snow surrounded the partially paved parking lot. The restaurant was a common meeting place for folks in the little hamlet of Haines, outside of La Salle.

I was early for my meeting with Mr. Jansen. On the phone that morning he had asked for the meeting. He was going to disclose some great secret, which he assured me would un-shroud the previous six weeks of confusion and frustration. I could hardly wait. I ordered a Rueben, fries, and an iced tea. I sat facing the double glass doors that led to the frozen parking lot so I would be sure not to miss him when he arrived. I reflected on the events that had led up to this meeting.

After arriving back in La Salle, I drove down to see my new clinic. It was a Friday and the grand opening would be on Monday.

As I approached my clinic, the first thing I noticed was there was no new sign by the road, only the old one with the name of the podiatrist and Dr. Bohjanen. I was disappointed, as it had been the first step of my marketing scheme to put up a new sign. However, I realized that new signs could take time.

When I entered the building, I gave my greetings to the front office staff, Sandy and Ann. At this point they were strangers, but would soon become dear friends. "Where did you ladies put the supplies?"

The two of them looked puzzled. "What supplies?"

What supplies? I had ordered a truckload before I left. Mrs. White the nursing supervisor at Mason Memorial was also the director of outpatient services. I had given her a long list of essentials, and she assured me they would be at the clinic long before opening day.

I got on the phone immediately. Mrs. White wasn't available but I spoke to her secretary. "Hello, this is Michael Jones at the East Clinic. I was checking to see if you know what happened to the supplies that Mrs. White was going to order for us."

"What is the East Clinic?"

"It is the new clinic the hospital is opening on the east side of the county–in Haines."

"I don't know what you are talking about. Are you sure you have the right number?"

"Yes, I am sure I have the right number. Would you please check into it for me and call me back?"

"What kind of supplies are you looking for?"

"It was a long list of supplies. All the things needed to start a clinic. Also, she was going to look into getting a sign for the clinic."

"OK, I will see what I can find out, but I am her secretary and I don't know anything about a new clinic."

She never returned my call. I called back later in the afternoon and the secretary told me, "Mrs. White doesn't know anything about the order. Can you send her another one? She also says she knows nothing about a sign."

Was I on *Candid Camera* . . . or perhaps *The Twilight Zone?* I had spent a whole afternoon putting the original order together, now I would have to start over–and with the clinic opening in only two days. The second time around didn't take as long. I faxed Mrs. White the new list. Now, however, opening day would come and I would have no basic medical supplies.

Monday, I showed up for my first day at work. I got busy moving my things in and setting them up. By the end of the first three days, there were still no supplies and none of the radio advertising I had planned on. I called Mrs. White's office again. "May I speak to Mrs. White."

"Mrs. White is in a meeting."

This is Michael Jones and I want to make sure our things have been ordered and I want to see what is happening to our advertising."

"OK, I will look into it." Again, she never called back.

On Monday morning, one week after opening day, I drove the 30 miles to the Mason Memorial. I was beginning to feel like Mrs. White was the most incompetent administrator I had ever known. I barged into her office. "Hi, can you tell me what is going on? Where are my supplies?"

"Mike, I think everything is in the hands of John in Central Supply."

I marched into Central Supply. "I want to speak to John," I said, thinking that he must be the incompetent one behind the scenes. Instead, I found a very nice older gentleman.

John was puzzled. "I know nothing of the order. I didn't even know we had an East Clinic." Fortunately I had kept a photocopy of the order and handed it to him.

"Wow, this is a lot of stuff. You see, my problem is that I have to have a department account number and authorization to order these things. Does the East Clinic have an account number?"

"We should. These things were supposed to be ordered five weeks ago."

"This is first time I have even heard of the East Clinic. Let me see what I can give you to hold you over."

He was able to come up with a few things: 4 x 4's, Band-Aids, and the like. However, he had to be stingy with them. I stopped by the office of Mr. Jansen, the CEO, and left a message that I wanted to talk to him. Unfortunately, he was out of town for a week.

I was starting to see patients now and then who had stumbled across the clinic by accident (there being no sign or advertising). They were word of mouth referrals–usually family members of Sandy and Ann or of Cathy, the gal who ran the lab and X-ray at the clinic.

I drove over and met with Mr. Jansen after he returned, to complain about the logjam with Mrs. White. "I feel angry," I said. "What is the big hold-up? I want to get the clinic going." At this point, I naively was placing all the blame on Mrs. White.

Mr. Jansen said, "OK, relax Mike. I will look into it."

The next major hurdle was the Air Force base closing. This would mean there were going to be hundreds of retirees and their families left in the area without a base to provide medical care. Champus, the military insurance program, was setting up a network of preferred providers for these families under their insurance program called Tri-Care. I had an inside line to this process because the woman in charge of setting this up was a personal friend of mine. I called her and she warned me, "Mike, make sure Mason Memorial does the paperwork to get your clinic on the Tri-Care provider list, otherwise, all these military dependents will think that they can't see you. If you aren't listed now, it will be really hard to get added later."

The cornerstone to this process was agreeing to certain fees and completing the paperwork. This presented no problem because my fees were already under their cap.

I obtained the application and sent it on to Mr. Jansen, pointing out how important it was for our clinic. A couple of weeks later, when the Tri-Care notice was published in the La Salle paper, our clinic wasn't listed as a participating provider, although the two other clinics owned by Mason Memorial were. To rub salt in the wound, I ran into one of my few patients in the mall that evening. I had followed this man and his family while I was in the Air Force. When he saw me he said, "Mike, no offense, but I called your clinic and asked them to send our records to the La Salle Family Practice Clinic because, according to Tri-Care, we aren't allowed to come to you any more."

That was the last straw. Again, I was operating on trust and was being disappointed. I called Mr. Jansen that morning. "Why weren't we included in the Tri-Care list? I told you how important it was."

"Don't worry about it, Mike. Hey, why don't I drive over and have lunch with you today? I need to tell you something that will explain what is going on."

Now that really got my attention. I thought, *Do you mean there is a purpose behind this madness?*

I had just taken a bite out of my Rueben when I saw Mr. Jansen's silver sedan drive by the restaurant window. In a moment he came through the glass door, stomping the freshly falling snow off his black rubber overshoes. He took off his gray wool overcoat, hung it on the rack, and came through the inside doors.

"Good morning, Mike. Good to see you."

I said, "Here, have a seat. I hope you don't mind that I started without you. I wanted to be done by the time you got here so my mouth would be clear to talk. Go ahead and order."

After a little small talk, Mr. Jansen looked at me and said, "Mike, I must level with you. While you were out of town, before the clinic even opened, there was a meeting of the hospital board (made up of older businessmen in the community where Mason Memorial was located). When I told them you were a Physician Assistant, they almost downloaded their breakfast into their Depends [my paraphrase]. They couldn't believe we were relying on a Physician Assistant to take care of patients, all alone, thirty miles away. They thought you were a physician. I tried to explain to them what a PA was, but it was no use. They decided that we can't invest one more cent in this clinic until we hire an MD."

He could see the dismay building on my face.

"I want to talk to them," I demanded.

"Mike, it is of no use. They were quite upset and there is nothing you could say to change their minds. In the end, I promised them I would hire a family medicine MD. I am new to this hospital myself and I don't want to start out on the wrong foot with the board. But, Mike, don't be discouraged. We are going to keep you, and as soon as we recruit an MD we will pour money into the clinic, buying all the supplies and marketing the place like crazy. In the meantime, we need you to just hold down the fort."

"Hold down the fort?" I whispered.

Reality began to grow more distant. The rest of his words grew faint until I could no longer hear them. I could see his lips moving, but nothing made sense to me.

Mr. Jansen took advantage of my silence with another bite of his food. After washing it down he added, "Mike, we also need you to be somewhat covert in your practice. If LaSalle General knows that we have planted a family practice provider in their territory, it could be a declaration of war. They would come into Haines and build a much bigger clinic—not to make money but to make sure that we didn't. That's medical business. Then it would be fruitless to hire an MD because this clinic could never succeed in their shadow. Once we have the MD on board, we will go public."

"How can you practice covert medicine?" I said rhetorically.

I sensed another deep betrayal. It was like Mel Gibson in *Braveheart* when he pulled the helmet off the English solider only to discover it was his dear friend, Robert the Bruce, who was now fighting for the English. The stonewalling had been deliberate—it was the result of back room meetings with a well-thought-out plan, all the while leaving me completely in the dark.

Dr. Bohjanen wasn't in on the plot, but remained very supportive. He had already been removed as my supervisor. Mr. Jansen had a legitimate reason. He was concerned that my practice would fall outside the "scope of practice" of Dr. Bohjanen since he was an obstetrician. I had great confidence in Dr. Bohjanen's judgment in all areas of family medicine. However, it wouldn't look good on paper to have an obstetrician supervising a family practice Physician Assistant. So another family practice physician, Dr. Bolton, who had been in practice about 45 years, was appointed as my supervisor. He had a clinic 30 miles away in the same town as Mason Memorial.

I questioned, too, what role the word "assistant" played in this whole matter. Johnny Cash sang a ballad about a boy named Sue. The boy's father couldn't be around to raise him (for some lame reason) so he named him Sue to make him tough. It worked. The boy had to literally fight his way through life. The founders of our profession chose to name us "Physician Assistants." Their intentions may have been good at the time, but we quickly outgrew the name, which became an albatross around our professional necks. The name "Physician Assistant" conjures up the synonym "Doctor's Little Helper" in the minds of many. Even my own son, Ramsey, described what I do (based on my title) as "holding instruments and stuff for the busy doctor." Maybe we are tougher for the battles we have fought, but there comes a time when such battles are not as amusing as they once were.

The process of recruiting a physician took much longer than anyone imagined. After several months without a single inquiry, I became impatient for patients. I was trying to make the most of each visit whenever I did see one. I gave each patient a lot of attention and even made a few house calls. I also did something I had never done before: I called every patient 24-hours after their visit, just to see how they were doing.

A few of my patients were "rejects" from other practices. These were people who were troubled in one way or another. Australia has its outback, and Michigan has its Up-back, with the "Up" standing for Upper Peninsula. Like the outback, so I've heard, the Up-back had a den of Ted Kaczynski types living there. Many were coming out of the woods to see me. Some of them were enlisted men who had retired from the military. They found out they could live off their retirement if they lived in a shack or an old school bus hidden way, I mean way back in the woods. They would come out a few times a year to buy dog food and beer and to drop by the clinic. Even those guys were welcome. Being the new clinic in town, I also had my share of–speaking of dog food–"my dog ate my Vicodin prescription" visits. Those I could have done without.

I had one sociopathic single father and his three children as my main customers for a while. The man always appeared to be in a state of mania. He had a very troubled past. To make matters worse, he was a gun collector.

Once he called wanting me to treat his girlfriend's STD. She could not come in because she was under house arrest and was wearing a police tether. He was screaming out every detail of her symptoms and the intimate description of their sexual activities. I said, "Why are you screaming so loud?"

"I am here at Sears getting tires put on my car. I am in the garage waiting room and I can't hear you for all the damn people in here talking." I could just imagine the scene and the looks on their faces.

I had seen his children several times and we were actually getting along quite well. Then one day as I was looking in his little girl's ears, he said, "Mr. Jones, could you give me a refill of my Valium? An ENT specialist put me on eight 5mg tablets per day for my severe Meniere's Disease. So I would need 240 tablets a month."

I finished looking in his daughter's ear and put away my otoscope. "Well, for one thing, I don't have a DEA number and Valium is a controlled drug. Secondly, I have never heard of using Valium at this dose for Meniere's Disease."

He started to fidget. "Well, could you ask your supervising physician for a prescription?"

"What I could do is make an appointment to see Dr. Bolton. He comes over here one morning every week or two."

The next time I ran into Dr. Bolton he said, "I saw that nut who wanted all the Valium. He's bad news. I sent him a letter telling him to stay the hell out of our clinic."

The patient was enraged that he couldn't get his medication. He came to my clinic twice looking for me, but fortunately I missed him both times. He left word that he was "angry as hell and was not going to let us get by with this." I spoke to Dr. Bolton about my concerns regarding the patient's aggressive behavior. Dr. Bolton's response was, "Let him come after me. I bet I have bigger guns than he does." This physician was a transplant from New York City to the Up-back, a dangerous combination. I was worried about getting caught in the crossfire.

I, on the other hand, never owned a gun, unless you count my BB gun I had when I was twelve. Not owning a gun in the Up-back of Michigan was about as odd as living in Aspen without owning skis.

I followed another family in the clinic that was made up of a single mom and her five children—from five different fathers. They were season ticket holders. I would be shocked when a week went by and they didn't make an appearance.

During one such visit, the ten-year-old daughter had a sore throat. She was a chubby little girl with dirty-blond hair (or maybe it was dirty, blond hair) and rosy cheeks. I had her on the table and, as I examined her, I was trying my best to make her laugh. Her wild siblings were going through the drawers and checking out the medical equipment. One had a blood pressure cuff around his little brother's neck, trying to pump it up. Another one had a vaginal speculum and was trying to stick it down his brother's throat. I grabbed these things away as the mom made no attempt to control them. I was feeling very critical of her parenting techniques.

I said to the girl, "You are so quiet. You're not like your wild brothers at all."

The mother was sitting in a chair to the side of the room, thumbing through a People magazine with Madonna on the cover. She said, in a very calm voice without even looking up, "Yeah, she's pretty shy. I think it is because her dad used to have sex with her."

By this time, you would think that nothing would shock me. However, the calmness of her tone and her saying it in front of the whole family got my goat. I looked at the little girl and my heart broke. "That is horrible!" I said almost as a reflex. The girl didn't bat an eye.

The mom added, "She'll get over it—my dad had sex with me when I was her age," and continued flipping through the magazine, like she was talking about the weather.

No, I don't think she will "get over it." There certainly can be healing but now I was a little less critical of the mom. The sins of the father are visited on the next generation. There is always the possibility of redemption, but short of that, I see another box seat in hell next to the warmongers and the lying TV evangelists. It is for those men—and sometimes women—who have inflicted mortal wounds on the innocent.

Out of boredom I decided to take matters into my own hands at the clinic. I set up a workshop in the basement and started making a large neon sign that read, "Walk-In Clinic." I had the lettering done professionally. While worked on it, I wore coveralls, and if someone stomped on the floor and screamed from upstairs, "Hey Mike, you have a patient," I would rip off the coveralls, a la Superman, and run up to see them. (Actually, maybe it was a little more like Mighty Mouse.) Once the sign was done, I placed it on top of the old sign by the road and wired up the internal lights.

The number of customers gradually increased. When I finally reached the 10-patient (in a day) milestone, I took the whole office out to nice restaurant to celebrate. However, the boredom was continuing to get to me. The only thing worse than being overworked is being underworked. I read every journal that I could. I even took the time to write a couple of articles for journals; and still I had time on my hands and we had no physician prospects. So, I decided to build a boat inside the clinic: a 21-foot wood strip sea kayak. During the process, I had several visitors from the medical community. They just couldn't believe what I was doing.

About the time I was finishing up my boat, I had a call from Mr. Jansen. "Mike, we have an applicant for the physician position. He is coming to town next week."

This young doctor, Bob Edgar, showed up on Tuesday. Mr. Jansen drove over with him to show him around. He looked like Adam Sandler with glasses and seemed like a really nice guy. We shared a lot of outdoor interests, such as hiking and biking. The only drawback was that he was very tangential, much like Chuck had been. He spoke in philosophical terms at every breath (at this point you have to lose the Adam Sandler image, especially his *Water Boy* character). It was hard to follow his thinking at times. He was really into heath care policy, Preferred Provider Networks, HMOs, and capitation. One of these three terms seemed to make an appearance in every sentence out of his mouth. The odd thing was that there wasn't one of these systems in place in our whole area of the state.

Dr. Edgar had completed the Family Practice program in Duluth a couple of years earlier. From my conversation with him, I couldn't quite tell what he had been up to since that time. He spoke of working with the Indian Health Service and a private practice as well.

It was about a month later that Mr. Jansen called to tell me, "Mike, you should be excited. We have called Dr. Edgar and offered him a very generous package (more than triple my salary). He has officially accepted the offer and will be moving over in about three weeks. If he hadn't accepted this position, we were going to terminate you and close the clinic." Something about the word "terminate" struck me as dehumanizing–as if I were a pest or a machine.

A couple of weeks later Dr. Edgar and Mr. Jansen came by to survey the clinic. At the end of their tour, they called a meeting. The podiatrist and his staff came. Dr. Bohjanen and his staff and I all showed up. It was the oddest meeting I had been in since the meeting with Chuck in Cyprus. I was feeling somewhat stupid because I couldn't make sense of Dr. Edgar's point. He spoke of "how terrible the facility was" and how as "part of his agreement with Mason Memorial, he was given complete control of a total make-over of the building." He lectured the whole group in a very condescending way. He said, "In the modern paradigm of capitation the hardware and environment of the medical practice must be in consistent compliance with the expectations of third-party payers to compete in a free market society, with the customer, our patients, finding our standards to surpass the traditional expectations . . . blah, blah, blah." I listened out of respect. Dr. Edgar didn't make a whole lot of sense but just sounded like a medical dictionary in a blender.

When the two of them left, Dr. Bohjanen expressed what I for one certainly was thinking: "What the hell was he talking about? If he is talking about remodeling this building, he better talk to me because I as far as I know, I still own it."

A couple of weeks later I had an urgent call from Mr. Jansen. "Mike, I have a major favor to ask of you. Dr. Scott, our ER physician, broke his leg this afternoon while mountain biking. He was scheduled to relieve Dr. Williams tomorrow morning at 8:00. I have called all of our physicians and, it being the Fourth of July weekend, none are available. Someone brought up your name. What do you think?"

I felt a little nervous taking over a hospital ER, but at the same time I was glad to have an opportunity to contribute after a year of sitting. I answered with a cautious, "Maybe. But will I have physician back-up somewhere?"

"Well, here is the strange thing. Dr. Scott is actually a patient in the hospital himself. He's alert but in a lot of pain. He would be your back up."

I arrived at 7:30 in the morning on the Fourth of July. Dr. Williams greeted me with a kind, "Hi, Michael." His soft demeanor and physical appearance reminded me of Dr. Jackson, my ER supervisor in PA school. However, Dr. Williams was middle aged and had paid back his commitment to the Air Force as a family practice physician. When he was done, he discovered the perfect job for him was one 24-hour shift in the ER per week, so he could fish the rest of the time.

"Mike, before I take off let me buy you breakfast and tell you how to run our ER."

"Sure." We made our way to the hospital cafeteria. Everyone we met, be they surgeon or janitor, said "Hi" to Dr. Williams and he greeted them back, usually swapping a quick fishing story.

Over breakfast an interesting topic came up. "Mike, how do you think you'll like working with that new Dr. Eager?"

"I don't know. He seems like a nice guy."

"Well, our ER nurses think he is a jerk."

"How would they know?"

"When he was here for his site visit, he had to bring his daughter into the ER for pyelonephritis. I was trying to cath her for a sterile urine specimen, and our nurse Brenda was helping me. She asked Dr. Eager to hand her a box of 4x4s, which was on the shelf behind him. He had the strangest response: 'I am a doctor. I don't hand nurses things, they hand me things.' Brenda was livid." Dr. Williams laughed and took another sip of his black coffee.

"So you are saying he seems a little arrogant?"

"Oh, arrogance is part of the work hazard of being a physician. This went far beyond arrogance. I just looked at him and said, 'You're not a doctor in my ER—you're a father. Now, please hand Ms Ryans the 4x4s.'"

That conversation was the most frightening event of my 24 hours in the ER.

The clinic doors opened at 9:00 a.m. for patients. On that first morning, Dr. Jekyll became Mr. Hyde. Dr. Edgar showed up at 6:00 a.m. and "cleaned" the clinic. There was certainly nothing wrong with that, except that he went through my personal things as well as those of the podiatrist. He threw away all of my books he considered outdated. He went through the papers on my desk, throwing away anything he thought wasn't important.

He threw away all sample drugs, including the podiatrist's drugs. He threw away every pen and calendar that had any advertisements of any kind.

I had two patients on my schedule that morning and both were "rejects" from other practices. The first patient had a somatization disorder and drug-seeking behavior. She had been thrown out of several practices for her overuse of narcotics for fibromyalgia and chronic abdominal pain. I was spending time with her, trying to divert her attention from her somatic complaints and to learn new techniques for dealing with her pain, other than medication. That morning she left in anger when I would not give her more Tylenol 3. The second patient was one of my headache patients. She had a terrible menstrual migraine. She was a very nice woman, but had been written off as a crock by every doctor in town because she hadn't responded to homeopathic doses of propranolol or amitriptyline. But, we were making progress.

When I had finished seeing the patients, Dr. Edgar called me back to the office. He said, "Mike, where are your patients? You didn't release them, did you?"

With an inflection of "duh" in my voice, I said, "Yes, I released them."

"Michael, I am the physician. You must present every patient to me, and you can't let them leave until I release them." I hadn't had this kind of supervision since PA school–the early part of school–and this guy was ten years younger than me, still wet behind the ears.

Although I had already discharged the two patients, I presented them to him as he had asked. He sat back in his high back office chair, the tip of his glasses frame in his mouth, looking every bit the Freud wannabe.

When I had finished presenting the first patient, the angry one, he leaned over in the chair and said, "Michael, what kind of necklace did the lady have on."

"I can't remember. I think it was silver. Why?"

"She didn't leave angry because you didn't give her Tylenol 3, she left angry because she knew in her soul that you didn't give a damn about her."

This struck me as odd, considering the hours I had spent with this woman when no one else in town would see her. "Really, now how do you figure that?"

"A woman only wears jewelry as a litmus test to see if someone else is honestly interested in her. It is a sublingual message. The very first thing you should have said to her was, 'That is a beautiful necklace,' then she would have responded to your treatment. From now on only I should see her."

I presented the next patient. I had placed the patient on Bellergal-S, which was working to control her very refractory menstrual migraine.

Dr. Edgar was reading through the patient's history as I spoke. "Michael, I can't believe that you are using such a barbaric drug. This is something they used 30 years ago. It is very dangerous because it contains Belladonna and an ergot (as if I didn't know). I want you to call her and have her stop this immediately. Her problem is obvious. From her family history, she recorded that her uncle–her father's brother–was an alcoholic. Now, that would imply that her father is probably a 'dry alcoholic.' It is very likely that her father had sexually molested her. When a woman has migraine at her menses it is often a sign she has been sexually abused."

Dr. Edgar was a regular Sherlock Holmes . . . a Sherlock Holmes who had gotten into a bad batch of mushrooms.

Dr. Edgar didn't know what he was talking about. It had been well established that the fall in estrogen prior to menses is a powerful migraine trigger. He began to reveal more and more of himself with each passing day. My initial positive impression of him was melting away as fast as the Wicked Witch of the West in a tsunami.

Dr. Edgar and I had to share a large office because what were two smaller offices had been combined into one. A social worker had rented the space for a year and needed a large space for a family therapy room, so the wall had been torn down.

Besides speaking of tangential theories of health care policy, Dr. Edgar began to share with me his true feelings. "You know, Michael, I wasn't the one who hired you. You were here before me so I will have to live with that; however, I don't usually work with PAs. I actually think PAs and NPs should be outlawed. We physicians are getting tired of being blamed for all their mistakes."

"Really," I said calmly, "where do you get the idea we make a lot of mistakes? Research doesn't support that. Have you ever seen a PA or NP make a mistake?"

He obviously had no firsthand experiences to draw from, so he reverted to philosophy. "It's obvious that mere assistants are trying to practice medicine and they are not qualified to do so. Most Physician Assistants are medical school rejects who then take a little two-year course and think they are doctors. Physicians, on the other hand, are the cream of the crop who then go through eight years of intensive training. It's a dangerous situation having non-physicians trying to practice medicine."

"Really? How do you know so much about the PA profession?"

While I was speaking, Dr. Eager spun his seat around and started urgently typing on his computer, apparently signaling that his half of the conversation was over. I got up from my desk and walked over to his side of the room, where I could at least see the corner of his eye.

"First of all," I said, "PAs are typically not medical school rejects. Most of us never seriously considered medical school for one reason or another. I also consider PA students as the cream of their crop. Out of three to four hundred applicants to my program, only twenty were chosen."

He continued to type, pretending to ignore me. I caught a glimpse of his screen and it appeared he was playing Solitaire.

"PA school isn't simply a 'little' two-year course and then you become a PA. Besides having good grades in college, the prospective PA student must have at least two years of prior health care experience before applying. Many of them have much more."

I did get a subtle response from him, a raised eyebrow and a "'hmm," but no eye contact. This was enough to allow me to continue.

"The wise physicians (and 'physicians' was a word I put a lot of emphasis on) who developed the first PA program realized they could cram the essence of medical school into 24 months of concentrated training. They did this partially by trimming the nonessential 'fat' from medical school. Now, if we were to compare a new PA graduate with a physician who just completed medical school and a three–or four-year residency in family practice, of course there would be a significant difference. There had better be. That is why PAs are required to work under the supervision of a physician. I am glad for that. But when you add years and years of practice experience under a PA's belt, the chasm between the two narrows significantly. But, even then, I am grateful for and respect physician supervision."

I could tell that Dr. Eager wanted to say something. At the last moment, however, he seemed to think he could get more mileage by just ignoring me, so he continued typing.

The next week, after our brief honeymoon period was over, Dr. Edgar started laying down the law. The most shocking rule was that only he would be allowed to see patients. Maybe, after his schedule was maxed out, he would let me see "very simple" patients, along the lines of a hangnail. My dream position was starting to become a nightmare. Dr. Edgar's rules in the beginning were just difficult, then they evolved to the strange and finally the bizarre.

One day, he was sitting in the office and said, "Mike, I noticed you were up in the front office speaking to the girls. That is very unprofessional. I don't want you talking to them again, ever."

"You must be joking. These women are my friends. Half of my patients are their relatives and friends. If it weren't for them, I wouldn't have the practice that I do." I was still in my keep-the-peace phase and was trying my best to adhere to his rules. The women in the front office hated him. He treated them like third-class human beings.

One day, after not having a single patient all day, Cathy called her husband to come by for ice cream. He dropped by about three o'clock and the two of them went across the street to the ice cream shop. It would have taken her 10 minutes.

Dr. Edgar just happened to have a patient scheduled at this time who needed a urinalysis. He took the patient back to the lab and called Cathy. When he found out she wasn't there, he was enraged. "Cathy didn't have my permission to leave."

Sandy, from the front office, ran across the street to get Cathy. The patient had to wait a total of 15 minutes. When Cathy entered the back door of the office, Dr. Edgar met her. "Where have you been? I have patients and you didn't have my permission to leave the building!" Then he turned to her husband, pointing toward the door. "Get out of here. You're not allowed in this office!"

Cathy's husband was one of my patients as were several of his employees. I knew that we just lost all those accounts.

Cathy had a long fuse as well. She had to think about how she had been treated overnight. The first thing the next morning she came into our office and began to vent to Dr. Edgar. "Don't you ever scream at me like that in front of patients and don't you ever treat my family so rudely."

When she was all done, she turned and walked out of our office. Dr. Edgar had a Grim Reaper grin on his face and said, "No one speaks to me like that. She's history." He threw his stethoscope across the office, jumped in his car, and drove off in the direction of the hospital.

He returned two hours later, still grinning from ear to ear. He said to me, "We will see who gets the end of this argument," and started laughing out loud.

By lunch, I saw Cathy sitting in the lab with tears in her eyes. I walked back there and she told me, "Mason Memorial just called me and told me they are terminating me as a cost-cutting measure." She was gone in a few weeks.

When I was trying to start the practice, the hospital board wouldn't give me a dime for supplies. They did reimburse me for the sign I made, but that was about it. Now with Dr. Edgar, the money floodgates opened wide. They were willing to finance the remodeling of the building, even for a $100,000. Next, Dr. Edgar was given an expense account of $50,000 for incidentals on top of buying him every state-of-the-art piece of medical equipment he wanted. A few weeks earlier, the hospital wouldn't buy me an electronic thermometer. One of the nurses and I were about to go in 50/50 to buy one with our own money. Now, Dr. Edgar was replacing all the furniture just because he didn't like the style.

The situation continued to worsen. Dr. Edgar decided to make life hell for me so I would leave. He would sit across the office and pick up the phone, dialing some number while staring at me. Once the other party answered he would say, "Hey Bob, how are you doing? Oh that's great! I'm here in LaSalle, Michigan. Yeah, I've been here about a month." Then he would look over at me. "I was hired to save the clinic from a PA. This PA had no equipment, just a few Band-Aids, and he was trying to start a practice. Ha! Ha! I think he just wanted to sit around and do nothing like he thought this was a country club. Of course, PAs don't even know how to order equipment." Then he would burst out with a hearty laugh. I was fuming, but I still managed to mostly ignore him.

When he got off the phone, I reminded him again, "I was seeing up to ten patients a day before you came, now our practice is down to one or two patients per day."

He would look across the top of his boyish glasses and say, "You are pathetic. I can't believe any patient would want to see you in this hole in the wall. You don't know a thing about how to set up a practice. You didn't even have supplies before I came." Another hearty laugh.

It took a couple of months before this nonsense reached a head. The day started in a bizarre fashion, which was typical. As soon as I walked in the door, the nurse Teresa stopped me to talk to me. I wore hiking boots to and from work because of the heavy snow. I knew the lug soles tracked sand from the parking lot so I always cleaned up after myself. As I stood there, a few feet inside the door with Teresa, Dr. Edgar came around the corner. He saw the white sand on the dark blue carpet between the door and me. He acted very angry and ran to the cleaning closet. He brought out the vacuum cleaner, plugged it in, and started vacuuming around me, hitting my heels with the carpet attachment. I ignored him like I would a spoiled child, all the while trying to listen to Teresa. Finally I said, "Just leave the sand, I'm going to clean it up." He simply continued until he was done.

I went into my office and took my seat, trying to keep the peace. On one side, I had my family wanting me to keep this job because they didn't want to move. On the other hand, I wanted to punch Dr. Edgar and walk out. For the sake of my family, I was dedicated to seeing this clinic work.

One of Dr. Edgar's early rules was that people couldn't use the break-room because the door was in sight of the lobby, visible through the receptionist's window. He reasoned that if a patient happened to come up to the window and the door to the break room was open, the patient might see one of the staff eating. If a patient got a glimpse of one of us eating, they might get the idea that we . . . were human! We couldn't have that, now could we?

To prevent staff from using the break room, Dr. Edgar ordered a small table and two chairs plus a small refrigerator. To make sure no one saw us eating, he set up his break area on the stair landing going to the cold, dark, unfinished basement. Of course no one used it.

The office staff and nurses tried to avoid speaking to Dr. Edgar, but on that morning Teresa came back and asked him, "Would you mind if we moved the little refrigerator and table to our break-room up front? We promise that if we use it, we will keep the door closed so no one would ever see us eating."

Dr. Edgar looked up from his computer, paused, and said, "Sure."

In a few minutes, Teresa came back into the office and asked me, "Mike, do you think you could help me move the fridge?"

Even with Dr. Edgar's approval, I knew we were treading on thin ice. I followed her to the landing and we started carrying the refrigerator toward the front of the clinic. Dr. Edgar came tearing out of his office and marched right behind us the whole way. We had his approval, so we ignored his silly behavior. As we were setting the refrigerator up Dr. Edgar was watching from the door with a stern, childish face.

When it was plugged in and running he said, "That is my refrigerator and you have no right to move it."

Teresa and I just looked at each other, rolled our eyes, unplugged it, and carried it back to the basement steps. As we were coming up the steps, Dr. Edgar was running down them. He grabbed the refrigerator, gave it a bear hug, and carried it back up by himself. Then he started pushing it down the hall to his office. I started wondering if patients would think that he was unprofessional for acting like a mad man, pushing a refrigerator down the hall. Once he reached his office, he put it under his desk where no one would touch it. By this time, I knew for certain that women are from Venus, men are from Mars . . . and Dr. Edgar was from Pluto.

During the afternoon I was quietly sitting at my desk reading journals, trying to avoid any conflict. I got up and walked up to the front office to make copies of some of the articles to put in my files. As I walked out of the office door, Dr. Edgar jumped up and came marching right behind me. While I was using the copier, he stood five feet from me with both hands on his hips and a big frown on his face making sighing sounds. Finally he turned around and strutted back to his office.

When I returned to the office Dr. Edgar was sitting in his chair, leaning back with his hands behind his head. He obviously was very mad. As I was filing away articles he said, "I can understand why no patient would want to see an idiot like you, but now you are ruining my practice!"

Biting my tongue, I said, "What are you talking about?"

"Mike, do you think if a patient came in the front door and saw a medical professional using a copy machine that they would want you taking care of them? Of course not! They would just turn around and leave!"

I screamed back at him, "You are nuts! They couldn't care less!" At that moment, the fuse hit the bomb. I began screaming at him and he at me. I had tried to keep the peace for two months—for the sake of my family, for the sake of the clinic—but now he had gone too far.

When we were done I collected up all my belongings and moved them right up to the front office to sit amidst the "low class office staff" in full view of the front window. I knew that would drive him insane, plus I was tired of sharing an office with him all day just so I could be the target of his cruel remarks. In the front office, at least I was among friends.

Next I jumped in my van and drove the 30 miles to Mason Memorial. I met with Mr. Jansen and Joe, the new outpatient clinic manager. I started to tell them the whole story of what was going on. When I was done, the response was very disappointing. "Mike, Dr. Edgar is a very nice man. We thought that you wanted a physician to come. Have you changed your mind now?" They thought it was some kind of turf issue.

"I did want a physician, but not a crazy one," I said

"If the two of you are having conflicts and can't work it out, you should find yourself another position. We have far more money invested in Dr. Edgar than you."

"This isn't an interpersonal conflict. I have never had a hard time getting along with another employee. I am telling you, this man is insane! Everyone in the clinic hates him. He is nuts. He got Cathy fired because she spoke back to him. He treats the ladies at the front desk very badly. You did check references on him, didn't you?"

Silence.

I said again, "Did you contact his previous place of employment to see what had happened there?"

More silence. Finally Mr. Jansen said, "We had a credentialing company check his medical degree and license."

Joe added, "When he sent us his CV, he had a glowing letter of reference from one of his residency supervisors."

"But, you didn't contact his previous employer? I don't doubt that he practices good medicine, but something is seriously wrong with the way he relates to others."

"For a physician, it would be rude to check up on him like that."

I couldn't believe it. When I was hired, they had gone over my background with a magnifying glass.

As I drove back to the clinic, I remembered a talk with a PA in another Upper Peninsula city who had known Dr. Edgar from a clinic in another state. When I got back to my office, I called him. It turned out that he didn't know Dr. Edgar well, but he did know the name of the clinic where he used to work.

I called the clinic. When the receptionist answered I said, "Do you have either a PA or Nurse Practitioner working there?"

"Yes, we have a Nurse Practitioner."

"May I speak to her?"

"Just a moment."

When she came on the line I said to her, "My name is Mike Jones and I am checking the reference on a physician who I will be working with. His name is Dr. Edgar."

After a long silence she said, "That man's a jerk! He is evil!" I had obviously pushed a button and she began to ventilate: "He seemed like a very nice man when he was hired. He had just quit his very first position with the Indian Health Service because of some interpersonal conflict. He made it sound like it was all their fault. Then, within days of joining our practice, he had his RN fired for insubordination. She was a wonderful nurse who had worked here for years. Then he started making crazy rules. I didn't work directly with him, but everyone who did hated him. Finally, he pushed a nurse into a filing cabinet when she wouldn't obey him. Our medical director thought he had Borderline Personality Disorder and wanted him to see psychiatry. We called an office meeting and the senior physician made an issue of his behavior; it was getting out of control. Dr. Edgar threw off his stethoscope and said, 'I'm not taking this abuse,' and left. He was never seen again."

We estimated it was six months between when he left there and was hired by us. Apparently he had remained unemployed during this time. This new information reassured me that I wasn't the crazy one. I called the hospital and told them what I had found out. I gave them the number of his old clinic and suggested they call it. They didn't have much to say and, as far as I know, never called them.

Mr. Jansen must have known what I was thinking. "You know, Mike, if we let Dr. Edgar go, we will just give up on the clinic and let you go as well."

"But why?" I said. "I can make this clinic work. Give me the resources that you gave Dr. Edgar and watch me succeed."

"Mike, the board has made up its mind. No physician, no clinic."

"We can start looking for another doctor and I can keep things going in the meantime."

"Nope," came his reply, "We can't do it. We spent a huge amount of money in luring Dr. Edgar here. If he doesn't work out, then we will just pull the plug."

I immediately started job hunting. For the next few months I would be caught up in a whirlwind of professional confusion. When I left my Internal Medicine position, I was jumping from the frying pan into the fire. Little did I know that the next jump would take me from the fire into the bowels of professional purgatory. But it would be OK–I had been there before and I knew my way around. My dream clinic would soon be completely in the hands of Dr. Edgar, a madman and clinic snatcher.

Chapter Twenty-two

Professional Pandemonium

The iron rich waters of the Coca River drift quietly behind the East Clinic. Although its headwaters cascade deeply into the interior of the UP's small mountains, as it approaches the big lake it meanders with barely any current. Through most of its final course, it is lined with homes at the top of steep sandy banks on either side. Each house has a series of wooden or metal staircases leading down to small boat docks, to which canoes or small craft are tied. The area is so densely forested, paddling there gives you the sense you are floating down the tunnel of love at an amusement park.

On autumn days, during my dinner break, I would jump in my yellow sea-kayak and cruise up and down the Coca chasing Coho salmon. I especially loved paddling down to the mouth of the river, where the dark organic waters of the stream met the clear crashing waves of Lake Superior.

Another river, the Dread, was about five miles away. Despite its eerie name, the Dread River was a wonderful place to paddle and fish. This river, though, had Chinook salmon spawning in it. These fish were huge, by Midwestern standards. For six years I paddled that river every fall, drooling for the chance to be pulled up and down the stream by the mother of all salmon.

For some of us, being out in the elements meant the fun of fishing. On a snowy or drizzly day, I loved to put on my rain gear, get in my kayak, and paddle up the Dread River. With my Walkman thrown into the mix, I was in utopia.

The Dread River starts as a chain of small man-made cooling ponds coming off Lake Superior, next to the main power plant. While paddling across the ponds I would encounter flocks of geese gathering for their trip south. Once I was heading up the river, my next encounter would be a subdivision of beaver lodges along the shore. The backdrop was a forest of maple and aspen trees so golden that it hurt to look at them.

This section of the Dread River had no land access and its shallow depth made it difficult even for watercraft to approach. The beavers weren't very happy when I invaded their privacy. Encountering a beaver from the cockpit of a kayak is quite an experience. They look like little saber-toothed grizzly bears with flat pressed tails. I have never heard of anyone being assaulted by a beaver but they appear as if they could rip your larynx right out with those huge curved incisors.

There was one narrow place of the river where a train trestle crossed. Just upstream from it was an especially large beaver lodge. I would try to paddle on the other side of the river, as far away as possible from their homes. The most water I could get between us was only about fifteen feet, due to the narrow passage. As soon as I would come around the corner, the beavers would stop what they were doing and climb on top of their hut. As I got closer, they started to get really mad. Next, the meanest looking one would dive into the river and head right toward me. He would get within a foot of my hand and then dive, slapping his tail on the surface with a loud "wham," then he would swim back to his house. I don't know much about beaver behavior, but I had a feeling this wasn't an invitation to come and have tea.

One time I was trying to pass by them as quietly as I could. I had just completed a pleasant morning of fishing and was heading downstream toward home. My beaver friends had been especially pesky when I passed them on my way up the river.

My fishing rod was tied securely to the aft-deck of the kayak. This time I was about in the clear without disturbing them when my kayak came to a curious halt. I couldn't figure out what was wrong. I was even paddling with the current but I wasn't moving.

Finally I looked behind my kayak and I was astonished. My fishing line had been coming out while I was paddling down the river. Of all things, the lure had drifted over and hooked onto the beaver lodge! With each stroke of the paddle, I was shaking the hut like an epilepsy ward during an earthquake. By this point, I had aroused the attention of all of the tree-eating man-killers.

I eventually had to paddle right over to their hut, speaking kindly to them: "Nice little beaver . . . nice little beaver." They became very agitated but I was able to unhook my favorite lure and move on downstream. I thought I had a clean get away, but as I was looking over my shoulder to make sure I wasn't being followed the tips of my kayak paddle caught two wooden pillars of the train trestle. With the force of the current, my paddle peeled the skin from my navel to my Adams apple and pinned me by the neck on the back deck of the boat. I looked like I was trying to do the limbo, but the limbo was winning and my head was about to pop off. Finally the boat started to rotate, spilling me out of it.

I got back to my parking place, drenched and with a skinned up face. I passed another fisherman who was shore-based. He was looking at me curiously. "Are you all right," he said.

"Yep. Bad encounter with a beaver," I said, leaving him looking quite confused.

I had to take another dive into the job hunting water, but, fortunately for me, it was still shark-infested. As soon as word got out I was looking for a job, I started to hear back from potential employers. This time, I was truly a man on a mission. My main goal was to find a stable job that paid at least an average salary. Secondly, I wanted to find a supervising physician that was supportive and someone I could respect. Thirdly, I wanted to work my buns off. And lastly . . . I wanted everything in writing!

I narrowed my choices down to two. One was a headache position at a world-class medical center in another state. The second was a rural clinic in northern Wisconsin. These two options lay at both ends of the medical practice spectrum. The first was in a major city on a huge medical campus. The second was tucked away in a national forest, a hundred miles from civilization.

I had an interview at the headache clinic first. I was impressed with the effort. The interview lasted eight hours as I met for one hour with each key player in the department. Dr. Singer, the head of the headache division, was enthusiastic about my coming. He made one statement that was like a breath of fresh air: "Here, the initials that come after your name aren't important. It is the care that you provide our patients." This sounded too good to be true.

The only drawback was the geography. Accepting this position would mean having to leave the beauty of the Up-back of Michigan and Lake Superior. I could no longer chase salmon on the Coca and the Dread.

I was planning on going to the second job interview regardless of how well the first interview went. The decision became easier when I had a call from the headache clinic. Dr. Singer started on a positive note: "The team here is quite interested in having you join us. The fact that you would be the first PA on staff means we would need to create a position for you. This usually takes a long time, but I think I can rush it through in twelve . . . months."

Twelve months! I thought. There is no way I could last twelve months with Dr. Edgar. Even if he wouldn't have me laid off, like he did Cathy, I would surely be in a straight jacket by then, just to keep me from killing him. Now the Wisconsin job had much more significance.

Denise and I made the three-hour trip to Lynette, Wisconsin. It is a small town of about 1,000 people and quite isolated by Wisconsin standards. The next town was thirty miles away and roughly the same size. It was at least an hour's drive to a city of any consequence. Lynette had one main street with a few businesses, such as the bank, grocery, restaurant, ice cream shop, and clinic. On the north edge of town was the chief employer, a family-owned sawmill. Huge piles of logs surrounded it on one end of the complex and piles of sawdust and lumber on the other. On the west side of town houses surrounded a small, picturesque lake.

Mike kayaking into the sunset on Gitche Gumee.

Lynette was looking for a PA to reopen its clinic, which had been closed for three years. We had lunch with the key players at the main restaurant in town. The nurse, Mary, who was trying to resuscitate the clinic, was there, along with the outpatient director of the hospital, which would be hiring me. The hospital was 50 miles away, back across the Michigan state line. Also present were a PA who was a rural health consultant and his pilot.

After lunch, we visited with the president of the bank and the key businessmen in town. Things were falling into place. The major issue brought up was the tight housing market. The small logging town was surrounded by a national forest and had no room to grow. I decided to look for a reliable housing market expert . . . so I went to the Gas-Mart.

At the Gas-Mart I asked the woman pouring slurpy mix in the machine. "Do you know of any homes around here for sale?"

She put down the gallon jug filled with a bright red liquid, and yelled out toward the front of the store, "Hey Maggie, is that Peterson place for sale?"

The woman in front, finishing up with a customer, said, "I talked to Joan on Wednesday. She said they are going to put it on the market in a couple of weeks."

The slurpy woman turned to me and said, "The Petersons have a beautiful log home outside of town. I will give you directions. As far as I know, that is the only home for sale around here." She pulled out a napkin from beneath the little hot dog merry-go-round and drew up a map for me.

As I walked back to the mini van, I felt like this was a sign from God. All my life I'd dreamed of a log home. Now after six months in Dr. Edgar's little island of hell, I sensed paradise just around the corner.

We went directly out to the log home and it WAS clearly my dream home. It had a foundation made of massive granite boulders. The lower layers of dark logs were about 30 inches in diameter. They slowly decreased in size through the second story. Coming out of the master bedroom was a beautiful log balcony. The living room had a massive stone fireplace. It was all custom crafted. The staircase was made out of logs with a natural curvature. To top it all off, the house sat on 40 acres of meadow and forest. Beside the house was a creek that had been damned up into a swimming and fishing pond.

The house wasn't officially on the market but the owner showed us around anyway. I spoke to the banker later that day. He knew they had paid $150,000 for the home three years earlier. He expected them to sell it for not much more since the local housing market was quite depressed in that price range. I was 98% sure this would be our new home.

Three weeks later, we took the family over to look at it again, confident it was going to be ours. Now it was officially on the market, and it was listed at $250,000. Certainly I understood the thinking of the owners. This is what it would cost to rebuild the home. However, I was surprised as the market in that area wasn't at this level. It wasn't a tourist area or someplace people would want to have a vacation home.

Our hearts sank with this news. A price of $250,000 might not seem like that much to many people; however, we had owned two homes and never had paid more than $70,000.

We left the area discouraged and my dream was taking on a shade not as bright as I had anticipated. During our long drive back to La Salle, Denise was quiet. Then suddenly she said, "We should just forget we ever saw that home. It is clearly out of our league." But I wasn't ready to pound in the death nail just yet.

Denise and I have always been a good match. I am a risk taker and have a tendency to do things off the cuff, hoping for a good outcome. Denise has Scandinavian blood running through her veins. She is much more cautious. She likes to think things through. This may be the result of thousands of years of cultural evolution. If Scandinavians made a mistake, it could cost them their lives in the harsh cold winters.

I still wanted to make this small town work. My heart had made the move already. Denise's heart was firmly planted in La Salle and she still held out hope that we could, somehow, stay.

Over the next three months I became obsessed with Lynette. I called the pastor of the small Lutheran Church, the school principal and teachers, the pharmacist, and of course Mary, the nurse heading up the clinic-opening committee. I about drove them all crazy trying to find housing. I enlisted the services of three regional real-estate agents. The only houses they could come up with were 30, 40, or 50 miles away. If I was going to make the clinic succeed, I wanted to live in the town and to be part of the community. I wanted to go to church with them. I wanted my kids to go to school with their kids, my kids to beat up their kids (or vice-versa). I wanted to be called in the middle of the night if Mr. Brown was having chest pain. I wanted patients to stop me at the local ice cream shop to talk about their hemorrhoids. Well, OK, maybe I could do without that last one. This was my dream medicine job–what being a PA in America was all about. Let us all face the flag and join stethoscopes and sing Kum-ba-yah!

I lost trust in one of the real-estate agents right off the bat. He called me one morning: "Hey, Mike, I think I have found the perfect house for you. Let me read you the specs. It has three bedrooms, a huge workshop, and an indoor pool. It is listed at only ninety grand. What a deal!"

As soon as the kids heard "indoor pool," they went nuts. We packed up the mini van and made the 200-mile trek through the birch forest. I met the agent at the driveway. He had never seen the house before. The previous owner had "invented" this home, but then afterwards, sadly died of pancreatic cancer.

I use the word "invented" because that was the best way to describe the place. It was a small house up on 20-foot metal stilts. The front of the house rested on the side of the hill and that is where you entered. The back of the house had a precarious metal fire escape stairway welded onto the supporting post, which led to the back door. The interior was a mess. The flat roof leaked everywhere, leaving black spots on the cheesy drop ceiling. The whole place listed to one side. You could feel each floor joist under the sagging underpinning when you walked down the hall. The so-called "indoor pool" was an area beneath the house walled off by sheets of clear polyurethane plastic. It looked like a giant version of one of my dad's homemade tents. The pool itself was an above-the-ground type. Since it leaked, it could only be filled to two feet deep. The water was slimy green with frogs and tadpoles in it. I wouldn't have taken the house if it were given to me! It would cost me money even to haul it away to the landfill. I was so disappointed when the sleazy real-estate agent continued selling us on the house when he knew it was a disaster. I have had good agents in the past. The good ones would just turn around and leave when they saw the condition of such a place.

I kept a picture of the log home on my bulletin board. Out of frustration one Saturday I drove over to the area again and met with the real-estate agent who represented the log homeowners. I also met with the banker and worked out a decent offer of $185,000. Then I returned home to La Salle. Denise was in the kitchen washing dishes looking out of the large sliding window above the sink. "Well, how was the house hunting this time?" she said.

I struggled to spit the words out: "I did something a bit impulsive today."

She looked over her shoulder at me and raised her yellow rubber gloves out of the soapy water. A little smile lit her face. She knew that when I said things like that, it wasn't a good sign. "Yes? What did you do?"

"I made an offer of $185,000 on the log home."

Denise freaked. "You are kidding me? You offered one hundred and eighty-five thousand dollars for that house? That makes me VERY nervous. If they accept it, we are stuck!"

The owners made a fair counteroffer, but I had to respond with an outright rejection, without Denise's support.

The owners of the main town business, a lumber mill, heard of my hold-up with the log home and offered to pay my mortgage for at least a year. Still, my hands were tied by Denise's veto. I wasn't doing this just to please her, but because I trusted her judgment, even when I disagreed with it.

During this time, I made thirteen trips to look at houses, land to build on, but came up empty. I was seeing this job slip between my fingers in great frustration. Before I gave up, I launched a campaign to find a simple room that I could rent. I could still take the position and continue looking for a house while Denise and the kids remained in La Salle.

I called Mary the nurse again: "Do you know of any rooms I could rent or anywhere I could sleep for a while?" I could tell that her patience was running out.

The townspeople had put up a large sign in the clinic saying, "Opening soon." I had already kept them in limbo for three months, contract in hand but not signed. I was growing desperate for housing. The nurse gave me the number for a woman named Betty who in the past rented rooms by the month.

I called Betty. "Do you still rent rooms? I am a Physician Assistant and I am coming over to open the clinic if I can find a place to sleep."

"Oh, I don't know. I have all my sewing stuff in that room and I don't want to put it away again."

I wanted to scream, "Lady, do you realize that time is running out! I want to open the clinic . . . you know the clinic that everyone in town has been waiting to open for so long. It all depends on you giving me a cot to sleep on!"

Mary next gave me a lead on the town motel. "They used to rent rooms by the week." I called the owner and she was quite cold to me: "I don't want you long-timers in my rooms. I have had people like you in my motel before for extended periods of time and they just wrecked everything." I offered to put a cot in the clinic and sleep there, but still they thought that wouldn't work. My 98% confidence level in taking the job was slipping on the technicality of not finding a place to sleep.

Dr. Edgar had been very supportive during this time. When I told him about the Wisconsin opportunity, he said, "Great–the backwoods of Wisconsin is a good place for you. All PAs should be so far back in the woods that no patient can find them." Then he threw in his belly laugh. When he thought I was going to the world class medical center, his comment was, "That is a good place for you. There, a lot of experts could keep a close watch on you and cover your mistakes. That is where all midlevels should be. Ha ha!"

I had a phone call about this time from a regional PA recruiter. "What kind of job are you looking for, Mike?"

"I would love to stay in La Salle, or at least the Upper Peninsula. I would also prefer family practice, ER, Urgent Care, or Neurology."

"I have a job that will be perfect for you: a family practice position in the U.P." As we talked, one thing made me lose interest quickly, and that was the issue of salary. The cap was below the national average salary, even for new graduates. I loved my patients, but I loved my children too. The driving needs of a growing family were turning me into a mercenary.

It was now June and I was attending the National American Academy of Physician Assistants conference in Las Vegas. I went to one of the pharmaceutical-sponsored dinners and sat beside a young man. He had just graduated from PA school and told me, "Yeah, I had a lot of offers. I finally settled on an ER position. They offered me ten grand as a sign-on and eighty grand a year. I had better offers but I really liked the medical director at this ER."

"Eighty a year?" I said, trying to hold in my surprise. Now what was this young single guy going to do with that kind of income–buy titanium hubcaps for his sports car? I was feeling quite frustrated now.

After my long career, I was being offered slightly more than half that. Every time I had mentioned a sign-on bonus with perspective employers, they looked at me like they needed to call the *Men in Black* to escort me back to my planet.

Now another guy at the table chimed in: "I remember when I used to ONLY make eighty a year. I would never settle for less than six figures now." Now why in the heck do I always sit by these guys who not only make a good deal of money, but are also not shy about telling the world? The next time I went to one of these dinners I would approach the microphone and say, "Uh . . . where are the PA losers sitting? Please raise your hand. Oh, thank you. Do you mind if I join you?"

A few weeks later the same recruiter called me back. "Mr. Jones, my client, the hospital, is now considering adding an incentive program for additional income to the package." I guess she was expecting me to jump up and down. Well, it was nice they were "considering it." I had been working under actual incentives for the previous three years with nothing to show for it. The thought of them considering an incentive wasn't very reassuring to me.

"If they ever do establish a real incentive program, you can call me back."

Meanwhile, back at the clinic, Dr. Edgar stepped up his harassment. From the time I moved to the front of the office, he pretended that I didn't exist. He wouldn't make eye contact with any of the staff members. If he wanted me to know something, he would tell his new nurse to tell me, like we were children having a tiff.

He had replaced Teresa, who was an LPN, with an RN because, as he put it, "I don't work with LPNs." He wanted the hospital to hire the most qualified RN they could find. Yet, once she was there, he treated her like an indentured servant.

It was his opinion that nurses should never speak to the physician unless asked something or spoken to first. He wanted a clinic where the nurse and staff would rely on a series of hand signals like a third base coach. I'm not making this up—who could?

This nurse was a fine woman. I had worked with her in the Air Force, but I didn't know her well. I felt so sorry for her during her recruitment. I wanted to get word to her to run for it while she had the chance, but Dr. Eager made sure I was never alone with her.

Because there were no patients, Dr. Edgar's first assignment for her was scrubbing scuffmarks off the baseboards. Before I resigned, I did manage a long talk with her. I wanted to assure her that she didn't have to take this kind of treatment and that she didn't need to waste a few weeks trying to figure out Dr. Edgar. Yes, he was insane.

I put in my notice, still with the job in Lynette being my top choice. Then one day the medical director of the other family practice, the one the recruiter had been telling me about, called.

"Hello, is this Michael Jones, the Physician Assistant?"

"Yes, it is."

This is Dr. Jerry Ward. I am the medical director here at Lakeview Hospital in Junction City. I would love for you to join us. We really need a PA, and from what I hear you are the ideal candidate. My colleagues down in La Salle told me you were a good PA. What do you think about coming up for an interview?"

"Well, my goals are to work in a stable practice where I could be very busy. I was in a very slow clinic for the past year and a half."

"I think this would be a great position for you. We just opened a brand new clinic and we have plenty of patients. The physicians have agreed to give the PAs an incentive income, the details of which they are ironing out. I know that you were not impressed with our salary offer."

"Unless I see an incentive in writing, I wouldn't want to come up to waste your time or mine. But, you can keep me posted."

There was no way I would settle for a below average salary again. Not, when I had above average salary offers elsewhere.

A few weeks later I had another call from Dr. Ward. "Hey Mike, we have the incentive formula worked out. I will send you a copy."

"Sure, go ahead," I said. I wasn't terribly serious about the position at the time and just wanted to see how they did incentive.

When I got the formula from them, I ran numbers through it. It was much more generous than the one back at the internal medicine or East clinics. Not only did it earn actual income, but the threshold was met when I averaged only 12 patients per day. That would be easy in a family medicine setting. Next, the cap of the incentive pay could be reached by seeing only 17 patients per day. This all seemed very doable. The average PA in family medicine saw 21 patients per day. Dr. Ward was starting to get my attention.

A couple of days later, I called him to set up an interview for the coming Saturday, which happened to be Labor Day weekend.

On that morning, I drove the scenic 100 miles through the pine and birch forest, along the shore of the big lake to the hospital. I parked in the almost empty employee parking lot and made my way inside. I took a seat in the marble and wood lobby of the 1930s-era building and started to scan their magazine selection. In a few minutes a gentleman came through the door and walked up to me. "Hi, are you Mike Jones?"

"Yes I am," I said as we shook hands.

"I am Dr. Ward. Come on back."

Dr. Ward was a stocky middle-aged man with curly, graying brown hair and glasses. We took a seat in the office of the CEO, Mr. Kinley. In a moment, Dan Cobb, the Human Resources Director, came in holding a styrofoam cup of coffee and wearing a white dress shirt with the sleeves rolled up. After introductions, he took a seat with us.

I thanked them for giving up part of their Labor Day weekend. It was a very cordial time together. I tried to explain to them about my previous two years and how I was hungry to work hard. Dr. Ward said, "Mike, if working hard is what you want then this is the place for you. We have patients coming out the wazoo. We really do need your help."

If anything, I was starting to feel like I might be going from one extreme to another. Yet, I was starting to think, "With five kids approaching college, I could live with being overworked for a few years if that is what it would take."

This time I wanted everything put in writing. I had their contract in hand. It had the formula carefully written out and I rechecked it several times. It *was* the same formula that I had run the numbers through a week earlier. The contract mentioned that I would be scheduled for 40 hours of patient contact per week. I added that my minimal number of patients that I would see per day would be sixteen to twenty-three.

About this time, Mr. Kinley leaned on his desk and said, "Mike, what is the maximum number of patients you could see in a day? Twenty-five? Thirty?" A big smile came to his face.

The contract looked watertight. It talked about vacation, office resources, support staff, and CME. I asked for a sign-on bonus. Instead, they gave me the equivalent in a 401K account for the first two years. I had them add wording about paying for our move. Every "t" was crossed and "i" dotted. These people were so much more reasonable to deal with than the big hospital in La Salle. At least that is what I thought at the time.

At noon I had an appointment with the two physicians who would be supervising the new PA, Drs. Kennedy and Shoemaker. We met at the new clinic across the river. It was a nice rented space in an upscale strip mall.

The physicians seemed cordial but our visit was brief. I made it clear to them as well: "My number one objective is to provide good care and to be very busy."

Dr. Shoemaker responded: "Oh, I think you will be plenty busy, but I want you to understand, I don't compete in the same arena as midlevels. We interviewed a PA a couple of months ago who thought he was a doctor. That isn't the kind of PA we want here."

When he said that, I imagined an arrogant PA who thought he was an MD and wanted total independence. I guess "thinking he was a doctor" was in the eyes of the beholder. It is like something Dr. Edgar used to say: "I don't like PAs playing doctor." I knew that what he really meant was, "I don't like PAs playing PA." Seeing patients and diagnosing and treating their illnesses isn't playing doctor, it's playing PA. That's what we do. We are locals in Medical Practice Land, not tourists.

After months of professional pandemonium, professional peace appeared to be on the horizon. I took Dr. Shoemaker's comments about not competing with midlevels with a grain of salt, in light of all the other information I had received. Little did I realize that grain of salt would someday come back to crush me like a boulder.

Chapter Twenty-three

Rural Health Roulette

I would put this part of Michigan's Upper Peninsula up against any place in America, as far as its natural beauty. On my drive back from Junction City I was feeling exuberant. I had found a wonderful job. The sun was shining brightly from a deep blue sky. On my right were the thick birch, aspen, and hardwood forests. To my left was my friend, Lake Superior, her waters shimmering turquoise, framed by light beige beaches and dark, wet granite outcroppings. For a stretch, the highway ran along the tops of high cliffs, a hundred feet above the shore. In other places, the icy cold waters lapped at the road's very shoulders. The air was a perfect seventy-five degrees. After three hard years, I was ready to settle down and establish some roots.

I was confident this new job was the one I had always wanted. As I drove up the hill beside our little farm, I looked out across our fields. Our sheep were lazily grazing behind the little red barn. I had loved that place as much as anyone could love a home. But, Dr. Edgar had soured everything. I couldn't wait to move on with my life. However, Denise and the kids weren't in the emotional boxing ring with the mad man each day. I knew that a move for them would be far more difficult. They were still living in the utopian mode that I had enjoyed before Dr. Edgar's arrival.

I pulled into our little white garage and walked toward the house. I walked through the kitchen door and met Denise, who was coming down the stairs carrying a large basket of dirty clothes. She asked timidly, "Well, how did it go?"

"Very well," I said. Tears immediately flooded her eyes and she sat down the basket, turned, and walked away. She knew what this would mean. I tried to reassure her: "But Denise, this sounds like a great job. They said I would be kept very busy. I can earn the incentive pay, which would go toward college for the kids. The area up there is beautiful–even more so than La Salle."

Through her tears she said, "But, I love my house. This is my home."

Awash in guilt, I said, "I will find you a house in Junction City that you will love just as much if not more. Trust me."

Late one night, a couple of weeks later, I put up a homemade sign by the road: "House for Sale by Owner." Early the next morning, Denise got a call from the family that sold us the house. The woman said, "We don't care what you are asking, we want that house back." It was sold instantly.

When I started the house-hunting process, I was confident that it would go much better than it had in Wisconsin. We were moving to an area with a population of about 25,000 rather than 1,000. Nevertheless, I didn't fare much better.

We found only two homes in the county. Each one had only two bedrooms. We knew we would have to add on if we bought either one. It was about this time that the idea of building first occurred to me. It was a moment of temporary insanity. This would be the perfect opportunity to build our dream house and I was driven to provide a living situation Denise and the children would love.

I had one good friend in Junction City named Rob, who was the youth pastor of a large Lutheran church. When I mentioned to him that I was thinking about building, he referred me to a friend of his named Tim.

Tim was six feet tall with a stocky frame and light blond hair, and he spoke with a slight Finnish accent–then again, everyone in that part of Michigan spoke with a Finnish accent. But Tim was a recent Finnish transplant. He came to the U.S. as a Lutheran pastor but had been a contractor back in his homeland. He continued doing general contracting on the side to help support his family.

The first trip I made to Tim's place seems like only yesterday. He had a brand new home in one of the nicer communities in the city. We took a seat at a large picnic table in his dining room. I had a large packet filled with our dream house ideas.

"Tim," I said, "if we were going to build a house, when could we start? When the ground thaws in the spring?"

Tim smiled big. "Why wait to spring?"

"Well, we are approaching the end of September. I don't even have land at this point. The ground will be covered with snow in a few weeks. How long would it take to build a house?"

"I had this one built in six weeks."

"Six weeks! You must be kidding."

"If you add a week or two for site preparation, septic work, basement . . . yeah, from that point it was about six weeks."

"My wife and kids have to be out of our La Salle house on December 15th. Do you think a house could be built before then? It would be wonderful if we could move straight into a new home."

Tim said with extreme confidence, "Oh, of course. No problem."

"Could we keep the total price below $150,000?"

"Certainly, especially if you do some of the finishing work, Mike."

After so many years of hearing, "It can't be done" by so many CEOs and administrators, I was actually starting to like this guy. But too much confidence and flexibility, I soon learned, can be just as bad.

"OK, let me explain what kind of house I want to build." I went on to show him our drawings of a Swiss Chalet style house, with two floors and a loft, all post and beam construction. With each description, he said, "No problem."

When we were done, Tim had a good understanding of our dream house. To save money, I agreed to do a lot of the inside work, including building interior walls and doors. I would finish the first two floors now and finish the loft later. He was going to start working on a contract and I was going to start looking for land.

Tim called me in a few days. "Mike, I have talked to the concrete guys. They said if we don't pour footings within three weeks, they can't pour them until spring." Now I was really starting to feel the pressure as I still had no land!

My friend Rob and his wife offered me a place to sleep at their house. I packed up my truck and moved on up to the area and starting to feel that I was entering a whirlwind.

I finally found three acres that I liked. To purchase the land, I had to have it surveyed, but the surveyor was tied up for three weeks. The concrete guys now had only two more weeks. So I did a ridiculous thing. I asked the owner of the land if I could excavate his property and pour footings before I actually purchased the land. He gave me his OK. Now, I was really committed.

The first day at my new, hopefully final, job arrived. I showed up at the clinic on a Monday morning. I pulled up in my little black Toyota micro-truck and unloaded my files and books. I sat them inside the back door. The office manager, Tina, a short, dark-haired woman, walked by. "You must be Michael Jones. Let me show you around."

We went through the clinic and Tina introduced me to the nursing and office staff. Drs. Kennedy and Shoemaker were at their desks as the nurses were putting their first patients in rooms.

The clinic was set up with two separate sections, which were a mirror image of each other; however, the east side was much smaller, with two treatment rooms, whereas the west side had six. A thirty-foot-long hallway separated the two sides. Between them was the waiting room and business office. Tina took me to the east side and showed me a cubical in the hall. "This will be your desk. Whenever you need a nurse, we will send Karen over from the other side."

By midmorning the west side of the clinic was bustling. I was eager to see my first patient. By noon, there were still no patients on my schedule. I knew things would start out slow for a few days so I wasn't too surprised. I looked over at the physicians' schedule and they were packed with 40-45 patients apiece.

I got home to Rob's that night, after a fruitless day as far as medical practice goes, to a really busy schedule. I was still trying to schedule surveyors, traveling to sawmills to have wood custom-cut for the interior, and I started restoring an old antique wood cook stove. I also started working like mad to custom-build the 14 doors for the house. Tim was still ironing out the specific details of his contract.

The next day at work I was bored out of my mind—not a single patient again. I heard one of the girls at the front desk mention that two patients in the lobby were very angry because they had been waiting for over an hour to see Dr. Shoemaker. I said, "Ask them if they want to see me."

The girl looked at me funny and said in a very serious tone of voice, "You'd better ask Tina."

"Sure." I walked over to the west side and found Tina at her desk. "Hi, Tina. There are a couple of Dr. Shoemaker's patients in the lobby that are mad from waiting so long. I would be happy to see them. I think I could calm them down as well."

Tina said with a sober expression, "Uh . . . well, I could ask Dr. Shoemaker."

I went back over to the east side and turned on the exam room lights and grabbed my stethoscope. I was pumped to start acting like a PA again.

Tina came around the corner and said, "No, Mike. Dr. Shoemaker doesn't want your help." Now I was really surprised. I wondered, *Why wouldn't he want me to help him out?* Usually physicians were glad to have my help in such situations.

The rest of the week continued likewise. Finally on Thursday afternoon, I had my first patient scheduled. He was a college student. The clinic had a contract with the local university to provide the student health needs.

On Friday I made the trek back to La Salle to see my family. I was missing them like crazy. The next week started to look a lot like the first week. I had two patients scheduled the entire week. I was so distracted by the house-building project and didn't have a lot of time to worry about the schedule. Our house site was now excavated and the footings poured. The construction had started.

One day, in the midst of all the confusion, Dr. Kennedy wandered over to my side to check on how I was doing. He was a really nice guy who was just starting his own career.

I didn't want to start my new "permanent" job by complaining so I hadn't yet brought up the issue of my very light schedule. I was just trying to be patient. This day I decided it was time to talk about it.

"Dr. Kennedy, I am a little confused about how light my schedule had been. I am averaging only one patient per day. I have never started a new practice that built this slowly."

Dr. Kennedy looked at me and said in a calm voice, "Well, Mike, you weren't really hired to see patients. Sure, it would be nice for you to see some of the students when our schedules are full, but the main reason you were hired was so we could get Rural Health Clinic (RHC) designation for this clinic."

It was like waiting for someone to laugh after telling you a joke you aren't sure was a joke. But Dr. Kennedy never laughed.

"What do you mean?"

At this point I knew very little about RHC. "The hospital wanted to get the federal Rural Health Clinic designation for this clinic to increase the reimbursement rates for Medicaid and Medicare. To get RHC designation, the law requires us to have a midlevel provider on staff. We had a medical meeting last spring and decided to hire a midlevel provider. The hospital calculated that even if you never saw a single patient, the income from RHC designation would more than pay your cost plus give us a nice profit."

It was another *Braveheart* betrayal. I tried so hard to have everything in writing after weeks of negotiations. This just couldn't be happening to me again. Now Dr. Kennedy wasn't the bad guy. He was only the messenger. Dr. Kennedy had no clue as to the impact this statement had on me. Three practices in a row had deceived me. I had a house under construction and our home that we loved had sold. How could I have been so stupid as to have ever trusted a hospital administrator again?

I immediately got on the horn. "Dr. Ward, I am a little confused. I was told that I would be very busy, now Dr. Kennedy tells me that the main reason I was hired was to help the clinic to get designated as a Rural Health Clinic. What is going on?"

Dr. Ward seemed to stumble for words and said, "Mike, oh don't worry about that . . . uh . . . I am sure things will pick up for you. Yes, the RHC designation was the main reason that we decided to hire a PA, but I am sure you will have plenty of patients in time. Mike, let's have lunch this week and talk about it."

Over the next couple of days I talked with Karen, the nurse, to try and understand more of the office dynamics. "You see, Mike, I'm not surprised at all that you're not busy. Dr. Kennedy had just started his practice a year ago. His schedule isn't full yet. I am sure he doesn't want to share patients—you know, he works on incentive too. It has been hard enough for him to start a practice in Dr. Shoemaker's shadow."

"Why is that?"

"Dr. Shoemaker is very stingy with his patients. If one of them sees Dr. Kennedy, Dr. Shoemaker will confront the patient and make them very uncomfortable until they swear loyalty to him and him alone."

I said, slightly astounded, "You must be kidding, Karen. I thought they were partners?"

"Well, Dr. Shoemaker is very possessive of his patients. He especially wouldn't allow PAs to see them. He thinks all midlevels are incompetent."

Normally I would've lost sleep over this situation, but I was too busy with the whirlwind of house-building around me. I remember as a child watching the Ed Sullivan Show. One night they featured this guy who did tricks with plates. He had two long carpenter's horses with about twenty thin poles sticking up from them. The juggler would start spinning plates on the poles. As soon as he had one spinning, he would have to go back and add more speed to the other ones before they slowed down to the point they would fall. Eventually he had all 20 plates spinning but he had to jump around like a crazy man to keep them all going.

This is exactly how I was starting to feel. Every day I was faced with calls from loan officers checking references, from the bank in La Salle closing on our house there, from the lumber mill sawing my wood and running into problems. I would hear from Tim writing out the construction contact, from the man who was selling the land, from

Denise in La Salle with a snow blower that wouldn't start, from the blacksmith making my door hardware.

On top of this, there was now a serious development with my new "permanent" job: no patients. The day of the meeting with Dr. Ward didn't come soon enough. We met in the basement of his clinic, next to the hospital, which was on the other side of the river. He ordered a couple of smoked turkey sandwiches from the hospital kitchen. Once we were seated, sandwiches in hand and past the small talk, he looked up at me and said, "So Mike, things aren't busy enough for you over there?"

"Busy enough? I am averaging 2 to 3 patients per day now and I have been at this for a month. I am working only 30 or 45 minutes out of an eight-hour schedule. Only after I was assured that I would be very busy did I accept this position. Now, Dr. Kennedy tells me that the real reason I was hired was so the clinic could get designation as a Rural Health Clinic. What's going on?"

"Well Mike, getting RHC was a big part of it. We had no choice but to have a midlevel in the clinic. This is mandated by the RHC."

"So, the reason I was hired wasn't to help out the busy practice as I was told? I understand now that Dr. Shoemaker doesn't even allow PAs to see his patients. Dr. Kennedy is still building his practice and isn't eager to share patients because of that."

"Well now, Bill Shoemaker is Bill Shoemaker. That is just the way he is. No, he doesn't like PAs to see his patients, but he doesn't like other physicians seeing his patients either. Don't take it personally."

"I'm not 'taking' it personally—it is personal! If I can't work as hard as I was told I could, my salary will drop by $40,000 a year. That is an enormous drop to me! Besides that, the most important thing to me, at this point in my career, is to be busy. I am tired of sitting around. I made that clear from the beginning."

"Mike, you worry too much. Just give it time." Then he offered a big, ear to ear, grin.

It seemed, judging from some of my work experiences, apparently I don't worry enough. I left the meeting feeling only slightly reassured. I now had the sense that I was on my own. I wouldn't be integrated into the practice as a team player, the way a PA should be. With a team approach, when the PA and physician work in tandem, the patient is the winner. When the physician sees the PA as a threat and the enemy, everyone looses. Now I would have to fend for myself. At this point, it was as if another five or ten plates had been added to the spinning ones. These new plates had to do with building my own practice, by myself, which is hard for a midlevel to do.

Since I have some expertise in headache disorders, I decided to capitalize on this as a marketing angle. I wrote an article in the *Junction City Herald* on headaches. I did two radio talk shows and an interview with the LaSalle TV news, which was broadcast to the entire region. Then I scheduled a public lecture in Junction City. The turnout was good: about 40 people packed into our little clinic waiting room on a Tuesday evening. Toward the end of the lecture, one woman raised her hand and asked me, "Do you take on new patients?"

I said, confidently, "Oh yes. I love to take on new patients."

When the lecture was over, as with all the headache lectures, a line of people came up to talk to me. One by one they described their headache problem and how it was being presently managed or mismanaged. I felt that I had a lot to offer these people. My first headache patient, the one who asked if I was taking new patients, scheduled for Monday morning.

On Monday, Mrs. Sorensen was very nervous when I came into the exam room. She said right off, "I don't know if I should be here. I didn't get Dr. Miller's (her family doctor) permission to see someone else. He might be mad."

Such an attitude of patient ownership by physicians gave me the distinct feeling I was in cattle country in the old west. "Hey boy, those are my little doggies out there in the canyon. Keep your dirty cattle-rusting hands off of them or I will give you a lynching. They got my brand, a circle D on each-n-ery one." (Maybe this is what a doctor at a New York hospital was thinking when he carved his initials, a big "A Z," on the abdomen of one of his patients while he was doing her caesarean section.)

I reassured Mrs. Sorensen: "As soon as the visit is over, I will call

Dr. Miller myself and tell him I am seeing you for your headaches. So don't worry about it. You're doing nothing wrong by coming here."

I reviewed her headache story. She was being treated with daily narcotics and making frequent trips to the ER for Demerol. She had very little in the form of good headache management. I was confident that she was a very help-able person. I had plenty of time so I spent over an hour with her, drawing up a comprehensive plan for management. She was still nervous at the end of the meeting, saying, "I'm not going to make any changes until I get Dr. Miller's approval. Now are you sure he won't be mad at me for seeing you?"

"Of course not. Don't worry, I'll talk to him."

As soon as this nice, but intimidated woman left, I gave a call to the other side of the river and asked to speak to Dr. Miller. The receptionist said, "Now, who are you?"

"This is Michael Jones, and I am the new PA over at the Division Avenue Clinic. I want to talk to him about one of his patients."

"Just a minute." Then I was treated to Neil Sedaka music for about five minutes. She came back on. "Mr. Jones, Dr. Miller is busy right now, but I can take a message."

I left a message for him to call me, but he never did. The next day I tried again This time the receptionist forwarded me to Dr. Miller's nurse. She said very sternly, "What do you want?" I told her the whole story. Then she said, "I will let him know."

I didn't hear back from Dr. Miller all day. I knew that the patient was waiting on my call before she would get the new medications filled, so the next morning I called her just to let her know what the hold up was.

"Hello, Mrs. Sorensen, this is Michael Jones and I just wanted to follow up with you."

Silence.

"I have been trying to call Dr. Miller and so far I haven't heard back from him."

Mrs. Sorensen said sweetly, "Oh, he called me yesterday."

"Really? Why did he call you?"

"He called me to tell me never to see you again, that you are just a PA and don't know what you are doing."

I felt sad for Mrs. Sorensen. I knew this woman didn't have to go on living with daily headaches. Out of frustration I said, "You know, you are the one suffering from headaches, not Dr. Miller. You are the one that makes the decision on who you see for them."

Then in a timid, shaky voice she said, "Oh, I do think you could have helped me, but, I better do what Dr. Miller tells me because he's my doctor."

To compound the problem, several of the patients who attended my headache lecture carried the BS brand on their hides for "Dr. Bill Shoemaker." It was months before I learned from the people in the front office that Dr. Shoemaker had instructed them, "When this PA comes, I don't want any of *my* patients to see him, ever!" So when these people tried to schedule with me, they were automatically turned away.

The plates were all still spinning . . . but just barely. With my focus on the job front, the home-front plates were starting to wobble. There were problems with the land purchase, which raised the cost a great deal more. The banker still needed our general contractor's contract so we could sign the papers, get the money released and the land purchased. In the confusion, I had to get Power of Attorney pages faxed back and forth between Denise and me. I called Tim several times to get a look at the contract but he was always "still working on it." The banker had scheduled a closing on the loan the following week.

I felt like I had started this house-building train in motion and now I had lost control. It had become a runaway. Suddenly there were deadlines and subcontracting problems that had to be worked out, little fires here and there to be stomped out. Finally the day of the closing came, and I still hadn't seen the contract. The big lesson I learned was to never build a house in haste. But now, I was committed; or maybe I should have been committed . . . to the farm where demented fathers lazily graze like zombie cattle on the hillsides.

I came into Steve's (the bank CEO) office. He was really a nice man. He was a tall man with thinning blond hair who spoke softly and smiled a lot. He had been very helpful. He even took our ewes to his farm to keep while we were in transition.

Steve showed me the piles of papers with one-inch yellow sticky-notes on every page marking where to sign. Finally Tim arrived with a folder in hand. He took out the infamous contract and I couldn't believe it. It was a very simple piece of paper with about five lines typed on it and virtually no details. Then Steve said, "I have to accept this and get things going. The land owners will be here in 45 minutes to close." Man, was I out on a limb now in a room full of saw-toting people.

Back to the professional spinning plates. Dr. Ward started looking for something for me to do since I didn't have patients. Certainly busywork wasn't the long-term solution and wouldn't help the salary, but it was one way I could make a contribution. The one area some of the doctors were willing to give up some professional territory was nursing home rounds. None of them liked to do it and it didn't help their incentive pay. That was fine for me because I really like older people. There were three nursing homes: two private and one actually located in the hospital.

When I arrived on the hospital floor to do rounds for the first time, I walked down to the nursing desk to introduce myself. It was a cold reception by the ward clerk and nursing assistants. The general surgeon, who was sitting at the nurses' desk, was, in contrast, very friendly. "Hello, you must be Michael Jones. Welcome. I am Doctor Wolf and I am one of the surgeons."

After some small talk, I collected Dr. Kennedy's patients' charts and carried them down to a conference room to review. As I was paging through the nurses' notes, the charge nurse heard I was on the floor and came down to see me. I knew who she was as the ward clerk had pointed her out down the hall at her med cart. She was a heavy blond gal in her late twenties or early thirties. Think of Mimi on the *Drew Carey Show*, with a little less make up, but the same personality.

As she walked in the room, I stood up to introduce myself. "Hi, I'm Mike Jones." I reached out my hand to shake hers and she didn't reciprocate.

She had a look of rage on her face and shouted back, "No one told me that you were coming up here. I just called the nursing administrator and she says that I don't have to help you in any way or take any orders from you because you are a just a PA. Next time you come up here you better call first." She whipped around and then left.

I was starting to feel that I wasn't wanted on the floor. Call it male intuition. I also was getting the feeling that my move to Junction City was a giant step back to the '60s, in terms of the physicians' and the nurses' attitudes. It was such a shame because, geographically, it was such a beautiful place.

I called Dr. Ward to discuss the situation. "Mike, be patient (his favorite phrase). The nurses were opposed to us hiring PAs so they aren't too eager to cooperate."

The next month I went back to do rounds again–calling ahead this time. As soon as I walked on the floor, someone must have pulled a "PA alarm" because Mimi came running down the hall to greet me. She said, "I found out that you are committing fraud by coming up here. I am going to report you to the state and they will take away your license!"

The whole situation left me feeling dumbfounded. I wasn't coming up to the floor to make the nurse's life more difficult or to boss her around–I was coming to help. I was there to write orders for a laxative for Mr. Johnson, whose severe constipation had turned his bowel movements into an once-a-week birthing experience. I was going to provide something for sleep for Mrs. Lindbloem, who had been walking the floors at night driving the late-shift crazy. I consider myself there to serve the patient and the nurses. The role of "The Enemy" was very uncomfortable for me, like a pair of wing-tipped shoes three sizes too small.

I picked up the hall phone and gave Dr. Ward a call. "Can you tell me what is going on here? Now I am being told that I am committing fraud by coming on the floor."

"Oh, Mike, the nursing administrator found a law that states if a PA is employed by the hospital, then he or she can't make rounds on nursing home patients in a facility owned by the same hospital. We are seeking clarification of this law. In the meantime, just forget about making rounds."

I had now completed my second month at work and my schedule had increased to 3-4 patients per day. These were exclusively patients who were transient, and thus not "owned" by any physician. I couldn't even see these patients unless Drs. Shoemaker and Kennedy had maxed out their schedules. Therefore, typically I ended up seeing students from the university.

One day I went up to the front office to check the Appointment Desk and one of the women said, "Mike, I put a patient on your schedule. He wouldn't tell us what his complaint was, only something personal. The odd thing, he is sitting out in the lobby with a white dinner plate on his lap."

"Why?" I said.

"We don't know. But he rode the city bus here from campus and was carrying the plate when he got off."

In a little while Karen checked him in, got his vital signs, and came over to talk to me.

"I don't know why he has that plate, he wouldn't tell me. Also, he wouldn't tell me why he's here."

I walked into the exam room and there sat the body double for the nerd-ish friend, Paul Pfeiffer on *The Wonder Years*–the guy that "urban legend" now suggests is Marilyn Manson. I introduced myself and said, "How can I help you?"

"Well, I am a worried that I have a sexually transmitted disease."

"Now, why do you think that?"

"My sperm looks a different color than usual."

"Really. Do have a penile discharge?"

"Uh . . . no."

"Do you have burning when you urinate?"

"No."

We went through the long list of sexually STD symptoms and his answer were all "no." Finally I said, "OK, now how does the dinner plate fit into all of this?"

"Well, I knew that you would want to look at my sperm under a microscope, so I donated a specimen on my plate before leaving my dorm room."

He started to reach for his plate when I said, "You know, that is OK. I really don't need to look at it. I just need to do a swab and other labs."

When I came out of the room to get a STD swab, Karen said, "Did he explain the plate yet?"

"Yes, he did. It has a semen sample on it." I saw her cringing as I went back into the room. I did the appropriate exams and labs, trying to reassure him. After I left the room, I went over to my cubical to finish my notes. The patient was inside the exam room getting dressed. He cracked the door, stuck his head out, and asked Karen, "Hey nurse, do you mind if I wash my dish in here before I go and get on the bus."

"By all means . . . please do."

After he closed the door again I could see the chill going down Karen's spine. I looked up at her and said, "Oh, Karen, this guy was so grateful for all the time that we spent with him that he invited you and me over to his dorm room for dinner tonight."

One day a fraternity president, neo-preppie-looking guy strutted in and Karen checked him in. I walked into the exam room and the guy said proudly, with a big smile, "Hey Doc, it looks like I caught me one of those sexxxxually transmitted disssssseases. I have been under quite the demand by the babes since coming to campus and I need to clear this up as soon as possible. They each think they are the only one. Ha ha."

"Well, if indeed you have an STD, then apparently you're not their *only one.*"

From the look on his face, it appeared he hadn't thought of that before. After he dropped his drawers, I could see he had one of the worse cases of jock itch I had seen in a while. "No, my friend, this looks red and cruddy, but it is not an STD. You're lucky this time. It is a fungal infection . . . along the lines of diaper rash." His departing strut wasn't nearly so proud.

Things on the home-building front seemed to be going from bad to worse. Tim told me that the house would be done by Thanksgiving and it was the week before with only the second floor finished. In two more weeks, my family would be moving up.

I was able to keep up with the contractors, putting my custom doors on as they finished a section. But the house itself had no interior walls and no electricity or plumbing. The amount of work falling on my shoulders was growing by leaps and bounds. I had been counting on incentive money to hire out many of the projects, such as plumbing and electric, which now I couldn't do.

A roof was put on the week that Denise was moving up, yet the house was like a three-story warehouse storing piles of lumber. The family went to stay with Denise's mom while I worked even harder, late into the night, trying to get things livable. I pushed myself beyond exhaustion. I put in one toilet on the first floor and one electric box. I had to build a staircase to the second and a ladder to the third floors. There were still no interior walls, just open space like a shed. Then we moved in.

I started working till midnight every night, putting up walls and doing plumbing. Denise was working throughout the day. I worked every weekend from sunrise to midnight. Even December 25th we worked without a pause, not telling the kids it was Christmas day. The cold warehouse was slowly taking shape, but not without some major setbacks.

It was around this time that I experienced the closest brush with a personal malpractice suit of my entire career. It was a situation that would leave me scratching my head for a very long time. Three days prior to Christmas, the co-owner of the bakery next door, Beth, came over to the clinic. Her long brown hair was tied back with a blue scarf. She had flour on her apron and on her cheeks. She appeared frazzled.

Beth was suffering from an intense throbbing headache. Dr. Shoemaker had taken off Christmas week and Dr. Kennedy's schedule was full, so by default Dr. Kennedy let me see her. Beth had a long history of menstrual migraine and this one seemed typical, except for being one of the most intense headaches she had ever had. But not THE most intense. Compounding the problem was the fact it was the holidays and her bakery was swamped with orders, requiring her to work sixteen-hour days. I was sure the intensity of her headache had been magnified by her extreme work schedule, and by the few hours of sleep she was getting. Another complication was the fact that she had no health insurance.

Her exam was normal. I didn't order a CAT scan of her head because it wasn't indicated, plus she would have to pay for it out of pocket. I gave her an injection of sumatriptan, an excellent anti-migraine medication. Unfortunately she had to immediately return to the chaos of the bakery. Her headache resolved for several hours, but it returned by the time she finished her shift at midnight. Beth then went to the local emergency room, where she got an injection of a strong narcotic.

The next morning Beth had to get up at 4:30 to start baking strudel and gingerbread men for her inpatient customers. Her headache soon returned, but this time accompanied by dizziness. Her worried mother, Mrs. Donaldson, called me as soon as I arrived at the clinic. "I am very worried about Beth. Could she have a tumor?" Her voice was intense.

I tried to calm her down by saying, "Oh no. I am sure this is her typical menstrual migraine. I'm not surprised at all that she's dizzy. She just got a powerful narcotic a few hours ago and followed it with only three hours of sleep. She really needs to go home and get some rest."

Mrs. Donaldson kept referring to me as Dr. Jones. I corrected her: "Mrs. Donaldson, I am a PA—a physician assistant, not a physician."

She responded with a startled, "Are you serious? You are just an assistant and not even a doctor? Well, I'm taking her back to the ER to see a real doctor."

"Mrs. Donaldson, I know what I am doing." I said. "I have been in medical practice for 15 years and much of that time specializing in headache disorders. Dr. Kennedy supervises me here in the clinic, if that's your concern."

That was no consolation for the worried mom. She took Beth back to the emergency room—being her second visit in two days—she got a spinal tap and a CAT scan. Both were normal and Beth's final diagnosis was migraine and she was sent home with more pain medicine.

The family was billed for over $2,000 for the ER visits and CAT scan. In response they wrote the CEO of the hospital threatening a lawsuit, complaining that, "Beth had seen only an assistant in the office and the assistant never even ordered a CAT scan. Apparently she needed one, because the emergency room physician ordered one. Because the CAT scan was delayed, and this put Beth at risk." The hospital in response forgave her bills.

Despite how desperate we were to get the house finished, all the carpenters left on the opening day of deer hunting season, not to be seen again for almost two weeks. "Opening day" was the most sacred of holidays in this part of the country—even the schools close. At the same time, Tim's father became ill back in Finland and he left the country to be with him.

Denise's worst day came the next week. One morning the sawmill came to deliver the huge truckload of tongue-and-groove interior wood. Since a heavy snowstorm was in the forecast, the driver insisted that the wood be put inside. If it got wet, $6,000 worth of wood would warp and be ruined. Denise and the kids worked like mad carrying the wood inside, armload by armload. The stacks filled up most of the first and second floors. Shortly after this, the truck from the lumber supply arrived with the kitchen cabinets. Denise was given two bits of terrible news. First, the cabinets (the order had been written up by a kid in the La Salle discount lumber supply), was entirely wrong. The cabinets, which had been custom made, were maple, not hickory. Denise loved the hickory look. We eventually got them for half price, but they couldn't exchange them for the right ones without having to wait three more months. I couldn't do the plumbing unless the cabinets were in, therefore we couldn't wait.

The next piece of bad news was that the truck driver wasn't allowed to help unload the cabinets. The union said he could only drive. Therefore, Denise and the kids (ages 4-12 at the time) tried to unload the twenty large, heavy boxes. Once they were inside, along with the six-foot stacks of boards, you barely had room to walk. The next bad news was that the moving company was due to arrive with our belongings at any time—a week earlier than expected. By this time, the snow was starting to come down quite heavily.

The previous night, our new furnace had blown up, pumping black soot all over the side of the house and making for freezing inside temperatures. I had to dig to find the name of the mechanical contractor since Tim was somewhere in northern Finland.

By late morning, the moving truck arrived. Denise backed the van out to make room for the semi. The street in front of our house had eight-foot-deep drainage ditches on each side. There was only about a foot of shoulder before the sudden drop. With three feet of snow on the ground, you couldn't tell where the road ended and the ditch started. As Denise backed out, the van slipped–actually fell–into the ditch. At this point she called me in tears. It took a major effort by a wrecker to get the van out.

Meanwhile, the movers were perplexed–there was nowhere inside to put our stuff. The house still had no interior walls, no closets, no cabinets, and only had stairs to the second floor. The movers got most of the stuff stacked inside, still in boxes. About a fourth of the shipment had to be left outside. This included things like lawn equipment, toys, and camping equipment. These things got buried in another thirty inches of wet snow that night. A hard freeze, plus much more snow, came later that week. These things became locked in a glacier until May. When the May thaw came, it was like the famous grasshopper glacier in Montana. As the glacier recedes, it leaves behind pre-historic giant mummified grasshoppers. Everything that emerged from our glacier wasn't preserved, but ruined.

The next bad thing to happen that same day was the mechanical subcontractor finally came. He unfortunately tried to park on the street since the moving truck was still in our driveway. The same ditch that had eaten our van that morning ate his equipment truck in the afternoon. He spent several hours getting it out. It is a day that Denise would love to forget.

I met with Dr. Ward again in the basement of his clinic. It was the same line; this time, however, I could tell that he was losing optimism. He was starting to say things like, "Mike, why is it so important to be busy? Why don't you just take it easy?"

"I didn't become a PA to take it easy, but to see patients," I told him. "I have taken it easy for three years. I am at the peak of my career. There is no greater punishment than to bore me to death. Besides, I would have never have taken this job without the opportunity to earn the incentive money."

Doubts about this position were growing by the day. I just couldn't believe it was happening to me again. I was tempted to think that the whole medical world had gone mad. But I knew that wasn't true. I had met many good physicians in my career. I knew many PAs who worked with really nice physicians like Dr. Bohjanen. Their practices had also been stable over decades, without major wars or turmoil. On top of that, I knew that these PAs were well compensated. Someone, somewhere, had to be earning an average salary, or otherwise, it wouldn't be "average."

I was also tempted to believe that something was wrong with me, that I was too naïve. This may have been the case sitting in a Cypriot swimming pool with Chuck a decade earlier, but I didn't think it was true any longer—that dragon had been slain. I had been very aggressive during my interview and had asked the right questions. There is always a factor of trust on both sides.

I came to believe that it all had to do with fate. I had run into a string of bad luck. It was like playing Russian Roulette and having the single bullet appear in the firing chamber three times in a row. I knew that my luck eventually had to change.

We continued trying to dig our way out of the huge house-building project. I had to finally find Tim again in northern Finland to force him to get his carpenters back to work and a new furnace put in. Soon after this, on a cold January day, as bad as things were, they would take a sudden turn for the worse.

Chapter Twenty-four

Redemption

Winter in this part of the country is so exotic; it is like visiting one of Jupiter's moons. The lake effect snowfall can exceed twenty feet. Fifteen-inch snowstorms are as common as an afternoon rain showers in other areas of the country. By December, the honking of southbound geese has given way to the whining of northbound snowmobilers. The roads become like deep channels of passage in the icy world around them. In the midst of this great winter of our discontent, across the river on Division Avenue, the day of reckoning had finally arrived.

To escape the world of snow and ice, Dr. Shoemaker took off for a family vacation to Mexico. I started the week, as usual, seeing one or two patients per day. Dr. Kennedy noticed that in Dr. Shoemaker's absence, the front office was turning away patients by the droves, and it was flu season. He took it on himself to confront the situation. He went to talk to the women at the front desk.

"It is ridiculous that we are turning away so many of Dr. Shoemaker's patients. From now on, offer an appointment with Mike to everyone who wants it." The women nervously agreed to do so.

Then he came over to the east side of the clinic. "Mike, get your stuff together if you want to come over to my side and see patients."

"Sure. But how is this going to work out?"

"Forget Shoemaker's rules. This is insane to turn away patients because of his possessiveness. I have opened the books for you."

I went over to the west side and set my things up on Dr. Shoemaker's desk. Within minutes my schedule began to fill: four patients, six patients, ten patients, and then eighteen. I had a ball working like a PA is supposed to work. For the rest of the week my schedule was full. I was happy, the patients were happy and were getting good care, and the clinic was making money from my efforts. I started to feel encouraged for the first time in months that this might, indeed, work out.

The following Monday, I returned to the east side, thinking that maybe this was the one act that would break the logjam. I thought once Dr. Shoemaker saw how well things went, how happy his patients were to see me, maybe his heart would change. That Monday morning I ran into Dr. Shoemaker in the break room. "How was your trip?"

He seemed distracted. In one of his rare moments he opened up and said, "My daughter has decided to go to PA school instead of medical school."

What pure irony! This must have been killing him. I couldn't help it, but a big smile came to my face. "Well, that's great!"

Dr. Shoemaker quickly grumbled, "I am sure she is doing this because she is in love and doesn't want to make the investment of time in medical school. She will come to her senses. PA school may not be a bad preparation for medical school."

Wow, he finally said something positive about the PA profession.

I got my cup of tea and returned to the east side. It took a while that morning before Bill figured out what Dr. Kennedy and I had done the previous week.

One of his patients that I had seen had a fracture of her proximal 5th metatarsal—a bone on the outside of the foot. I saw her early the previous week and reviewed the X-ray carefully, making sure she didn't have a notorious fracture called a Jones Fracture. Later in the week, after the swelling was down, I painstakingly applied a cast—a well-done cast, I might add.

While I was sitting there drinking my tea, Karen came over to get the cast saw, which was stored on my side. She said (I think to play devil's advocate), "Mike, you know Mrs. Olson's cast? Well, Dr. Shoemaker is taking it off."

"Why?"

"He was really upset when he found out that you had seen his patients. Without even looking at her, he said, 'Get the cast saw, I want to take the PA cast off.' I guess he doesn't trust a PA to put a cast on." Karen left with the saw in hand.

I usually don't react impulsively; I tend to think about things for a while and brew, like my tea bag. I decided it was time to confront Dr. Shoemaker. The diplomatic approach with Dr. Ward wasn't working. Yet, I was walking on thin ice. I had a house that was half-built and a wife and five kids who would be in deep dinosaur dung if I was laid off by a pissed off physician.

I walked over to the west side and hung out in the hall while Dr. Shoemaker was in the room putting on a new cast. When he came out I said, "Was there something wrong with that cast?"

He said politely, yet condescendingly, "Oh, I had to examine her foot and X-ray it to make sure she didn't have a more complicated fracture. There is one called a Jones Fracture that needs special attention."

"Yes, I know what a Jones Fracture is. I X-rayed her foot and reviewed it. It wasn't a Jones Fracture." I wanted to say, "As a matter of fact, the Jones Fracture was named after my grand pappy who invented it." Instead I said, "Did you look at my X-rays?"

"No, I didn't look at your X-rays. I have my own special views when I order an X-ray."

That's too bad, I thought. The patient is going to be billed for two casts and two sets of X-rays and for no good reason.

I could tell something was bothering Dr. Shoemaker. In a moment he turned to me and finally vented, "You know, I'm not putting up with you seeing my patients behind my back. I'm a doctor. I don't compete with midlevels. I'm the one with power at this hospital and I'm going over there at lunch and demand that they get you out of this office 2-½ days a week. The Rural Health Clinic Act requires a PA to be in this clinic only 20 hours a week."

"What are you talking about? Put me where?"

"I'm going to have them put you down in Lake Baines." With that he grabbed his coat and went out the back door.

Dr. Kennedy was finishing up his morning about this time. I walked over to him and said, "Dr. Shoemaker wants to have me put in Lake Baines 20 hours a week. Do you really think he could do that?"

"Don't worry about it. He is just blowing smoke. They had talked about putting a clinic down there but that would be a huge financial loss. Just ignore him."

Lake Baines was a small mining town of a few hundred people about 15 miles away. What made putting a clinic there unlikely was the fact that the town was only 5 miles from Clairmont. Clairmont was the next town of any size to our area. It had the Clairmont Memorial Hospital, which was in great competition with ours. The two hospitals had been at war for a couple of years. It was like the old Risk board game using real territory and people as game pieces. Dr. Shoemaker wanted to put me deep behind enemy lines so I wouldn't have access to anyone who could possibly become his patient.

Back on the spinning plates of home building, we were still slowly digging out of the avalanche of work. For three months it had been only Denise, the five kids, and me working our butts off, and we were exhausted. I was stressed out and the kids considered me a raging lunatic and slave driver. I tried to make it fun by calling the industrial adhesive "dragon snot" and the table saw "the widow maker." Yet, that didn't help much.

Although Denise was stressed out by the hard work, she was trying to keep a positive attitude. She started making friends, as did the kids. Bryan and Daniel entered the combination Middle School-High School. Denise continued home-schooling Tyler, Amy, and Ramsey in the little time she had between putting up walls and kitchen cabinets.

About this time, I called Sandy at the old clinic in La Salle. "Hi, Sandy, this is Mike Jones."

"Well, PA Jones, how's it going?"

"Not as good as we had hoped. How are things there?"

"Dr. Edgar is still an asshole and finally the hospital is realizing it. It looks like they are going to get rid of him. Besides, La Salle General just built a family practice clinic a block from us.

Dr. Edgar had put the clinic through a slow and painful death. The RN quit the day of her one-year anniversary. The patient he said you had offended because you hadn't asked her about her necklace, well, she and Dr. Edgar just had a huge fight in the lobby this morning, with her screaming her head off. Otherwise, things are going well."

"Sandy, we are desperate. We need help!" I think she could hear a quiver in my voice.

Like the cavalry coming to rescue the ranchers under attack, those women and their families came up for a Saturday to help us. Those office women, whom Dr. Edgar told me never to associate with, were friends indeed when we needed them most. They accomplished a lot on the house, but it was their boosting of our spirits that made the greatest impact. Later we had other friends from our church in La Salle, Mike and Laura, come up and give us two whole weekends. They worked with their whole hearts. We couldn't have made it without them.

Then followed an ironic twist. While Tim, our contractor, was on another trip to Finland to visit his dying father, his associate embezzled the company's money–our money. She was caught but the money was never recovered. Tim had to declare bankruptcy and his construction company folded. It was a mute point trying to get any more help from him. OK–the Russian Roulette bullet appeared in the chamber for the forth time in the row.

Back at the clinic, I returned to seeing my two or three patients per day. One day a young coed called our front desk. She was in tears, being worried that she had "gangrene in her feet." The receptionist told her to rush right over. When I heard about her, I was a little excited to be taking care of something besides sore throats and STDs. Maybe it was a relic of the "emergency high" I enjoyed back in the 1970s. I doubted if it was going to be an authentic case of gangrene, but it must be some kind of nasty infection.

After the worried young lady was taken to an exam room, I came in. She was upset, but otherwise she looked healthy. "Hi, I hear that you were having some problems with your feet."

"Yes. I just woke up this morning and they were green. I called my mom in Chicago. She said it sounded like 'gang-green' and that needed to be seen right away–that I could die from it."

"You're telling me that your feet are actually green?"

"Yes!"

"Can I see them?"

She quickly took off her running shoes. The soles of both feet were bright green–not grass-stain green–I'm talking chartreuse–a color of green that does not occur anywhere in nature. She stared to sob again.

"Just a minute, I'll be right back."

I ran down to our procedure room, got a stainless steel basin, filled it up with soapy water and retuned. I kneeled before her and scrubbed off her feet with a surgical scrub brush. The water took on the same color of green while her face became fuchsia. She put her hand over her mouth and her tears of fear turned to tears of hysterical laughter.

"I'm so embarrassed. I just remembered I bought insoles for my hiking boots that were that color and I wore them last night without socks."

One typical quiet afternoon I heard a page from the front desk, "Michael, Dr. Ward is on line three for you."

I picked up the phone in the hallway. "Yes, this is Mike."

"Hi Mike. How's it going?" Without a pause for a response, he continued, "Say . . . Michael, the hospital has decided to put a clinic down in Lake Baines. It looks like you will be spending half your time down there and half of it back at the Division Avenue Clinic. What do you think?"

"Well, I see that Dr. Shoemaker got his way." With a sigh of hopelessness in my voice, "I'll do whatever the hospital wants. It doesn't matter what I think anymore. So the clinic will only be open twenty hours a week?"

"No. It's going to be a full-time clinic. Cathy is going down and working the twenty hours a week when you're over at Division Avenue– that way, each of you can meet the requirements for RHC status for your perspective clinics."

Cathy was the other PA employed by the hospital. She was well established in Dr. Ward's office–three years prior to my arrival. What made it sad about moving her to Lake Baines was the fact that she was actually busy. Dr Ward didn't consider her as a threat and shared his patients with her freely.

During the interview process, I had taken Cathy out for Chinese food, to get the inside scoop of the hospital. During dinner she warned me, "Mike, Dr. Shoemaker is the least PA-friendly of the doctors, however, (she reassured me); I am sure you can charm him and win him over in time." Neither one of us had a clue how entrenched his attitudes really were. Besides, I had been working with the mother of all PA-haters for six months. Dr Shoemaker's "hesitation" seemed trivial-at least at the time.

I'm not sure why they decided to hire me in the first place. Dr. Kennedy told me it was to obtain RHC designation. Cathy could have easily rotated between her clinic and the Division Avenue clinic, fulfilling the RHC requirements for both. At the time, they must have figured that they didn't want to take Cathy away from her practice. But now they were going to do it anyway.

Cathy and her husband Bud gave us great support during those difficult days. Besides encouraging us to "hang in there," Bud freely gave of his time to help us work on our house. They were lifesavers.

In June, I started my new post. The hospital rented a downtown office space. It was very small. They spent several thousand dollars to remodel it, turning a very old insurance office into a makeshift clinic.

Even before the clinic was finished being remodeled, the Clairmont Memorial Hospital found out about the "enemy" clinic going up in their territory. The next thing you know, there were two 18-wheelers coming down the mountain from Clairmont, each one carrying half of a large, modern, pre-fabricated clinic, complete with X-ray and lab. There was no way they would let my hospital establish a foothold in THEIR territory. It was like a scene from Mayberry with Barney Fife directing traffic and the townsfolk sitting on their porches just laughing at the "Battle of the Clinics."

As one old man told me, "We've been here 100 years without a clinic and within one week, two pop up. It is like someone suddenly discovered gold here—ha!" They set their clinic one block down the street from our remodeled hole in the wall. It was a race to see which one would open first. Clairmont won by three days. Now the Lake Baines people wouldn't even have to drive up the hill for health care.

Our clinic was a sinking ship from the outset and I was being chained to the wheel. I was determined to give it my best try and to go down swinging, or in this case swimming. For the Fourth of July parade, my family and I sat on a clinic float and threw candy to the kids of Lake Baines. That may have been the only part that was fun.

Our days in Lake Baines were extremely slow, seeing one patient every two days. After months the practice finally built to 1-2 patients per day, but most of these were Dr. Ward's patients getting allergy shots. Back at the Division Avenue Clinic, patients were being turned away left and right when the physicians' schedules were maxed out. I didn't have the money for supplies to build another boat or I would have.

Finally Dr. Ward conceded that I would never be busy and there was nothing he could do about it. During a visit to the Lake Baines clinic, he said to me, "Mike, just forget about seeing patients. Find some good mystery novels and spend your days reading." I knew I had to get out of the situation.

I called a PA recruiter to see what kinds of jobs were available. There were no longer sharks circling. The recruiter said there had been a dramatic fall in PA job opportunities over the previous two years. Then, he added, "Mike, you're no longer employable."

"What do you mean I'm not employable?"

"If a prospective employer sees your record of job failures, they'll know that something is seriously wrong with you. You apparently can't get along with people or something." I would have loved to work for Dr. Saper, Dr. Bantle, Dr Bohjanen, Dr. Greg, or even Dr. Kennedy. They were wonderful doctors and wonderful people as well. But my destiny seemed to reside with the asshole doctors. The hope of finding my dream job was gone. It was even time to start looking for another career.

One day I was sitting back in the Division Avenue clinic and had a call from Dr. Singer, the director of the Headache Division at the world-class medical center. "Mike, when did you move from La Salle?"

I felt a wave of embarrassment. "Well, it has been about a year and a half now."

"I had a hard time tracking you down. I wanted to let you know that the institution has cleared the way for us to hire you. Are you still interested?"

"Well, yes I am. However, I'm in the middle of building a house here and have to finish that first. Hopefully it will be done in a couple of months."

The family and I took another 10-hour trip down to the area of the medical center. It was very different from Michigan's Up-back. The natural beauty of the area paled in comparison. We looked at a few houses, just to get a taste of the market, and left discouraged. There was no way we could afford a home near the level of the one we were building. We would have to give up Lake Superior. I had already given up my love, sea kayaking. I had to sell my kayak to buy lumber to finish the house.

Our second love was cross-country skiing. All our skiing equipment was lost during the move and we had not skied in a year. It would be hard to give up skiing permanently.

There were times that I skied every day from October to early May, using the same ski trail that some of the U.S. Olympic team members trained on. It was an excellent workout, but it could be terrifying as well. I used to think that cross-country skiing was softly gliding across the snow.

As a Tennessee boy, the best way I can describe cross-country skiing on these world-class trails was like climbing a mountain . . . while doing the splits . . . with 2 x 4s strapped to your feet. Then, once on top, you clamp your shoes to a narrow, greased railroad track. The diagonal grooming leaves two deep, ice-bottomed tracks. Then you head down a mountainside that is only two degrees short of being a cliff. You approach the speed of sound with your knuckles scraping the bark off the birch and hemlock trees that snuggle up to the trail. Your ears fill up with frozen tears being whipped back from your eyes. At the bottom, a mile and a quarter later, the track makes a sudden 90-degree turn. You dare not step out of the tracks or you will go head over heels into some old-growth white pines, smashing your skull like a watermelon and then bursting into flames. Once at the bottom, you start the climb up the next mountain.

Dr. Bohjanen grew up in such parts. He told me that as a high-schooler he tried to set a personal cross-country ski speed record. The 30 inches of snow was met with a few freak days of 40-degree temperatures follow by another deep freeze. This left an inch-thick crust on top of the snow. He carried his skis to the top of La Salle Mountain. Once there, he clipped on his skis and took off down the wild side of the mountain, skiing on the ice crust. As he approached the sound barrier, the most unfortunate thing happened: his skis broke through the ice. This brought him—or at least his skis—to a sudden dead stop. He still had tremendous momentum, which ripped his feet right off the skis, leaving only the soles of his boots still attached. He sailed a hundred feet down the mountain like Superman still holding onto his poles and his boot's uppers still on his feet. He landed headfirst on the ice. As his head broke the ice, the sharp edges separated his scalp from his skull. He collected his scalp and headed to the ER.

The decision to leave this Shangri-La wasn't going to be easy. We wrestled with it for weeks. The world-class medical center offered me a slightly above average salary for the first time in my career. Yet, they didn't work on contracts, just trust. That was scary, but yet what the heck. I had a great contract in my job with Dr. Ward's outfit, but it hadn't been worth the paper it was printed on. Another harsh reality of life is that a contract can be a false security blanket—being limited by your ability to get a lawyer to tramp a hundred miles through the snow drifts to take a case with minuscule returns.

The kids were finally getting settled. By late summer, the house was starting to look like a house, and we could start to unpack at just about the time we needed to start packing up again.

I agreed to accept the headache position on the condition that we could sell our house. We put it on the market even before I was done with the third-floor walls. The interest at first was high, with about ten showings, but no offers.

By October, I had another call from Dr. Singer. "Mike, we have been holding the job for you for five months now. We have another PA candidate coming out for an interview. We would like for you to have first shot at it, but we can't hold the position forever. Where are you at with it?"

It was confusing times, but after some praying and talking it over, we were on the edge of making the plunge. Dr. Ward got drift of what I was thinking and gave me a call, "Hey Mike, let's go to lunch and talk about things."

I met Dr. Ward at a local restaurant. We quickly ordered and got down to business. "Mike, I know that you are thinking about leaving. I've spoken to Mr. Kinley. Since you can never earn incentive money, I think he has agreed to increase your salary by ten grand. What do you think about that?"

"That would be helpful. That would then put us up with the average salary of new graduates. However, the loss of income is only one issue, and not even the most important one. Some of the doctors believe that they have to protect their patients from me because I–being a PA–offer inferior care. That is false and it really gripes me. Secondly, the reason that the RHC Act mandates a midlevel provider is to improve health care access for the patients. The hospital is reaping the benefits of RHC through higher reimbursement rates, yet the patient is being short-changed. They still have to wait days or weeks to get in and when they do get in, they may have to wait over an hour to be seen. Meanwhile I sit doing nothing. I find that unethical."

"Well Mike, I can't change Bill Shoemaker, but maybe you can. I would like to invite you and Cathy to the medical board meeting this week to present your case."

Dr. Ward, spinning greasy spaghetti onto his fork, looked up at me. "So you'll come?"

"Yes."

The hospital had rented a large meeting room at one of the hotels for the quarterly medical staff meeting. Cathy and I had never been invited because we weren't considered real medical staff. Several issues were discussed before it came to the PA agenda. Cathy was sitting next to the podium and was the first to speak. Certainly she didn't feel as compassionately about the matter because she was seeing 15 patients per day, except for her days in Lake Baines.

A nice obstetrician, Dr. Finley, was present. He had just moved to the area and was still wet behind the ears. "Oh, I think the PAs are a great asset and we can capitalize on their positive contributions. For Cathy, she is the only female in the family medicine group, and many females prefer a female. Mike has an expertise in headache disorders. I had to call him once already for his advice. I think we can keep them both busy." Obviously he was speaking from reason and hadn't yet fallen under the local spell of the ownership of patients.

I wanted to say something but wanted to wait my turn at the podium.

Next Dr. Shoemaker spoke. "Oh, come on now. The real issue is that the PAs are just greedy and want to make money from the incentive. Like I have always said, PAs don't deserve an incentive. They're not doctors."

I was about to crawl right out of my skin, snakelike. I made my way, quickly, to the microphone. "First of all, I can never be busy in my headache practice because our own physicians won't let their patients come to me, even if their lives depended on it, and sometimes it, or at least the quality of their lives, does. Secondly, Dr. Shoemaker, so you think we are in this for the greed? I will make a deal with you: open my schedule so I can practice like a real PA and I will forego all incentive money. You can have it! How can you call me greedy when I average 1-2 patients a day, while, at the same time, you are cramming 45 or more patients into your schedule?"

I rested my case and returned to my chair. Cathy and I were excused as the private policy meeting was going to continue.

The next day I had a call from Dr. Ward. "Mike, you guys left an impression on the staff last night. Several rose up against Dr. Shoemaker to support the PAs. As a result, the official policy was changed. Now if a patient has to wait more than four weeks for an appointment, one will be offered for the PA. Now that is exciting, isn't it?"

"Do you mean to tell me that the hospital had an official policy that patients couldn't be offered an appointment with a PA?"

"Well, the policy in your clinic at least, was that a PA could not see a patient who had established care with one of the physicians."

"But, also, I can't see new patients, right?"

"Well, that's a reimbursement issue. Besides, Dr. Shoemaker doesn't believe that a new patient should be seen by a midlevel."

"OK, so you are telling me that I cannot see new patients, and I cannot see old patients. Who does that leave? Am I missing something?"

"Well, Mike, there are the students. You can see a student if they haven't established care with one of the physicians and if the physicians' schedules are full that day. But, I am telling you that is all going to change. If a patient, even an established patient, has to wait more than four weeks to get in, they will now be offered an appointment with the PA. Give it some time and let's see if your patient load doesn't pick up–at least while you are in the Division Avenue Clinic."

"Dr. Ward, we should let the patient decided if they want to wait four weeks to get in or see the PA the same day." It was like pissing into the wind. It was simply a matter of way too little, far too late.

The house had been on the market for four months with no offers. With each wave of price reductions, we saw our life savings melting away like a sandcastle in the rising tide. We were sweating bullets but made a confident decision to take the headache position. It was a great risk, trusting the house to sell soon. I would give the PA profession one last chance. If I were deceived again, that would be it. I would leave the profession. My dream job had always been to live in Zermatt, Switzerland, write children's fiction books for six figures a year, and take periodic trips to provide health care to the poor of the Third World. Now, only one thing stood between my dream and me: reality. I relayed my decision to Dr. Ward, who of course was disappointed.

The empty chalet.

We made another trip to the medical center. Due to the loss of our life savings and the burden of a huge mortgage, our buying power for another house was quite limited. I started doing my homework several weeks before our trip to civilization. I had been speaking to a banker who was trying to do some creative financing. The only money we had left anywhere was our 401K. Gone was our kid's college fund; also gone was our retirement money. We were going to have to cash it in to make a down payment.

We had to settle on a home in very poor repair, in the middle of town but thirty miles from the medical center. We were once again burdened with yet another huge construction project.

With the long drought of owning two homes, we came to financial ruin. I had to take a weekend job in an ER 90 miles away. We lived from paycheck to paycheck with no reserve. While some of my PA friends were saving up to buy midlife crisis Harleys, we could barely buy groceries.

To find the happy ending to this saga, I have to flash forward. It has been over four years since we left the beautiful and the ugly backwoods of Michigan's Up-back on a pilgrimage, looking for a resting place. The physicians at the world-class medical clinic have treated me with more respect than I imagined possible. Some of them are leading authorities in their areas of expertise. Yet, these kind physicians treat me as a peer. If anyone had the right to be arrogant and obstinate, it would be them. This is quite a contrast to where I had been. I started here as a physician extender, but once I had proven myself I was promoted to a full, independent headache consultant. I have patients coming to see me from across the country and from around the world. My faith in physicians as being hard working, talented, and nice people has been restored.

I wish I could say I left a positive first impression on all my new colleagues. When I first arrived at my new position, I was quickly introduced to the "electronic environment." We greatly depend on computers for patient care. In front of me sits a large monitor, where I read patient notes, send orders, research the literature, and communicate with other colleagues. My monitor also has constant T-line connection to the Internet.

I had experience with the Internet before in Michigan's Up-back, but with the combination of our slow, first-generation modem and the over-taxed phone line connection, it was like a starving man trying to eat a steak dinner through a straw. I imagined I could see each individual byte of data crawling down the phone line, jumping into the computer, one by one like fleas.

With the constant T-line connection I quickly became an Internet jockey. If I wanted to know about any disease, within two seconds I could have volumes of information about it, as well as the names of hundreds of support groups and Web pages devoted to the disorder and quacks of all kinds that offered unorthodox treatment. Besides the medical information, I could find out about anything—even the mating habits of albino aardvarks.

One day, I discovered E-Bay. It changed my life. From that point on, I could never take out the trash again without thinking, item by item, hmmm—I wonder how much that would sell for?

One of the first times I was looking at E-Bay, I was amazed at the variety. It was like visiting one million garage sales all under one well-managed roof. There was anything you wanted, as well as a lot of things you would never want. I was sitting in my new office one day with a pause in my busy schedule. I quietly searched for more and more bizarre things like pieces of alien spacecraft and Elian Gonzalez's ear wax (which was thought to harbor supernatural powers). Then I typed in "used enema bags" and came up with two pages of them with photos. I couldn't believe it. Not only were people selling used enema bags, but, stranger still, people were actually bidding on them!

About that time, from over my right shoulder someone said, "Uh, Mike . . . I need to talk to you about a patient." I looked up and there stood one of our consultants. I wasn't sure how long he had been there. He was the first visitor in my office all day and his timing was terrible. Not knowing how to disconnect the computer quickly, I spun around in my chair and discussed the patient with him. I notice his eyes wandering from my face to the computer screen still donning the heading "Used Enema Bags for Sale," and then back to my face.

On the positive side, the Internet did introduce me to literally hundreds of other Physician Assistants through professional forums. We swapped stories, which gave me the feeling that I was not alone in this journey.

The improved Internet access in our area was, for my son Daniel, the only redeeming quality about our new home. It was a depressing move for him. Being an isolated farming community, when our kids started in school—the second mid-term move in two years—they weren't well received.

Amy was the exception, being our little social butterfly. During our brief stay in Junction City, she had developed many close friends. We had only been there a few weeks when she had a birthday party attended by 15 little girls.

Amy was quick to make friends in our new town as well. The first one was a little blond boy, Kyle, from next door. He was the closest reincarnation of Dennis the Menace I had even seen. Kyle introduced us to half the town. He did this by leaving our front door constantly wide open, allowing our 150-pound, hyperactive Saint Bernard named Oatmeal to have free reign of the city to terrorize people. She is very affectionate, but like the fictional dog Clifford, our Oatmeal doesn't appreciate her own size. When people scream and start running, she thinks they want to play.

Unfortunately, across the street from our house sits the town's senior citizen's apartments. There is nothing more frightening to an 85-year-old, 90-pound woman with a walker than being tackled by a hyperactive Saint Bernard. We got to know the town's two police officers quite well.

Denise has seen radical changes in her life. She was able to be a stay-at-home mom for seventeen years. To help with the finances she bravely decided to go back into nursing. After a refresher course, she got her RN license back. To be close to the kids, she took a job in the nursing home down the street.

It is amazing the transformation our family life has had to make. In the Up-back, Denise was a stay-at-home mom and quality family life was a top priority. In the Up-back, miles of untamed nature and the sense of freedom surrounded us. Now, at least until our Michigan house sells, we live in town—surrounded by gas stations, fast-food restaurants, and asphalt. Against our strongest beliefs, we have watched our children become "latch-key" kids with Denise's return to work.

It is also ironic that when Dr. Shoemaker has headache patients he can't handle, he sends them to Dr. Lesson. If Dr. Lesson can't manage the patients, she might send them to our medical center. The neurologist here would send the patients to me for consultation. Go figure. I offered the same level of care in Michigan's Up-back, but no one could get past the two letters, "P" and "A."

At the time of this writing, our dream house still sits in the beautiful north woods with no family to own or enjoy it—even with an asking price far below the construction cost and appraisal. If the tongue-and-groove aspen walls could talk, they would tell of the dark days of working to midnight with exhausted fingers; of nights with Amy and

Ramsey, Bryan, Daniel, and Tyler sawing boards and pounding nails and squirting dragon snot out of a caulk gun. These were dark days when we thought would never see the light again. In an unexpected change of events, during the biggest real-estate boom in history, our house couldn't be sold.

One day, while sitting in my new office, I had a page: "Mike, I have Cathy from Michigan calling. She says she's a PA and used to work with you."

"Sure, I'll take the call." This aroused my curiosity. I had seen Cathy only once since leaving Michigan and that was at a national PA conference.

"Hi Michael. This is Cathy."

"It's great to hear your voice!"

"Mike, I just wanted to fill you in on things in Michigan since you left. After you left, Mr. Kinley called me over to his office one day and said, 'Kathy, you're terminated. You're not a team player. Our experiment with PAs is over! I want you out of your office by this afternoon.' I had no clue this was coming."

"Cathy, of course you were a team player. You were fired because you stood up for me. I feel terrible! What about all your patients–they loved you?"

"It's OK, Mike. I found a new position just fifty miles away in Bay Harbor. It is totally different here. I'm glad I left Junction City. Here I work with a great group of doctors who are very supportive and do not feel threatened by me. We are a team here. I will miss my patients though."

As I hung up the phone, I noticed that Cathy's voice had stirred up a million memories of the Up-back. A huge piece of my soul still glides softly across the north woods snow. A huge piece of my heart still glides over the waves of Gitche Gumee in a yellow kayak with the sound of sea gulls calling from the cliffs above me. In a perfect world, I could've had it both ways: the opportunity to practice my skills and profession, where I would have professional respect as I do here while living where nature is still untamed. I would love to return to the Up-back, the Pacific Northwest, or even the Third World. I would love to be giving away my services to patients in deep need in some distant land. But we all know this isn't a perfect world, and sometimes there must be compromise.

Sometimes the call of God on one's life isn't written by brazen fire in the heavens, but rather dances softly in the shadows and makes itself known gently, in the twilight and in the dawn. All of us are wrought by the narrow places in our lives through which we are drawn. What we may have understood as the call of God can be forged during that process into a direction that seemed unimaginable before.

The circle's complete–a family hike in the Tennessee hills.

I looked out over the audience, the tones of gray and navy, each sitting up tall, with somber faces, in antique wicker and leather chairs. I cleared my throat and began: "Hello, my name is Michael Jones and I am a Physician Assistant. I will be looking today at an entity that we now refer to as Transformed Migraine."

A journey that started twenty years ago with an employment classified ad in a jeep on a cool autumn day in Tennessee has taken me around the world and back. I have traveled to the depths of depression and despair and to the peaks of exhilaration. Our family has weathered some terrible storms that could have destroyed us, and almost did. But we have survived and have been "wrought" together. As a kernel in a pod, a so-called midlevel clinician in a top-level world, I have finally found a place of rest, where the pod of peas is big enough for a kernel or two.

Postscript

Thank you for accompanying me on my little adventure. I hope you at least found the story entertaining if not inspiring. If it was either, I would be most grateful if you would recommend the book to your colleagues, friends, and family.

Mike Jones

Additional copies of the book can be ordered online at Kernelnpod.com